# ONE
## FOR THE
# BOYS

*John Wayne Blake's extraordinary story*

## CATHY SAINT JOHN

SINJIN PUBLISHING CO.
ST. JOHN'S, NL CANADA

**Praise for**
**ONE FOR THE BOYS**

This well-deserved tribute was absolutely riveting!

A Newfoundland war hero's life of bravery, persistence and struggle is brilliantly remembered by a loving sister and family. I know of no other text that better captures the true essence of a person challenged with the life-altering illness/ injury known as PTSD.

Being an advocate of those suffering with debilitating stress injuries, I highly recommend this book to those with injuries and those who assist the affected. It is also a must-read for those craving non-fictional accounts of our history of war and its effect on humanity.

In a section of this meticulously written account Saint John quotes a medical doctor who decades ago exclaimed, "I regret to have to advise you that at this time, not only Newfoundland but in all of Canada, medical and government health providers...are probably decades away from understanding and coping with chronic Post Traumatic Stress Disorder." Saint John's book gives the reader an up-to-date solid understanding of this often misunderstood injury.

I am a better person for having read this brilliant and timely literature. My only regret is that I never got to meet this amazing individual, Sergeant John W. Blake. His selfless actions throughout his life will be well and proudly remembered for generations to come.

**Staff Sergeant Elwood Boyd Merrill**
**Royal Canadian Mounted Police (retired 2018)**

**Praise for**
**ONE FOR THE BOYS**

A detailed and vivid look at the heroic life and tragic death of an Airborne Ranger, who as a Canadian, voluntarily served our country in Vietnam.

When he returned, the book chronicles his attempt to heal the strife of our Veterans and the contemptuous divisiveness felt by our citizens by marching across the entire country in full uniform while carrying the US flag.

While this brave soldier suffered and died from PTSD, his family endured the ultimate dishonor from his native country's Canadian politicians, who disrespected his service to its southern ally.

A poignant and heartbreaking story!

**Gary Dolan**
**Company C (Rangers)**
**75th Infantry (Airborne)**
**US Army Ranger Hall of Fame—2011**
**Author: Of Their Own Accord**

## Praise for
## ONE FOR THE BOYS

### Cathy Saint John's 'ONE FOR THE BOYS' hailed
### "A tour de force." by Tracey Arial, Canadian author

Not many family members have the courage needed to write an honest book about a family member they loved who died in hurtful circumstances. Cathy Saint John has succeeded in combining her personal desire of eulogizing her beloved brother with a journalist-like attention to getting the facts right and telling the entire story, warts and all. It's a rare trait, and it couldn't have been easy.

Her beloved brother John Wayne Saint John Blake made many choices over his lifetime that brought his family pain. From the moment he and his younger brother David volunteered to serve with the United States Armed Forces during the Vietnam War until the night he took his own life, Mr. Blake's actions constantly worried everyone who loved him. At the same time, they couldn't help but be proud of his achievements.

As a Canadian, Mr. Blake could have avoided Vietnam if he chose not to go. Instead, he rushed onto the front lines in part to keep his younger brother safe. He was in Vietnam from January 1970 until August 1971. During February, 1970, he volunteered and served with the 75th infantry of the 173rd Airborne Regiment and earned the Bronze Star. Ms. Saint John writes about the type of actions that earned him his medal. She also details several more personal moments when her brother stood up for justice during his time in Vietnam, as related to her by veterans with whom he served.

After Mr. Blake came home, despite flashbacks and mental health episodes, he willingly spoke about his service to help other veterans and to get public attention about their needs. The most impressive of these post-war actions took place over seven months in 1982. He took on the persona of 'the walker' by donning full combat gear to carry an American flag 3,200 miles across the United States from Seattle, WA to Yorktown, Virginia on foot to garner attention for Vietnam veterans. In addition to relating these positive attributes of her deceased brother. Ms. Saint John also writes in great detail about the many difficulties and struggles he had trying to survive. Reading her book, you can't help but tear up.

Although I've had the honour of interviewing many Canadian Vietnam Veterans over the years, I never got to speak with Mr. Blake. However in the spring of 2001, I participate in his burial service with his brother David, representatives from his unit and an honour guard from Fort Lewis, WA , which made the ceremony particularly meaningful. It's even more poignant now reading about his life and death as portrayed by Ms. Saint John. In many ways, she's written the book he might have completed had he lived longer.

Anyone interested in the Vietnam War and its social repercussions read this book. I highly recommend it.

**Tracey Arial, Writer**
**Author: I Volunteered/Canadian Vietnam Vets Remember**
**Montreal, Canada**

# ONE FOR THE BOYS

Editing by Lynn Rajala Schultz

Cover Design by Germancreative-Fiverr
Front cover photo of John Blake 1982—courtesy of Ron Whelan
Back photo cover of Ranger John Blake 1970—courtesy of Michael Swisley



This is a work of non-fiction. All real names of all judicial, medical and first responder characters in the writing of this book have been changed and any resemblances to actual people are purely coincidental. Similarities are not intentional.

Published in Canada 2018 by Sinjin Publishing Co.

Printed in The United States of America

EBook ISBN 978-1-7753739-1-9

Paperback ISBN 978-1-7753739-0-2

Contact the author at: johnblake.thewalker@gmail.com

DEDICATED TO

Rachel, Joy, Cory, Paula, Michael, Nancy, Sera, Will, Jack,

Evan and Allie

This is not a combat book. However, it is a true story about a Canadian family who originated from Newfoundland, Canada and of their only two teenaged brothers who voluntarily joined the United States Army. They were both deployed to Vietnam within weeks of each other; at a time, when tens of thousands American young men were exiting the United States and crossing the borders into Canada. Both John and David survived the 'Nam with the exception that the war followed John home in the form of Post Traumatic Stress Disorder.

This is John's and our family's extraordinary story.

## AUTHOR'S DISCLOSURE

**THE REAL NAMES OF ALL JUDICIAL, MEDICAL AND FIRST RESPONDER INDIVIDUALS IN THE WRITING OF THIS BOOK HAVE BEEN CHANGED; SIMILARITIES ARE NOT INTENTIONAL.**

## WARNING

**THIS STORY CONTAINS INTENSE EMOTIONAL CONTENT AND MAY TRIGGER PTSD. IT ALSO CONTAINS HARSH LANGUAGE THAT MAY BE OFFENSIVE TO SOME.**

## CONTENTS

## Acknowledgements

The largest compliment I can give to my late brother, John W. Blake, was to have written his story and gotten it right. It has taken two decades of writing, research and editing to succeed. The reasoning rests in John's story.

A special heartfelt thank you is extended to the November 75th Airborne Rangers, who without their guidance, assistance, and trust John's military storyline would not have been completed with historical military accuracy and photos. I am especially thankful to the following Airborne Rangers, many of whom served alongside John in Vietnam and agreed to be interviewed: Patrick (Tad) Tadina, Rodolfo (Rudy) Teodosio, Robert Hendriksen, Michael Swisley, Herbert Baugh, Carl Millinder, Ronald Thomas, Reed Cundiff, Richard Baker, Charles (Chuck) Moseby, William Jeffery (Jeff) Horne, Gordon Baker, John Bryant, Brian Danker, Don Bizadi, Fletcher Ruckman, John Wilkofsky, John Jersey, Rob Purvis, and Jerry Herrera.

I am forever grateful to my new-found Ranger brothers and the brotherhood that was forged in Vietnam and continues to flourish throughout the years in North America among all the battalions of the United States Airborne Rangers. Warriors, who lifted-up and embraced a fallen Vietnam veteran SF Ranger's kid-sister, taking her under their wings, allowing her to run with the Herd. Rangers really do lead the way!

My sincere thank you to the following contributors Rachel Blake, David Saint John, Lynn Rajala Schultz, Stephen Ratcliffe, Lynn Mowry, David Keall, Mark Reid, Gary Dolan, David Walker, Sonia Marie Kelly, Michael Ormiston, Roberto Patino, Douglas Clarke, and Ron Whelan.

I would like to express my sincere gratitude to the Vietnam veterans and their families in Canada, the United States of America, Australia, Britain and Saigon who contributed their support, experience, advice and friendship to me and my family throughout the years.

Thank you for your service and my freedom. Welcome home.

We, the Blake/Saint John families, are proud to acknowledge that the Canadian Mental Health Association, Newfoundland and Labrador Division is the recipient of an annual 3% donation of net profits from the sale of this book.

# Preface

Our little family's universe, while living in Montreal, Quebec during 1968, turned upside down the day both of our teenaged Canadian brothers arrived home and announced, "We have joined the United States Army in the fight against communism in Vietnam."

Mom shook her head in disbelief, buried her worried face in her hands and moaned a sorrowful sound of disbelief. Then she retreated to her bedroom for three days and grieved her sons' decision.

Two years prior to the boys' enlistment decision we had moved to Montreal, Quebec where life there was surreal; especially during the mid-sixties. It was a time when most people who watched television followed the daily news release that depicted the Vietnam War.

Morning, noon and night we were exposed to the constant coverage of America's efforts in Vietnam—wins and losses. Occasionally, the Vietnam War protesters achieved media coverage. Throughout Canada, the Vietnam War became 'the war on television'. However, the reality was that it was not a fictional story. It was ever so real.

I originally wrote this book for the next generation of children in our families who did not have the opportunity to meet our remarkable brother, John. He was an extraordinary man who they knew only by name and reputation.

My family and I now recognize more than ever that it is necessary to share John's story with the public, largely due to the continuous struggle that modern veterans, first responders, civilians, and their families endure. Communities and governments in North America, especially in Canada are mostly inexperienced and unprepared to live with the many facets of Post Traumatic Stress Disorder (PTSD). The heartbreaking day-to-day battle in understanding persons who live with (PTSD) is compounded by the lack of timeliness in discovery of the illness and the delivery of supports. The intentional and unintentional stigma attached to mental health issues is an ongoing concern.

Most importantly, John's story will offer some clarification as to why too many military personnel and civilians have chosen to die by their own hand as a result of their injuries pertaining to PTSD.

It is with hope and a prayer that our brother's story will make a difference in other families' lives and assist communities in understanding, accepting and respecting our veterans and civilians in their newly formed life. It is a life that they cannot openly discuss for fear of traumatizing the people they love with their own painful experiences and their world in living with PTSD.

John's story, with a few unique historical exceptions, is not so very different from those of others who have died due to injuries pertaining to Post Traumatic Stress Disorder. His story offers the reader an understanding and acceptance of those who live with mental health issues.

If this book engages readers to rethink this serious issue, we will have honored our fallen brother with the respect, dignity and understanding he and so many others rightly deserve.

The following passage and poem were written by John W. Blake while he and David were both going through the process of attaining landed immigrant status (permanent residency) into the United States of America for the purpose of joining the United States Army.

*As my brother, David (17 yrs.) and I (19 yrs.) move forth unto the threshold of our careers, we endeavor to answer a very common question. Since we are both citizens and residents of Canada, many people have asked: "Why bother to become soldiers in the service of the United States Army?"*

*To some people our reasons might seem more idealistic than factual, but to my brother and me, they are very real. Here are our reasons and answers to this question.*

**Why Bother?**

To defuse the spread of communism
To save the freedom for us all

ONE FOR THE BOYS

To discourage moves of socialism
And aid our allies, however small

To make this world a better place
To earn our right to live in peace
To serve and save our country in face
And force oppression to a decrease

To stand with those who have gone before
To show the way for those who have not
To encourage the same of many more
To respect Robert F. Kennedy's, "Why not?"

John W. Blake©1968

Isaiah: 6-8 "Whom shall I send? And who will go for us?"
And I said, "Here am I. Send me!"

# Prologue

## Canada and United States of America: Officially Allies

The Government of Canada has continued to bawl from the steps of Parliament Hill in Ottawa that they "were not involved in that war" in Vietnam. However, history has since proven, and the Canadian people have known, the real truth of that enormous falsehood for decades. Why the deceit?

Canada's involvement started in July of 1940, when Canada and the United States of America (USA) officially became allies. Canadian Prime Minister William Lyon Mackenzie King, along with a growing number of Canadians, became increasingly concerned during WWII that Britain would fall and that Canada, with its small population and abundant natural resources, would become Germany's next target. Therefore, the *Ogdensburg Agreement* was hatched and the agreement was signed on August 17, 1940, between Prime Minister Mackenzie King of Canada and the United States President Franklin Roosevelt in Heuvelton near Ogdensburg, New York.

The agreement outlined a permanent plan for mutual defense overseas between the United States and Canada. The Ogdensburg agreement was the beginning of a long military relationship between Canada and the United States that would allow for the development of many military projects. For example, had the agreement not been in place the idea of the North American Air Defense (NORAD) would not have been able to take place because the Americans and the Canadians would not have been able to do it without each other. However, with the Ogdensburg agreement in place, the Permanent Joint Board on Defense could draft an agreement between the two countries' top military leaders. Therefore, the Ogdensburg Agreement set the ground rules that permitted both Canada and the United States of America to unite in a military and economic fashion; and each would make a contribution, whether directly or indirectly, to the Vietnam War effort.

After World War II, Canada, the United States of America and Britain were the founding members of what later became known as NATO

(North Atlantic Treaty Organization). The two most significant rules of the agreement were:

1) No member nation can attack a fellow member nation

2) Any attack on a member nation shall be interpreted as an attack on all member nations. (http://en.wikipedia.org/wiki/Ogdensburg_Agreement)

The Ogdensburg Agreement was essentially a blanketed reciprocal agreement. However, where the Vietnam War was concerned, it basically meant that Canada conveniently turned a blind eye to its own involvement in Vietnam and kept its hand in the back pocket of America.

During the Vietnam War, the American Armed Forces used Canadian airspace as U.S. bomber pilots practiced carpet-bombing over Suffield, Alberta, and North Battleford, Saskatchewan, for training purposes. The American recruiters softly recruited the Canadian young male population to volunteer with the American armed forces; by coupling an arrangement that pertained to landed immigration status and a promise of American citizenship, if desired.

Canada contracted, developed and tested seventy percent of the defoliant Agent Orange at Canadian Forces Base Gagetown, New Brunswick, the defoliant was used by the United States in Vietnam. Canadian aid during the war was solely directed towards South Vietnam and totaled $29 million from 1950-75. Canadian aid was routed through the Colombo plan and the Canadian Red Cross. Although humanitarian in appearance, Canadian assistance was an integral part of the Free World Assistance Program coordinated by the US Department of State with the International Security Office of the Pentagon.

War proved good for the economy. Canadian unemployment fell to a record low level of 3.9 percent; the gross domestic product rose by 6 per cent yearly. Nearly 500 Canadian firms sold $2.5 billion of war materials to the USA for use in Vietnam. Among the many items that Canada exported were raw materials, aircraft engines, military transportation, TNT, munitions, napalm, Agent Orange and the famous Green Beret tam. Canada exported over 1,000 military products necessary in the action of the war. However, Canada was deemed, then and now officially, "not involved in that war."(Victor Levant, Quiet Complicity, *Canadian Involvement in the Vietnam War,* 1986)

**Americans Run for the Border**

Across the border in the United States young men had become restless. A resistance to the draft erupted and a movement of young men who resisted the call of their country decided to make a run for the Canadian border to escape the draft.

Throughout the duration of the Vietnam War, Canada held the door wide open at the boundary of the US-Canadian borders and permitted the immigration of Americans and vice versa. Canadians exited Canada and joined the United States without fear of being prosecuted for committing treason by participating in a foreign war. Canada received approximately 90,000 American draft-dodgers and deserters, some with wives and children. (www.vcn.bc.ca/~jjones/hstrnt.html)

In 1964, President Lyndon B. Johnson stated, "If we quit Vietnam tomorrow we'll be fighting in Hawaii, and next week we'll have to be fighting in San Francisco."

Those impressionable words rung loudly throughout North America. Moreover, impressionable young Canadian men with high moral purpose answered the call.

The American government subsequently welcomed the Canadian 'boys' who had chosen to volunteer with the American forces in their fight against communism. Many Canadian young men joined the American forces—destination, Vietnam. It is believed that approximately 40,000 Canadian young men took the place of draft dodgers and deserters. This figure is difficult to prove because many Canadians, during their enlistment, used addresses of relatives who resided in the United States. Our brothers, John and David, were accepted into the United States under a permanent visa status with a directive to immediately enlist in the American Army.

John and David arrived together at Fort Dix, New Jersey on January 12, 1969. The next day, they stood proudly beside each other and pledged allegiance to the American flag of Canada's ally and were officially sworn into the United States Army.

This book is an emotionally charged visual of John's journey throughout his lifetime as the first and only Newfoundlander who intensively trained and earned the 'Green Beret' then served two tours of duty in Vietnam as a Long Range Reconnaissance Patrol (LRRP) with November Company, $75^{th}$ Rangers, $173^{rd}$ Airborne. Hooah!

In 1982, John relied solely on his Ranger skills and experiences in Vietnam when he became the first person to have ever walked 3,200 miles across the nation of the United States of America as he carried the American flag 'Old Glory'. He made history, without the technology of a GPS, cellular telephone or the support of an entourage. And he was Canadian.

On February 13, 1996, at the age of 47, John died as a result of his injuries pertaining to Post Traumatic Stress Disorder (PTSD). This is John Wayne Blake's extraordinary story.

# PART 1

# JOHN'S LIFE BEFORE, DURING, AND AFTER THE VIETNAM WAR

# Chapter 1

## Vietnam Then Not Now

JOHN BLAKE WAS JUST ONE-OF-MANY SOLDIERS who had arrived in Vietnam on that sultry afternoon. The deployment journey had started early the day before on a filled to capacity commercial flight that departed the United States of America with hundreds of fresh military replacements commonly known as 'cherries'.

Upon arrival, an unfamiliar odor compounded by excessive humidity, tropical heat and putrid fumes of burning jet fuel pierced his nostrils, in a most sickening manner when John disembarked the American Commercial Airline flight at Cam Ranh Bay military base. It was his welcome to the war zone.

After hours of standing in line due to the lengthy processing procedure for new arrivals, a cherry's first evening in Vietnam was spent jet-lagged and sleepless. Many of the soldiers chilled out by sitting on the bleachers at the base soccer field, viewing the distant mountains across the bay. Each was amazed that Vietnam was so very beautiful and picturesque.

John's first impression of Vietnam, minus the disgusting never-to-be-forgotten stench of what was later discovered to be burning human excrement mixed with diesel oil, was that of an island paradise. This was a place to surrender all inhibitions and tribulations while basking under tropical temperatures amidst the lush green foliage as the gentle waves of the South China Sea caressed the pristine sand-covered beach. Many of the American troops agreed that Vietnam resembled Hawaii. Moreover, John felt that the vast ocean and mountains reminded him of his former home beside the great Atlantic Ocean in Newfoundland, Canada, and the times he frolicked carelessly in the frigid Atlantic water. John also visualized the days that he ran freely throughout the hills and valleys of Topsail with his younger brother, David, and childhood friends. John's brief reflection of his home was quickly interrupted by real-time sounds of war.

The riveting burst of machine gunfire from a Huey helicopter in flight pierced the blackened sky with red bullet tracers while the enemy 'commies' returned fire with green tracers from a mountainside across the bay from the soccer field. From a distance, the soldiers quietly watched the fireworks of an actual firefight, and it was then they all realized that soon it would be them who would be in the fight. Many felt the despairing 'oh heck' moment that led to. "What now?"

Cam Ranh Bay is a deep-water harbor in Central Vietnam that is located on the southwest end of a long protective peninsula adjacent to the South China Sea. The peninsula is surrounded by crystal clear blue water and dense granular white sand. Today the Bay of Cam Ranh is the most valued gem in all of Vietnam. It is believed to be the best and most beautiful deep water port facility in the world. But it wasn't always that way.

During the Cold War years between 1962 and 1979, the United States presence escalated in the Vietnam War and developed Cam Ranh Bay into a major supply entrance port and constructed off-loading docks, warehouses, and barracks. The peninsula was home base for the US Army transportation units who distributed supplies throughout South Vietnam. The US Navy based their patrol crafts at Cam Ranh. The Naval Support Facility was nestled between two hills away from the main base. The United States Air Force base was constructed with eastern and western runways capable of accommodating massive transport aircraft on the supply base. The military base was not very large by today's standards, but it was functional and isolated away from the more densely populated northern half of the peninsula.

The military base housing barracks were located on the beachside, while the messing facilities, headquarters, and other related buildings were on the opposite side of the man-made road. The base became the main arrival and departure point for many of the 3.2 million military personnel assigned to the American war effort in Vietnam and for personnel lucky enough to be stationed on or near Cam Ranh Bay, the site of the Bob Hope Annual Christmas Show.

The United States military contracted American Commercial Airlines to transport troops from America to Cam Ranh Bay, Vietnam. The troops were fresh, energetic and filled with pride, anticipation and cautious nervousness surfaced as they loaded aboard the flight to a distant, war torn country and culture. The airline flight was like any other civilian flight with young and very pretty stewardesses, plus movies with all the other amenities of food and beverages. The flight time to Vietnam from Seattle, Washington, was approximately sixteen hours; generally with a one hour stop in Tokyo.

During the Vietnam War, approximately 1.5 million military personnel either fought in combat or provided close combat support. All of them were at least fairly regularly exposed to enemy attacks. Troops were deployed not as a unit but as individuals whose orders commanded a twelve-month tour of duty. Each new arrival was a replacement for a soldier returning home. This instilled a sense of aloneness among the young soldiers.

On the landing approach to Cam Ranh Bay, the Bowing 707 aircraft flew in high and swooped down in a touch and go landing. When the exit door opened, the troops were immediately blasted with hot and humid tropical heat as they departed the aircraft. Most were over-dressed for the excessive heat in their new fatigues and perfectly spit-shined boots.

The entrance doorway to the terminal was located adjacent to the exit doorway. It was there that the 'cherries' first met the seasoned warriors. The sight was sobering and respectful. As both groups passed beside each other, the rowdy chatter and newly formed comradery of the cherries that was forged aboard the incoming flight suddenly fell silent. The sight of the warriors who had just completed their tour of duty, and were now scheduled to depart Vietnam on the Freedom Flight to America, had a profound effect on the cherries. The warriors soiled and tattered fatigues quite suited the dried red mud that stuck to their worn-out boots. Their non-military hairstyles reflected their hellish tour of duty in Vietnam. Those who had made eye contact with a departing warrior received a first-hand glimpse of the thousand-mile stare that mirrored the horrid experiences of trauma, death, and grief in the eyes of many returnees. It was a silent message that screamed to the 'cherries' that war is horrible. John and the others would soon find this out for themselves and, ultimately, they too would develop and own the thousand-mile stare.

Once inside the terminal, the new arrivals were herded and bused off to a compound of tropical buildings near a beautiful beach. They were processed through a supply building where each received additional fatigues, a couple pairs of jungle boots, a cap and a steel pot helmet plus several pairs of socks, t-shirts and boxer shorts. Most never wore the boxer shorts due to the dreaded 'crotch rot' that generally occurred due to the excessive heat and humidity in Vietnam.

The barracks consisted of canvas tents with the wall-wings rolled up to allow the excessive heat to vent throughout the day and night. The floor was constructed of wooden pallets and the entire area was filled with bunk beds. As each of the new troops entered the barracks, more and more of them became further subdued as they watched the regular personnel—who now sported longer hair and mustaches and dressed in washed out fatigues-move about the base wearing personal guns. However vulnerable and defenseless the 'cherries' felt at that moment, they would have to wait a few more days to be processed out to their new fighting units before they too would be issued a gun with ammunition.

John, like many of the new arrivals never slept during his first night in Vietnam. The next day they were moved out of Cam Ranh Bay and closer to their destination, but before they left the base they were issued a poncho for the monsoon season. Without a gun and feeling vulnerable, they were uplifted to An Khe, Phu Cat, or elsewhere in South Vietnam to a designated repositioning depot where they were briefed on the 'ins and outs' plus advised of the 'to do' and what 'not to do' while in the country. In short order, they were each assigned to their teams or platoons. Finally they were issued weapons and ammunitions. It was at this point that the new troops were either airlifted or transported by truck to a landing zone base closer to the war zone. Generally, the practice in Vietnam was that each combat 'cherry' be paired with an experienced soldier for the first few weeks of duty. Work orientation was baptism by gunfire.

∞

# Chapter 2

## John's Journey

OUR FAMILY ORIGINATED FROM TOPSAIL, Newfoundland and Labrador, Canada. Our siblings, Annette, Wayne (known later in life as John), David, my twin sister and I shared a special understanding and camaraderie. Our Dad was a much older man than our Mom, and for what it mattered, he was much older than our friends' fathers, too. Still, we never noticed the difference.

During our young, formative years Dad had greatly influenced each one of us; he was strict but fair. He taught the boys rugby and boxing, especially Wayne, his oldest son. At just eleven years of age, Wayne engaged in regular boxing lessons and became extremely skilled during the following two years with Dad as his coach.

Wayne was an eager student and learned well the art of boxing; he thrived on the knowledge and precious time that Dad shared. David, just two years younger than Wayne, constantly followed his brother and observed Dad's life lessons. Decades later in Vietnam, Wayne's talent for boxing would prove to be quite memorable to those who challenged his ability to physically defend himself and his values.

It was September 21, 1962, when my siblings and I had arrived home for our evening dinner after our daily adventures of running throughout the hills and valleys in Topsail. Mom instructed Wayne to take my twin sister and me across the street to the neighbor's home. Dad had been released from the General Hospital in St. John's several months prior due to a terminal disease and died just minutes before we arrived home.

Wayne returned from the neighbor's home and Mom sadly informed both Wayne and David that Dad had died. Wayne immediately bolted through the back door and could be heard, deep in the garden, far behind the house, as he screamed gut-wrenching howls, the painful kind that emerged from deep inside one's heart and soul. Wayne was gutted with a deep emotional loss of his father and mentor. He never did cry.

David witnessed Wayne in utter distress, and quickly ran to the home of his friend, Patrick. Tears streamed down his face as he told Patrick's mother, "Dad is dead. May I come in?"

The evening our Dad died, both my twin and I, at almost nine years old, were at the neighboring house and observed the activity at our home through a small bathroom window directly across the road. We viewed the front entrance and watched the movement of people through the window of our parents' bedroom. The hearse arrived and removed what we later learned was Dad's body from our home. It was shortly after the hearse left that we were summoned home.

My twin and I felt stunned and bewildered by all the commotion when we entered our home, and we were told to go to our bedroom and wait for Mom. Within a few minutes, she entered our room and seated herself on the bed between my sister and me. She then explained that Dad had died; his life was over. My twin and I were too young to fully understand the scope of death and dying. We simply understood that he was gone, and he wasn't coming back.

Mom told us that Dad wanted us to have something special now that he was gone. My sister said she would like to have a bicycle and I requested roller skates. Our discussion was interrupted when the doorbell rang. It was Dad's nephew, Paul, and his wife who lived in St. John's. They were relatives from Dad's former marriage and had arrived as quickly as possible when they heard the news of Dad's death. Mom left us in our room with the knowledge that Dad was gone and we were getting something special. She greeted the relatives who had arrived at our home bearing a basket of fruit. That was the extent of our grief therapy.

Our little hearts were hurting. Without a word spoken between us, my twin and I both knew that it was little consolation that we were to receive gifts. A thousand bicycles or pairs of roller skates would never alleviate our loss and feelings of emptiness and sadness. A tremendous loneliness swept over both of us. The news was permanent, and we understood that we would never again see our Dad. He had left us. I could sense my twin's deep hurt and anger as we sat silently on the edge of our twin beds. We quietly stared at the bedroom floor for what seemed like hours until sleep took us away from our thoughts. We never did cry.

On that sorrowful day, the very foundation of our existence was fractured by the sudden loss of our Dad. Consequently, those shattered pieces of our lives would ultimately be prematurely filled by the impending lost childhood of his children.

**Life Without Dad**

During the months that followed Dad's death, and at the tender age of thirteen, Wayne asserted himself as the man of the house and watched over his younger siblings. He often cooked a meal or escorted us to and from school. He mostly refereed our childish quarrels and taught us to be more understanding and respectful to each other. Sometimes he was stern, but was generally kind and provided us with much-needed stability.

Wayne, David and my twin often took the time to be children. We ran with their friends throughout Topsail Hill and engaged in a form of reconnaissance. Cowboys and Indians were the general themes of the day. They would dash throughout the forest and path areas of Topsail Pond Road. If necessary, they would climb trees along the way to avoid being captured by the enemy, a local group of equally imaginative youngsters.

Mom's life had changed drastically, too, after Dad's death, and she decided that she would return to work. She consulted with engineers, and against their better judgment she reinstated the former Woodstock Cottage Club, our previous family business. She forged ahead in life at what she knew best, cooking, hosting, and hospitality. During early 1964, the newly constructed Woodstock Cottage Club restaurant was completed near the old ruins of the original Woodstock on the meadow adjacent to ours. Mom recruited and trained her staff in the art of advanced cooking, serving and hosting.

Our sister, Annette, who was sixteen years of age, worked part time alongside Mom at the Woodstock during the first summer of business.

The first year of business was quite successful; therefore, Mom expanded and added ten cottages to the entity. In 1965, the business name changed to the Woodstock Colonial Inn. Her dream had been realized and there was hope for a somewhat financially stable future. Later that fall, Annette moved to Ontario and lived with Mom's youngest sister. The following year she moved to Montreal, Quebec.

Long before Dad's death, in the early fifties, the original Woodstock Cottage Club had accidently burned to the ground. Three-year-old Wayne, unattended by the nursemaid, located some matches, paper, candles, and a cupcake. Innocently, Wayne tried to light the candle that he had placed in the cupcake. He struck the match that ignited the paper. Startled by the burst of flame he threw the burning paper into a closet that was filled with Mom's evening gowns, which fueled the fire that destroyed Woodstock during the wee hours on April 1, 1952.

The nursemaid, who had enjoyed a late evening out with her friends slept in and was unaware of Wayne's activity. She became trapped upstairs and jumped from a bedroom window. Fortunately, she injured only her leg. Thankfully, all occupants exited the burning building with just the clothing on their backs and minor injuries. Dad suffered minor burns as he retrieved David, an infant, from the crib in the nursery. My twin and I were born the year following the fire.

Dad's business associate in 1950 was an aspiring entrepreneur who neglected to arrange insurance on the building; hence, the structure and business were a total loss for the Saint John family. Decades later that same young businessman became a pioneer in Newfoundland communication mediums. Oddly, our paths would cross in 1996.

Wayne was sixteen when he ultimately restored his previous self-image regarding the accidental destruction of the former Woodstock. He saved the newly constructed Woodstock Colonial Inn from a kitchen fire. He fought the kitchen fire until the extinguisher had emptied. Wayne sprinted the two hundred yards from the restaurant to our house and returned with an additional fire extinguisher to douse the remaining flames. The incident was without any major damage to the structure and Wayne became an instant hero.

During the following years at Woodstock, Mom worked eighteen hour days every day and some days even longer until the spring of 1966 when her failing health and diminishing business put an end to her lifelong dream.

During the summer of 1966, Newfoundland's first "Come Home Year," our family departed from the island to begin a new life away from our beloved home. We traveled across land on the local railway system commonly known as the Newfie Bullet. The journey proved to be both lengthy and exciting for approximately five hundred miles from St. John's to Port Aux Basque. Then we boarded a ship to make the watery crossing to North Sidney, Nova Scotia. Upon arrival in North Sidney, we immediately boarded another train for the destination of St. Catherines, Ontario.

Mom obtained a job as a nutritionist/chef for the local clergy. Wayne found employment as a welding apprentice at the local dockyard. David, my twin sister and I continued our education. It was an uneventful year until Mom required surgery, which gave us a good reason to move once again, and join Annette in St. Hubert, Quebec.

**Enlistment and Vietnam: Times they are a changing**

In the fall of 1968 and at the age of nineteen and seventeen respectively, Wayne and David announced their decision to volunteer and enlist in the United States Army. Mom was devastated by her sons' decision and buried herself in disbelief and denial that her two boys' departure was indeed on the horizon.

In her youth, Mom had witnessed the many difficulties experienced by the men who served during both World War I (WWI) and World War II (WWII). Men who had returned from both wars broken and tattered were, forever changed. She fully understood the path that her sons intended to embark upon. It was a journey that would ultimately change their lives, as it had changed hers and that of her late husband, our father, during WWI. She remembered all too vividly the many injured soldiers who had returned home from overseas during both of the great wars, maimed and mentally changed.

At fifteen years of age, neither I nor my twin sister truly understood the magnitude of our brothers' decision to volunteer in the United States Army. We also lacked any understanding of future repercussions. We simply continued with our high school education in Quebec. We were regular teenagers. My twin was extremely active in sports, and I, not being the athletic type, was more academic. I tutored a young girl, who was born with cerebral palsy and assisted her with her academic program each day after school. Every Sunday morning, I lectured Sunday school lessons for neighborhood children at a nearby church. We simply continued our daily lives as was expected of us in our age group. We didn't quite grasp the fear or concern that loomed over our family.

While both Wayne and David awaited their birth certificates from the Government of Newfoundland and Labrador they continued to work at their regular jobs. Wayne worked as a marketing representative for a magazine publisher, and David was employed at the Montreal Stock Exchange. Neither was overly enthused about their employment, which no doubt enhanced their decision to make a change. Wayne was an avid reader and writer; he constantly wrote poetry. It was his way of recording events and rationalizing his thoughts and feelings on paper.

Pauline, Mom's cousin, had also been a WREN (Women's Royal Canadian Navy Services) during WWII. She had made a career with the Canadian Armed Forces after the war and was stationed in Montreal. One day she encouraged Mom to join her at the local Air Force Base for a social event. It was there that Mom met Thomas, a Canadian Air Force serviceman, who was nicknamed Paddy simply because he was formerly from County Cork, Ireland.

Paddy was an interesting, confident, and a kind person. We instantly liked him. He constantly referred to Mom as his 'darling girl'. They were happy; hence, we were happy. Within a few months of meeting, they were engaged and planned to marry the following year. Paddy was a bachelor, and we considered him very brave to want to settle down with a crowd of ready-made teenagers like us. With Paddy in her life, Mom became a different person or perhaps just more like the person we knew when we were very young children. She enjoyed dressing up for socials and cooking her specialty meals, but most of all she enjoyed the companionship. She laughed more often and looked rejuvenated. Paddy was good for her; we all appreciated this next chapter in Mom's life as both she and Paddy planned their wedding. She deserved happiness. They both deserved happiness.

**Mail Call—Discovery of a Family Secret**

It was mid-November and a Wednesday when two distinctive brown envelopes boldly stamped with the official seal of the Government of Newfoundland and Labrador Coat of Arms arrived in the mail. On that very day, David arrived home before Wayne and opened the brown envelope addressed to him. Inside was his birth certificate. Just as Wayne arrived, David waved the second brown envelope in the air as he excitedly announced: "They have arrived; here is your birth certificate."

Wayne excitedly snatched the envelope from David. He fully realized that enclosed within that envelope was the last major document that would set the pair of them on an adventure with the United States Army. He ripped apart the envelope and pulled out the letter with the enclosed birth certificate. The color drained from Wayne's face as he read the certificate and then suddenly his face reddened with anger as he roared, "What the fuck has happened, and who the fuck is John Wayne Blake?"

The next day, Wayne telephoned the Department of Vital Certificates in Newfoundland. The person who answered the call verified that he did indeed have the correct birth certificate. The spokesperson could not offer any explanation as to why the surname was Blake and not Saint John. Immediately, Wayne marched down the hallway towards Mom's bedroom. He stood in the doorway and waved the birth certificate in the air as he asked, "What is this all about? Why isn't my name Saint John? Is John Saint John my father? And if he is not my father— then who is?"

Mom stared at Wayne in a daze, knowing full well that this day was long overdue; she would not answer his questions that day or the next day. Unknowingly, he would have to wait decades for the answer. Instead, Mom quietly replied, "You figure it out." She gently closed her bedroom door and retreated into a depression. Fortunately, Paddy was in her life and helped her to regain her mental health and disposition.

The rest of us siblings never knew what the big secret was that shattered Mom and Wayne that day, but we did recognize that it was not a good day. Wayne, right then and there, decided to accept what he could not change, and stated, "Fuck it—I'll make something of this name!" From that day forward, John Wayne Saint John became John Wayne Blake and insisted that we call him John.

Christmas of 1968 was bittersweet. Each of us wondered if we would all be together again next Christmas or, for that matter, any future Christmases. Was this to be our last Christmas together?

David required Mom's permission and signature to enlist; he was only seventeen and would turn eighteen just two weeks after enlistment. Defeated and tormented, Mom reluctantly signed the necessary documents with a verbal understanding from a padre in the United States Army that David would not be deployed to Vietnam. John and David concluded the enlistment procedures and both were inducted into the United States Army. They immediately engaged in Basic Infantry Training.

**Return from Basic Training**

On a cold, rainy St. Patrick's Day weekend after weeks of Basic Infantry Training, our soldier boys finally arrived home. The taxi cab stopped directly in front of our home on Prince Charles Street in St. Hubert, Quebec. John and David had returned from Fort Dix, Burlington County, New Jersey, smartly dressed in the uniform of the United States Army.

I watched the boys from the living room window and felt an immediate sense of pride as they collected their duffle bags from the taxi and marched swiftly into the driveway. Running down the hallway I screamed with excitement, "They're here, they're home, the boys have arrived!"

My twin sister was first at the door as John and then David entered the house. She greeted John with a closed fist and punched him directly in the mouth, splitting his bottom lip as she asserted, "Just because you're wearing that uniform, don't think you're so smart."

Mom and I stepped back into the hallway, lost for words and half afraid to speak as we observed John's surprised reaction. David even looked somewhat concerned. It was obvious that John and my twin sister clearly understood each other. She cherished both her brothers equally, and she was obviously still very angry at the pair of them for leaving her behind. The silence was deafening. John stared down at her for what seemed like minutes. He had completely understood her and grinned as he wiped the dribble of blood from his bottom lip. Then with a warm, humorous gaze he replied, "Don't worry buddy, I won't."

After the excitement of their return had settled, we each sat on the end of our respective chair waiting to hear about their experiences and the next phase of their training in the Army. Surviving six weeks of Basic Infantry Training was the first step in military training for all new enlistees. Success meant that you were on your way to more advanced and specialized training. For the next three years; John and David were now assets of the United States Army.

During their brief time at home, they each continued to impress us with their physical strength and agility. John would press and hold his body weight on the tips of his fingers and thumbs while balancing his knees on his elbows in an upside down positional squat. We were constantly amazed how the pair of them could easily complete fifty single-arm-push-ups with one arm tucked behind their back, then switch without skipping a beat to the other arm and complete fifty more push-ups.

Every day we heard John singing Staff Sergeant Barry Sadler's song. *The Ballad of the Green Beret*, as it echoed throughout the house. We never realized that he aspired to become an actual Green Beret. We just thought that he liked the song because of the movie that starred the renowned actor, John Wayne. The two weeks we shared with the boys went by far too quickly.

At the beginning of April, both John and David returned to the United States. John traveled to Fort Gordon, Georgia for Advance Infantry Training, while David traveled to Fort Rucker, Alabama, and attended Air Craft Maintenance School.

**Next Stop—Vietnam**

One month later, John and David were both reunited in Basic Airborne Jump School, a three-week program, at Fort Benning, Georgia. After Jump School, David's official training was completed, and he was assigned as a company clerk to the 82nd Airborne Division Aviation Platoon, stateside position, just like the Army padre had promised Mom. He mostly typed transfer orders for soldiers who were to be deployed to Vietnam.

John volunteered for the U.S. Army Special Forces largely because of his enlistment officer, Staff Sergeant (SSGT) Gary L. Flaherty, whom John admired as a 'soldier's soldier'. John passed all the difficult selection tests and placed in the upper third of the class with excellence in conduct and efficiency. On July 28, 1969, John began Special Forces Phase 1. He then completed the 19-week intensive training requirements, which included advanced training in weaponry. In December, he earned the honor of donning the Green Beret. John was subsequently selected for additional military training as a Vietnamese interpreter.

John held great admiration for the instructors who conducted the Special Forces training. He regarded several instructors as mentors and friends, but most especially Roy Salinas, his principal instructor during Phase I of the Special Forces. John also regarded his instructor and teammates as unique soldiers, all of whom he fully believed he would lay down his own life to protect.

Suddenly, a change in plans occurred. Two weeks prior to John's sudden transfer to Vietnam, David had met with John and informed him that he had immediate orders to Vietnam. Apparently, after a short period as a company clerk, David had become very fed up with typing other soldiers' deployment orders to Vietnam. He proceeded to type his own request to be transferred to Vietnam, which was granted. David was scheduled to leave the United States by mid-December. John was furious.

On December 8th, at his own insistence, John was assigned to the 4th Battalion (Airborne) 503d Infantry 173rd Airborne Brigade, and within a few weeks he too was in transit to Vietnam. We believed at the time it was a gallant effort to catch up with David and somehow have him returned stateside.

David arrived in Vietnam just one month shy of his nineteenth birthday. The unofficial previous agreement between the United States Army and Mom was now moot. She was sick with worry about David's deployment to Vietnam. John was equally worried that his younger brother would be in Vietnam two weeks before him and was certainly not as well trained as himself. John dismissed his own expectations for additional stateside military training as an interpreter. Now, he was on a mission to get to Vietnam. John fully understood that a lot could happen in Vietnam in two weeks.

Mom was desperate when she contacted the U.S. Army who had unknowingly sent her two sons into a war zone, within weeks of each other. The Army didn't realize that they had issued orders for two brothers from Canada to be stationed in Vietnam at the same time, quite possibly because of their different last names. Regardless, Mom was going to have her say and attempt to get one of the boys back on safe soil. After a lengthy conversation with an Army Commander, he reassured her that the younger of the two boys who was not so extensively trained for combat as the older son would not be stationed near an active combat zone. But he would remain in Vietnam to finish his tour; there was no turning back. Orders were orders, and that was the end of the conversation. Mom sadly hung up the telephone with understanding that David, who was assigned to the 20th Trans Group and stationed at Cu Chi as a ground crew member would be safe. She tried, without much success, to imagine her sons in a safe place anywhere in Vietnam.

On the home front, a heavy atmosphere thick with the unknown constantly hung over our lives. We often wondered and worried if and when the boys would return. Moreover, would they be the same sons and brothers who had made it their choice to volunteer in the United

States Army ultimately fighting alongside approximately 500,000 soldiers in a foreign war against communism in Vietnam?

**Kill or be Killed**

John arrived in Vietnam on January 12, 1970. He was designated a rifleman and assigned to Company C 4th Battalion, Airborne, 503d Infantry 173rd Airborne Brigade (The Herd). The 173rd Airborne Infantry's mandates engaged soldiers in search and destroy, and clearing missions, which were a critical part of the combat strategy. The idea was to insert a platoon of soldiers into a pre-determined area, search out the enemy, destroy them and withdraw immediately afterward. The soldiers were transported by helicopter to a landing destination in the war zone. They would have been dropped off near the designated area, regroup, carry out their orders and complete the mission. Most missions generally lasted three to four days; then the platoon would be picked up by helicopters from a designated landing zone and returned to LZ English.

Within a week of John's arrival in Vietnam, he was assigned to a platoon. The platoon's assignments consisted of search and destroy missions that would occasionally lead to overkill and destruction of villages. John witnessed atrocities that were horrid, criminal behaviors and actions completely against his training as a soldier and as a human being that shocked him to his inner core.

John was the cherry out on his first mission with a platoon when they came upon the target, a small village that needed to be searched for NVA combatants and supporters. The action started very quickly and the platoon commenced their work in searching and destroying the village. John witnessed a few 'bad' soldiers commit indecent, inhumane assaults on the local village people, and no one in the platoon attempted to stop them. These hard-core soldiers took bizarre satisfaction in unjustified, unnecessary, extensive torture and beatings of villagers, men and women alike. Young women in the village suffered horrible indecency acts when they were dragged off to a secluded area by a few out-of-control soldiers to suffer rape and assassination.

The overkill was followed by grotesque dismemberment and separation of body parts by the same soldiers in an effort to prove body-count and in other cases some soldiers understood that Vietnamese spiritually believed that if the corpse was not intact then the spirit would not be able to move into the afterlife. The collection of freshly severed ears hung as war treasures on a few soldiers' belts as a sign of their military prowess. John's first mission in Vietnam was horrid and the experience would last him a lifetime. This was the barbaric and darkest side of war that occurred when soldiers turned into crazed animals. Appropriately, the 'bad' soldiers were charged with criminal offenses in Vietnam.

The vast majority of combat soldiers in the Vietnam conflict served with distinction, honour and valor. War is itself the greatest inhumanity inflicted on the souls of the combatants and also has far-reaching, deleterious effects on countless generations. Some soldiers in every war committed atrocities after witnessing and reacting improperly to the deaths of their best friends. War turns a few others into soulless, uncontrollable beasts who deserve to be incarcerated for their war crimes.

The American jail in Vietnam, nicknamed LBJ, in reference to Lyndon Baines Johnson, the 36th President of the United States, was located at Long Binh Post near Saigon. The facility was established in 1966 by the US Army as a temporary stockade. It was designed to hold about four hundred American prisoners who were separated by the seriousness of the charges or convictions and housed in tents with wooden floors. There were minimum, medium, and maximum security areas for the prisoners as well as a mess hall, work areas, and an administrative building.

Maximum security prisoners were housed individually in five-foot by seven-foot sheet metal and wooden boxes. The tents used in the minimum and medium security areas were designed to hold about eight men. However, each designated secured area reportedly contained almost double the number of prisoners until the end of the American occupation in the Vietnam War. Men who committed felonies that required sentences of less than one year were assigned to LBJ for confinement. LBJ also served as a holding facility for more serious crimes that required confinement in the United States Disciplinary Barracks at Fort Leavenworth, Kansas. Others confined at LBJ included those who were awaiting trial, as well as those who had served their sentence and waited to be returned to their assigned unit. Often these soldiers were not wanted by their old unit, which refrained from issuing orders for their transfer out of the stockade. This left the soldier to serve the remainder of his tour at LBJ until he DEROS'd (Date of Estimated for Return from Overseas) and returned to the United States to be discharged from service.

John quickly realized that what he had witnessed on those first few missions was not his way of soldiering. He was a man of high morals and strong beliefs. His integrity dictated his actions. He could not, nor would not, remain in a situation and condone the heinous behavior that certain platoon members practiced. John wanted out of that platoon, and he immediately requested and received a transfer to the 75$^{th}$ Airborne Ranger Unit and was assigned to November Company 75$^{th}$ Rangers. The rule on Ranger Hill for new volunteers to the Ranger unit was that regardless of where you were assigned to when you first arrived in Vietnam—on Ranger Hill you were considered a cherry until you were deemed not a cherry.

As soon as John arrived on Ranger Hill at LZ English base he began to run missions as a cherry with the Long Range Reconnaissance Patrol teams who regularly faced extremely dangerous, deadly work. His missions involved a six-member reconnaissance team that forged deep into the jungle and spied on the enemy. John's ascent to Ranger from cherry was recorded in an article recorded and published by the 173$^{rd}$ Airborne Brigade newspaper shortly after he arrive—view article on page 74. The team had gathered intelligence for current and future missions.

Quite often, the team's mission entailed setting up an ambush to capture a prisoner. Occasionally, the team made contact with the enemy, and there would be losses on both sides. John suffered his first tremendous loss on February 15$^{th}$ when his friend Ranger John Kelly, a Canadian volunteer and a member of the N/75$^{th}$ Rangers, died from a gunshot wound during an ambush. He and Kelly had trained together at Fort Bragg, NC. John Blake became John Kelly's replacement on Charlie Team. Then, on May 5th, John experienced another loss when his good friend, Ralph Martin, died as a result of a gunshot wound, also during an ambush. Then again on May 30th, John's friend, Santa Cruz, died. Plus, on June 28th, another friend, McGinn, (first name unknown) died. The list of lost friends grew and the cruel realities of Vietnam sank in; John had to learn to bury the pain of his losses.

In the spring of 1970, David had been re-assigned to the 187th Helicopter Assault Co., which was located just seven kilometers from the Cambodian border, and was primarily a base for the renowned Fish-Hook operations. The 187th Helicopter Assault Co. was the only American military group at Tay Ninh base camp. The purpose of the unit was to fly and provide air support for the South Vietnamese paratroopers and other allies. David, being a mechanic, repaired the helicopters, called 'hueys', daily. Once the hueys were repaired, the pilots always made a test run of the choppers with the operative mechanic aboard to assure quality workmanship was performed.

Occasionally, David would meet up with John at the 173d Airborne Brigade, LZ English base, Bong Son, Binh-Dinh, Province, for a few hours. Those welcomed visits from David would jolt John back to a reality that promoted a level of normalcy in an abnormal environment. On one occasion, David arrived at LZ English during a time when John was in the jungle on a radio-relay mission. The chopper crew radioed the relay team who were just a five-minute flight out and advise John that they would be out to pick him up because he had an unexpected visitor, his brother! This sort of service rarely happened in Vietnam, but because David was a chopper mechanic, he had friends with benefits when it came to the pilots.

John returned to LZ English and spent a couple of hours with David. During that particular visit, they both threw a few concussion grenades into the Bong Son River, which stunned the fish. Local people quickly collected the readily available catch to feed their families. After their short reunion, John returned to the radio-relay team. Before the boys parted John insisted that David keep a promise that he would never volunteer for any field combat. John reinforced his request to David when he stated, "I will do enough fighting for the both of us."

**MACV Recondo School**

While on Ranger Hill in Vietnam, John had been recruited to volunteer for specialty training at MACV (Military Assistance Command Vietnam) Recondo (reconnaissance and commando) School and immediately reported to Nah Trang in Central Vietnam, 5th Special Forces Group (SFG). He successfully participated in the three-week Long Range Reconnaissance Patrol, (LRRP) pronounced *Lurps* training program at Nha Trang, just outside of Saigon. In December 1967, the abbreviation LRRP changed to LRP meaning Long Range Patrol.

(*For the purpose of this story, the author will continue to use both LRRP and LRP as LRRP/LRP simultaneously in referencing the members of the 173 Airborne 75th Rangers so as to include members who have served multiple tours of duty prior to the abbreviation change in 1967.*)

MACV Recondo School was an elite school that taught its students how to operate in stealth as they walked silently in the foliage of the jungle and listened to the sound of the jungle. The jungle was the classroom; one error and the student could answer to the enemy's bullet. MACV Recondo School was considered the deadliest school on earth. The final exam was an assigned actual combat mission deep in the jungle. Returning alive was the passing grade.

The teams at Recondo School were made up of six members. Before the three-week, eighteen hours-a-day course was finished, half of the airborne qualified recruits would have been dismissed or simply left of their own accord. John persevered. MACV Recondo training was exactly what he wanted to do, and he held great respect for the men who operated the program.

On the first day at MACV the recruits were ordered to run a six-mile trek around the perimeter of the base as they carried a sealed thirty-pound ammo can covered by a poncho liner and placed in a rucksack. Failure to complete the run in one hour resulted in dismissal from the program and an immediate return to their former platoon. Generally, one-third of the recruits were dismissed in the first hour due to poor physical ability, largely due to poor nutrition. Those that completed the trek headed to the communal shower where everyone noticed the large red welts on each other's back and shoulders from the friction of the rucksack.

The program was headed by a Special Forces Major who shouted a welcome to the newly formed volunteers and then immediately engaged in a poignant no holds barred lecture. He first informed his audience of the meaning of the Recondo patch, which each would receive if they survived the three-week course. The word Recondo was embroidered in black letters across the top of an arrowhead emblem and derived from three infantry words: Reconnaissance, Commando, and Doughboy (a WWII Ranger term). The 'V' that is formed by the arrow head represents valor and the mission in Vietnam. Additionally, the arrowhead pointed downward represents air to ground infiltration into enemy territory and also symbolizes scouting and survival skills. Recondo involves reconnaissance, patrolling, ambushing, POW snatching, collecting intelligence and more. There would be times in the jungle when a Ranger would be so well hidden and camouflaged that the enemy would literally urinate directly on him without being discovered. A Ranger had to have nerves of steel.

The food at Recondo School was a nutritious, high protein balanced diet with vegetables and starch. A significantly better diet than to what they were accustomed. The tents housed fifteen students, and they were expected to dig their own outhouse. Cohesiveness and teamwork were a huge factor in successfully completing the mentally and physically challenging program.

The LRRP/LRP training program was intense from the beginning. Each six-man team had to function as one unit. Failure to do so would result in dismissal of the whole unit from the program. That meant that each person in the unit was required to eat and finish their meals together, sleep together, shower together and tend to their other bathroom needs together. No one person of the unit was permitted to fail a test, drop out of a drill march or be alone at any time for any reason. After two warnings, failure to comply by the third offense would result in the whole team being dismissed.

The new recruits met with instructors who specialized in varying disciplines, such as assault and reconnaissance, logistics and mapping, repelling, weaponry and explosives. The instructors were firm but fair. The school's enhancement program was critical and rigid. Occasionally, during the second week, a few more recruits would leave due to their inability to comprehend the material.

A typical day would consist of a six mile run, multiple physical training exercises, repelling from a tower and class instruction. An unspoken rule existed: Don't be a smart-ass, but do be proactive and competitive...and never outperform the instructor.

Seldom did a Ranger repel into the jungle, but it was a necessary skill. Repelling was practiced down a wall and/or from a helicopter. John thrived on tough training. Most of the training came easy for John, as he was a strong runner, excellent swimmer, and an expert with firearms. John enjoyed repelling from the towers, but repelling from a Huey chopper was pure excitement. He was an astute student in map reading, navigation and many other aspects of MACV training. He conquered all required disciplines, mastered the materials and graduated with little difficulty.

Since all Rangers are marksmen, instruction on weaponry and explosives classes were more geared to the care and maintenance of the equipment prior to a mission. Before going out on a mission the Rangers had to make sure that all magazines were disassembled and cleaned by hand with a towel and then refilled with clean ammo. Grenades were checked to ensure that the pins or the spoons were not cracked, and then the pins would be lightly taped as a safety measure.

Prior to a mission, MACV recruits were taught to anticipate and to think like the enemy, live like the enemy and eat the same type of food as the enemy. Ultimately, they would smell like the enemy. The final test was scheduled during the last few days of training. The goal was to go out on a three to four-day authentic long range reconnaissance patrol mission with the probability of engagement in real-live gunfire with the enemy and survive without causing injury to the team.

The team prepared by ensuring that all the items they carried that could rattle or reflect light were covered or secured with black tape. The soldiers dressed in camouflaged garments and blackened their white skin. They each packed enough ammunition and various types of explosives, such as grenades, claymore mines and C-4 (an explosive), web gear, radios, food, water, medic kit and most importantly their hand weapons. They carried nearly 100 pounds of gear. A helicopter would land and unload the team into a drop area; then the Rangers would disburse to the target area that required patrolling. When the mission was completed or compromised, the chopper would collect the team. A designated pick-up zone would be determined prior to departure. Recondo School was just the beginning of the many challenges that John would face as a Long Range Reconnaissance Patrol (LRRP) Ranger.

John, being a member of the Special Forces (Green Beret) and MACV Recondo School, was considered a highly trained intelligence specialist, an experienced combat soldier, and a 75th Ranger of the 173rd Airborne. He often volunteered to run missions with other team leaders when an additional member was required He became a respected, trusted and well-liked member of Company N (November Rangers) 75th Infantry, 173d Airborne Brigade.

Prior to graduating MACV Recondo School, John assisted his new friend Kang Kwang Ki, a Korean soldier, who desperately wanted to befriend a Canadian female. John thought about his friend's request and decided to give the soldier my address. John knew that I would understand and would write to the soldier. He then scribed a letter for Kang Kwang Ki. Upon receipt of the soldier's letter, I promptly responded. Unfortunately, there were no additional correspondences between us, yet I still possess the one letter from him. Years later, I asked John if the young Korean soldier Ki had survived; John stood quietly and stared off into the distance. He then turned and walked away without responding.

**Rangers Lead the Way**

The 75th Rangers of the 173 Airborne who served in Vietnam were an elite special operation force. Composed of small, heavily armed long-range reconnaissance patrol teams, they patrolled deep into enemy-held territory. Rangers in Vietnam lived by their oath; moreover, none would ever leave a member behind. The rule stood strong, even if the Ranger was wounded or killed, you never leave him behind.

The Ranger mission was to sneak up and spy on the enemy while hiding in the jungle—harrowing events for young men to experience and witness as the enemy walked within a few feet of their location. A simple cough or a snap of a twig could give away the Ranger team location, and then all hell would break loose. The Rangers communicated using hand signals, but when it was necessary and they were near they would whisper directly into the other Ranger's ear. Most missions ran three to five days in length. Occasionally, a couple of teams would run in the same vicinity as part of a larger coordinated mission. The prime goals were to collect intelligence, discover enemy troop locations, survey trails, and enemy hot spots plus direct artillery and air strikes. They also assessed bombing damages, performed ambushes and conducted sniper attacks. The Rangers were the eyes of the command. When the occasion presented itself, the Rangers often captured enemy soldiers for interrogation.

The LRRPS/LRPs were a rare breed of men who could read tracks in the jungle, set ambushes and detonate claymore mines just ten feet away from their hidden position. To stay awake for several days without sleep while out on a mission, Rangers were often supplied with Pep pills commonly known as Dexedrine (dextroamphetamine). They paid little attention to the recommended dose or frequency of use. The drug gave the Rangers a sense of fearlessness as well as keeping them awake. Every sight and sound was heightened. Not only did the drug boost the fighter to fight without fear, it also reduced the harmful impact of combat on their psyche to prevent mental breakdown from combat stress. Many military personnel, doctors and soldiers believed that this resulted in an unprecedented low rate of combat trauma during their warfare tour and a widespread outbreak of PTSD among combat veterans in the aftermath of the war.

The LRRPS/LRPs were a well-known force by the North Vietnamese Army (NVA) and the Viet Cong (VC). The enemy placed a bounty of one thousand dollars on the head of each Ranger, dead or alive.

**The Renowned Patrick Tadina**

One Ranger who personifies the history of the N/75th Rangers in Vietnam is Patrick (Tad) Tadina, a most respected and renowned former team leader of the N/75th Rangers.

Tadina, a native of Maui, Hawaii, led hundreds of patrols deep within enemy controlled areas during his five tours of Vietnam. Depending on the mission, he often dressed as a North Vietnamese soldier, wearing khakis or black pajamas, Ho Chi Minh sandals and a floppy hat. Tadina carried a communist AK-47 assault rifle, the NVA choice of weaponry. He knew his enemy well; they had taken the life of his only brother in An Khe, Vietnam.

Tadina's success on the battlefield was due to his combat expertise, but his attire, dark complexion and small stature also contributed. He always walked point, the most dangerous position on a patrol. If confronted by an ambush, his enemy would be surprised by his appearance, thinking that he too was Vietnamese. This enabled Tadina and his team to shoot first and stay alive. Tadina devoted his time and expertise in training the men under his direct command to become highly skilled Rangers and return home alive.

During the five years that he had been a combat infantryman more than 200 men served under his direction and returned to America without so much as a scratch. Although Tadina was wounded three times during different missions, his wounds healed and he returned to combat after each occasion. During Tad's last tour of duty 1969-1970, John experienced the honor and privilege of running several missions on his team.

Apart from scheduled leave between tours of duty, Tadina's service during the Vietnam War spanned five straight years. This record of service established Tad as the longest continuous serving Ranger during the Vietnam War. While serving five years as a team leader, not one of his team members was killed. He accomplished this at the risk of his own life many times and was cited for extreme valor, including two Silver Stars, ten Bronze Stars (seven with "V" Device), four Army Commendation Medals (two with "V" Device) and three Purple Hearts.

The wealth of confidence, experience and knowledge which Tad shared with his team members was invaluable and made the difference between life and death when on patrol in the jungles of Vietnam. Ultimately, his lessons would be passed on throughout Ranger Hill at LZ English in South Vietnam.

Tadina was eventually ordered out of Vietnam when it was discovered that the enemy had placed an unusually high bounty on him. He returned to America in July 1970. Tadina is a soldiers' soldier and highly respected, admired and loved by his fellow Rangers.

In 1995, Patrick Tadina was inducted into the Ranger Hall of Fame. He retired after Desert Storm with the rank of a Command Sergeant Major. Patrick "Tad" Tadina is a living legend.

### John's Choice of Weapon—M60

John embraced his work as a Ranger as equally as he embraced his M60 machine gun, which fired 7.62mm bullets, from a disintegrating belt of M13 links. He serviced his weapon of choice with regular cleanings and loaded the 22-pound weapon with ammunition and tracers. John, being a small-framed male with a stature of 5 feet 7 inches and a weight of 135 pounds soon became well known among the Rangers for his endurance. He often carried a hundred pounds of ammunition and necessary supplies while out on missions.

Whenever John was forced to provide suppressive or cover fire for his teammates he would engage the M60 and blast the enemy. This action protected the Ranger unit when they were in close range of the enemy's weapons, or if his team was escaping a hot pursuit. The effect of the furious M60 inflicted heavy casualties on the exposed enemy.

John's ability to perform the classic 'duck walk' while carrying the M60 was impressive and memorable. To this day, his Ranger brothers still boast that nobody could 'duck walk' an M60 like John Blake!

**Dangerous Work in Vietnam**

Decades later in 2016, Ranger Mike Swisley told me of a mission that he and John participated in during John's first tour of Vietnam in 1970. John and Mike were out on a mission that turned hot with four other Rangers: Golf (G-team) team leader Roberto Patino, George Morgan, Golf assistant team leader and Paul (full name unknown), plus one other Ranger.

They had been dropped off near a tree line at the designated LZ by helicopter just before dusk. The team immediately took cover for a short period of time to ensure that they had not been detected by the enemy. Patino signaled for the unit to move out, so they quickly and quietly blended into the jungle foliage. The team moved in stealth and covered their tracks behind them to a location where they could set up a safe perimeter with claymore mines. In the darkness of the night, they watched and listened for movement of the Viet Cong. Rangers rarely slept while out on a mission in the jungle as sleeping could mean death. The mission was strictly a hunt and destroy: set an ambush, kill the enemy and collect any documents.

John carried his M60 with eight hundred rounds of ammunition, plus enough water and rations for three days. The load weighed approximately one hundred pounds. Other team members frequently offered to carry some of the bandoleers (M60 ammo belts). Each bandoleer weighed seven pounds and was usually carried until needed in a metal box strapped over the shoulder, but John generally carried his own load without help.

Just before daybreak the following day, the team broke camp and traveled to the pre-determined location to set up the ambush. Under a triple canopy of foliage that darkened their environment, they slowly and quietly proceeded for several hours through the jungle. It was early morning when they suddenly happened upon a group of

Viet Cong soldiers who had the same intent. The Ranger unit had walked into an ambush.

Patino, who had walked point—the most dangerous position—was first to see the enemy. He immediately opened fire; it was them or him. John generally walked behind the point man in the third position. The unit jumped into action, they covered all sides, firing their M16s and tossing grenades. One Ranger was shot in the shoulder and unable to use his weapon. The uninjured team members fought furiously to protect the wounded Ranger and each other from any additional injuries. John stepped up and opened fire with the M60, providing the cover fire necessary for his team members to escape.

The Ranger unit quickly moved to a higher elevation with the injured Ranger in tow. Mike remained near while John mesmerized the enemy with machine gun fire peppered with red tracers that seared through the darkness of the jungle. The unit watched the tracers from a distance as John sprayed the countryside. He emptied nearly all of the eight hundred rounds he had carried as he single-handedly fed the rounds into the M60. The last burst of pre-set arrangement tracers from the M60 warned John that he was down to his last five shots. Mike had also witnessed the warning markers and roared at John to follow while he covered John's retreat with gunfire. John made tracks to catch up with the team; he felt much lighter without the additional ammo. His boots barely touched the ground as he bolted past Mike.

Mike shook his head in disbelief and laughed when he stated, "I will always remember saying to John, 'Hey you were the real John Wayne back there—Hooah!'"

The mission was compromised and the unit had to leave the area as quickly and quietly as possible as they traveled to the pre-designated pick-up zone. The team had run for many hours, zig-zagging the territory and hiding in the jungle for short periods of time to rest. Then, they radioed in the situation and requested an immediate pick-up.

Just before dusk, the chopper pilot advised them that they were a few minutes out from the pick-up zone. It was a welcomed sight when they saw the Huey drop down for a few minutes, just enough time for the Rangers to scramble aboard with one wounded.

Once the Ranger team returned to base the wounded Ranger was medivaced to a hospital and the other Rangers were debriefed on the mission. Each was exhausted and collapsed onto their bunks after they had showered off the stress and debris of the jungle. Sleep came easy to the exhausted but triumphant Rangers.

The next day, the team undertook some unpleasant housekeeping as they decided that Paul, one of their team members, was deemed not suitable to be a Ranger. He was immediately removed from the unit. One thing was certain in the Ranger world: If a Ranger failed to be a dependable or a trusted part of the team, then he was a liability. Liabilities meant death.

On October 18th, Randy Krisely, John's closest friend during Phase 1 of Special Forces, was killed in a helicopter crash. John felt deeply hurt by the loss.

A few days later, on October 22nd, tragedy struck once again when Roberto Patino, Golf team leader, was killed in action during a mission. On that fateful day, John was out on a mission with a different team. When he returned, John was informed of Patino's death and felt crushed by the loss. He deeply respected Patino and had run many missions with him during the previous months. John had also considered him a trusted friend. Since John's arrival in Vietnam, he had already suffered the loss of six close friends.

Team leader Sgt. Robert Lerma Patino was John Blake's trusted friend, and his death affected John tremendously. As he stated in his journal, "Sgt. Patino was killed here with us, because of multiple frag wounds. Pat was on a special mission in the Tiger Mountains and on the second to last day he tripped a booby trap and was killed. Patino's nickname, *The Ragbag,* held a special meaning to him, Morgan and me. No one will forget *The Ragbag,* for he should never have died that day. Left to mourn were his wife, children, family and the November 75th Rangers.'

The following is an excerpt which John wrote from the original poem Ragbag:

> "I remember now, the way you fought...the way you felt, and the way you cared...in life you've passed a lesson, well taught...the end you found wasn't what you feared! Things will go on, and I, somehow...will join you somewhere, by and by! I'll keep on fooling around, for now...remembering you, Pat, you didn't die!"

John also wrote that it should be known that Sgt. Patino was killed during a twelve-day mission, the purpose of which was to locate and destroy an enemy radio center. John wrote that the whole mission was a jinx.

**The Ranger Brotherhood in Vietnam**

Ranger work in the jungles of Vietnam was constant; seldom would a team have more than a couple of days off before they would be sent out on the next mission. During their off time, Rangers often practiced repelling on Ranger Hill and hung out together discussing upcoming and past missions.

Ranger Hill on LZ English base was the Rangers' home away from home. It was a more relaxed lifestyle than soldiering in a rifle platoon, which often required regular inspections. On the downside, Rangers were constantly on alert and ready to be called out to search and destroy the enemy due to mortar attacks on the base or to verify intelligence on enemy activity.

Each Ranger team of six members lived together in the 'hootches', which consisted of a tin roof covered in tent-like canvas material attached to wooden studs with a screened doorway. Sandbags were layered on the outside walls for additional protection. Inside the hooch, walls were covered halfway up the tent walls with plywood attached to the wooden studs. Bed bunks were scattered around the interior perimeter. On the plywood walls were protruding nails that doubled as hooks for clothing and other military gear.

Laundry facilities were operated by assigned military personnel. The Rangers simply dropped off their bag of dirty garments and collected them later. All garments were labelled prior to laundering.

Homemade shower facilities consisted of a 50-gallon drum of water that was heated by the sun and flowed by gravity. The drum was suspended above an outdoor single wooden cubicle. A hose was attached to the drum with a valve which enabled the Ranger to turn on and then turn off the water. No frills.

Toilet facilities were even more basic. At some point and time during a tour of duty, each Ranger would take their turn in 'burning human excrement mixed with diesel oil' and suffer the horrid stench. Kitchen patrol, (KP) duties were assigned to non-Ranger military personnel on base.

Rangers often went into the nearby town for haircuts and to visit the local saloon that generally served warm skunky beer. Occasionally, a Ranger would get dysentery from eating a flavored ice treat or other items made with local dirty water.

The recreational hall on base was a large meeting room where the Rangers could hang out, have a few beers, sing a few songs and relax. The hot meals at the mess hall were considered good.

Occasionally, the Rangers would retreat to nearby Phu Cat Airbase by hitching a ride. The airbase was comparably a luxury facility with a tennis court, swimming area, cold beers and a larger variety of food and entertainment. On one particular occasion, the Phu Cat Airbase came under rocket attack, and its commander requested the assistance of a Ranger team to search and destroy the enemy that inflicted the attack. A team was sent and found a whole cache of rockets and mortar. They destroyed the munitions and became honored guests of the Phu Cat Airbase. From that point forward, the Rangers' money was refused at the airbase. They were all welcomed to the amenities, especially free cold beer.

Prior to Patino's death and during the summer of 1970, Patino, Morgan, Blake, and Swisley borrowed a medical jeep without authorization and drove to Phu Cat Airbase to enjoy a few cold beers and celebrate Mike's 21st birthday. It became obvious to them early in the evening that other military personnel would deliberately move in the opposite direction rather than confront the Airborne Rangers, and that gave the boys a sense of security. Perhaps it was because they had each worn their T-shirts with the Ranger logo clearly displayed. The Ranger logo was enough warning to other military personnel not to mess with them. Not surprisingly, they each drank far too much and decided to sleep it off at the Air Force base before they returned to Ranger Hill on LZ English base. That evening, Blake and Morgan slept where they fell, on the grass outside of a barracks. However, Patino with Swisley managed to stagger into the barracks and found two soft, comfortable, clean bunks.

In early November, Ranger Mike Swisley was wounded during a firefight. He was transported to a hospital in Japan, where he quickly recovered from his wound and returned to his unit by early December. Mike's tour in Vietnam had come to an end; his Date of Estimated Return from Overseas (DEROS) was reached. He returned home just in time for Christmas.

John missed his friend. They had become trusted buddies and confided personal experiences from their civilian lives, experiences, which were both profoundly enlightening and tragic. Rarely would soldiers become close confidants. Personal friendships were seldom established during a theatre of war. The probability of loss was tremendous, and the distraction of that loss could be devastating. John felt contented that Mike had gone home to the United States where he would reunite with a young lady whom he had known since kindergarten. Ultimately, they would fall in love and marry.

John felt peaceful knowing that finally this friend, Swisley, would be safe from the war. The pair had spent many months together on LZ English running missions. When they weren't on missions they would practice repelling skills, and hand-to-hand combat maneuvers. They shared their experiences and knowledge of jungle survival. Everyone understood that shared skill sets enhanced the team members' survivability.

John's friend, John 'Limey" Ormiston returned to Vietnam after a month of leave at home. He had become a proud father of a baby boy and upon his return to Vietnam, he had chosen to stand down from running dangerous missions. He wanted to ensure his new son had a father after the war. There was a clear understanding in the volunteer Ranger units that once you decided to no longer continue running missions, you could stop without question.

John Blake enjoyed the sport of boxing in his younger years. He had gained a reputation as a boxer in Vietnam, an attribute that served him well when attitudes or tempers got out of hand on Ranger Hill. A round or two with John and the problem was resolved. In due course, a rumor spread throughout the LZ that John was a Canadian light-weight golden glove boxing champion. The take away message seemed to be, "Don't mix-it-up with him. You'll lose!"

Team Golf had been restructured after Patino's death. George Morgan became the new Golf team leader, and John was designated assistant team leader. The pair continued to run missions together. They were good friends and respected colleagues, and became inseparable. George appreciated John's poetry, which reflected the many great soldiers and friends with whom they had served, a number of whom had been wounded or had died in combat.

**Vietnam—Lack of Leadership**

The Year of the Monkey began on January the 30, 1968. This would be the Tet holiday known as the day the opinion of many Americans changed from supporting U.S. policy towards South Vietnam to opposing the Vietnam War.

On January 31, 1968, some 70,000 North Vietnamese and Viet Cong forces launched the Tet Offensive (named for the lunar New Year holiday). A coordinated series of fierce attacks on more than 100 cities and towns ensued in an attempt to bring about the quick and total defeat of South Vietnam. This occurred just as many Vietnamese families began their observances of the lunar New Year. Since the celebration of Tet was the most important holiday on the Vietnamese calendar, the date had been the occasion for an informal truce. It was expected to be a 36-hour cease-fire for the holiday.

Within hours of the ceasefire, the People's Army of Vietnam (PAVN) and Viet Cong forces struck targets throughout South Vietnam, including cities, towns, government buildings, and forces of both the United States and Army of the Republic of Vietnam (ARVN) military bases. The PAVN and Viet Cong intended to take over the capital city of Saigon but only succeeded in taking over the city of Hue in the far north of South Vietnam. The final result was a military failure for North Vietnam and the Viet Cong whereby they suffered enormous casualties and significant destruction of military assets.

Officials at the White House and the Department of Defense were very satisfied with the result over the NVA and Viet Cong defeat, but the major media reacted differently. A particularly bold attack on the U.S. Embassy in Saigon stunned the United States and international observers, who saw images of the carnage broadcast on television as it occurred. During the actual fire-fight, several American journalists in Vietnam had reported that suicide commandoes were inside the U.S. Embassy and had seized the first floor. They reported that snipers were on the rooftops near the Embassy shooting at American military policemen and paratroops when in fact not one invader was successful in getting in any building of the U.S. Embassy Compound. The reports amounted to fake news.

The renowned Walter Cronkite of CBS reported to his American audience, "Early Wednesday, Vietnam time, the Communists struck at the heart of Saigon and seized part of the new American Embassy. At dawn, American military police tried to storm into the Embassy but were driven back by the Viet Cong force, estimated at twenty men. The Communist suicide squad held part of the first floor." Then in February 1968, in the wake of the Tet Offensive, Cronkite announced, "it seemed more certain than ever that the bloody experience of Vietnam is to end in a stalemate." Those comments gave the North Vietnamese and the Viet Cong tremendous pleasure as they enjoyed a major psychological victory due to the reporting by much of the U.S. media. Despite its heavy casualty toll, and its failure to inspire widespread rebellion among the South Vietnamese, the Tet Offensive proved to be a strategic success for the Democratic Republic of Vietnam (DRV).

Before the Tet Offense, General William C. Westmoreland and other representatives of the Johnson administration had been claiming that the end of the war was in sight. The General had earned the nickname Tiger for his aggressiveness. He drove his subordinates hard and some would say mercilessly. Westmoreland requested more than 200,000 new troops to mount an effective counteroffensive, an escalation that many Americans saw as an act of desperation. As antiwar sentiment mounted on the home front, some of Johnson's advisers that had supported past military buildup of troops in Vietnam now argued for scaling back U.S. involvement. The Vietnam War became more about re-election in the government than arguing about the Vietnam War.

On March 31, the beleaguered President Johnson declared that he was limiting the bombing of North Vietnam to the area below the 20th parallel (thus sparing 90 percent of Communist territory) and calling for negotiations to end the war. At the same time, he announced that he would not be running for reelection in November. However, peace talks would drag on for another five years, during which more American soldiers were killed than in the previous years of the conflict. Johnson's decision to halt escalation after the Tet Offensive marked a crucial turning point in American participation in the Vietnam War. (http://www.history.com/topics/vietnam-war/tet-offensive)

In addition, another significant battle that negatively impacted the support of Americans against the Vietnam War was the battle of Hamburger Hill, also known as the Dong Ap Bia Mountain or Hill 937. The mountain is located on the Laotian border of South Vietnam, rising up from the floor of the western A Shau Valley. The entire mountain is a rugged, uninviting wilderness blanketed in double and triple canopy jungle, dense thickets of bamboo, and waist-high elephant grass. The battle, which was fought May 10-20, 1969, was a direct assault against a heavily defended and strategically insignificant hill, resulting in over 400 U.S. casualties and causing an outrage in America.

The Hamburger Hill battle had run afoul of a fundamental war-fighting equation. Master philosopher of war Karl von Clausewitz had stated almost a century and a half earlier, "Because war is controlled by its political object the value of an object must determine the sacrifices to be made for it both in magnitude and also in duration." He went on to say, "Once the expenditure of effort exceeds the value of the political object, the object must be renounced." That is exactly what happened. The expenditure of effort at Hamburger Hill exceeded the value the American people attached to the war in Vietnam. Public opinion had turned–not on ideological grounds, as the anti-war movement would claim, but for pragmatic reasons. The prevalent sentiment was, "Win the damn thing or get the hell out!" When the Johnson administration seemed unable to do either, the American people's patience ran out. (June 1999 issue of Vietnam Magazine)

Not everything that was presented to the public was as it appeared. The 'Tet Offensive' became a motivating factor for many young men to volunteer and for others to report to their draft enlistment in the fight for the people of South Vietnam against Communism. The battle at Hamburger Hill helped prove that American forces were quite capable of delivering a strong military attack. That became instrumental in the eventual withdrawal of military troops from South Vietnam. The enemy had lost its punch, so to speak.

Vietnamization of the war then began in earnest. At the same time, President Nixon gave orders to General Abrams for withdrawal of 25,000 U.S. troops by July 8 and removal of 35,000 more by early December. The U.S. military was on its way out of Vietnam, and the fighting on the ground would gradually be turned over to the ARVN. At the strategic level of the war, time had run out.

**American War Protesters**

The return home from Vietnam for several hundred thousand soldiers in the late 60's and early 70's to America foretold of turmoil and chaos long before they left Vietnam.

American and non-American protesters took part in protest marches that would ultimately cause humiliation for the United States. It also would cause the Cambodians and South Vietnamese the loss of their nation after already incurring the loss of millions of lives. The American military that served in Vietnam would be blamed and shamed by those protesters, who knew not what they were doing.

On October 15, 1969, two hundred thousand protesters traveled down Pennsylvania Avenue, Washington, D.C., toward the White House in a protest demonstration as they screamed, "What do we want—Peace! When do we want it—Now!"

Many protesters carried sticks held high, fashioned as flag poles, with the flag of North Vietnam or the Viet Cong attached, while others held the American flags hoisted upside-down in protest. This caught the eye of then North Vietnam Premier Pham Van Dong, who encouraged and praised the protesters in America. Due to this notoriety, during a weekend on November 15th, a much larger gathering of protesters marched to the United States Capitol grounds. In fact, it became the largest protest ever held in Washington, D.C.

At least a quarter of a million students and representatives of labor unions formed up and chanted as they marched: "One, two, three, four; we don't want your fucking war. Ho, Ho, Ho Chi Minh! The NLF is going to win!" NLF is the acronym for National Liberation Front, a political organization formed on Dec. 20, 1960, to affect the overthrow of the South Vietnamese government and the reunification of North and South Vietnam (https://en.wikipedia.org/wiki/Viet_Cong)

The protest became violent in front of the U.S. Department of Justice building when they began to break windows and approximately 50 people were arrested. Protesters threw rocks and bottles at the police, and tear gas had to be used to control the crowd. The United States flag that hung above the Justice building was torn down from the flagpole and burned. The protesters then raised the flag of the Viet Cong. The protesters believed in their constitutional rights to freedom of speech, at any cost, as they basked in their moment of fame in front of television and media crews.

Many protesters were manipulated by up and coming entertainers, such as Peter, Paul and Mary and the cast of *Hair,* plus many other seasoned entertainers who should have known better than to influence the youth of America with their misguided opinions. Young people who never really understood that their actions and the deliberate actions of those entertainers, two of whom were Vanessa Redgrave in Britain and Jane Fonda in America, would cause grave consequences to the people of South Vietnam and the Americans who were still on active duty in Vietnam. Military returnees from Vietnam were vilified upon arrival in America and were regularly greeted at airports by protesters who pushed and taunted the troops, spat in their faces and on their uniforms and shouted obscenities at the troops. Some protesters were punched as a self-defense action and righteous retaliation by the veterans.

During that weekend of protests in October, the daytime consisted of destructive and shouting protesters while their nighttime morphed into a love-in. The protesters camped out south of the Lincoln Memorial. Usually two or more people, male and female, shared a single sleeping bag. The youthful protesters soon forgot what they were protesting during the dark of the night. Their party turned passionate with the acrid smell of marijuana fermenting the air that was filled with laughter and music. Most exercised their protest chant: '*make love not war,*' when they blatantly situated themselves directly across the river from Arlington National Cemetery, the graveyard of heroes.

In early 1970, orders from President Nixon were implemented, which reduced troops in Vietnam from 500,000 to less than 50,000. It was the beginning of the end of American involvement in Vietnam, which pleased the voters of America. In Vietnam it was business as usual: excessive air strikes, combat operations, Rangers running dangerous missions and soldiers becoming wounded or dead.

The impression in America and Canada was that there was little or no sign of a scaled down effort to the Vietnam War by the American Forces. In America, the draft law was due to expire at the end of June 1971; but the Department of Defense and Nixon's administration decided the draft needed to continue.

The lack of leadership in an army that was pulling out of a war was evident by the absence of responsibility or caring; compounded by low morale of young soldiers, who continued to experience needless incidents of maiming and death. No one wanted to be the last American soldier to die in the abandoned effort of Vietnam. Indeed, it was a difficult time to be a soldier in a war that had lost its popularity.

The poem, *'A Soldier Is a Lonely Man,'* was written by John Blake, while in Vietnam, during 1970, at the end of his first tour of duty. John had begun to lose faith with the American people who were not supporting their troops and him in Vietnam. The following is an excerpt from the original poem: "Take a problem sent from home...Sent to a soldier; all alone...Let him play with it in his mind...And watch, as he becomes entwined...Entwined, with problems greater still...So great they may destroy his will...Understand me if you can...A Soldier is a lonely man."

As if the misguided opinion of American people couldn't be any more demoralizing for the troops in Vietnam, enter movie actress, Jane Fonda who further exacerbated the situation. In November 1970, Ms. Fonda told approximately two thousand students at the University of Michigan and at Duke University, "If you understood what communism was, you would hope, you would pray on your knees that we would someday become communists. In July 1972, Fonda stated to the people of North Vietnam on Radio Hanoi, "I loudly condemn the crimes that have been committed by the U.S. government in the name of the American people against your country. I want to publicly accuse Nixon of being a new type of Hitler whose crimes are being unveiled. To the U.S. servicemen, who are stationed on the aircraft carriers, those of you who load the bombs on the planes should know that those weapons are illegal and the use of those bombs or condoning the use of those bombs makes one a war criminal. The tragedy is for the United States and not for the Vietnamese people because the Vietnamese people will soon regain their independence and freedom." When Ms. Fonda returned to the United States she stated, "The prisoners of war are the best-treated prisoners in history." These words were spoken despite a report that the Red Cross was refused all requests for inspection of North Vietnamese Prisoner of War camps throughout the duration of American involvement in Vietnam. Ultimately, the fall of Saigon on April 30, 1975, would prove Jane Fonda wrong on so many different levels. http://mainemilitarymuseum.info/wp-content/uploads/2013/09/Fonda-ledgersize.pdf

Decades later in 2012, the only regret and apology that Ms. Fonda offered for her despicable behavior during the Vietnam War in 1972 was that she was sorry for posing for photographs. Photographs that were visibly anti-American that were published worldwide of Fonda smiling while sitting at a Vietcong anti-aircraft gun that had killed Americans.

During the return of American military troops from Vietnam there was a tremendous degree of rejection of veterans. In the United States, the war protesters and the media's harsh criticism of the war and condemnation of the military and its traditional values became widespread. The lack of leadership at the end of the conflict weakened the traditional bonds of gratitude in American society and history. There would be no parades, no offering of pride, understanding or acceptance for the soldiers who served in Vietnam. There would be only confrontations, misunderstandings and abuse. The soldiers expected nothing, and when they got home that was exactly what they received. http://www.discoverthenetworks.org/individual

∞

# Chapter 3

## The Boys are Home for Christmas

IN CANADA, OUR DAILY FAMILY LIFE went on as usual; we continuously worried about the boys. The daily news reflected less about Vietnam and more about Canadian current affairs. Mom and Paddy had married in Montreal prior to accepting a transfer for one year to Summerside Air Force base on Prince Edward Island (PEI).

My twin and I were uprooted from our civilian life in Montreal and became Air Force brats while settling into our last year of high school. It was a nice change. Mom also enjoyed base living on PEI. She spent most of her time in the kitchen baking the traditional family recipes, delicious treats that consisted of dark fruit cake, shortbread cookies, mincemeat pies and other delicacies. She filled the freezer by mid-December and awaited the expected return of John and David. In just a few months the boys would be home and safe from harm's way.

Not a day went by in our lives since January of 1969 that we didn't worry and think about our boys in Vietnam. We wrote and sent letters on a weekly basis. Each of us would take the time to write both John and David to let them know how much we cared. We also provided them with up-to-date information about family and current events. We looked forward to reading their letters; however, neither of them ever mentioned what they were actually doing in Vietnam. They simply wrote about the country they were living in and advised us that they were well and looked forward to Mom's home cooked meals. We constantly watched the mail for those bluish American Air Mail envelopes, trimmed with red and navy lines accompanied by the postmark, 'Postage Paid by the Army Postal Service' boldly stamped on the top right-hand corner. The return address showed their handwritten address that consisted of name, rank, organization, and finally USA/Vietnam. I can remember as a teenager being excited beyond belief when I saw one of those envelopes in the mailbox.

Then another letter arrived for me from John. I quickly opened the envelope while Mom nestled herself in her favorite chair and waited to hear the latest letter read aloud. Naturally, I omitted anything John or David occasionally asked me not to mention.

Excerpts from John's letter from Vietnam dated October 1970

Dearest Sister:

Time to drop you a few lines to let you know that I got your letter; enjoyed reading it very much. I like to get mail, though I find it difficult to find the time to write myself. Glad to hear that all is well with you all there and that there are no major problems.

My job is very exciting and time goes by very quickly. I will be coming back to Vietnam for six more months then I'll be finished with the Army. (Don't tell Mom—I'll explain when I get home.) I've done well with all the training and experience I've gained. Things generally are going fine with me and so far I've only gotten non-life threatening shrapnel wounds.

Upon my return, I will stay about six weeks. I'm looking forward to the rest I will get, and a few other things, you know. I will also visit Newfoundland and collect my share of the inheritance from Dad, plus visit some of the family, maybe even run into some of my former friends. It will be nice to dance and ham it up, etc. To drive a car, drink cold beer and eat good food, all the little things that have come to mean so much to me. See movies, places, people, and things. It will be a wild experience for me.

I'll be leaving Vietnam on December 15th and should be home about the 17th or 18th. (Don't tell Mother exactly when I will be there). We'll make as much of a surprise out of it as we can. David will be home about the same time, give or take a few days either way.

The weather here now is wet. The monsoons are in now and it stays wet all the time. The only good thing about that is I have to carry less water on my missions with me. We stay wet day and night out on the missions. All of my work is done high in the mountains so when we get wet like that it is very cold and very miserable. The enemy feels the same as we do about the rain so they tend to make mistakes. And we get them when they do. It works out pretty good.

Sorry to hear you are disappointed with your choice of courses at school, but I wouldn't worry about it. Now I must dash so take good care of yourself and the family; have lots of fun all the time. See you at Xmas, for sure! Bye!

Love, John

**White Christmas in Canada**

By mid-December, the snow banks were enormous in Summerside. We had just experienced the first large snow storm of the season, which deposited twenty centimeters of snow on the ground; just in time for Christmas. We wondered about the boys' return and how they would react to the sudden climate change from the heat in Vietnam to a frosty winter on PEI. This would be our first Christmas on base at Summerside, and we were certainly looking forward to making new memories during the boys' homecoming.

Mom and I chatted and giggled while we cleaned and prepared John's and David's bedrooms. Then we laundered their winter clothing in preparation for their return. Winter jackets were sent to the dry cleaners and winter boots were polished and weather proofed. Christmas presents were purchased, wrapped, and placed under the Christmas tree. The house was festively decorated with holiday lights and garland. The fridge, freezer, and cupboards were filled with every possible food and drink that the boys' imagination or desire could muster.

We were grateful and relieved when David arrived home on December 14, Mom's birthday. Each of us was reduced to tears when we saw him enter the house after a year of constant worry and turmoil since his deployment to Vietnam. Mom could not have wished for a more special birthday present than to have her youngest son safely home. This past year had taken its toll on each of us in its own way. Soon, all of us would be together when John arrived. The anticipation of waiting was exhausting.

Over the coming days, my twin and David were inseparable as they spent long hours in conversation; catching up on lost time. She simply refused to leave the house unless David was with her; therefore, she skipped the last few days of school prior to the Christmas break. Mom was lenient and understood my sister's feelings when she gave her permission to stay home from school.

Mom was concerned when John did not arrive home with David. She became more suspicious as each day passed. She constantly wondered as to his whereabouts. We giggled with excitement as we kept John's pending arrival a secret from Mom and Paddy. John desperately wanted to surprise her.

A few days before John's arrival, David asked Mom to make her famous Prime Rib roast with Yorkshire pudding for Friday's dinner. Naturally, she was delighted to cook a special request for David, but she questioned that a prime rib dinner was a more suitable meal for a Sunday dinner. David insisted that he couldn't wait until Sunday, adding that he had been dreaming of a prime rib roast with all the trimmings since he'd arrived home. "My son, you will surely have your dream," she cheerfully replied.

David was quite satisfied with himself as he had just arranged his brother's homecoming meal. John's flight was expected to arrive in Charlottetown, PEI, at 3 p.m. on Friday. After an hour of driving to Summerside, John would be sitting at the dinner table once again with the family.

We could hardly contain ourselves Friday afternoon. The three of us needed to keep busy and stay away from Mom and Paddy. They would surely sense our excitement and certainly question the cheeky smiles on our faces. We decided that we'd stay in the basement and tie-dye two dozen white cotton tee shirts. It was the rage during the seventies. The process was time-consuming as we wrapped elastic bands in a pre-set pattern to optimize unique pattern formation of white streaks against the dye color. We had six buckets of different colored dye water ready and submerged the elastic bound tee-shirts to soak overnight. The following day, we would remove the T-shirts and rinsed them in clear water. We were certain that John would be interested in a few funky T-shirts for Christmas.

Mom opened the basement door and announced that dinner would be served at 5 pm. She then asked me to come upstairs and set the table. I winked at my siblings as I replied, "I'll be right there, Mom."

David and my sister were instructed to keep a lookout for John's taxi from an upstairs bedroom window and to alert me when John had arrived. The plan was to sneak John into the house and summon Mom to the front vestibule to advise her that she had a visitor. David and my sister would be on the stairs in full view and I would be directly behind Mom so that I wouldn't miss a second of John's arrival. The table was set with napkins, cutlery, and glassware, plus an additional place setting was conveniently placed out of sight for John. We had everything planned for his arrival.

Just as I stepped directly off the front vestibule into the washroom to fix my hair and makeup, I heard Mom mumble to herself as she rummaged through the hall closet. Immediately, I thought, "Lord, I hope she doesn't have plans to leave the house."

Suddenly, the front door opened while Mom was standing just ten feet from the entrance. Then I heard her cry out, "Wayne! Wayne! You're home!" David and my sister ran down the stairs just in time to witness Mom and Wayne (John) as they cried tears of joy and relief. Mom had never accepted Wayne's chosen name, John Blake. In her heart, he would forever be Wayne Saint John.

I had missed the homecoming. I suddenly ripped opened the washroom door and accidentally startled John. He swung around abruptly with a wild glare in his eye, and for a few seconds I thought he was going to jump at me. Everybody went silent, and I stood frozen in my tracks. Instead, he took a deep breath and smiled as he pulled me into his chest, kissed my forehead and thanked me for all the letters. John then turned his attention to David and poked him in the arm, just like the way best buddies do. He playfully motioned a left and right boxing jab at my sister. We siblings were grinning like sly foxes.

Paddy heard all the commotion and joined us in the hallway. John extended his hand to Paddy in appreciation for taking such great care of his girls. Paddy shook John's hand with gratitude that both of his wife's sons were finally safely home. John's arrival was the happiest time Paddy had seen his wife experience since their recent wedding. The stress of having both of his wife's sons serving in Vietnam had taken a toll on his newly acquired family.

John gently placed his arm around Mom's shoulder and with a devilish grin asked, "What's for dinner, Mother?"

"As a matter of fact, your favorite meal, Prime Rib with Yorkshire pudding as specifically requested by your brother," Mom replied as she smiled and winked at David.

"Right on, bro!" exclaimed John.

**Time Passed to Quickly**

Christmas Day came and went, and we truly appreciated the togetherness we shared as a family. We felt blessed and grateful for having both John and David safely home, seemingly without a hair on their heads out of place and certainly no visible scars. Everything seemed quite normal, just like the days prior to their enlistment into the Army. Ignorance is a blessed state of mind sometimes, and this was one of those times.

As planned, just before the New Year, John and David boarded an Argus aircraft that departed from Canadian Forces Base Summerside, for a week together in St. John's, Newfoundland. They intended to blow off a little steam with their friends. David enjoyed his last week of leave with John before he returned to Fort Leavenworth, Kansas on the fifth of January to complete his enlistment obligation. He was assigned as a rifleman in the Honor Guard as part of the burial detail for deceased soldiers whose bodies were being returned from Vietnam.

John had an additional three weeks of leave before he was required to return stateside. While in Newfoundland, John reunited with the family of his first teenage love who was killed in a car accident while he trained at Fort Benning, Georgia.

John's first true love was a remarkable young woman whose memory he constantly carried in his heart. During the visit with her family, John met his former sweetheart's younger sister and her infant daughter. Immediately, John noticed that the sister had grown into a lovely woman. The pair became instantly smitten. Prior to John's departure from Newfoundland, they became engaged and planned to marry in the fall upon his return from his second tour in Vietnam.

At the end of January, John returned to Summerside, PEI, for one additional week, primarily to get himself in the proper frame of mind and continue his journey to Fort Lewis, Washington. This journey would ultimately end with John's arrival back with his unit, the N/75$^{th}$ Rangers, in Vietnam on the afternoon of February 16. John had told Mom that he was resolved to return to Vietnam for another tour of combat.

Mom had placed her fears about John's return to Vietnam aside during Christmas and enjoyed every minute of the holidays with her sons. Once again, she felt terrified and emotionally distraught that John had volunteered for a second tour. In lieu of an additional twelve months stateside, he opted for six more months in Vietnam. She had counted her blessings when John returned safely after a year of heavy combat in Vietnam, and now she feared the worst. She felt John was tempting fate.

Within a few days of John's arrival from Newfoundland, we each noticed a major change in him. His mood had sharply changed as he readied himself for his return to Vietnam. We noticed that when we engaged him in a conversation his mind was elsewhere, and he rarely smiled. He became moody and ate less and less. He showed little interest in the fabulous treats that awaited him in the cupboards and refrigerator. He only ate and drank what he felt was necessary. Perhaps that was his method of preparing for Vietnam, but his withdrawal placed him in a dark and secluded frame of mind. It was as though he had numbed out all the enjoyment he had experienced during the past month of relaxation and family gatherings, including his engagement. John never spoke about his first year in Vietnam or the type of work he engaged in, or the losses he experienced, or the living conditions. No one who went to the war, especially John, wanted to talk about Vietnam. We never pried into his war experiences; we simply communicated with him as if nothing had changed.

∞

# Chapter 4

## John's Journal—Memoirs of Vietnam

EXCERPTS FROM JOHN'S JOURNAL in Vietnam, during his second tour in Southeast Asia from February—August 1971

"If I should die, for Freedom's sake, that's a lick,
on no one else, but Blake!
To my enemy, I grant that he should be, as sure of himself;
as I am of me!"

**23rd Feb/71**

Thoroughly enjoyed my whole leave; needless to say, was very reluctant to return to the military, especially Vietnam. Fell very much in love while I was home and didn't want to leave her. She understood. I miss my sweetheart and love her very much! She will be my wife very soon. I shall never leave her on her own, after this!

My stay at Fort Lewis was extensive and I note - those were easily the most miserable days of my entire life. Now that I'm back at my unit, 22 years old and engaged, a lot of changes have taken place while I was away and it shall take me some time to adjust totally. The old First Sergeant is gone and Captain Tanaka left yesterday. We have a new set up here and everyone generally is pleased with it, so far. Very few of the old guys are still here, and I am very lonely. I will merely exist for the next five months and go on home and settle down (a bit).

We had mail call a few hours ago and I received four letters from my fiancé with a picture of her in one of them. At first, I had been thankful that I did not have a picture to stare at all day long. Now I see I was a fool, I needed something material to believe in and I've found my reason in that picture of her.

**25th/Feb/71**

I spent the morning putting the Team House and Arms Room into order. Showered at noon and went to the club with Ranger George Morgan, (Golf Team Leader), and enjoyed a T-bone steak. Helped Garcia and Morgan with the resupply for 103I and went to the PX (Post Exchange) to buy some junk.

Had mail call today and I got one letter from my fiancé, of course! It is always so nice to read her letters. They pick me up a lot! I thank God every day that I have her waiting for me. I'll have a good life with her when I'm finished here with this place.

Ranger Garcia wants to go out on a mission soon! I'll go with him I guess; he'll need someone to help him. Morgan is far too short on DEROS to go. All the while I've been back here now I've not run any missions. I'm fine now. I'm ready to go at it for another five months or so. Yesterday was miserable! I miss my fiancé very much. Today—the letter helped! Miss the family as usual. I'm well and just starting to get into the swing of things here. Hopefully, I won't have anything unnerving happen to me, too soon.

**26th/Feb/71**

Left LZ English (Landing Zone compound/base) by chopper at ten this morning and went south to Duster Hill, which we found to be heavily secured by the 1st battalion. We dropped off three men there to set up the Radio Relay (a communications unit) and maintain it for the Super mission, which went out today. I returned to LZ English at two this afternoon. All is well today and I am feeling pretty decent.

Our new C/O or 'Old Man' is Major Shippy and is really a straight fellow. He's not easy, but he is fair. That's the only big thing. He went out today with the Super mission. A Super mission is a raid directed at a specific target or objective. Sometimes they work! We shall get our berets soon! Black Berets for the Rangers, finally! All the other Ranger units have had them for some time now.

The 173rd Airborne Brigade is going home in a couple of months from what we hear. It is slated to be cut out of Vietnam by the summer anyway. We aren't sure what will become of the N75th, but I guess they have something in mind. I miss the family very much. I've had my sweetheart on my mind most of the day. God, I miss that girl. Everything is going okay—little action today.

**01/Mar/71**

I decided today to take on a new team of my own. It probably will be Golf Team. Morgan wants me to have it, but I'm still only thinking of it really. It's a large responsibility taking on the position of Team Leader and the lives of five other guys.

Activity is picking up a lot now, and almost every team, which goes out gets in a firefight or two. They usually kill some gooks and most of the time capture weapons. There's no doubt that the enemy has been ordered to step up the war to draw some of the pressure off of Cambodia and Laos. About five of the guys have been wounded in the past few days. Tomorrow I'll go out to Elevation 606 with Morgan on Radio Relay for a few days. After that, I shall take missions once again. Morgan and I'll get some sun anyway. Get away from drinking for a while, Thank God!

Miss the family and most especially my sweetheart. I am well and have no real problems.

**02/Mar/71**

Activity is up and morale is high. Things are really hopping around here now and from what I can see it is going to be a hell-of-a five months for me.

We had another team in contact early this morning. They had a few kills, etc., no one was injured. Tonight on the Tiger Mountains, five GI's were wounded and three dead. No one can get to them. They are of my old unit in the 4th battalion Recon and they're messed up pretty badly. They were in heavy contact and there's as much fire power on the enemies side that Gunships and Dustoff/Medevac can't get down to where they are. Gunships/ Dust Off and, Slicks are on the station but can do nothing to alleviate their situation.

Earlier today Fire Support Base (FSB) Salem was beaten up pretty badly and suffered heavy causalities. That was an American FSB. Everything is tightening up! The enemy definitely is working new directives concerning their function here in South Vietnam. It may well get worse before very long.

Reset all of my equipment today and did a little rappelling with Morgan. Had a lot of fun! Checked the machine gun, and all is in order. Tomorrow we should go to Radio Relay at Elevation 606. Been keeping busy these days; yet, I must write my sweetheart tonight. It's really wonderful the way she's behind me now. I love her all the more for that; miss her and the whole family.

**04/Mar/71**

Left LZ English yesterday at 4:00 pm and set Radio Relay 103I at elevation 606—just 5 miles from LZ English. No idea of how long we shall have to stay here but I guess it isn't important really. Morgan and I made a shelter and there's not a lot to do today except to keep an ear on the radio etc., slept under the stars last night.

The countryside below us here is very picturesque. At night the stars are beautiful and at day it is very hot. Morgan is suntanning—he is soon to go home, finally after three tours.

I should like to have this mountain top and bring my sweetheart here for our honeymoon. I know she'd love it—it is very foreboding up here! Death could be anywhere down there below us. Miss her and my family. I am well and in good spirits. Time is going very slow as always.

**06/Mar/71**

Not a great deal to write about today at all. I'm well and on the third day here on Elevation 606. Last night was very cold on the mountain, but I slept pretty well.

It's about noon now and the wind is blowing quite cool over my mountain top. I made dinner for Morgan and myself. I won't do much of anything today at all. Oscar Team found a small cache yesterday but had no contact with the enemy at all. Not a lot happening, to be factual. Morgan got a call on the radio today and he will be leaving here tomorrow to head on home to the world. He got a 27-day drop and was quite surprised by it all. He's a day late now! That's the end of three years of service in Vietnam for him. What a great guy! He was the only buddy I had left from last year. Happy for him! We all may go in tomorrow. I wrote a long letter to my sweetheart today. I am well and miss the family.

## All Hell Broke Loose on Elevation 606

Sgt. Robert George Morgan, Golf Team Leader died instantly on March 7, 1971, as a result of an accidental grenade (frag) explosion.

It was determined that the grenade had an altered short-fuse, which detonated immediately. Some Rangers carried such a grenade on missions in the event of capture by NVC or VC. Mostly, the short fuse grenades were normally used when securing a booby trap with a trip wire. This was not the case during the Radio Relay mission.

A few Rangers on Elevation 606 were indiscriminately blowing off ordnances during that fateful morning; expelling munitions, a common practice before returning to base. Morgan pulled the wrong grenade at the wrong time.

The wounded received shrapnel from the 360-degree radius explosion resulting in two Rangers being medivaced to the hospital. Sgt. Blake received a deep wound to the left thigh and Sgt. Jetter received a serious wound to the front neck region. Sgt. Baugh received a less threatening wound and remained on Elevation 606 engaged in the Radio Relay mission until later that day.

(Medivac) chopper personnel and remaining Rangers on Elevation 606 removed Morgan's remains, which were then wrapped in a poncho and placed on a chopper and returned to the Landing Zone English base. The accident would prove to have a lasting traumatic effect on the surviving Rangers; those who were on Elevation 606 at the time of detonation; notwithstanding, the entire N75th Ranger unit. The Duty Officer's Log (DA1594) recorded the event as RR 103I per discharged HG accidently causing 1xKIA and 3xWIA. The following is a continuation of John's journal regarding the loss of George Morgan.

**09/Mar/71**

Morgan is dead. Fate, once again, had seemingly deemed it necessary to hurt me. This time it will be awhile before I give a damn about too many things. Morgan was killed in an accident with a Frag grenade the morning of 07/Mar/71, while we were getting ready to return to LZ English. I'd just left him on his own for a few seconds when I heard him say "Come, check it out!" I started walking toward him and I was looking at the smile on his face waiting for him to say something to me. I was still walking and looking at him/and he was looking at me. There was something he wanted me to watch, see or that he was going to say when I was about ten feet from him, the 'frag' he had been holding went off and blew him all to hell. He died instantly. Two days over his DEROS. I lay the blame for his death on US Army Red Tape or more precisely "Brigade". He should have been taken out of the field days before. Bastards!

I caught a large piece of shrapnel in my left thigh, which bounced off the bone and came out. Average wound and today, March 12, I was released from B/Med. I shall try to get over seeing Morgan die like that, but I don't think I shall. I'm having flashbacks! I liked Morgan very much and I shall miss him. Morgan is dead along with all of my other friends. I'm fed up with this! Wish I could be with my fiancé and my family right now. I'm feeling very poorly. The wound is healing—no infection yet.

John wrote a tribute poem for his friend Sgt. George Morgan, Golf Team Leader who was accidently killed on elevation 606.

On February 27th, at Morgan's request, John had written a poem for "Ragbag No.1," Sgt. Patino, who was killed during the previous fall.

In a tribute to Morgan, John wrote: "Now I write for Ragbag No.2, who died an instant death. On his third and promised, last tour - yes! He kept his promise to me. Hopefully, there is a life after death; Patino—Morgan—one day me! Morgan was without any doubt my most loyal and honestly sincere American friend and comrade. I shall lose no more "Friends" in this war, or because if it! The good do die first! Left to mourn was his immediate family and the N/75th Rangers."

The following is an excerpt from the original poem, *Yesterday*. "I'll not forget, the friend you were...The many ways you cared about us all...Sometimes I know I will refer... to you and yesterday; if I should fall!"

**10/Mar/71**

Things today are very quiet and so far I've accomplished nothing. I formally took charge of Golf Team; though, it has been mine for quite a while. I'm getting around well on my leg now and healing very quickly

The big mission will be coming off in a few days; regretfully, I shall be left behind. I loaned my machine gun to one of the guys, Jeff Horne, because they will no doubt need it. I will not be running any missions for a while because of my wound; two or three weeks at least, I suspect. Showered today for the first time in ten days; felt good too!

**17/Mar/71**

Things generally are routine these days and not a lot has been happening. We had a ceremony and were officially presented with our Black Berets. It's nice to have a beret on my head again! I think I like this one over the Green Beret. I guess it doesn't really make any difference. The cold weather has finally broken and it's getting warm again. Very little mail had been received the past few days. The investigation of Morgan's death is finished, from what I gather: Accidental death! What a humbug!

My leg is just about healed up now and I expect I'll be at work before very long. It will be good to go on a mission after so long. The days, hours and minutes pass so slowly this way. I'm feeling pretty good generally and don't think there will be any real problem getting into shape to run again.

Larry Peel came back last night from his two-week leave in the world. His pretty young wife just had a baby recently and I know how he must feel over it. He'll not run anymore in the field because of this. He will drive for the C/O (Commanding Officer). Received a shipment of new guys today and hopefully one of them will come to my team so that I can have a full run of it; we're down by two.

**Canadian Flag Incident—John Standing Down**

**21/Mar/71**

Today I had a Visual Reconnaissance in preparation for my mission, which was to come off tomorrow. When I returned to the unit I was told I'd have to take down my Canadian flag and put it away for a few days. I took it down because I was ordered to, not because I ever wanted to. That was my last order from the United States Army.

I resigned my Team and they have cut orders for me to leave the Ranger Company. I also requested to be released from the U.S. Army. Discrimination against my Country's Flag—The last straw! They will try many things to cover up what they have done and before it is over I shall look pretty bad in most cases.

The majority of the Rangers here feel bad about the incident and some even agree with what I've done. In actuality, I've blown the whole deal and all my benefits, but it makes me feel that I still can identify with something material. A piece of cloth and all it represents: My heritage. My whole life is in what stands to make that piece of silk what it is to me. In supporting it as I have, I cannot be wrong.

I was sent to Battalion Headquarters for the incident today and after writing my charge on paper was kept waiting while the Officer Corps built a story to cover its mishandling of the issue of my flag coming down. They think they can ruin me even though I told them I'm merely a Zombie for their cause. Tomorrow I'll go to see the WACO and find out if I'm crazy. Silly fools! They'll put me through a lot more than this before it's all over—I know.

I've put my weapon down and they know I'll never pick it up again. Jeff has my M60—he'll need it for the next mission. I am sincerely finished with this Army; opinions are in my favor with the Ranger Company and the men know I'm getting a bad deal. The whole company is on my side; though I'm up against the whole system and may lose anyway. I'm confident and feel I'm right to stand by my beliefs!

**24/Mar/71**

I wrote a heartfelt parting poem, *You Are This To Me* dedicated to my Ranger brothers—the N/75$^{th}$ Rangers. Friends and Comrades, Forever, plus one day!

The memory of this will carry, I'm sure...Yet, the memory of you guys will carry more...With me, no matter what I do...I never shall forget any of you...Take care, my friends...Until we meet—At home...At peace...On the street!

Leaving Company now 15:30 hours.

**26/Mar/71**

The day before yesterday I moved all of my junk down to where I shall be living until I leave to go home. I've dispensed with the idea of seeking a release out of the Army because I will certainly lose my G.I. Bill, my future. I feel as though my rights as a human being were ignored during the flag thing at the company—matter of fact—they were!

In the meantime, the new job is good, clean and safe. The people I work with are very good indeed and I expect that my time will go quickly. Captain Gilbert is in charge here and he seems to be a very mature, cool and collected man. SFC Crawford is next in command and he truly is a great guy. The rest of the fellows are fine people and it should work nicely.

I still spend a lot of time at the hill (Ranger Hill) with all the guys and nothing really is changed except that I won't fight anymore from now on. Miss my old work considerably and really feel weird without my machine gun. The past!

**29/Mar/71**

I'm near the end of my 15th month in Vietnam today and I must say it all has been an experience thus far. Found out today that four more of my friends with the 'Green Beret' have been killed.

They are; Captain Dennis Becker, SFC Euhouse, and SSG. Roy Salinas, my Principal Instructor Phase 1 Special Forces who died as a result of a friendly fire accident on January 16th. And SSGT Krisely, who was my closest friend in Phase 1 Special Forces, died in a helicopter crash on October 18th.

That brings it to 15, the number of friends I've lost over here since I first arrived. Average, one for every month! Very depressing for me!

My time is going by quite quickly and there's nothing much to complain about. John Ormiston, 'Limey', and I press weights in the evening and ran about two or three miles. Just to stay in shape. Limey is short on his DEROS and has decided not to run any more missions.

John wrote a poem for his friend 'Limey' John Ormiston's first son Michael. The following is an excerpt from the poem, *My*

*Little Man—Michael* 'One day, I'm hoping, we shall be...In a place of love and serenity...Where boys can grow up to be men...And never have to fight, again...Don't worry, my son... I'll soon be home... And you won't have to learn on your own...You'll walk at my side and never see...How important you are, in this life, to me'!

**More Unnecessary Losses**

**01/Apr/71**

Things are generally going well these days and my time is passing very quickly. Have received a few letters from my girl with pictures, which was nice.

November Rangers have experienced a lot of changes, over 10 people have left the Hill already and more Rangers plan to leave. Presently they are all out on a Super Mission west of Beaver and I don't think it has been too prosperous, thus far.

My orders for re-assignment still have not come down, though I have been working in my new capacity for some time. I enjoy my new work and the people I am associated with. I am very happy nowadays.

Roy Doster will go home in a few days and get out of the Army. I'll miss him a lot; we've been together since Special Forces Training.

Enemy activity is normal now and I hear that the North is getting hit a little more. Miss all the family.

**05/Apr/71**

My friend D. Phillips, Ranger, who took over my Team Golf, was seriously wounded on his first mission in my place. They say he'll be okay, but his injuries are extensive, no doubt he will go to the U.S.

All of my friends get it over here, one way or the other. Reason: my friends are good men and don't lag behind waiting for someone else to do their job. When the luck goes bad, it gets them first. That's par! The battalion lost over 70 men – dead or wounded in Suoi Cau. November Company is to go to the Suoi Cau as enforcements—they will lose men!

**08/Apr/71**

Yesterday, some officer from S-5 (Civil Affairs) came to ask me for another statement concerning Morgan's death. I sent him away once, but he came back again, so last night I wrote a new statement for them; not that it really makes any difference anymore.

Visited Ranger Hill November Company a few times since, but don't really have a lot in common with the leaders there anymore.

Limey came to see me late last night and was very upset about something that someone has said to him concerning his leaving the Rangers to take his new job. Some people just don't have any common sense at all. Gannon has made two enemies!

**12/Apr/71**

Three more of my friends have been hurt in a booby trap a few days ago. Welsh, was hurt the worst and he almost died of shock. He was hit pretty badly and so was Hines. The other guy was not so bad.

Have not had any mail for about one week now; don't know what the problem can be. I'm operating the film counter now and in some ways, it's a good job, yet in more, it's not. I don't like to serve the public so it's difficult for me to get along. I'm short of patience these days anyway.

They say we had a lot of mail down at the airport so I guess maybe we'll have a letter or two tonight. I wonder about my girl and often think of the family and her. One day soon I'll be home.

**17/Apr/71**

Gary Butts, a Canadian from Montreal, came into the army at the same time I did. We went to Advance Infantry Training and Jump School at Ft. Benning, Georgia together. He was KIA (killed in action) on the 3rd of April by a AK47 bullet that pierced his chest, when he and five other men walked into an inverted L-shaped ambush. All six men were killed. The dead men and Gary were brought back and sent home.

Gary was assigned to D-CO 4th Battalion Airborne 503d Infantry 173d Airborne Brigade. He was stationed at landing base North English about 10-12 miles from LZ English.

I saw Gary last month at the N.C.O. Club and he gave me a pack of Export A cigarettes; we had a long talk and enjoyed the conversation. He would often come to see me at the Rangers. Now he is dead and I am really pissed off again. He was just 19 years old!

**22/Apr/71**

There is a massive operation in Suoi Cau Mountains and the A Shau Valley. The ARVN's are in the A Shau Valley in masse to block and discourage a drive into Vietnam by the NVA who were originally sent from North Vietnam to repel the ARVN invasion of Laos, earlier. The NVA are avoiding a major confrontation for some reason.

The command is finally starting to use the Intel we collected for them on activity in the Suoi Cau Mountains back in December. They didn't believe us at first so they sent the 4th Battalion in there. They had twenty some odd killed and over seventy wounded. What does that imply? They've got all the Koreans in there now. They have the Rangers, Battalions 1st Field Force, and a few other units in there now too so they should come up with something; at least some more dead for both sides.

Had guard on the perimeter the other night, and four rounds went over my head. Received mail from my girl, made me a little happier! Feeling poorly today! Miss everyone.

**01/May/71**

The past few days have been bad for Golf team Rangers, on April 28, the unit lost five guys. Two dead and three wounded. My old team, under a new Team Leader walked into an ambush, which killed my good friend, Ranger Larry Peel. He was killed by an AK-47 round just above his heart; he died instantly. I am sad for his wife and new baby. Dave Cummings was wounded and the Kit Carson Scout was hit. Mistakes were made during the mission, which leads up to the Team getting hit. I feel very badly about it all.

Another friend, SSG Juan Borja, Ranger, Team Leader of Kilo Team, was killed and Ranger Campbell wounded when they walked into a widow maker set out by the 1st Field Force, and who are being held responsible for the whole thing. It's too late to be losing men over here; it's a goddamn crime!

**08/May/71**

For the most part, today has been very sad. I attended memorial services for Peel and Borja at the Ranger Company. It hurt very much to look at the Ranger Company and think that these particular guys are dead. I feel the deep sorrow of having lost two more close friends. Even now when we are about to turn things over to the gooks, we still send young men out there to die. I hate to think that these men died for nothing.

**13/May/71**

The war goes on, but there has been very little making the news. The papers show that they finally are wondering about the advisors from Korea, China, and Russia etc. Silly fools; of course it's true, we, the grunts know it is. It'll all come out in the wash one day! The ills of both sides will shock the hell out of a lot of people.

**31/May/71**

On May 29$^{th}$, my friend, Ranger Joe Sweeney was killed and Bizadi, Curtien, and Whitlook were wounded by a sniper's bullets.

Militarily, the enemy still holds the Suoi Cau Mountains Region. We've lost well over 100 men there and countless wounded in the past few months. There's no way we can drive them out for they are well entrenched. They are well equipped and obviously have been ordered to hold those mountains. I ran my last four missions there and I know how it is for those guys now. We should not be taking on jobs like that if we really are pulling out. One thing seems to have led to another and there we are.

Had a letter from my girl yesterday, which said in effect that we have little in common, at this stage. I wrote a very long letter to her, and don't really know what effect it will have on our plans. I'm more set in my ways than she is in hers and she will have to make a decision. I'll take it from there; entertaining thoughts of hitting the road after the army. I'll see what happens when August comes by. Refuse to be hassled; everyone should know that by now.

**09/June/71**

Barney died a couple of days ago with a fever from pneumonia, they say—that's just a waste!

Finally, it is definite that I shall wear my Sergeant's stripes before I leave the army; went before the E-5 Board on the 8$^{th}$ and passed. Major Shippy was President of the Board. My family and everyone else will be happy to know that I can still get promoted on my ability. I've worked as a sergeant for over a year and never got paid for it—though, that's the way it goes—takes all kinds!

I'll be glad to get home, no word from David for a long time. The war goes on and we lose a few guys every now and then. I'll be on my way in about two months—miss everyone a lot.

**19/June/71**

For the last five days, I have been in the hospital with a high fever of 100 degrees and a very bad throat infection. I've been going through hell and have never been sicker in my life. No real idea when I will recover and generally don't believe it will be for a while; too bad really.

Ranger Company had another man blown to pieces the other day. I believe they've given up, all of a sudden, in the Suoi Cau Mountains. I know that sounds stupid, but that's how the fighting has been since I've been here. 2nd Battalion left for Cam Ranh Bay this afternoon. This unit will go home soon.

**27/June/71**

Dustoff (flight out by helicopter) to 67th EVAC at Qui Nhon for more extensive care. It's been two weeks now and no improvement with a severely swollen throat.

The 173rd Airborne Brigade has been alerted that they will return to the CONUS (Continental United States) by the end of August. The enemy has started his campaign against the unit and has begun hitting LZ English with small arms and sapper attacks. Soon the mortar and rockets will start and in the end, the NVA will tell the people that they drove us from the land. The people will believe the enemy too. Most units within the "Herd" are standing down from combat operations even now. Hard to believe that only a few weeks ago they were fighting like hell in the Suoi Cau Mountains. I am hoping for an improvement in my health soon. Miss the family.

**05/July/71**

Still in hospital at 67th EVAC, but things are going generally well for me now and my health is much improved, but my nerves are pretty much shot. Made a friend here Ben, who is awaiting Dustoff to the world (the United States) for further attention to his wounds; the night before he left we pulled a real 'humdinger' by sneaking off the LZ with him in a wheelchair and both of us in patient attire. There was a reason for it all, which owing to the fact that both of our attitudes are a little off, was good enough for us. We enjoyed the evening immensely. Ben has since been flown out of Vietnam en route to the world.

**24/July/71**

Was released from 67th EVAC on the 19th as an outpatient with anemia; my blood count is still down to 34% when it should be 45%. The doctors believe that I may still have some parasites in my system somewhere, but the B/Med., at LZ English can continue the treatment. I returned to Phu Tai by helicopter and got my pay, and returned to LZ English by truck. My extension went through and I will leave the military on the 16th of August/71.

Finally received paperwork for one Bronze Star Medal, paperwork for two Arcom Medals, but I haven't got any paperwork for my Air Medal. I declined three purple hearts for my shrapnel wounds because most of us Rangers don't allow B/Med to write us up for Purple Heart awards due to shrapnel wounds unless they were life-threatening.

My fiancé and I have drifted apart. I will go see her as I did last year upon my return but am doubtful this time—a bad break for all of us. I'll be okay, no sweat on that; still, it really is too bad. No more making plans for me. It's good to be alive today, but it's an empty world.

The war around here is very quiet, also no mortars or rockets yet, and believe me, that helps. The whole unit is just about stood down except for security patrols, etc. Everyone in the 173rd will be out of 'Nam by the 25th of August or so. Most of the guys will go to Fort Campbell, Kentucky where they should enjoy themselves a little. This unit was the 1st combat unit in Vietnam and is easily the most fighting unit in the United

States Army. As General Westmoreland said, "They call it the HERD because we are all ANIMALS."

**30/July/71**

The anemia persists but may be only one of my problems at this point. At any rate, I find it very difficult to maintain my composure. I'm leaving the Army with less than what I came into with—three years older—in poor health. All will work out—I feel that at least. Captain Gilbert has gone home to his wife and family, and he too will separate from the Army. The unit (173rd Airborne Brigade) is in the final stages of shutting down its role in Vietnam. They'll all be gone by 25th. I'm so glad they'll all be leaving here when I go. Now I'll be able to remember rather than worry about my friends. A fitting end.

**07/Aug/71**

I'll begin to clear out of the 173rd on the 9th and should be finished by the 14th so there's lots of time to stop in at 67th EVAC at Qui Nhon for some tests, but physically I'm feeling fine so it shouldn't amount to anything at all. Still worried about reentering civilian life, but what can I do? That's life; I only wish now that David was getting out with me.

**10/Aug/71**

I have begun my journey home. It's all over now, but the memories. I departed LZ English and my unit at 1300 hours this day. All of my friends spent the morning bending my mind and gearing me up for the trip homeward. Everything now seems different to me and I think that I am very, very happy. I only wish I could take those friends of mine, who are still living, with me as I go. The dead—God, I should love them until I join them, they are and were wonderful. I made a trip similar to this one, before, but this time I'm finished. These should be roads I shall never walk again. Somehow, I know I was happy here, especially when I was in the fighting. I would flatter myself to say I am a peaceful man. Yet, I rather believe myself as one who is hoping for some kind of peace. Few would ever believe that I came here to die following the death of my childhood sweetheart. I am glad my death never came to me in Vietnam. The chopper ride out of LZ English, at Bong Son was a unique experience for me as I looked down knowingly, for the last time, at my faceless enemy of so long. I saw places where I had almost died in the past; and where my friends did. Some of the places where I had killed could be seen. The hurt came out of the realization then that little has changed, except that I have been and gone.

**14/Aug/71**

I signed out of the 173rd Airborne Brigade on the 11th of August and spent the next two days at Phu Cat airbase; on the morning of the 13th I departed the Airbase and traveled to Cam Ranh Bay and processed in at 1500 hours; presently waiting to be put on a flight manifest to the world. Currently, have a very bad headache and I am in a pretty miserable mood. I am very, very depressed. There are about one thousand guys here now and they all seem just as bad off as me. When my unit sent the first lot home to Fort Campbell they were ill-received by the people there. No one should get on me when I am home. Not a lot to look forward to.

**17/Aug/71**

At Seattle Washington—I haven't had much rest the past two weeks and I am fatigued right now. I'll leave here at 11:35 and fly to Vancouver then make a connection for Winnipeg to Mother and Paddy for a few days then settle in Newfoundland. Now that I am a civilian I am completely lost; I've very few plans.

**05/Sept/71**

Engagement is broken off; I feel saddened. Enrolled at the Memorial University of Newfoundland and shall soon be counting my blessings.

∞

# Chapter 5

## John's War at Home Began

AIRBORNE RANGER JOHN BLAKE, AKA CIVILIAN, returned home to Canada and arrived in Winnipeg by mid-August. We were all very happy to see him and confident that this time there would be no going back. Vietnam was finished business, and both of our brothers were on safe soil. We felt relieved and hopeful that, finally, the worst was over.

John spent one week in Winnipeg and hurried back to Newfoundland just in time to enroll for the fall semester at the local university. His benefits from the G.I. Bill included tuition for one year. During the second year, John worked part-time as a bouncer at a local pub in Conception Bay Central and earned tuition for an additional year of study in Accounting. After university, John obtained steady employment as a junior accountant. In 1972, John married the girl to whom he had previously been engaged during his second tour in Vietnam. The following year they had a daughter whom they named Rachel.

During the onset of winter, David and my twin sister moved back home, too. I finally arrived in Newfoundland during spring of 1973, leaving Mom and Paddy with an empty nest. Finally, we had all returned after seven years away from our beloved island.

We each found employment relatively quickly and settled down living among the people we loved and the culture we cherished. The freshly scented salt air and the beauty of the surrounding hills and ocean was a welcomed sight. Moreover, the accent of our heritage, mainly Irish, nurtured our souls. We especially cherished the music and songs of the island. In my opinion, per capita, the people of Newfoundland are still the most talented people in Canada. Almost everyone can sing, dance, or play a musical instrument.

Six months later, David and my twin, plus a few of their friends, decided to drive across Canada and live in Vancouver. Ultimately, David settled in British Columbia, and a few years later my twin settled in Ontario; neither would return to live in Newfoundland. In the years to follow, they would only return for a brief vacation.

In 1975, it was John's intent to walk me down the aisle at my wedding. Unfortunately, the night before the wedding John's wife telephoned and said that they would not be attending the wedding. John was sick. I didn't quite understand why he felt sick, but in my heart I suspected that he really hadn't been well since his return from Vietnam.

As soon as I returned from my honeymoon, I visited John and his family. It was clearly apparent to me that John was suffering, mentally and emotionally. It was only then, on that very day, that I realized my brother, John, the boy who became a man overnight, when Dad died, and had become the good soldier who survived two tours in Vietnam, seemed to have died spiritually and emotionally in Southeast Asia. He now was simply a stranger who looked like John. I felt sickened by what the war had done to him.

When John returned to the world in 1971, life and living was nothing like he thought it would be. He expected that everyone would welcome him home with open arms, and we did. But the society had mixed feelings about that war and the people who served in it. With the exception of a few childhood friends, most of his Newfoundland friends and acquaintances were only interested in him as the guy they knew before 'Nam, but not the man he had become. Those former friends and new acquaintances were more interested in the traumatic details of the many losses and casualties of war for the wrong reasons. John was very guarded about the losses of his comrades and the killings. What mostly troubled John was the immaturity and lack of character he witnessed on a daily basis in these individuals. Moreover, he realized people of his age failed to understand the importance of life and freedom and seemingly also lacked the intelligence or experience to know the difference.

Some people believed that John's life would be the same as it was before he had left for Vietnam. But life had changed for John, and nothing remained the same. His dreams and fantasies that preceded his return were just that: dreams and fantasies. His world had changed as had ours.

No one in the family, especially John, wanted to talk about Vietnam. It was a subject he never brought up. He buried the experience of Vietnam, hoping that it would never resurface. But he was wrong. There would always be nightmares and memories to remind him of his lost friends and his own traumatic experiences. Sometimes he would welcome the dreams and remember the times he spent with his Ranger brothers whom he admired and deeply respected. Then there were times when the dreams were unwelcomed. Those were dreams of his friends' death. Of course he had no control over those dreams, and they often left John devastated. He could never shut the door on Vietnam; the war had followed him home for better or for worse.

There were very few, if any, Vietnam veterans in Newfoundland, and this added to his need for the brotherhood that was forged among the Rangers in Vietnam. John felt alone in his misery.

When the Canadian Vietnam veterans returned home, many did so exactly as John. They tried to fit into a society that held little or no respect for them as veterans. Most hid their war experiences and tried to move on. While some succeeded, others did not.

I continued to visit John and his family weekly for a few months. Eventually, John told me more details of his struggle and that he constantly experienced nightmares of the 'Nam since his return. He mentioned that at times he often became uncontrollably angry and despondent. We both knew that few people, especially in Newfoundland, could ever understand what had happened to him, partly because he had difficulty in understanding what was going on in his own life. He told me that he intended to leave Newfoundland and return to the United States. For the safety of his young family he asked his wife to go back to her original family.

He felt alone and out of step with everything and everyone around him. To say that he marched to the beat of his own drum would be an understatement. He felt lost and he felt that he didn't fit into this new world that he had formerly called home. He missed his friends who were lost in battle. Those were his most painful days. He was home in a physical sense, but in his mind, he was still in Vietnam. Nothing—not man, woman or child could replace the bond of friendship that he had formed in Vietnam. Nothing in his life could come close to The Brotherhood.

I arrived at St. John's Airport on a bone-chilling January evening in 1976, with John, his wife, and daughter Rachel. It was heartbreaking to see him leave again, but we understood it was for the best. John needed to make sense out of what seemed senseless. Perhaps he would find some understanding and acceptance in the United States. Perhaps he might even find some peace and purpose in his life. I gladly loaned John a thousand dollars toward his travel and living expenses. He promised to pay me back within a few months.

I'll never forget the moment John kissed his wife and child goodbye at the airport. Then he reached out and pulled me into his chest, kissed my forehead, turned and walked away.

My tears flowed freely this time as he left home. I watched him through an observation window as he boarded the plane. Suddenly, I felt overwhelmed by a premonition that he and I would never see each other again. We never did.

**Back in the United States of America**

John settled into an apartment in South Dakota and immediately obtained a job. Soon after he arrived, he located some fellow Vietnam veterans. He was surprised and somewhat reassured to notice that they, too, suffered from many of the same symptoms that he experienced. This gave him hope that the nightmares, anger, and rage he experienced, were normal for a Vietnam veteran. America became John's home, a place where he could walk down the road and feel connected. A nation that accepted him and understood his war experiences as a Vietnam veteran, without any explanation. He continued to write poetry, which served as a venue to express his feelings. He promptly repaid my travel loan but he never discussed his war experiences with the family or advised us of any mental health difficulties during our many telephone conversations.

We, the family, never really understood much of what John was going through mentally and emotionally. We did, however, understand that he intended to protect us from whatever was troubling him. Although his memories and experiences rendered him sad and angry, he did not seek professional help. He simply worked and sought some solitude in being a survivor of Vietnam. In 1977, John left his job and started working at more dangerous jobs. With danger there was familiarity in the adrenal rush, something with which he could easily connect. He continued his life without seeking any medical intervention.

Then in 1979, John started looking for trouble, and he became self-destructive as his life was falling apart. He had an impulsive suicide attempt when he ran his car into a bridge after he experienced an earlier flashback. Unknown to everyone, medical personnel included, John was living with undiagnosed Post Traumatic Stress Disorder that would wreak havoc in his life if left untreated.

John realized that he was on the wrong path and joined the National Guard, a reconnection with the military, which regenerated and reinforced his self-worth, pride, and dignity. During that same period, John obtained a job as an advocate for migrant workers. He enjoyed his work, but the job created animosity among the locals and the migrant workers. As a result, after about nine months of advocacy work, John was shot by a local man. He immediately quit that job and went to the Veteran Administration Medical Centre to seek medical attention for his gunshot wound.

We all found it difficult to understand that John survived Vietnam, when he received shrapnel in his hands, arms, and legs during three different occasions, only to return to the United States and be shot. He still refused to seek professional assistance. John held onto the belief that he could work out his difficulties by himself. John recovered from the gunshot wound and accepted an employment position as an apprentice painter while he embarked on becoming a volunteer veterans' advocate. In a letter to a close friend John wrote:

> For years after the Vietnam War, I searched for some meaning of it all—but there was none. The meaning, if it existed at all, had been lost somewhere along the way. Finally, it came to me that the real meaning must lie not in the win or loss of that particular war in Vietnam, but more likely in what would

> come to be as a result. Upon this realization, I saw a road open up before me. I began to see that my buddies had died not at all in vain. I began to see that because of their sacrifice it would not be possible for America to simply flounder along. That indeed our nation would be mandated to grow in many ways, special ways that would not likely be possible were it not for these young men. Now I have my reason and meaning. And now I have my work.
>
> Other veterans' advocates across the nation have their priorities and I have mine. I am pained to see so many of them being compromised to one political camp or the other. I realized further that so much of this is necessary for them since so much of their interests are political, to begin with. We can all look forward to Vietnam veterans playing an increasingly significant role in the shaping of a better America and I'm confident that if we can keep them from fighting unnecessarily among themselves then their potential can be realized.
>
> I believe that my buddies held true to a profound tradition of duty and service to their nation. I am upset that they were made victims of their nation's lack of determination and support for their efforts and sacrifices. America did not fall into Vietnam and indecisiveness as some suggest. I believe America grew to that level of apathy and must necessarily grow out of it. Here is where the survivors of Vietnam have their responsibilities first and foremost.

John set out on a mission in life to make a difference, this time without a M60 machine gun.

∞∞∞

**Southeast Asia**

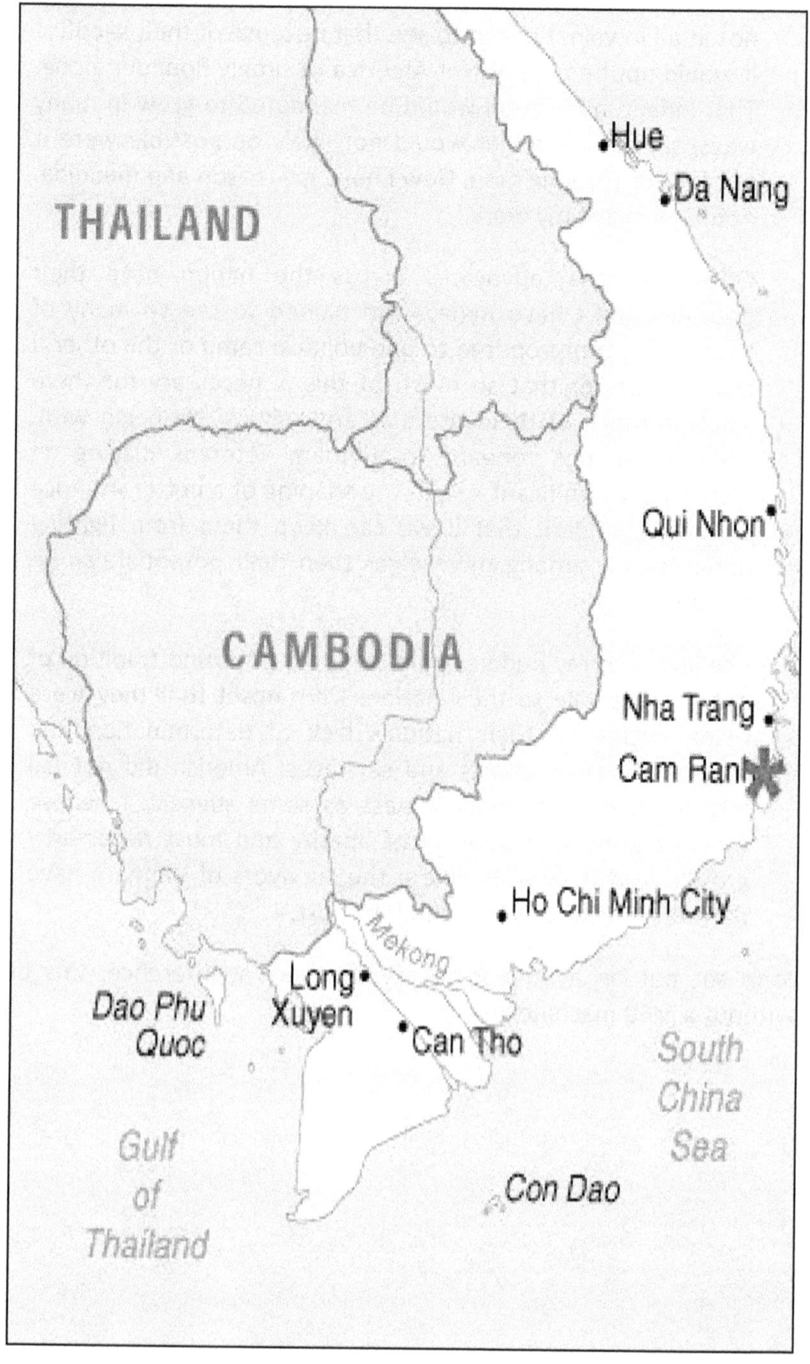

*Below*: Article written by the 173 Airborne Brigade Newspaper, Vietnam, 1970. The cherry was John Blake. (*photo courtesy of John Bryant*)

# Rangers Bust Cherry

LZ ENGLISH – A team of rangers from N Co., 75th Rangers killed two NVA on a jungle trail in the Soui Ca Valley, about 40 miles north of Qui Nhon. One turned out to be a "cherry"...a new man in country.

The rangers were checking out a well used trail when they spotted an enemy OP (Observation Post). The Red dived for his rifle, but the team leader, Sgt. Charles Cash of Houston, opened fire first.

At that point the second NVA jumped up only to be greeted by an M-60 machine gun carried by Spec. 4 John Blake.

The rangers captured two rucksacks, pistol belts, medical supplies, and an AK-47.

Some personal documents tipped off the rangers about the "cherry"...he had been with his new unit two days.

***Photos of John Blake and his N/75th Ranger brothers in Vietnam***
***February 1970—August 1971***

*Above: 1st arrow left to right*: John Blake. 2nd, Sven Henriksen, 3rd, Herbert Baugh, 4th, David Walker, author of <u>Cyclops in the Jungle: A one-eyed LRP in Vietnam</u> *(photo courtesy of David Walker)*

*Below:* Landing Zone (LZ) English, Bong Son, Vietnam N/75th Ranger Hill (*photo courtesy of M. Swisley)*

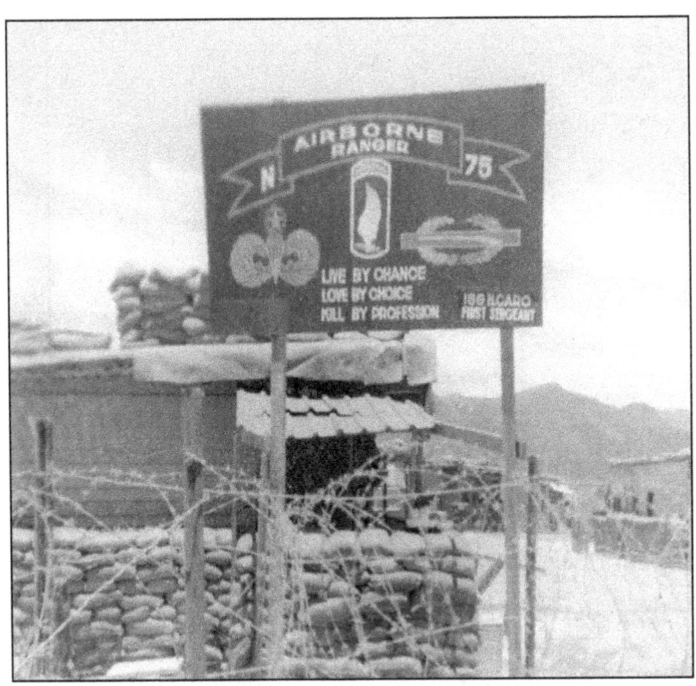

*Right:* Orderly room on LZ English *(photo courtesy of M. Swisley)*

1970-71
John Wayne Blake

*(Photos courtesy of M. Swisley)*

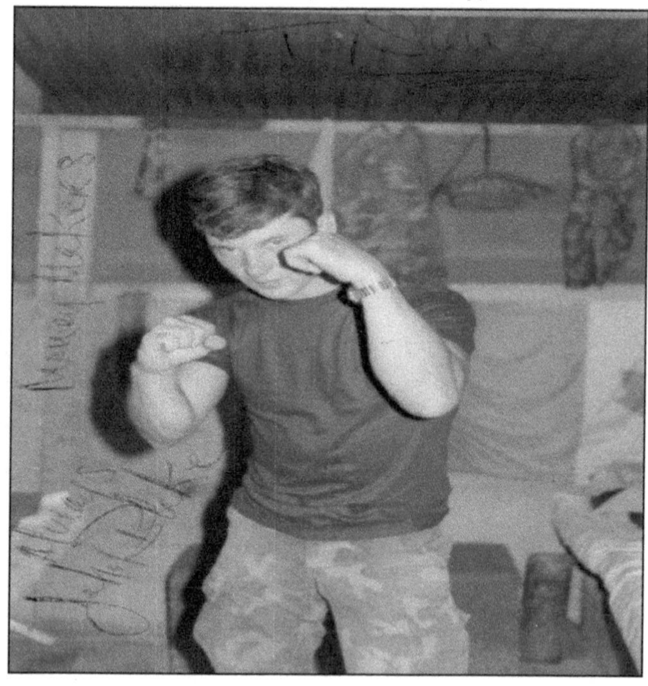

*Photos courtesy of Brian. Danker, Robert. Henriksen, Carl. Millinder and Herbert. Baugh*

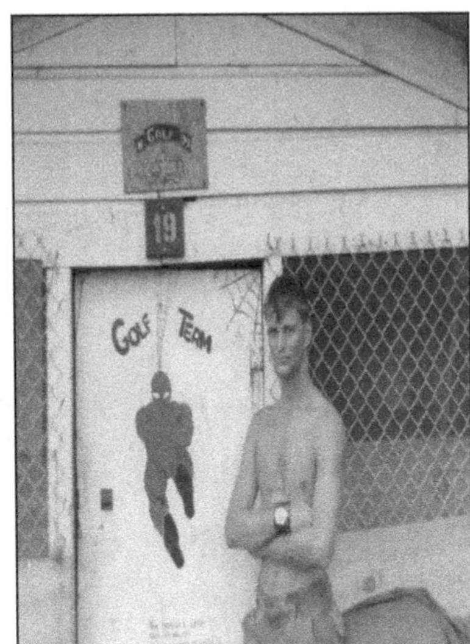


*Above Left*, Brian Danker/ *Right*, Robert Henriksen

*Above Left*, Carl Millinder/*Right*, Herbert Baugh

*Below*: Memorial service for Larry Peel and Juan Borja, both Rangers KIA as indicated in John's Journal May 8, 1971. John Blake is standing directly behind the Ranger reading from the Bible *(photo courtesy of J. Horne)*

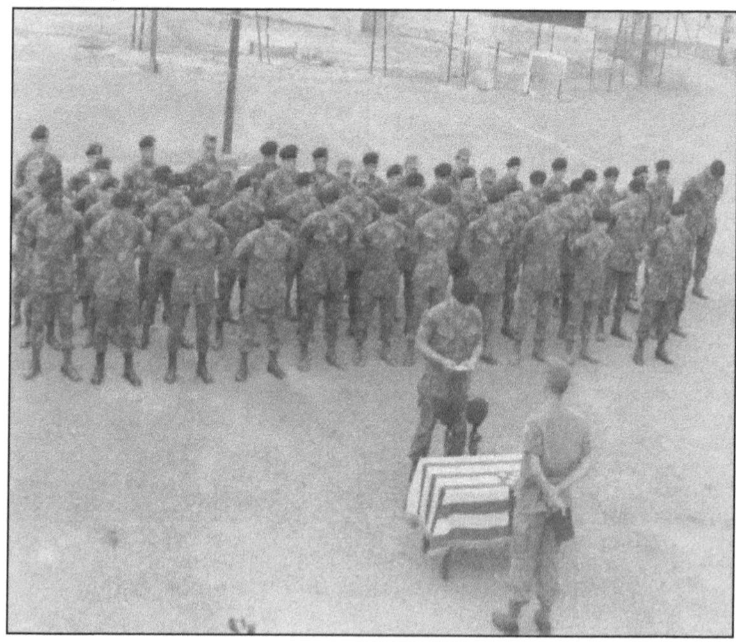

*(Photos courtesy of M. Swisley, J. Horne and J. Bryant)*

Above left: Chuck Moseby, Right, Jeff Horne

Above left: John Bryant, Right John Blake

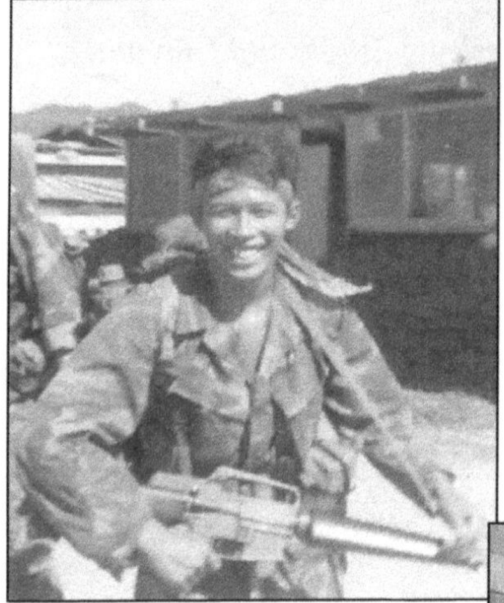

*Left:* Rudy Teodosio, my first contact with my brother's unit, the N/75th Rangers, in 2011 *(photo courtesy of R. Teodosio)*

*Right:* Sgt. Roberto Patino, KIA. John wrote the poem 'Ragbag' in memory of his friend. I would finally meet his son and name sake in 2016 *(photo courtesy of M. Swisley)*

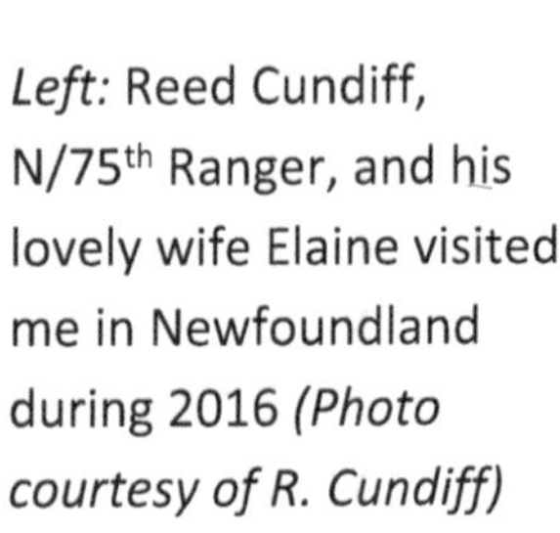

*Left:* Reed Cundiff, N/75th Ranger, and his lovely wife Elaine visited me in Newfoundland during 2016 *(Photo courtesy of R. Cundiff)*

*Right:* George Morgan died suddenly on Hill 606 – a terrible loss to the N/75th Rangers, especially John Blake

*Left:* John Kelly KIA and Brian Danker

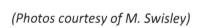

*Right:* Michael Swisley repelling.

*(Photos courtesy of M. Swisley)*

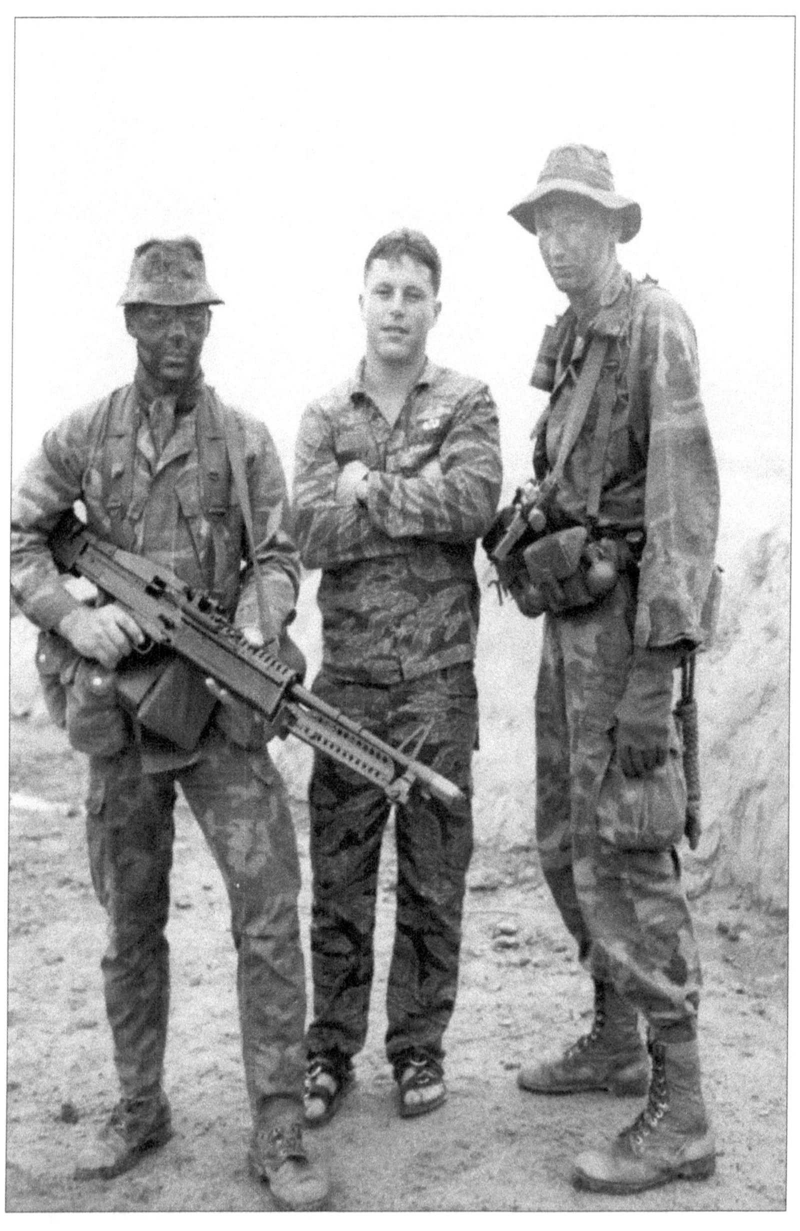

Left to Right- John Blake, Michael Swisley and Charlie Cash
*(Photo courtesy of M. Swisley)*

*Left*: Cpl. John Ormiston commonly known on Ranger Hill as "Limey" largely due to his British heritage. A soft spoken Ranger with a gentle smile. But, when it came to running dangerous missions he was a trusted and respected warrior. John Blake wrote a poem for Limey's son titled *My Little Boy, Michael*

*Right:* Patrick (Tad) Tadina, renowned Special Forces Airborne N/75$^{th}$ Ranger who completed five tours of duty in Vietnam

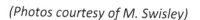

*(Photos courtesy of M. Swisley)*

*Above*: Cpl. John William S. G. Kelly was a N/75th Ranger and a Canadian originally from Nova Scotia. John Blake suffered his first tremendous loss in Vietnam on February 15, 1970 when his Ranger friend, died from a gunshot wound during an ambush. He and Kelly had completed Special Forces training together at Fort Bragg, NC. Blake became Kelly's replacement on Charlie Team. His daughter, Sonia and I have since become long distance friends *(Photo courtesy of Brian Danker)*

*Above:* John W. Blake's genuine Zippo lighter from Vietnam was placed in my hand by the person who found it. John returned from Vietnam with the lighter in 1971. In 1974, he moved from a house in Avondale, Newfoundland when he unknowingly left behind the lighter. That was 44 years ago. Approximately ten years ago, Douglas Clarke, found the lighter during the final demolition cleanup of the property when the rake he was using came in contact with the lighter. He heard a clink, picked the lighter up, cleaned it and set forth to locate me. He succeeded in 2018.

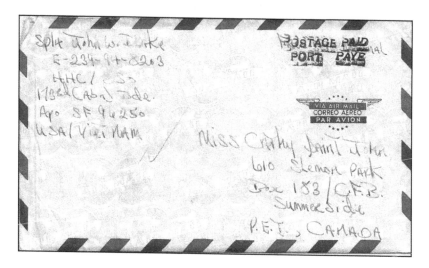

# PART 2

## THE MISSION AT HOME
## ONE FOR THE BOYS
## TRANSCONTINENTAL MARCH 1982
## FROM
## SEATTLE, WASHINGTON TO WASHINGTON, D.C.
## PHASE ONE
## BY
## JOHN W. BLAKE
## UNFINISHED MANUSCRIPT

# Chapter 6

## The Planning Stage

FROM THE TIME I RETURNED from the conflict in Southeast Asia on August 16, 1971, I had been plagued with an apprehensive feeling of unfinished business. I kept these feelings to myself and tried to at least act normal while hoping that time would somehow make some change. Well, what time did was to provide me with a better understanding of just what had been dogging me for all those years, such as:

- The way we had put our young military service people in a very dangerous environment while tying their hands behind their backs, rendering them up as "sitting duck targets" to the communists' hit and run tactics.
- The way we had some half-hearted efforts to make tangible military gains, only to neglect follow-up; thus destroying any sense of accomplishment.
- The way we were still losing people while pulling out under the mantle of our 'just and honorable peace'.
- The way we left Vietnam, leaving almost 2,500 of our people unaccounted for and missing; only to find more and more reasons to believe some were still captive and being used as pawns in the game of international politics.
- The way we have been having such difficulty separating our feelings for the conflict from our feelings for the people who served there.

- The way we had to stand by and watch as the communist effort flourished throughout South and North Vietnam, Laos and Cambodia. People suffered untold deaths, deprivations, and migrations while we knew it didn't have to be that way.

- The way our ineptitude had exposed unknown numbers of our faithful troops to Agent Orange and the deleterious effects of dioxin (the most toxic substance known to man).

- The way we stood by idly at home while an average of 60 Vietnam veterans a day wasted themselves through suicides and other uncaring, reckless acts.

You might say I was having a ten-year restless night from which, as I awakened, there was an even greater sense of spiritual loss. That loss was not just for me or for other veterans and their families. No, it was for America. We had fallen from grace and didn't seem to know how to deal with it.

I further realized that the role of the Vietnam veterans and approximately 9.2 million military services personnel had indeed become confused. Many veterans had returned to become successful in their chosen fields, but the vast majority specifically the 3.2 million veterans who actually served in Vietnam experienced a constant struggle of not fitting in, including myself.

Feedback from the Vietnam Veteran community was quite simply that the Veterans had been heartbroken for a long time. By the eighties, that heartbreak had become agonizing. When feelings change directions as the wind changes, the only constant is a sense of struggle. This struggle and conflict bred a sense of something missing, a sense of need.

Those who survived the conflict, the thoughts of suicide, and the neglect at home are finally in a position to give the nation a lesson in courage. They are ready to project the prodigal son's image all the way down the road to coming home under more appreciative circumstances.

The only solution to the problem that faced the Vietnam veterans, and indeed the whole nation, was a renewed sense of purpose, which when applied might give back the personal and national dignity that had been lost or taken from us Vietnam veterans upon our initial return. The Vietnam veterans were robbed of respect at the same time that America lost grace.

The idea for a *Transcontinental March* came to me near the end of the first week in October, 1981. The continued plight of the Vietnam veterans and indeed the nation necessitated some significant action. We were going into the decade of the eighties with so little promise. The plight of the Missing in Action (MIA) and Prisoners of War (POW) was still unresolved, a stinging slap in the face to us. Moreover, the information of continued suffering because of exposure to Agent Orange had begun to reach us and suggested to us that the price tag on Vietnam was not concluded. Perhaps we would not fully understand the true cost of the Vietnam War for several more decades or generations.

- I saw the potential for a further rift between the veterans and the general public over the eventual price tag.

- I saw that though the years had changed many things at home and abroad, society and government had done little to lessen the stigma attached to Vietnam veterans, at least as far as too many people were concerned.

- I saw that there was still a lot of misinformation regarding Vietnam veterans, although there have been innumerable attempts at reconciliation with little impact.

- I saw that the dedication of the Vietnam Veterans' Memorial was merely a scheduled event which could have had a profound impact on the veterans and the nation if more positive reinforcement, respectable communication and awareness of the veterans had been generated.

- I was reminded of the prodigal son, and I thought there should be some visual representation of the road leading home, and not just of the veteran arriving home.

I remembered we had run numerous missions against an enemy in Vietnam with nothing more to show for it than disenchantment at home. So, I surmised, "Why not a mission at home, which might just accomplish some of a goal to appreciate the Vietnam veteran?"

The purpose of the Transcontinental Walk would be to recreate the physical impression of the Vietnam combat veteran, to put him on the long road and allow the people an opportunity to see him firsthand. I wanted the people to see part of the suffering that was his lot in a bygone era, to enable an opportunity for civilians to talk openly with him and to receive up-to-date and accurate information from the veteran. It would remind the public of our unfinished business in Southeast Asia where our MIA/POWs are top priority with us. The American community needed to be encouraged that we are less concerned with any bitterness or difference there might exist between civilians and veterans than we are in having a successful monument dedication at Washington.

This event represented the first real opportunity veterans would have to speak openly to the American people and have them respond. It represented the opportunity for the Vietnam veterans to say something on behalf of our war dead and their families. Finally, and not the least important, was the potential that the Vietnam Memorial held in uniting America in a feeling we have too seldom experienced: cohesiveness.

This potential was as contingent on the positive attitude of the Vietnam veterans present as much as it was the depth of the coverage by major media shared with the people to the maximum degree possible. Further, by the dramatic and positive nature of the event, the media could undo some inaccuracies and injustices attributed to Vietnam veterans. It would be interesting to see how the major media would handle it.

One morning after the planning for the mission had begun I was sitting in front of the television when a Bob Hope commercial that advertised the Vietnam Memorial was being aired. I'd seen this commercial several times before and each time I saw it, I was left with an uneasy feeling. The reason for this feeling became clear to me that morning. The damn thing was low key! It was just too low-keyed; almost as if it wasn't meant to have any impact at all! Everyone in America was not necessarily expected to be as interested as the average veteran, but it did seem to me to be important to at least suggest to the people that the event might be significant.

I finally discovered what had been bugging me. I became aware that we had no guarantee that the Vietnam veterans would be there in significant numbers, or that the nation would be tuned in, or that major media would apply their expertise to the event and do some really in-depth broadcasting. It was obvious to me that without some prelude event or events, we would have no guarantees at all. This once-in-a-lifetime situation could go off without significant positive impact. The media were already dwelling on the controversial aspects of the event and not the event itself.

I thought, "Oh no you don't—not this time, there will never be another shot at this!"

Jan Scruggs, the founder of the Vietnam Veterans' Memorial concept, had definitely made some great moves, not just for the veterans, but for the entire nation. He undoubtedly could use some positive input about a prelude event! Sure. What else could be more appropriate than to send a combat veteran under full combat load walk across the nation? The picture would be self-explanatory: a tradeoff from weapons to our nation's flag and to leave from a former embarkation area where countless thousands before had been shipped to Vietnam. This would be the journey home. The long journey home!

It had been suggested that the American people had been standing in the shadows for so long that this event had the potential to provide a truly significant sunshine ray of hope.

The potential for positive impact was tremendous. If all I had to do was help, I would gladly do it.

I would walk across the nation under a full combat load and carry the American flag to remind all who would bear witness that the Vietnam veterans are proud and patriotic fellow citizens. I knew also that the veterans would have their batteries recharged by this action. It was with these things in mind that the serious research and planning started.

Well, I sure needed a second opinion and my friend Verna, had never let me down. Verna thought it was a fantastic idea. Her response was especially important because she was an American who had no involvement in Vietnam veterans or the conflict. I was talking to 'Miss Jones', an average citizen, about this thing which was primarily the concern of veterans and families of veterans. Verna said it would be terrific and that it would indeed open a lot of people's eyes. From that point forward there was no turning back. It would be done, and I was going to do it!

I spent the next few days thinking of nothing else. So many questions! I suffered a brief period of self-doubt concerning whether I could bring it off. This would be a tremendous physical test, so I really had to look hard at myself. I asked myself some serious questions, which disturbed me because I didn't know if I could do it.

Then it became clear to me that there had been a lot of things in my life that I was not likely capable of or intended to do, but I had managed to do them nonetheless. Was it just that I'd been lucky? Well maybe, but more likely it was the way I'd been raised. I was lucky enough to stand in the shadow of my father, John Saint John. My father was one of those rare people with inner strength and outward courage; he represented everything I aspired to become. My time with him was less than I expected, but I learned a lot in the short time we had together.

Mind over matter was the biggest lesson he taught me. Mind over matter helped me make it through Vietnam, as it had in other tough situations. I was content thinking that I would have to let myself regress to when I had been a young soldier to do this right. I would have to allow myself the very feelings I had been denying all these years. Regression to traumatic events that had improved a person's ability to perform extraordinary things under extraordinary circumstances, such as in a theatre of war, enhanced both mental and emotional disturbances and sensitivities. It seemed a dangerous game!

The planning progressed and was near completion by the end of October. There would be continuous updating and modifications until I actually got going, which would be in the spring of 1982, whenever the weather on the west coast was favorable.

Since I would be doing the walk, I had no trouble deciding on the starting point. It would be from near Ft. Lewis, in the Seattle, Washington area. The area from which I had embarked twice and twice returned. This is also where I had been discharged on August 16, 1971.

The plan called for me to move from west to east coast. I'd already researched this endeavor historically and had satisfied myself that this would represent the first time anyone had walked across this land from sea to sea under a combat load and carrying the nation's flag, 'Old Glory'. I must admit I was especially happy in knowing this since I just knew it would be a good shot for us Vietnam veterans. Heaven knows we needed it, and more!

### David's Support and Approval

Around Christmas time I called my brother David, who was living in Vancouver, Canada to check in with him. I hadn't planned to tell him about this project for a while longer, but I just couldn't hold back my excitement.

At any rate, I broke the story to David, and he was delighted. His approval made Christmas for me because I needed to hear that from him. We discussed the plan and David volunteered right away to monitor the weather on the west coast and keep me posted.

During Christmas and the early New Year I was laid off from my work for a short period, but fortunately I got called back in January. This mission endeavor was going to take some bucks to get started. Rumors of lay-offs kept me unnerved all winter. Then I finally received a layoff notice, but luckily my friend Chuck came to my rescue and offered me work with his painting company. I worked steadily with them for several months and was able to save some money. I gave written notice requesting a leave of absence when it was time to start the Transcontinental Walk.

David, Verna and I decided the best way to work a resupply system was simply to alternate use of funds belonging to David, and what was left of my funds which Verna had access to. Therefore, when I needed money I would contact David or Verna and they would arrange a money order at a Western Union Office at my next destination. We thought this would work to ensure there wouldn't be money changing hands unnecessarily on the road. We established a rule that I would not accept donations from the public in order to secure our credibility.

As I mentioned earlier, the plan was perpetually modified. I continually consulted with other veterans in and out of state. They frequently misunderstood my reason for being so interested in their views. I was determined to keep my plans to myself until I was actually engaged in the walk. No one knows better than the Vietnam veterans that 'talk is cheap'.

Planning was finally completed and funding for expenses was established. I was just waiting for the word from David that the weather on the west coast would allow me to start. It was the second week of April 1982, when David telephoned and said, "You've got a green light, brother. Go for it!"

I submitted the leave of absence request from work during the third week of April and arranged to be paid on my last day at work. I got real lucky and worked Saturday, April 24th , for overtime. That was my last day at painting for a while.

Monday, the 26th, Verna and I drove from our home in Beulah, North Dakota to Fargo, North Dakota to pick up my gear and supplies from the Army Surplus Store. The total price of the gear and supplies was about $350, but the store owners discounted that by a hundred dollars, as support for the walk. Good people!

We traveled approximately six hundred miles to and from Beulah to Fargo, and it just about wore us out. While driving that day, I found myself paying more than the usual attention as the miles went by. I have no problem confessing I had another brief encounter with self-doubt. By the time we arrived back at Beulah that night, I had a chance to play with all my new toys. My first noticeable regression took place, and I was encouraged by it. For a few minutes before I went to sleep, I felt very primal. That was good as that ingredient would be necessary to be successful, and I knew it!

It goes without saying that I was an early riser on Tuesday, the 27th. Working and pawing over my new survival gear, I checked the gear out the way we always had prior to a mission years before, and double-checked the webbing and stitching to insure the load bearing equipment and rucksack would carry the weight. I packed and repacked everything to get it all in, accounting for frequency of use and weight distribution. All the while I made mental notes on where each item was stashed.

The following is a list of equipment and supplies I started out with:

Clothing:
2 camouflage bush caps
2 camouflage sets of fatigues
3 O.D. Green undershirts
4 O.D. Green pairs of socks
1 issue-type pair jungle boots
Notice—no underwear briefs travel commando style

Equipment:

1 American flag and staff
1 Combat survival knife
1 Rucksack issue (nylon) with modified frame
1 Set of L.B.E. load-bearing equipment or web gear
2 ammo pouches M-16 issue (not carrying ammo)
2 canteens—1 quart each, cups & camouflage cover
2 ponchos
1 heavy duty sleeping bag with protective cover
1 small flashlight

Supplies:

First aid kit
Writing materials—journal, notebooks, and pens
Assorted small waterproof bags
Assorted vitamins
12 ft. Nylon rope ¼-inch width and 6—6-inch nails
Misc. personal items (shaving kit, etc.)
4 days' food (dehydrated)
2 towels, issue O.D. Green

The approximate loaded weight of clothing, equipment, and supplies was 60 pounds.

*You think it weighs a lot right now.*
*Wait 'til you reach the hills.*
*Lord knows it'll bend you over son.*
*It's going to test your will.*

*John W. Blake©1982*

**Departing North Dakota: Destination Seattle Washington**

Well, it sure started to look like someone was going somewhere. David had taken annual leave from his job in British Columbia and planned to meet me at Sea-Tac Airport in Seattle, Washington, for my arrival. Two of our friends would also be present: Brian, from British Columbia, and Ron Whelan, a fellow Newfoundlander. They would drive down from Vancouver in David's truck so we would have transportation while doing business in the area. My flight itinerary had me depart from Bismarck, North Dakota, on Northwest Orient Flight 105, April 28th , and arrive on the west coast at 1:15 p.m. PST. I would need a couple of days to set things into motion with media, etc., prior to the start date, which was now scheduled for May 1st . This was indeed a paramilitary operation, one that would be addressed as *The Mission at Home, 1982, One for the Boys*.

It should be considered that within the planning of this walk significant points were decided:

- There should be no advance publicity either in North Dakota or elsewhere since, to the Vietnam veteran, "talk is cheap" and it has no significance until you're doing it, or you've done it.

- No others should accompany the lone walker since the symbolism of one was representative of all veterans.

- No security or advance personnel would be required since this represented a unique opportunity to find out once and for all just how the senior veterans and other citizens really felt about the Vietnam veteran in 1982. Therefore, it was important to keep this in the natural flow and rely on spontaneous response as a prime indicator of those feelings.

- That the walker should behave in a military manner, remembering always that he was representative of so very many others.

- That the walker should promote the issue of our MIA/POWs and Vietnam Veteran Memorial and accomplish the distance as quickly as possible from coast to coast.

- That the walker should be highly visible and always accessible to the public and media.

- That the walker should keep detailed notes, letters, endorsements and documented media coverage plus any other pertinent documentation for future reference.

During my last day, in North Dakota, I packed the rucksack and spent a quiet day with my dearest friend, Verna. With most of the business completed, we were left with only a few minor chores to accomplish before the end of the day. I had photocopied a one-page fact sheet and prepared a map overlay of the projected route (tentative at this point), which I intended to carry with me and make available to individuals and media wherever appropriate.

The next day, Verna and I reached the airport in plenty of time, so I checked in and paid the man two hundred and nine dollars for my one-way ticket. Verna knew the man, so we started to discuss the mission with the attendant. He said he wished he had known sooner so that he could have attempted a complimentary fare, but it wasn't possible on short notice. What he did do was immediately upgrade my reservation to first-class accommodations from coach at no additional charge, which sure was nice of him.

In the short distance from the terminal to the airplane, I had a wonderful experience. In my memory, I was taken back many years to another place and time when, as a younger man, I had taken similar walks to a surprisingly similar aircraft. I was consciously aware there would be more similarities. Surprisingly enough I sensed myself looking forward to them. I knew that no matter what happened on this walk. It could not be much worse than what I had already experienced in Vietnam. With some luck, it could be a lot better.

Once we were airborne my heart started beating as though it was on its own private frequency and dancing to the rhythm of some ancient tribal tune. Once above the clouds, it either slowed down or the rest of me caught up. No matter. It just felt great! My mind's eye wandered out beyond the expanse of beautiful white fields of clouds to again see familiar faces I thought were gone forever.

In my mind, I thought I heard someone say; "Good to see you, Blake. We knew you were coming. It's all part of the plan, you know!"

Plan? What plan? But of course, my plan.

During most of the trip, I remembered bits and pieces of faded memories which came from as far back as my childhood and as recently as just a few months ago. No matter where my thoughts landed, the memory would be a vivid picture, as though I were there again. Although it was strange, it was beautiful. I wondered why I was thinking this way when I had much important work to do.

Those memories offered up a healthy mixture of happiness and sadness. The flight from the Dakotas to the west coast seemed to go by quickly. As I disembarked the aircraft, I suspected some forces had been present on the journey. I felt I was not so much leading as being led. The young stewardess thanked me for flying Northwest Orient. I was fully aware that the easiest part of my journey was finished.

**Reunited with David in Seattle**

I spotted my brother and friends almost immediately in the airport, standing there full of silly grins, but they were a sight for sore eyes. I guess it had been four years or more since I had seen David and even longer since I had seen Ron. I had never met Brian; although I had spoken with him several times by telephone at David's house.

Walking the corridors of Sea-Tac Airport, I was haunted by the memories of the several times I had been here before. I thought of the countless others who had, under similar circumstances, traveled these corridors. Now, all these years later, I was back.

Once the baggage was delivered I grabbed my gear, and we headed out. For the sake of having some direction, I asked David to drive to the waterfront in Seattle. I had two reasons for wanting to go there; I'd been landlocked in the Dakotas for several years and very much needed to breathe the salt sea air, plus I wanted seafood, fresh seafood. In the early to mid-seventies, David and I had been around the Seattle/Tacoma area quite a bit. I was happy to see that he still knew his way around as he drove directly to a seafood restaurant on the waterfront.

David and the boys decided that they would pick up the tab for all expenses over the next couple of days. We booked two rooms and arranged that David and I were together while Ron and Brian were in an adjoining room. The boys made it clear that although helping me to get a good start was their main reason for being in Seattle, they'd still like to do a little celebrating. I took the opportunity to emphasize a few priorities and left them to their better judgment. They were good old boys who wouldn't go far off center.

We still had the evening to share before I would start setting things up for the next morning. While being brought up to date on the happenings back in Newfoundland, Ron broke the news about a dear friend's death. Roy, a gifted guitarist and a fellow Newfoundlander, had taken his own life. The news hit me the way such news does with anyone who cares. I remembered the times when I would worry over Roy. On quiet evenings, he would come by to share a pot of tea and try hard to explain his anger. Roy wasn't a Vietnam veteran nor was he ever in combat, but he sure knew about war, the war inside. He fought it every day and night—except one.

Around midnight the boys left for points unknown to go "fox hunting," they said. Before falling to sleep, I wrote the following media alert notice.

# MEDIA ALERT
# E PLURIBUS UNUM
# (One Out of Many)

AN EVENT OF NATIONAL INTEREST begins May 1, 1982—at Seattle, Washington.

From there, on that day, a Vietnam veteran—in full combat uniform—will begin a 'forced march' across America; coast to coast. This action is not a protest in any way, but rather is a **TRIBUTE** to a great nation—of great people.

**SPECIAL TRIBUTE**

To our Vietnam era war dead and their surviving families

To the courage and sacrifice of those seriously wounded and their supportive families

To ALL surviving Vietnam veterans and their families

**SPECIAL APPEAL**

To all Americans to show solidarity with the families of the estimated 2,497 of our 'boys' missing in action—many of whom are being held prisoner

To all Americans to appeal to the Vietnamese government and its people for the safe return of our boys

**SO THEN**: On May 1, 1982, and for as long as it takes, let's have

## ONE FOR THE BOYS

John W. Blake, Vietnam Veteran

# "One for the Boys" The Original Map for the Transcontinental Line of March

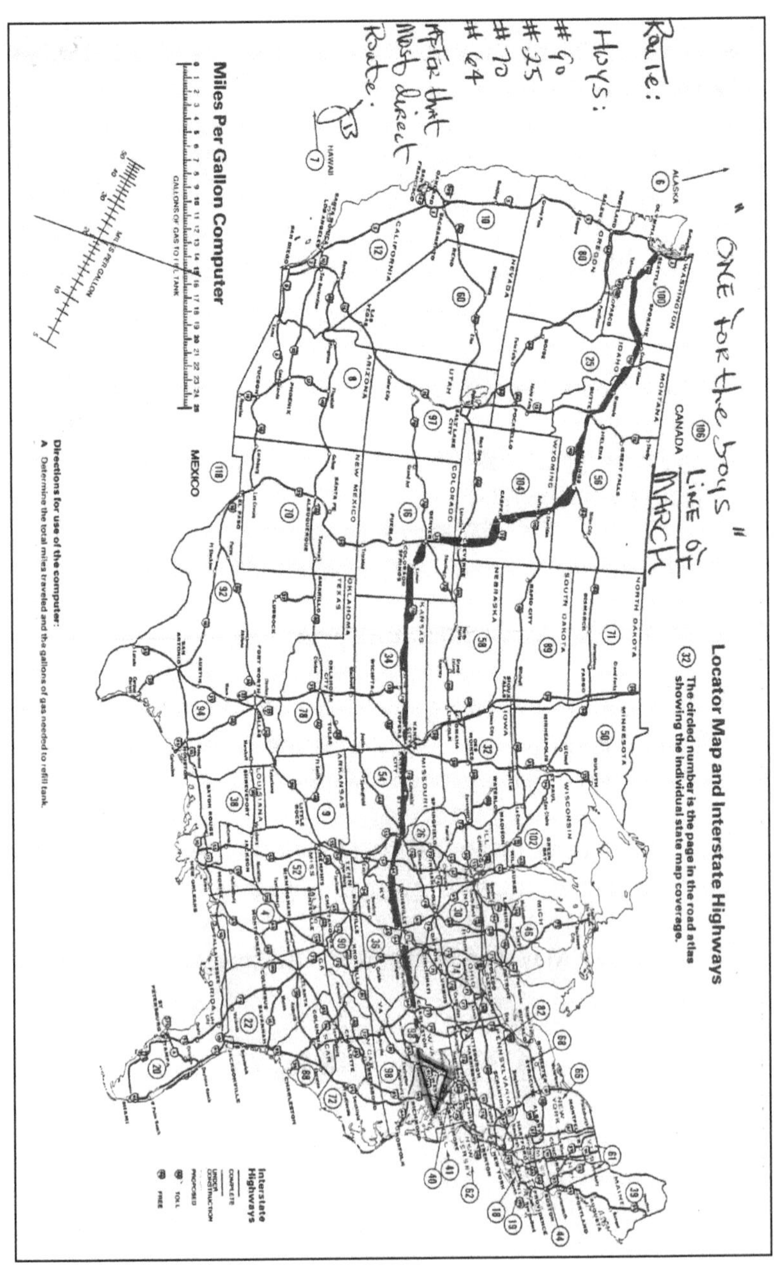

**Seattle Washington Media**

I woke around 7 a.m. on Thursday morning, April 29th. The boys were sleeping soundly after their forays; I had no idea what time they had returned, so I left them to sleep. I showered, dressed and walked a block up the street to a cafe to have breakfast. Directly across the street from where I was seated was the *Seattle Post-Intelligencer* office.

Stepping through the doorway of the newspaper's building, I introduced myself to the information receptionist. I showed her a copy of the media alert that I had prepared, so she made a telephone call which cleared me to go upstairs in search of Mr. Jon Hahn, writer.

Once upstairs, I introduced myself to the receptionist and passed over a copy of the media alert. Within a few minutes, I was greeted by a distinguished-looking gentleman who introduced himself as Jon Hahn. He suggested that we chat over coffee in the cafeteria. During our conversation, I realized Mr. Hahn was well informed about Vietnam veterans. When we parted company that morning, I felt encouraged by the receptiveness Mr. Hahn had expressed concerning my planned venture. I stepped out into the morning air and breathed a sigh of relief before moving down the street to alert other media. The people at KOMO TV were very nice, and I felt certain they would come out on the starting day.

With these things accomplished, I returned to our motel rooms where I found the boys still soundly sleeping. Since it was noon, I didn't feel the need to tiptoe around. Soon, the sleepy hunters woke to report that the woods were alive with game but that they had bagged none. They would try again that night for they had learned from their mistakes of last evening, or so they said.

While the boys dressed and prepared for the day, I made some notes on things that still needed to be done before starting the mission. I had an uneasy feeling that I had forgotten or overlooked something, but I'll be darned if I could figure out just what. One of the most important things was media for documentation of start-up. At no point did I want or need a lot of hype. I just needed it recorded that the March was here and now and actually happening. This project and I would be tested equally and any credibility due would come on an ongoing basis. This project had to acquire a hard-earned respect. Getting it would suggest that respect was due all Vietnam veterans, especially our KIAs, MIAs, and POWs. What could I be forgetting?

When the boys were finally ready, we piled into David's truck and traveled downtown, where we spent the rest of the afternoon picking up needed food items, maps, and other items required for the journey.

We returned to our rooms after dinner and spent a couple of hours together looking over the maps. We decided on a specific starting point location and set the time for departure at 10 a.m. on Saturday, May 1, 1982.

I double checked the equipment, supplies, and route; everything seemed okay. I forced myself to relax as the boys prepared to resume 'the hunt'. When they left, I wrote a few entries in my journal on the things we had done and then fell off to sleep fully clothed. Sometime during the night I awoke to find myself still alone and thought, "Those boys are certainly determined hunters, although it is getting more difficult to tell the hunters from the hunted these days!" With that thought, I drifted back to sleep.

On Friday morning, I was anxious to see the morning paper. I wanted to see how Jon Hahn handled the story. I dressed quickly and went out to the same cafe I had been the day before. I purchased a newspaper, entered the cafe and ordered a coffee as I began thumbing through the pages. Finding the story, I read through it feverishly. I was eager to see what sort of impact Jon had created. It was positive! On a second reading I realized that I had put Jon on the spot and that he had come through in fine style. With this story, the first media input was documented, and the mission was publicly known.

The following are excerpts from an article by Jon Hahn published in the *Seattle Post-Intelligencer*, April 30, 1982.

**A Viet Vet's March for Dignity**

Seven years ago, today, U.S. troops pulled out of Saigon. We Americans went through agonies of belated revulsion then threw-up in public and then set about getting-it-all-together.

Tomorrow, a former Special Forces soldier in full 50-pound field pack and uniform and carrying an American flag will start a march from this Washington to the other Washington to help end the Vietnam conflict here at home.

There's an unwritten rule about never doing a story on something that someone may say that he's going to do tomorrow...But John Blake, 33, is different. With just a hint of his native Newfoundland accent, he talks about the need for Americans to accept their Vietnam veterans. Call for recognition.

"A lot of us have felt for a long time now that there is still an unfinished business about 'Nam...There's a need in each of us to sort of clean up the impression left by Vietnam and 'Nam vets. We need our dignity to be given back," Blake said.

So his march isn't so much—if at all—a protest as it is a call for recognition.

"This is for all the boys who didn't get welcomed home after 'Nam," Blake said. "It's for the families of all the boys who were killed or turned into invalids over there and for the families of the thousands of MIA's (Missing in Action) still over there."

"I chose Seattle as the starting point for my march because I left for 'Nam from Fort Lewis. I spent one year and one extension, in total 18 months in Vietnam. I was with the Special Forces Airborne Rangers, November

> Company 75th Infantry. I was lucky. No serious wounds, but I lost a lot of good friends. We all did."
>
> Seven years after they hauled down the American flag in Saigon, John Blake is going to begin carrying it across the United States. Not in any gung-ho display of misguided patriotism, but in a sincere effort to heal all the wounds left from Vietnam. There is a scar, of sorts, apparent in one of Blake's comments. "We have to be together on this thing, and then it has to be let go."

I quickly returned to the room and woke my brother. While he read the newspaper story, I prepared notes on things to be done that day. Again, I felt that I was overlooking something. David finished reading and said he thought that the story was "a good, clean shot."

I telephoned Jon and thanked him for the story. We spoke briefly, and I informed him we had decided on a starting point. I confirmed the time and arranged to call the paper's city desk in the morning so they could get a photographer out there for pictures. Then I telephoned the other media contacts, gave them an updated time and confirmed the location of the starting point for the Transcontinental Walk.

The boys and I spent most of the day driving around Seattle. Starting at the waterfront from where I would leave the next morning, we drove approximately twenty miles along the projected route out of the city proper. With this accomplished, I was satisfied I knew my way out of the populated area and would be okay heading into the rural areas.

**We Stand Beside You**

When we returned to the motel, I collected my messages. A return call to Jon Hahn put me in touch with a local Vietnam veteran who offered moral support and the use of his Ranger patches, plus the use of other items of equipment. I explained to him I would wear no particular unit patch or rank. The whole idea of the mission was 'one walker represented the many'. He would be as universal in appearance as possible so he could represent any veteran and anybody's son. The Vietnam veteran thanked me for that as if he meant it, and so did I. Several anonymous messages were left, but the one that stood out the most read, "It is great what you are doing. We stand beside you."

I felt deeply moved by the media support and other veterans getting on board with offers of assistance and moral support. I had been self-driven for so long that I hadn't even tried to imagine how I might be impacted by these favorable responses. I walked out of the room and down the hallway, because I didn't want the guys to see me cry. I thought to myself that no matter what happened from here on, I must remember this moment.

Back at the room, the boys had poured drinks to toast the successes of what I titled, *The Mission at Home, 1982—One for the Boys*. We spent the evening in leisure discussion, plus we captured some pictures of ourselves for posterity before turning in for a restful sleep. When I took off my clothes that night, it dawned on me that it would be several months before I would wear civilian clothes again. For the duration of the mission, I would be in camouflage fatigues, a prescribed uniform for a prescribed effect! David would inherit the civilian clothes I had brought with me to Seattle.

While lying in the bed aching for sleep, I had a sudden realization. I finally realized what had been bugging me the whole time at Seattle. Of all the people I have ever known, I had to be the dumbest!

I had forgotten to clear this venture with all the local authorities. The police at Seattle and the State Highway Patrol had to be notified. I had a sick feeling with shades of distress. David offered to go around in the morning and take care of it as best he could on such short notice. "That would help," I thought, as I spent a fitful night trying to sleep. I vowed not to repeat this mistake.

∞

# THE MISSION AT HOME
# ONE FOR THE BOYS
# TRANSCONTINENTAL MARCH 1982
# FROM
# SEATTLE, WASHINGTON TO WASHINGTON, D.C.
# PHASE TWO
# BY
# JOHN W. BLAKE
# UNFINISHED MANUSCRIPT

# Chapter 7
# Boots Start Walking

WE CHECKED OUT OF OUR HOTEL ROOMS' early and skipped breakfast. Then we headed down to Coleman Park from where I would begin the long journey across the continent. I was dressed in full combat gear minus weapons, and we hammed it up for a little while as we waited for the media photographer to arrive. I had planned to kick-off at 10 a.m. and now it was 10:30 a.m., so I couldn't wait any longer. I just had to get that gear on my back and go for it; so we said our emotional goodbyes.

David and I had emigrated to the United States of America together from Canada on January 12, 1969. We were sworn into the nation and its army the very next day. I was nineteen years old and David was only seventeen years old at the time. We had stood side by side on that day so many years before, so full of pride and self-esteem. We were joyful as we raised our right hands and pledged allegiance to the flag, along with all those other young Americans and Canadians who stood there doing the same thing for the same reason.

There was no further need for words, as that familiar feeling returned. We hugged each other and parted. I quickly turned on my heels, picked up the gear and swung it upon my back. Then, I raised the flag staff to rest upon my shoulder while the flag fluttered in the gentle breeze. I didn't look back as I walked away!

The boys went on ahead of me by a short distance to snap a few pictures and then were gone. I moved heading due east from Coleman Park to the Memorial Bridge and headed out across the bay.

David, Ron, and Brian had really gone out of their way to help me get off to a good start. They departed to advise the authorities of the route and agenda at the police station in Seattle. Hopefully, the local police, as requested, would pass the information on down the line to other police authorities. In a couple of hours, David and the boys would be back in Canada, while I hoped about the same time to be out of the heavily populated area.

I traveled across the bridge and noticed people waving and sounding their car horns in appreciation of what they were viewing. I then sensed something was happening behind me. As I turned and glanced over my left shoulder, I found myself looking straight into a T.V. video camera. Talk about a shock! All I could do was keep walking and try to ignore their presence. With no real media experience, I began to feel unnerved with all the attention. The thought that they were just doing their job helped me settle down. After all, the formula for exposure was: "Veteran plus media exposure multiplied by people equaled impact!"

The media camera captured my movement across the bridge. I began thinking that whether I liked it or not, I was simply going to have to do my very best with this project, for better or for worse, I would simply project myself with no performing or grandstanding!

As I neared the end of the bridge, the media raced ahead. People in cars were still waving and honking their horns, so I felt a little more reassured. It was not so much that I seriously doubted they would approve, but I didn't know for sure. There was no book written on this sort of thing. If there had been, I sure as heck would have read it!

With a few more steps I closed the distance between myself and the media, who had gathered to set up their equipment just off and to the right of the bridge in readiness for a live interview. For me, it was 'baptism by fire', and I reminded myself to think beyond the impending interview and just deal with it. I did not want to make a big thing of it and get all nervous or shook up. That is how I got through the first interview. The reporters wanted to know who, what, where, why and when, so I told them. Just like that it was done, and I was on my way thinking, "That's not so hard. Now, let's get some miles behind us." The 'us' in my thoughts meant the tens of thousands Vietnam veterans who never made it home. Soldiers, whom I spiritually represented and constantly carried in my heart, soul and mind. I could feel them all traveling with me. I traveled along Highway 169; a two-lane blacktop with narrow dirt shoulders to a town called Enumclaw, and continued on to Highway 410 up to the Cayuse Pass. It looked as if it would be easy going as far as Enumclaw but that I would be climbing steadily afterwards.

I was a little unnerved to find that the two-lane blacktop offered me no rear security. I realized this danger when I narrowly missed being hit by a speeding car, which was simply passing another car. At one point, the speeding vehicle shot between the other car and me. It was a real close call and a nasty scare for me. I would have to use my sense of hearing to protect myself against things behind me and off to the sides. While I sensed some danger, I also sensed some welcomed regression. Old instincts were being alerted; former LRRP training provided me with strong observational and awareness skills to protect myself and others in Vietnam. Now those same skills would help protect me here.

I was still adjusting to the newly recovered hypervigilance when I noticed a pickup truck.It had passed me earlier and now returned pulling off the road just ahead of me. I approached the parked truck and met two local guys, one of whom was Vietnam veteran Vince Humble. We chatted, and he told me that as they drove past earlier, he had sensed I was a Vietnam veteran and excitedly expressed, "I knew it. I just knew it!"

I explained to him what I was doing and asked him what he thought of it. He said, "It is a good idea and it makes me feel proud."

I told him, "Making the Vietnam veterans feel proud is one of the main reasons I decided to do the mission."

Vince and his buddy described the immediate terrain, and then I took off to find a campsite. The sun was already going down so I wasn't too fussy about where I pitched my make-shift tent for the night. I climbed over some railroad tracks to my left and moved into the tree line. There, I found some dense overhead cover offered by the trees. I tied a line between two trees and hung a poncho over the line. With the poncho secured and fastened on both sides by six-inch nails pounded through the corner center holes, my tent was secured in the ground. I had shelter for the night. I threw my second poncho down as a ground sheet inside the open-ended shelter and spread out my sleeping bag for a goodnight's sleep. I folded the flag and climbed inside my cozy, humble abode. Once settled, I laid there rethinking the day's events. What a day it had been! I was completely exhausted. Sleep came easily.

**Walking in the Rain**

I woke to the sound of falling rain. Soon after I roused myself from my cozy sleeping bag, I realized that this was going to be another tough day. My entire body, muscles, joints, and bones, were stiff and sore. Since it was a Sunday, I thought at first I would linger in camp for the day, but I soon decided it was still early enough to make a few miles and maybe even find a better place with more shelter.

The rain began to flow steadily through the trees, and I was in a hurry to break camp. I quickly packed up everything and moved out of the tree line and back over the railroad track onto the road. Here in the open, the rain seemed to pour down like the monsoon rains in Vietnam, falling straight out of the sky with little or no wind. I had a moment of confusion as I tried to decide if I should open and expose my flag to the rain. Then I remembered recent changes in regulations allowed that the nation's flag could be flown in all weather, even at night when it could be illuminated. With this resolved, I let Old Glory wave over my shoulder and took off walking.

After a few miles, my boots were sopping wet, as were my arms and head. I had neglected to pull the hood of my poncho up over my head when I started walking. By now my bush hat had soaked up water, which ran down the back of my neck. The aches and stiffness of my body were somewhat diminished only to be replaced by the misery of being wet and cold. My flag no longer proudly waved in the air with each stride since it was laden down with rain water. There wasn't much traffic on this rainy Sunday morning, but what traffic there was seemed more bewildered than enthusiastic about seeing me walking. I reckoned these folks had not seen the media report from yesterday. I wasn't at all encouraged. As a matter of fact, this shaped up to be a totally uninspiring day.

I traveled a few more miles and noticed a car, which turned around up ahead of me and returned. The vehicle pulled onto the shoulder of the road. I noticed that the driver was a woman with a little child bundled up on the front passenger's seat. She told me that she had been driving along listening to her cassette player when the tape began to unexplainably mess up as she passed by. She couldn't get the tape to play again and took this as a sign to turn her car around and speak to me. She said, "I sensed something."

I stood there in the rain and explained to the lady what I was doing out in the rain and why. She was impressed and wrote a telephone number on a scrap of paper, which she gave to me and said, "You must call this number. A friend is there who has something for you!"

The lady went on to say that she had a long journey ahead and offered me a ride, which I declined. Then she was gone. I was confused by this encounter. As I moved on down the road I tried to figure it out, which made me less aware of my rain-soaked misery. After a few more miles, I stopped for a rest in a sheltered area where I intended to ponder over the note the lady had given to me. Unfortunately, I couldn't find it. I had lost the piece of paper. At first, I was disappointed, but then I realized that I still had the memory of her warmth and concern. The fact that she had taken the time to brighten my day meant a lot to me.

Back up on the road, I was moving along pretty well when I noticed a car pulled in on the shoulder of the road opposite me. An elderly gentleman rolled down his window and said, "What the hell are you doing with the colors (flag) out in the rain? You're not supposed to get them wet!"

From across the way, I hollered, "This is not my first choice, but that revised regulations on the usage of the flag now permitted the flag to be flown in all weather conditions."

"I should know the regulations because I had a career in the military. What the hell are you doing out here, anyway?" He asked.

I resolved myself to the probability that there would be a lot of this, so I stayed calm and briefly explained, 'what the hell I was doing'. He listened attentively. When I had finished speaking, he told me that his son, who is a Vietnam veteran, had returned home and settled in after fighting in the war. The gentleman went on to brag so much about his son that I began to envy his son for having such a proud father. This gentleman then said, "I'm tired of hearing about of all those Vietnam veterans who were so sore about their reception after Vietnam. I don't think they care about this nation anymore, and that they should quit their belly-aching."

I remained calm even though I felt wounded inside as I responded, "There is no need for anyone to add to the damage that's been done to us guys; major media and circumstances have done a good job of that already. A lot of the time, you folks have been hearing from and about our 'walking wounded' while the vast majority of us veterans have kept quiet and taken care of our own business. Now, after all these years, we're looking at a situation that is not going to resolve itself. So if this march is anything, it has to be an example of just who we are and what we still believe in. This is 1982, and we are determined to make sure there is no further misunderstanding about these things. The fact is that as nations go, America is still a baby that has not nearly finished growing."

I returned to the other side of the road and noted that I would always remember that moment of despair caused by the gentleman's words. I thought, "I shall never know if he got anything out of what I said, but I do know he wished me good luck and success. And I think he meant it!"

I continued walking in the pouring rain. Within a mile another car pulled over. I could see just one person in the car. As I came broadside I was impressed to see a young, tremendously beautiful lady step out into the rain. She stood by the opened door of her vehicle and asked, "Would you like to get in out of the rain and ride a bit of the way?" I replied, "No thank you. It is significant for me to only walk the distance I have left to travel."

Nothing more was said; she understood. The beautiful young lady slipped back into her car and bid me good luck as she drove off. It sure didn't do me any good to have had this temptation, although I did the right thing. However, that knowledge seemed like poor consolation as I hobbled into the little community of Maple Valley, Washington.

On that quiet rainy afternoon I decided to pitch camp discreetly under the bridge. By walking in the continuous rain under the weight of the gear, which was now soaking wet, I had developed some concerning blisters on my feet.

I expected blisters to be a problem. I had counted on a few dry days of walking to toughen up my feet building up some calluses. The calluses would protect my feet from further blistering. I now had to deal with a number of serious blisters, which had developed and broken inside my boots. My feet were too soft from being wet all morning, and now there was also a risk of infection. Once I was settled in my camp under the bridge, I removed my boots and socks and reassured myself that I was wise to stop for a while. The Cedar River was just a few feet away, so I was able to wash and care for my feet. Lying comfortable in my snug and dry bunk, I watched the rain fall on either side of my make-shift camp, but not a single drop of rain touched me.

I made a small fire among the rocks and heated some water to make instant hot soup, which turned out to be so good that I had to have another. I felt regenerated by the warmth of the soup and a full belly.

I thought of how little one really needs to be happy, and it dawned on me that what I thought was the same thing I said to myself many, many times before in Vietnam under similar conditions while in the jungles. I had been fully aware of this reality although somewhere along the complicated road from Vietnam to here I had managed to forget it. I began to wonder about all the guys we had lost at home since we finally returned from Vietnam and how many of them might still be with us had they not forgotten the reality of simplicity. It was normal to want the finer things in life once we came home. But having learned such basic lessons and appreciation of life through the many sacrifices in combat, it just didn't seem right that so many of us had become victims of superficial wants or desires.

I reviewed the previous days of the mission and reasoned it had been a good test to evaluate the resiliency of the mission and me. For the time being, I was content just to walk along, checking with the veterans as I did and observe their feelings of approval and note where their priorities stood. Instinctively, I knew that by the time I walked over the Cascade Mountain Range, I would be more physically conditioned for this venture. The vision of me walking over those mountains seemed like an eternity away.

Before dark settled in, I found the energy and ambition to wash out my dirty fatigues and hang them over the top of my poncho tent for the night. Everything about me was damp, though I was happy just not to be soaking wet. Dressed in dry fatigues, I was comfortable for the night, which I suspected might be chilly at best. Several people had come down to the river during the afternoon, although none had attempted to find out more about me than what they observed.

I spent some time in significant regression before finally falling off to sleep. I encouraged myself in these regressions, as I have stated, it would be necessary for me to project as close an image as possible to the Vietnam soldier so that I could share with the people some of the intensity of our feelings. Regression would accomplish part of that projection, and I trusted the physical activity to accomplish the rest.

The only drawback with regression is that one cannot pick and choose the emotional attachment to memories. Often, I had to re-experience the sadness of some of my memories in order to find my strengths. Those times of regression were the most difficult.

My walk was for the benefit of the American people as well as for the Vietnam veterans. I hoped they would see our veterans in a better light than that in which we had been previously cast. I hoped the people would finally realize the difference between the Vietnam veteran and the Vietnam War. We would soon see!

I was up and about bright and early Monday. The night had been a little more than chilly, although for the most part, I had slept well. The sun peeked through the darkened clouds, which appeared as though the clouds would shortly pass over. I dismantled my camp and spread everything out over the nearby bushes so that the sun would draw out the dampness. Yesterday's fatigues and socks were still wet, and I thought I'd let those items dry a bit more before I repacked them. My feet were raw and covered with broken blisters. The condition of my feet would make for tough going over the next few days, but with time they would heal. I shaved, brushed my teeth and washed my face in the river. The water was predictably cold since it was the spring runoff from the mountains. I enjoyed a breakfast of several granola bars and put the gear back together before breaking camp.

The sun was shining as I made my way back up to the roadway. I had a feeling that in a few more miles I would be well on my way into the rural area. The forest that surrounded me was quite dense, and the road was like a corridor with angles. Both sides of the road were heavily lined with trees. The tree line was within a few feet of the road edge, so it felt as though I was walking through a maze. My feet continued to bother me, but I made up my mind to ignore the pain. Mentally blocking discomfort sometimes worked...for a while.

**Community of Black Diamond**

When I entered a rural community called Black Diamond, I noticed a police car coming my way. Two young officers asked what I was up to and checked my identification. When I expressed concern for my safety in the heavier populated areas, one officer said, "I don't think you'll have any problem in places like this, though I'm not sure about towns and cities—a lot of kooks around."

I told him I thought that even the bad boys would let this "Walk" go by them because of what it represented. The same officer replied that he hoped so, for my sake. They both wished me well in my travels as they returned to their vehicle.

I had figured out by now that David's efforts with the authorities had fallen short. It certainly would have been beneficial if law enforcement had passed the word on down the line that the 'Walker' was headed their way. But that could be a difficult task to communicate.

Black Diamond was a quiet, rural community. As I walked down the main road that passed right through the town, a couple of guys standing in the doorway of a tavern called me over. One of them had heard the news about me.

"Well, that was encouraging," I thought, as I asked one of the guys to go back inside the tavern and fetch me a cold soda. I relished every luxurious mouthful of that cold soft drink right down to the very last drop. I pondered over my map for a while and decided I ought to make it to Enumclaw by sundown. I picked up my gear and headed out with the sun shining brightly high overhead in a brilliant blue sky.

After an uneventful afternoon of walking, I approached the community of Enumclaw. Several vehicles had stopped and each driver asked the same question, "Why are you walking?"

I kept my explanations brief since it was getting near sundown, and the cloud buildup, coupled with a chill in the air, indicated a turn in the weather. Plus, I needed to get into the town before dark to avoid the confusion of night movement in unfamiliar territory. All who stopped were pleased with the explanation I offered and wished me well.

With only a half mile left to go, the sky opened up, and a hail-like sleet started to fall. In a matter of minutes, I was chilled to the bone. I noticed sidewalks on both sides of the road. "So, this is Enumclaw," I remarked to myself just as a young man with a camera came up to introduce himself as a reporter for the local paper. He questioned me briefly and took a few pictures. Just as he finished his interview, a city police car pulled in beside us.

The police officer asked me what I was doing and requested identification. Again, I found there had been no advance notice to this area. I was thinking that I would have to make some provision for this situation. The natural flow principle was still important to the project, but I started to think that it wouldn't hurt to work more closely with the media and the authorities. The police officer returned from his car to ask me if I had any lodging for the night. I explained that I hadn't, so he offered me a warm dry bed at the Enumclaw Police Station, which I welcomed and gratefully accepted.

Other officers were in and out of the station all evening, and the several brief conversations I had with them helped me to feel very much at ease. I was offered the use of and enjoyed the shower and kitchen areas. After making a hot cup of soup and other snacks, I washed my clothes by hand and set them over the radiators to dry. I brought my journal up to date and slept soundly throughout the night.

In the morning, I woke early and spent some time working on my travel route through the state. The original media alert I carried had a map illustration of the route I had first intended to take. I simply traced the alternate route onto that illustration and made a few copies.

I met with Enumclaw's Chief of Police and other officers before I stepped out to have breakfast at a local restaurant. After I had eaten my first decent meal in a few days, and while I lingered and enjoyed my second cup of coffee, local V.F.W. Post Commander George Austin approached me. George and I talked openly about veterans' issues, and I was glad we had the opportunity to meet. George dropped me off at the police station where I thanked everyone for their generous hospitality. I collected my gear, secured the flag onto the staff, headed back to the point of pick-up from the previous evening and continued onward with the mission.

**The Cascade Mountain Range**

I walked towards the outskirts of Enumclaw, where I turned east-southeast on Highway 410 and started uphill. Within a few miles, I was in the Cascade Mountain Range and continued to climb steadily to an elevation of 4,694 feet. Although the weather was probably comfortable to most people, I felt quite hot under the load that I carried. The hills were covered with trees, and I experienced the corridor effect again. Amazingly beautiful!

Once in the mountains, I had a unique sense of space and depth, even though I was surrounded by forest. There was always a ridge line, mountain peak, gorge, or hill to view, all of which was food for the soul. Memories flooded back to me as I recalled so vividly the foreboding ridgelines and mountains of Vietnam. These were places embedded in my memory where I could sense danger and smell death.

Traffic on the road was light as I steadily climbed. I soon noticed the entrance to an army mountain training camp located straight ahead and off to the left of my location. I paused to rest and reflected on my surroundings. In Seattle, I had read about an Airborne Ranger unit permanently stationed in the Fort Lewis area, and I presumed they had used this very camp from time to time.

During World War II and Korea, the Army had used Rangers but had discontinued their use at the end of each conflict. In

Vietnam, the Rangers were first known as Long Range Reconnaissance Patrols (LRRPs) and were later re-designated LRPs for Long Range Patrols. My buddies and I had again proven the effectiveness of small unit tactics in Vietnam. The Army now saw fit to keep this concept going, and here I was resting in an area where these young Rangers would train. It made me feel proud of my buddies and myself. I thought, "We don't need these brave young people today, but until we do, we'd better have them ready and well trained. Sometime in the future, we will certainly need them again simply because Rangers Lead The Way!" I lifted my rucksack onto my aching frame and sadly thought, "We always will!"

Later in the afternoon, after I traveled a few more miles, I met Mrs. Daryl Abbott and several other people from the nearby community of Greenwater who had recognized me from the media coverage. Ms. Abbott informed me there were many people there who would enjoy meeting me, including her husband, and that I should stop at the Naches Tavern. She also informed me that several Vietnam veterans lived in the area. We parted, and I quickly headed out with a new-found energy. The anticipation of meeting a bunch of people and some veterans added a skip to my walk.

I pushed on without any further breaks and arrived at Naches Tavern at approximately 5:30 p.m. I strolled into the tavern and sensed that these mountain people were laid-back folks because no one seemed to notice me. But of course, they did notice. They just don't get surprised very easily. I sat at the end of the bar and ordered a soda.

Mrs. Abbott's husband, Terry, arrived and greeted me with a brotherly handshake and hug—the kind that veterans offer to each other knowingly when they have shared a common history. We all enjoyed a wonderful evening together, and I even helped drink a pitcher of beer. I found Terry and the people of Greenwater to be most welcoming. I felt especially fortunate to have met these wonderful people and accepted an invitation to spend the night with the Abbott family, at their home.

Mrs. Abbott and her young family settled down for the night leaving Terry and me to spend an hour or so talking about old times. We shared ideas about where we wanted to go in life. If I hadn't been so worn out, I am sure that we would have greeted the morning sun. We both began to chat a little more cautiously and slowly near the end of our evening, not necessarily for the benefit of the other, but for ourselves. There was a lot more going through each of our young minds than what was being said. We had both fought in Vietnam and still, almost a decade later, we had difficulty speaking about our experiences. Our experiences and losses were still raw and deep. We both recognized that from our collective war experiences we had become the walking wounded.

In the early morning we shared a wonderful breakfast. Terry and I talked about the route I would take over the mountains. We enjoyed the morning air when Terry advised me that the Chinook Pass was still blocked with snow. However, the Cayuse Pass had been open for about a week. He mentioned that the snow line was still low, therefore within a day's walk I could be up to the Cayuse Pass. Temperatures at the Pass were well below freezing at sundown, so I must not get caught on top of the Pass overnight. I agreed!

Terry had advised me of one other family that lived between Greenwater and the top of the Pass. They lived there and operated a resort which was closed for the winter. I made up my mind to visit if they were home.

We said our goodbyes, and I moved on and climbed steadily toward the Cayuse Pass. Within no time at all, I was back into the wilderness. I pushed onward for the rest of the day at a steady pace and made camp beside the White River. I wished that I had brought a fishing pole along, for surely I would have caught a fish or two for supper. I wasn't about to complain since I had eaten two large home cooked meals in one day. Somehow, I knew that would be an exception for me while on this journey.

As soon as the sun went down beyond the ridge line, the air became chilly. I scurried into my sleeping bag to keep warm and laid there awake just thinking for the longest time. While walking that day I reflected on my memories of the guys I had served with in 'Nam, the guys who had made it home and the ones that had not. I needed to remember them every day since we parted so that they would never be forgotten.

I lay bundled up and cozy in my simple camp when I had a profound feeling. Although I was undoubtedly walking alone and lying here by myself, I wasn't at all lonely. I could feel a spiritual presence, a purely sensory experience, and it sure was a good feeling. It was the 'boys'. They too were here in spirit.

I thought about how our nation had been so negatively impacted by the Vietnam experience, and how fitting it would be if the veterans could promote the healing. It sure would be wonderful if the guys could do something to bring America back into the sunlight again. What a lasting tribute that would make to the veterans, the soldiers we lost, plus their families. Somewhere during these thoughts I fell asleep.

I woke early the next morning to the chilly mountain air, skipped breakfast, quickly broke camp and took advantage of an early start. I located the cozy resort, Alta Silva, which Terry had described. I walked from the highway up to the garden and was greeted by a middle-aged man chopping firewood. He must have been surprised by the sight of me fully camouflaged and in combat gear, so I quickly introduced myself and told the man the nature of my business. He smiled, and introduced himself as Bill McMahan. He told me about the resort he and his wife were carving out of the wilderness. His pioneering spirit and efforts were indeed impressive.

I was good and hungry by now, so I asked if the dining room was open this time of year. He advised me that the diner was not open yet, but said I would be more than welcome to join him and his wife, up at their house for lunch. I gratefully accepted.

Mr. McMahon and his wife were both concerned that I would have a problem farther up the road because of the Cayuse

Pass, which had been closed for the winter due to snow. It had only just reopened during the past week. They assisted me in contacting the park rangers who instructed me not to attempt a walk through the actual Cayuse Pass at the top of the mountain. The park ranger reported that the snow was piled fifteen to twenty feet high along the roadway, creating a narrow winding corridor for traffic with no road shoulder for ten or twelve miles. After that distance, the road would widen and I could possibly walk from that point onward. I was disheartened by this news, and told myself that I would take the chance, though I said nothing of my intention to the McMahan family or the park rangers.

Mr. McMahan offered to let me stay at his resort/motel for the night so that I would have a full day to climb up and over not only Cayuse Pass, but also the White Pass, which lay immediately beyond. For the life of me, I don't know why I declined his gracious offer, except for the fact that I felt drawn to the challenge that lay just ahead of me.

**Cayuse Pass**

Even though the day was half gone, I fully intended to push up and over the Cayuse to a position somewhere between it and the White Pass before sundown. The highway climbed more acutely, and with the Snoqualmie National Forest surrounding me, I had a true sense of adventure. I was now at an elevation of 4,000 to 4,200 feet, and there were mountain peaks and ridgelines on both sides dwarfing me amidst the rugged terrain.

A Park Ranger arrived, pulled his vehicle off the road and then spoke with me. He cautioned me not to go much farther that day since the snow line was just up ahead. He also suggested a campsite nearby that wasn't covered in snow, but I was not satisfied to make camp in that location. I thought I would be better off pushing on since I had a couple of hours of daylight that remained before nightfall.

Nearing the top of the Cayuse Pass the climb became quite steep. Walking became arduous and the temperature was freezing. Surrounded by snow and a shrinking road, I stopped briefly to view Mount Rainer from an area located near the mouth of the Cayuse Pass. It was a stunning sight to behold. I continued my journey and soon came face to face with an equally stunning sight directly in front of me. Cayuse Pass had an enormous wall of snow fifteen to twenty feet tall on both sides of the road, which reduced the road bed to one and a half lanes without a shoulder for walking. The view created an awesome appearance that reminded me of a cave or a bob-sled run.

"So, this is what they had warned me about!" I thought. I dropped my gear by the side of the road and walked fifty or sixty feet to where the road shoulder ended. The area where I stood looked like a tunnel without a ceiling. My map indicated the Cayuse Pass would snake its way in twists and turns for about ten miles. The sun was beginning to drop behind the ridge line and I realized that I should not go forward into the Pass during the night.

I sat down on the guardrail and smoked a cigarette while I calculated the mileage and time required to walk through the Pass. I realized that it would be foolhardy of me to attempt a walk through there without road shoulders. I sheepishly recalled the warning that I had been given not to walk through the Pass. If I were to proceed ahead against those warnings I could be run over by some unsuspecting motorist. I realized it would not do the veterans any good to have me wiped out or injured up here doing something that I had been advised against for good reason.

At this point, it dawned on me that there had not been much traffic on this road for the past hour. I looked around to see where I could pitch a campsite for the night. The only place I found was a small area on the west side of the highway outside of the guardrail. The area was about eight feet along the guard rail, but just six feet beyond that spot was a very steep embankment. I assured myself that it would work in a pinch.

I put the flag away and stored the gear under the guard rail out of the way of any traffic. I quickly slipped into my sleeping bag. The sun had set for the evening and it had become increasingly colder. The wind blew about fifteen miles per hour, which increased the chill factor. I was in for a rough night, but with my camp lowly contoured, I figured I would not be much affected by the wind. Unfortunately, I lay awake under there for several hours and heard only one vehicle pass by the guardrail. The temperature continued to drop well below freezing. The wind had picked up considerably. This project was going to be difficult enough, but I made matters worse by not taking darn good advice. This was a lesson learned.

I woke before the sun came up and prodded around under my shelter, until I finally poked my head outside to find an accumulation of two or three inches of snow. "Well," I thought, "this is going to be some day!" I wasted no time in breaking camp and kept my poncho wrapped tightly around me to guard against loss of body heat. I packed my gear and took up a position at the mouth of the Pass.

I finally heard the approach of a vehicle and discarded my poncho to make myself a little more presentable. I hailed the driver of the car, who pulled to a stop beside me as she opened her window. There were two beautiful young women who listened attentively to my story. They both smiled and advised me that it would be no problem to drive me through the Pass. As we traveled, I learned that both of these ladies were married to soldiers stationed at Fort Lewis, Washington.

The highway through the Cayuse Pass twisted and turned more than my map indicated. I thought about how I had planned to attempt a walk through this area and was infinitely thankful that I had changed my mind. As we traveled, I watched the road and the car's odometer. I was getting quite anxious as I saw six miles go past, then seven, and finally ten before there was a road shoulder. Right between ten and eleven miles, I asked the ladies to drop me off in the pouring rain. We had chatted along the way, and they knew what I was doing and why I was doing it. Before we parted, I thanked them, and they both wished me success.

The rain was heavy and a cold wind blew. I hurriedly draped a poncho over the rucksack and covered the top of my head. With the flag in hand, I walked quickly downhill until I came to the intersection at Highway 12. Turning east I began the long, steep climb up to the White Pass at an elevation of 4,500 feet. I figured that I had lost approximately 2,500 feet descending the Cayuse, which placed me standing in the saddle between the two peaks. The rain lashed at my hands and face while the wind continued throughout the day, but I kept steadily moving onward. The air around me was pristine, along with a magnificent forest and a rugged terrain.

As I approached the top, the rain turned to sleet then to light snow. I stopped briefly to boil some water for soup and then pushed on to make the top by 4:00 p.m. The White Pass represented the first level ground I had walked on all day, and it felt great to be finally up there. I was delighted. I had climbed my last mountain in the Cascade Range. From this point forward it would be downhill all the way to Yakima.

**The White Pass**

The White Pass area of the Cascade Mountain Range is known to many for its skiing facilities. It is also well known as the place where two of America's foremost skiers, the Mahre brothers, learned their skill. I had walked past their family's home on my way to a chalet and restaurant.

As I approached the restaurant I met Al Mathis, the driver of a highway department truck. He seemed especially pleased to know about the project. Al informed me about this region, which led me to believe I would have little or no problem making it off this mountain and into a more populated area by nightfall. Al advised me that I would only have ten more miles of downhill walking to Silver Beach. This was the kind of news I needed to hear to end my day of travel.

Once inside the chalet's restaurant, I enjoyed a hearty meal with plenty of hot coffee and good conversation with the staff members. They each took a special interest in me and the project. I was so happy and comfortable that I almost did not want to leave, but of course, the time to depart did come. I paid for my meal and headed to the foyer area where I had stored my rucksack. I reached for the door just as it snapped open and two young men entered. One of whom fixed his eyes on me and kept them locked in place with my eyes. Within a few quick questions and answers, we found our level of unity. Not only were we Vietnam veterans, but we were both Airborne Rangers and not only Rangers but brothers of the November 75$^{th}$ Rangers! The Ranger introduced himself as Ernie Davis and explained that he had been in the outfit just a bit earlier before my time. This was just too much for either of us. I dropped my gear and settled in with a member of my Ranger brotherhood.

We sat there in the lounge for approximately half an hour and I learned that Ernie Davis had been in Patrick "Tad" Tadina's team. Tadina was a legend to us at November Ranger Company. Ernie spoke briefly about those days with the company until it became evident to me that he was becoming emotionally upset. Actually, we both were. We went on to talk about the way life was after Vietnam and he told me that it had been an uphill battle ever since he came home. Ernie felt he was more fortunate than many other Vietnam veterans because of his loving wife. My time with Ernie passed by too quickly. Ernie's friend offered to drive me down the mountain on their way home, but I refused the offer. They both understood when I informed them that this mission was *"One For The Boys"* and we weren't going to slack it or cheat.

As they drove away, I grabbed my gear and took off in a hurry. I would need to travel downhill nine or ten miles to where I would find some people who could provide me with shelter for the night. With only one hour of daylight remaining, I traveled as quickly as my legs could carry me. My body was starting to adapt well to the fast walking pace, but my knees were becoming problematic.

On the downhill with a steep incline, one inherently tends to put a lot of pressure on all lower joints, especially the knees and ankles. The weight of my gear pushed me forward and forced me to brake myself and avoid jogging. I had to maintain a smoother, more rapid movement of the hips as opposed to the knees. For this reason, I began to walk with a straight-leg stride, which gave my knees and ankles some temporary relief. Having suffered numerous injuries to those joints over the years, I knew that they were my weakest parts and should be somewhat pampered.

My feet, which had built calluses, were now getting a good workout, especially around the toe area. The added weight and steep incline tended to force my toes forward into the front of the boot, which began to rub the tip of my toes and created new blisters.

Halfway down the White Pass, on my way to Silver Beach for the night, I met up again with Al Mathis. This time he brought his wife to meet me. They were also kind enough to bring me a lunch, which was certainly a much-appreciated treat. We talked for just a few moments, and with their blessings I was off again.

It was dark when I finally walked into Silver Beach. The owner of Silver Beach Motel was very kind and gave me a room for half price. I hurried to my room, stored my gear, threw off my dirty clothing and stepped into a wonderful, hot shower. I changed into clean clothes and joined the motel owner and his wife for some coffee and conversation. They seemed quite pleased to have me stay there for the night and agreed with me about the Vietnam veterans and America.

A Christian organization had gathered in the convention room of the motel, so the sound of hymns sung by the energetic group echoed throughout the motel. It was a most welcomed sound. I returned to my room and relaxed while I wrote my journal entries for the day. I could still hear the singing quite clearly and was reminded of the few times I had joined in with a few thrown-together church services while in Vietnam. I also remembered the all-too-numerous services we would hold for the guys lost in battle: Patino, Morgan, Peel, Sweeney, Borja, Santa Cruz, McGinn, Martin, Salinas, Krisely, plus Kelly and Butts who were both Canadians. There were many, many more losses to be forever remembered. Tears stung my eyes as the memory of each of the boys flooded my mind.

Every time I thought of those guys I had a profound sense of their presence. I cared not if it was real or imagined because I knew they would always be with me! I will carry them in my heart for eternity. I was especially aware of their presence since I started this march across the nation, their nation and homeland which they had loved so dearly.

I wished that this nation could have known them as I do, and loved them half as much as I do. But now, that chance is lost, and the only way America will ever come close to knowing those brave souls will be through the rest of us, the survivors. We must always be at our best, for as long as we can in whatever we do with our lives. The only lasting tribute to our fallen will be our on-going positive contributions in the love of God, America, and remembrances. We must salvage something positive from the ashes of the sacrifices of those young men, our buddies. All those thoughts and more raced through my mind as I listened to the hymns being sung nearby. Sleep stole my thoughts as it softly engulfed me.

I slept late into the morning after that hard push through the mountains. About mid-morning, I enjoyed a hot breakfast at a restaurant near the motel. Then I was on my way again. The weather was nice, though the sky exhibited some cloud build-up, which threatened rain. I walked alongside Rimrock Lake and became more impressed with the natural beauty of this part of America. At the east end of Rimrock Lake near the Tieton Dam, I stopped to enjoy the breathtaking view while I studied my maps. It seemed that I could arrive in the resort area of Trout Lodge by sundown on Saturday with a relatively short walking day. This would provide an opportunity to enjoy a rest period before a hard day's walk on Monday. It made sense for me to rest on Sunday in a sparsely populated community while I coordinated the entry into Yakima, my first major populated area. Traffic continued to be light with people who honked their horns and waved as they passed. Some stopped to chat and offered moral support and praise. At times, people offered me money, which I declined and suggested that they donate the funds to the Memorial Fund or the National League of Families in Washington, D.C.

Having crossed the Cascade Mountain Range, I had achieved additional credibility for the mission and could anticipate additional public interest. During the approach to Trout Lodge, a sheriff's department vehicle drove towards me and stopped. Two young deputies approached me to say they had a report that some guy was walking out of the mountains carrying combat gear, a flag and two sawed-off shotguns. The officers had no problem clarifying this misconception when they soon realized that the supposed shotguns were merely the protruding rods of my modified pack frame. The rods extended several inches over each of my shoulders and could be used to affix more gear as needed.

The deputies and I talked briefly. I explained that the major oversight in the planning of this event was my failure to clear the path of travel with the authorities. It was my intention at Yakima to pick up the slack on that point and meet with a Department of Transportation representative to discuss the specifics of my route throughout the rest of Washington State. Satisfied with my explanation, the deputies wished me a safe journey and drove away in the direction of Yakima.

I continued my journey to Trout Lodge and stopped at the Sportsman's Cafe for a coffee where I was greeted and pleased to meet Phil Wharton and Roly Lounsbury, fellow Vietnam veterans. We talked for quite some time, and Phil offered me a comfortable room at his house, which was next door to the business. Both Phil and Roly confirmed their support with long-suppressed pride. They both agreed that the mission was a darn good idea, and they were eager to help. After Phil closed the cafe for the night, we went next door to his house where we spent several more hours locked deep in the conversation. We discussed everything from long-standing issues concerning the veterans and the nation to subjects of local interest, such as hunting, fishing and tales of Big Foot.

Sightings of the ape-like creature, commonly referred to as Big Foot, had been reported throughout those hills for decades. I must confess that I had hoped to see one as I crossed the Cascades alone and on foot. But with the mountains behind me, the chance was lost for the time being. On the other hand, if I ever ran out of ideas for an adventure, I could always come back and search specifically for Big Foot!

I awoke Sunday morning at a respectable hour to meet with Phil's sister, Jenny, and her husband George Chisholm. George was also a Vietnam veteran, which pleased me immensely. After a hearty breakfast, I decided to go with Jenny, George and Roly to fish at a nearby lake. Before we left to go fishing, I made a quick collect telephone call to my friend, Verna, in North Dakota and advised her to contact my brother, David, in Canada and coordinate the next financial re-supply. I needed it to be mailed to the Clarkson Post Office for pickup when I arrived there.

We fished most of the afternoon, but only caught a few average-size trout and maybe a head cold. I was especially pleased to be in the company of those wonderful people, I was not in the least discouraged by our fishing outing. I helped cook the fish as fast as they were caught, and we ate the day's catch of tasty morsels right there beside the lake. The afternoon was an unexpected treat. I recalled many days, as a young boy with a fishing pole by the brook that ran parallel to our home in Topsail, Newfoundland. I needed a day like this to reflect on those childhood days, even if was early in the mission.

Upon our arrival at the cafe we were greeted by a large gathering of people from the local V.F.W. Post at Yakima. Phil, a member of the Post, had advised his fellow comrades about the mission. A livelier group of people could hardly have been found. We talked and talked until they simply had to leave and return home. Each assured me that they would handle everything at Yakima upon my arrival. "These folks are wonderful!" I thought, as we said our goodbyes.

Later that same evening while Phil and I talked, he informed me that he had sought the help and support of the Veterans of Foreign Wars, (V.F.W.) members and that they were very enthusiastic about the whole project. Phil kept the lounge open that evening until about midnight, so I sat there and drank coffee and chatted with the clientele. I also met Larry Kalvano, the person who admitted reporting the sawed-off shotguns. We had a great laugh about the incident when Larry explained to me that a customer had come into his store to make the initial report. "No harm was done," I assured him as we laughed even harder.

Phil and I talked briefly before we finally called it a day. He told me I would have an easy walk all the way to Yakima and that I could walk along the banks of the river until I was out of the foothills. In all, it would be a thirty-two to thirty-four-mile trip, which I wanted to accomplish by 6:30 p.m. I reflected on the day and finally realized that I was about to earn a solid mandate for the mission. It was significant that support had already been forthcoming from the senior veterans and the long-established V.F.W.

Roly came by the house at 7:30 a.m. to make sure we were up and at 'em. We shared morning coffee while I finished packing the rucksack. Once I was ready, we spent a short time voicing our goodbyes, and I must admit to a pang of regret at having to leave them. They were just a couple of 'good-old-boys' with one exception. They were Vietnam veterans, my buddies. I knew there would be many more similar experiences, so I had to become emotionally stronger. "I'd have to work on this," I thought, as I walked on through Trout Lodge and out of the foothills.

I felt extremely well rested, and calculated my rate of movement to be about three and one-half miles per hour. My body and mind felt quite in tune for the first time since I had started the journey out of Seattle. I knew the next physical test would be the heat. With the mountains behind me and

Yakima Valley just ahead, I noticed the amazing contrast in both the weather and terrain. I stopped briefly beside the Tieton River to boil some water for soup. The past and present seemed to be with me now, and once again I had a sense of being carried along.

Soon I arrived at the intersection of Highway 12 and Highway 410. At this point, the Tieton and Naches Rivers married up and continued the journey as one to Yakima. I stayed with Highway 12 parallel to the river and soon reached the rural town of Naches. People there were instinctively curious about what was going on, so I explained as much as time permitted, though I was aware of being slightly behind schedule. After I passed through Naches, I stopped for a short rest. I had walked for an hour when a car pulled over and stopped directly in front of me. It was Willie Ablerdinger and his veteran friend, Bill, from Yakima.

Willie and Bill brought me up-to-date with the arrangements that were scheduled upon my arrival in Yakima. The media would be waiting. Reporters from TV Channels 29 and 35 would capture my arrival live as I approached the city, plus a reporter with the *Yakima Valley Sun* newspaper would meet me at the V.F.W. Post #379 shortly thereafter. Before they left, they advised me that I had approximately twelve miles to go with only three hours remaining as per my schedule. I stripped the sleeping bag from my rucksack so that I could pick up the pace. Willie took the sleeping bag with him in the car, which reduced the rucksack to about fifty pounds of gear. For a while I felt much more comfortable.

It was evident that the public was more informed of the mission because they honked their horns and flashed the 'right on' symbol of thumbs up, which was tremendously encouraging. "Boy, this is great!" I thought as I realized the people were just as impressed by what they saw as I was with their reaction. There was no doubt in my mind that *The Mission at Home, 1982—One for the Boys* was necessary.

America, largely because of its people, understood and appreciated the message of the mission, and it had become increasingly clearer that a new beginning with a refreshed attitude and understanding for the Vietnam veteran had blossomed with a win-win situation.

**Welcome to Yakima**

Nearing the city of Yakima, I was filmed and interviewed. Many people stopped to shake my hand, and a couple of the veterans walked beside me for a half mile and offered me their blessings.

At sundown, I arrived at the city center where Willie and Bill were waiting. They escorted me straight to the V.F.W. Post and Golf club. A banquet event was in progress, and the facility was filled with many wonderful people for me to meet. We were invited to join the buffet where I readily filled my plate with my favorite home-cooked foods.

We settled into a corner of the facility with Post Commander Bob Lounsbury and *Yakima Valley Sun* reporter Patricia Brown. I seized the opportunity to lean back and rest while I regained my energy before I mingled and shook hands with many others. At the end of the evening, I returned to the home of Willie and Kappy Ablerdinger, where I enjoyed a fresh shower and change of clothing. We settled in for the evening with coffee and conversation. I was impressed to find that both Willie and his Hawaiian wife, Kappy, had been in the service. One of their sons was also a Vietnam veteran. Their two daughters still lived at home, one of whom was to be married the following month. They were simply a down-home, USA, fantastic family.

After everyone had gone to bed I lay awake for a short while and reflected on the journey thus far. I recognized new aspects about myself and the mission. I could see the weakness and strength in both. The apparent strength of the mission was that it provided people with a forum with which they could make their true feelings known as they sensed that the lone walker represented the many. People talked not just to me, but through me, and it had become quite apparent that I had to communicate these feelings to the Vietnam veterans.

I knew even then that I had generated an impact which, in turn, had impacted me.

I had planned this mission to communicate to the people the true feelings of the Vietnam veteran community. I had not counted on the responsibility of communicating to the Vietnam veterans on behalf of the people. I had felt for years that the Vietnam veterans and the people wanted to reconcile. The mission suddenly took on an additional cause to its mandate. To what degree and how do the people of America want reconciliation and why?

I strongly believed that the plan for the mission was to keep with the natural flow and rely on spontaneous responses as the prime indicator of people's feelings. But the response to the mission was more than an indication of people's feelings and beliefs. It was an appeal for me to represent those feelings and beliefs back to the Vietnam veterans. The realization that I was being positioned squarely in the middle of a long-standing rift was more at this point than I could handle. Once again, sleep saved me.

The next morning I awoke to the delicious aroma of Willie and Kappy's home-cooked breakfast. I spent the day in the community and took the opportunity to meet the authorities in an attempt to tie up logistical loose ends. My first resupply from Verna would arrive later in the day. Willie helped me plan my various local projects. After breakfast, we left for a brief visit at the V.F.W. Post and met with several of the senior veterans, who approved of the mission.

I picked up a copy of the *Yakima Valley Sun* published on May 20, 1982, and read the half page article written by Patricia Brown titled *"One it is...one for the boys."* Along with the familiar reporting of the mission the article stated, "Food and a place to sleep he accepts; donations he does not. Blake suggests that monetary gifts be forwarded to the National League of Families or to the Vietnam Memorial Fund."

Willie and I made the rounds and stopped at the Sheriff's Office, the Department of Transportation, and the Western

Union Office to pick up my resupply funds from Verna. My next resupply from David would be waiting for me at Clarkson, Washington. We shopped for a few items to replenish my supplies, and I purchased a pair of sunglasses.

Back at the Ablerdinger home we relaxed and enjoyed the rest of the day while I worked on my rucksack. Willie had a rucksack frame, which I fancied, so we swapped. I also decided to swap the heavy sleeping bag I had used in the mountains for a lighter blanket and protective cover. Before sunset, much to my satisfaction, I had the gear perfectly packed in my newly acquired rucksack. I then retired to my sleep feeling more at ease than at any other time since I had begun the walk at Seattle. The next morning, we gathered at the V.F.W. Post with a group of local veterans and media before I finally walked away from the gathering at 9:30 a.m.

I genuinely appreciated the impact of yesterday's local media coverage as just about everyone knew about the Mission: *One for the Boys*. Some folks even yelled their encouragements and blessings from their vehicles as they passed. I headed east by southeast as the Department of Transportation had advised, so I traveled the long way around. The route would take me several miles out on Highway 24, toward Moxee City, to a point where I would turn southward and walk through Union Gap, paralleling Highway 12 headed south.

It was still early in the day, but I could feel the temperature increase, which predicted a hot day. I stopped once to participate in a live broadcast interview for a local radio station. Once finished, I picked up the pace and passed through the populated area as quickly as possible. Nothing I did in the past had prepared me for this kind of attention. Though common sense told me it came with the territory, my instincts drove me toward the rural area.

I passed the fire station at the end of town where I noticed a group of firefighters had gathered at the entrance. One firefighter called out, "Come have a cup of coffee!"

Without delay, I joined them. We retired to the air-conditioned lunchroom where we sipped our coffee. The visit was short since we all had a day's work ahead of us. In parting, I assured them that what I was doing was appropriate and well received. They advised me that they would try to see me again farther down the road when their shift rotated in a couple of days. Good solid support and handshakes put me back on the road under the blazing high noon sun. I traveled along Highway 24 until I reached my designated route southward through an area of vineyards for several miles. I cut back to the west where I traveled around a ridge line and turned southward through the Union Gap. Other than being cooked under the blazing sun, I experienced no problems.

I walked with my head tilted downward so as not to look far ahead of myself. Suddenly, I realized that just one step ahead of me was a big snake sunning itself. Imagine my horror of the ominous sound, the unmistakable rattle of a rattlesnake. I moved as quickly as I could to the right and watched closely for movement in the snake. I carefully bypassed the snake, which made only a half-hearted movement towards me. I stood a safe distance away and watched the rattlesnake resume its former relaxed position as though nothing had happened. For a moment, I felt insulted that my presence had disturbed the snake so little, and I actually thought about taking its rattler with me on my journey. Thinking better of it, I continued on my way.

I traveled through Union Gap until I was finally parallel to Highway 12, where I noticed some fanfare. People sounded their horns, and some even stopped to holler the usual well wishes. A photographer from the *Yakima Herald-Republic* arrived and took pictures to accompany the story that would be published the next day.

The rural community of Donald and my arrival at Sawyer were just a few miles ahead, so I stopped briefly at a restaurant for a hamburger, fries and a cold soda. The owners and their staff generously refused to let me pay for my meal. They had viewed some media reports that informed them of the mission, and they simply wanted to help.

Between the towns of Sawyer and Buena, I met Vietnam veteran John Wilson. He, too, had seen and heard about the mission in the media so he had been on the lookout for me. We sat there by the road and talked about the upcoming memorial dedication. He said he wasn't pleased with the design, but I maintained the position that it was already decided upon, so we should focus on making the dedication a success. We talked a little about what it was like to come home after Vietnam, and it soon became evident that John, like most Vietnam veterans, had encountered some bad times. Unfortunately, we had to cut our conversation short because I needed to make it to the town of Zillah before nightfall.

I reflected on my bad times as I continued the walk and remembered the anger and loneliness that I and most Vietnam veterans felt as a result of our reception home from the Vietnam War. I recalled the airport assaults from protesters upon our arrival and the people who hit veterans with their protest signs and threw urine at their uniforms. They shouted "baby killers," a title that was furthest from the truth and absolutely wrong on so many different levels.

We were strongly advised upon our return to change out of our uniforms as quickly as possible and wear civilian clothing in public to avoid conflicts. Some of us, myself included, grew our hair long within a few months of returning home to "fit-in" with the civilian male populations. But what was most frustrating was that American civilians had reacted to incorrect information. Regardless of the political disagreements over the Vietnam War, it was time to 'let it go' and express appropriate support for the Vietnam veterans.

I felt that this was what the mission had discovered: Civilians and veterans alike were on the same page, so to speak, and it was reasonable to believe that never again would a generation of veterans and civilians abandon each other.

It was still hot and muggy under the gear as I pushed along the road, and I wondered how long it would take me to become acclimatized. My pores were wide open and I was losing fluids too fast. I recalled my former military practice of water discipline: The act of conserving water by providing the body with just enough water to replace some of the losses by simply sipping water instead of drinking in volume to quench the thirst. This had been a tough lesson the first time I mastered water discipline years ago during basic training in the Army. Today, it seemed impossible to replicate.

**Hello Zillah**

The sun was just setting as I wandered into town. I stopped briefly to speak with the few people who had heard about the mission and had anticipated my arrival. I learned that City Hall and the Police Station were in the same building, which made it convenient to advise the authorities before I did anything else.

As I entered City Hall, I left the rucksack and gear in a hallway within full view. I approached the courtroom where a sizeable crowd had gathered, several of whom were uniformed police. Immediately, I met Chief of Police George Bazin, who recognized me from media reports. He explained that he was also a Vietnam veteran and then welcomed me to his community. He introduced me to Zillah's Mayor Richard Brousseau, several other officials and officers. Luckily, they had been engaged in evening court, so I located everyone I required to speak with. I stored my gear in the police office and accepted an invitation to join George Bazin, Richard Brousseau, and several others plus their wives for coffee in a nearby cafe.

There, in the company of some of Zillah's finest people, I briefly spoke about the mission. During our conversation, I clarified the point that it was not a mandatory rule for me to camp out each night; whereupon, George and his wife quickly invited me to stay at their home, which I happily accepted.

Upon our arrival at George's family home, he served sandwiches and milk while we enjoyed our conversation until it became obvious that we were worn out. After a hot shower, I climbed into bed and lay awake thinking about several ideas I had tossed around in my head over the past few days. I finally drifted into a deep sleep.

Early the next morning, George and I arrived in downtown Yakima to pick up several copies of a local newspaper article about the mission. Boy, was I ever shocked! The article took up half of the front page. No complaints about that! We went to the local restaurant where the servings were plentiful and delicious. The folks at the diner would not allow me to pay for the meal and generously gave me their blessing accompanied by a delicious desert. After thanking the good folks at the restaurant, we hurried over to City Hall. George had arranged a few speaking engagements for me for later in the day. I spoke briefly with a representative group of Zillah's residents, a group of student reporters from the local High School paper and a disc jockey named Trapper at KENE Radio. Trapper interviewed me by telephone and assured me he would give the recorded interview a lot of air time. George also arranged that we meet newspaper reporter Linda Baker from *Toppenish Review* for an interview and coffee.

Mayor Richard Brousseau joined George, Linda and me during the interview and coffee at the restaurant. I was touched by the sincerity of these people. Moreover, their concern for the mission, nation and for me was genuine. Time went by too quickly, and I felt privileged to have met these wonderful folks, but it was time to move onward.

The *Toppenish Review* article, "Walking Washington to D.C. Viet vet honors lost 'Nam buddies'," by Linda Baker was handed to me, and I quickly read the article. She had stated, "There was no casualness in his voice when he told a handful of Zillah residents that he was on a march to regain lost dignity and to honor the dead and injured, the crushed families and, most of all, those officially listed as Missing in Action."

I immediately felt that familiar emotional shot in the arm, which continued to fuel my drive to proudly continue the walk each day. Sunday was the exception; it was my day of rest and solitude in remembrance for my buddies who didn't come back.

We returned to City Hall to collect my rucksack and other gear. I was surprised to find that both George and Richard had prepared letters of support, which they gave me to carry to Washington, D.C. I accepted the letters on behalf of the Vietnam veterans and felt overwhelmed with the support building around me and the mission.

Once we bid each other farewell, I climbed back under the load and raised the colors. I walked out on Main Street with a renewed strength and between rows of people who came out to wave goodbye. Possessed by an abundance of inner strength graciously bestowed upon me by the City of Zillah and its proud representatives, I felt supercharged. This was indeed 'Our Mission'. It had taken some time and many miles for me to finally realize this, but now that I had I wasn't going to let it slip away. This whole venture was insignificant unless the people gave it a mandate. All the way down the road from Seattle I had sought this mandate from the people; today, it took ownership. "Okay, folks let's do it—*One For The Boys*!" I thought, as I briskly walked away from Zillah.

**On the Road Again**

It was a hot day, but the wind blew softly in my face and kept me comfortable. The colors flew freely in the breeze, which added to the ambiance of pride and determination that carried me onward. The terrain was smooth to rolling and posed no difficulty as I proceeded to my next destination. Horns honked and people yelled encouragements as they passed. Their gestures of support were naturally inspirational. My body had adjusted well to the rigors of my new vocation. Even my feet were beginning to toughen under the load. The various stages of blistering had passed. Calluses started to form a protective shield on the bottom of my heels, toes, and feet.

A late start out of Zillah combined with being stopped frequently en route limited the distance I travelled that day. I resolved that where there was a special interest on the part of the public and veterans in a particular area, I would adjust my priorities and give special attention to interested persons. I would take time from walking to do my very best and provide answers to questions. I reminded myself that this was the intent of the mission.

Occasionally, a few people stopped me to ask what I was protesting, and it struck a raw nerve each time I heard the word, 'protest'. I did my utmost to clarify the distinction between a protest and this patriotic action. When I noticed a look of bewilderment in their eyes I explained the reasons for the walk. Many confessed that they were not able to remember the last time they had seen an action so positive and patriotic. I survived those incidents with diplomacy, although I was not at all happy with the way I had handled some of those situations, nor was I happy about the way my temper was so easily triggered. I further resolved that I was going to have to 'Ranger Up' and become a bigger man emotionally than I had been for a long time. If this mission was going to benefit anyone, it became imperative that I maintain my self-control, regardless of any personal feelings or issues.

On the road to Sunnyside, I passed through the rural communities of Granger and Outlook. When I arrived at Sunnyside just before sundown, I went directly to the local police station, and advised them of my arrival and intention to stay overnight. The Sunnyside Fire Station was next door to the police station so I visited there and met Abel French. He and I talked at length, and Abel decided that the mission warranted support from the local media and the V.F.W. Commander, Mr. Williams. Abel contacted the press and within a few minutes a young woman dropped by from the local newspaper and conducted an interview. Abel told me that the Ministerial Association of Sunnyside had reserved a room for me at a local motel. I thanked him for their generosity.

Mr. Williams, Commander of the V.F.W. Post, arrived and joined Abel and me during our conversation. He was very impressed with the mission and explained that the V.F.W. would have been more than happy to put me up for the night. I explained that lodgings was already in place, but a ride to the motel would be much appreciated. Once we arrived at the motel, Mr. Williams and I confirmed a time to meet the next morning for breakfast. I quickly settled into my room, showered and changed into clean clothes. I then enjoyed a late supper at the restaurant. After the hearty meal, I returned to my room, washed clothes by hand in the sink, made my daily journal entries while lying in bed and then drifted off to sleep.

Mr. Williams arrived early the next morning, and we returned to the downtown area. We stopped at both the police and fire stations. Last evening when I arrived, I didn't have the opportunity to meet many of the people in town, and I thought I would like to introduce myself before I moved on. At the police station, I spent time with Officer Bourdage and several other officers. We enjoyed a discussion until I was called next door to the fire station for a photo opportunity. I met a few more firefighters before I joined Mr. Williams at an informal gathering at the local restaurant for breakfast. One of the men at the breakfast gathering was a local radio announcer who invited me to do a taped interview before I left, which I did. Within the hour, I was on my way out of town.

Just outside of Sunnyside, a car pulled over to the shoulder of the road, and I met Keith Tupper. He said that he had just listened to the radio interview, when he saw me walking and decided to stop. Keith told me that he was on his way to Washington, D.C. to begin a new career with the Reagan Administration. I thought that it was ironic that both of us were on the way to the same place. Keith pointed out that he was driving and expected to arrive in Washington in approximately six days, whereas I was walking and had no idea how long it would take me. Jokingly, he offered me a ride. Keith snapped a few pictures of me and then gave me his address in Washington, D.C. He returned to his vehicle and shouted back to me as he slowly drove away, "I'll tell them you're coming!"

I laughed and waved goodbye to Keith and the ride he had offered. I continued walking while the sun beamed its burning rays down on me as it had for the past several days. Temperatures were in the mid-eighties, and it seemed even hotter as I carried the rucksack and flag. Naturally, I wasn't about to complain as I reflected on the earlier experiences of rain, snow, and freezing temperatures. I knew that I had experienced worse and that the climate would soon again become nasty.

**Community of Prosser**

Along the way I was approached by a young man who said that he represented his high school newspaper and wanted to do an interview using a tape recorder. Again, I was pleased with the interest that the young fellow showed. All but one of his questions were well formed and required in-depth and soul-rendering answers

The young man had asked, "What was it like to be in a war that the people at home did not support, even while you were there?"

Intuitively, I had responded, "Horrible!"

In Prosser I experienced what was by now the usual fanfare. I spoke briefly with the ladies of the V.F.W. club who had just served supper and invited me to join the group. They informed me that most of the club's men were out on a fishing trip.

Among the few men I met that evening was fellow Vietnam veteran, Fred Freeman. Fred and I chatted about the mission and other points of interest. He invited me to spend the night with him and his wife at his home, and I accepted their kind offer. We drove out into the countryside for about ten miles to where Fred and his wife Arlene lived. We spent an enjoyable evening together, and I even had the opportunity to machine wash some clothes. Fred telephoned the Prosser police to inform them of my location and also advised them of my travel route to Benton City the following day. I was extremely happy for this couple when they informed me that they would celebrate their wedding anniversary the next day. The Freemans provided me all the comforts of home, and I slept like a king that night.

After an enjoyable breakfast the next morning, Fred proudly showed me the vegetable garden that he and Arlene had recently planted. I could tell right way that they would raise a good kitchen crop because the soil looked and smelled like rich countryside farmland. Soon it was time to pack up my belongings and head back into town. The Freemans drove me into Prosser, where they gave me a quick tour of their pretty rural community. Then they drove me to my starting point for the day, and we said our goodbyes.

I had become a veteran of greetings and especially of partings by practicing a policy of seeming to be in a hurry during farewells. It was a conscious behavior I projected to protect my newfound friends and myself. This was a numbing practice I had learned in Vietnam. Developing intimate feelings causes additional emotional pain on an already heavy heart.

The Freemans had barely left and I had just started my day's journey when a man in a car passed by and yelled, "Stop at my store up ahead and get anything you need—free!"

I knew the store was located at the crossroad just ahead, but since I didn't need anything and was already behind schedule, I didn't stop. I turned right at the crossroad and headed east, parallel with both the Yakima River and Highway 12. I traveled several miles through farmland and orchards. Soon I was in the rural area again where the terrain was desert-like and seemed more so because of the intense heat. I spotted quite a few snakes as well as other critters that lounged at the edge of the grass. I also heard a lot of scurrying varmints as I walked along, even snakes get out of the way most of the time but not all of the time.

A little farther along I met a couple of guys who were fishing. They shared their ice water with me, and we talked. One had heard of what I was doing, and they both expressed their approval of the mission.

Moving into an area where there had obviously been some gravel work done in a bygone era, I was unnerved to hear gun shots. Confident that it was only small caliber target shooting in the gravel works, I picked up my pace and quickly cleared out of range.

When I entered Benton City just before dark, I noticed a fast food restaurant, and in no time I chowed down a burger, fries and a cold soda. The young fellow working there gave me directions to the Police Station, and it was there that I met Officer Mike Fluharty. We discussed the reasons why I was walking and details about the mission. I asked Mike, "Where would there be an appropriate place for me to lay over for the night and Sunday?"

Mike made a phone call, and then we went for a short ride up the street to meet Ken Carlson, a former military person, and now a man of God as minister of the United Methodist Church in Benton City. Ken and I chatted for a few minutes before he offered me the use of the church for the weekend. He showed me around the church as he explained the Sunday schedule of events, which he invited me to attend. After Ken had gone home, I showered and made a bunk on the floor for the night. With the day behind me again, I brought my journal up to date before drifting off to sleep.

Prior to my arrival in Benton City, I consulted a Department of Transportation representative at Yakima about my route, and he informed me of an area of difficulty I would encounter. The area was at the Tri-Cities of Richland, Kennewick, near Pascoe. The bridge that I would use to cross the Columbia River was part of a freeway system, which meant no pedestrians were allowed. I would be required to walk my way down to the bridge then parallel along secondary roads through Columbia Park. At that point, I would need to climb the embankment and cross over the bridge as quickly as possible to pick up secondary roads on the opposite side before continuing into the rural area. A local couple, Jerry and Diane, who I had met at the church, decided that we should drive down there so that I could familiarize myself with the area before I would have to pick my way walking through it. This reconnaissance was a good idea. Satisfied after scoping out the route we returned to their home in Benton City. We continued our many conversations over coffee before Diane drove me back to the church. As I dug into my pocket for the key to the church, which I had been so graciously entrusted with, I wished all the veterans could see and feel what I had experienced, especially today!

I settled in for the night and lay awake on my bedroll as I reflected on my travels to this point of the journey. The convictions I had at the beginning were reinforced by the people I had met. Most people were convinced that indeed something was missing from everyday life in America. This belief dealt with interrelationships within the United States. People struggled to put words to their feelings and regrets regarding past social behaviors after the war. It felt as though this mission had provided them with a rare medium to communicate their current feelings and opinions. The spontaneity, nature and short-term lay overs, coupled with an onward movement in the mission that I represented, appeared to relieve people of an inhibition they might have had about expressing themselves. The feedback was genuine and heartfelt. I constantly felt humbled by the show of support and kindness, which was generously reflected in each community by their providing for my modest needs. Quite possibly, this venture also allowed for greater freedom of expression among the people.

This mission was an American venture that brought out the real and genuine heartfelt concerns of the people for the Vietnam veterans. I recognized that not only would we have an opportunity to address certain issues while on this journey, but also that when it was completed, we would be further able to tell the nation something of value about itself. "A lot of potential 'waits'," I thought as sleep finally arrived.

The following morning, it rained softly as I hurried to the Cafe and ate a hearty breakfast. I lingered over coffee, hoping that the rain would soon stop, but alas, it did not. I climbed under the rucksack as always and quickly said goodbye to Benton City. I traveled as far as the Tri-City area before I sought shelter from the rain at Richland.

**On the Road to West Richland**

When the skies cleared and the rain stopped, I pushed onward to rural Highway 224 toward West Richland. Just outside Benton City, I was approached by a woman I had met in the church on Sunday who insisted that I take the lunch she had prepared. She added that her husband was a Vietnam veteran and that they both believed whole-heartedly in the mission. I thanked her for the wonderful gesture and moved onward.

After I ate the lunch, I was enjoying the elevated view of Benton City when I noticed some activity just downhill off to my left. A little goat was making quite a scene and appeared to be attempting to free itself from a rope that tethered it from harm in the safety of a back garden. I thought little else of the small goat as I moved upward to the top of the hill. Before much longer, I realized I had some company. The little goat now flanked my movements, on my left and kept pace slightly behind me while bleating, almost childlike, as it followed after me.

When I stopped, the goat stopped, and when I moved on, the goat moved too. I smiled as my appreciation of the little fellow heightened as we traveled together along the road. I felt satisfied to let the goat follow me to a populated area where I could make some arrangements for its safe return. I soon realized that this plan wouldn't work because the little goat took a fancy to walking on the roadway. Now I had a problem.

I tried to frighten the little creature away, hoping it would go home. I even tried to catch the running end of its broken rope; however, with each attempt, the goat ran just out of my reach. All my efforts proved to be futile. The goat remained just out of reach with a pleasant look on its face that seemed to say it liked what I was doing and wanted to go with me. Perhaps it would have been feasible under a different circumstance. I knew that a combat veteran under the colors with a companion goat just didn't fit the scenario.

As an alternative, I decided to flag down a passing motorist to see if the driver could get someone from the local animal shelter to recapture the little guy. The first car passed by, but the second vehicle that approached from Benton City area immediately stopped. I explained my problem to the woman driver, while her male companion listened. She quickly jumped out of her vehicle and in a few quick strides captured the little goat, cuddled him in her arms and politely placed him in the back seat of her car. Naturally, my ego took a major drop as she accomplished the task with such ease. Nevertheless, I was grateful to the lady when she assured me that the little guy would be safely returned to its owner.

The couple and the goat drove off, and I continued my walk alone towards West Richland. Throughout my journey, most animals seemed interested at the sight of me as I passed. I reasoned that it was probably a combination of things, not the least of which was the brightly colored flag, Old Glory fluttering in the breeze.

I enjoyed a relatively easy walk on Highway 224 to West Richland. Plus, I hoped to make Richland before sundown. I also realized that I had walked out of the effective range of media coverage at Yakima. This situation would likely repeat itself many times until the mission had built up enough miles and credibility to be worthy of major media coverage. I decided that I would have to continuously explain myself and the mission, as though it were just the beginning. I further resolved that these responsibilities would have to be met with continuous determination regardless of the repetition. Very little in the way of support was evident as I walked into residential Richland. Some folks sounded their car horns, though I knew by now it was on the merit of appearance and not because the people knew the nature of my business. Still, it felt good to know some folks were patriotic that the mere sight of the flag held aloft by human hands moved them to respond.

I reported to V.F.W. Post 7952 at Richland, introduced myself, signed the register, and met Commander Dan Carty, a fellow Vietnam veteran. Dan and I spoke in depth about the mission, and he offered me the full support of Post 7952. He also arranged for media coverage the next morning and my lodging that night. Dan introduced me to the Supreme Court Judge and his wife plus a wonderfully supportive group of people at the Post. They all appreciated the intent and design of the mission and promised me that they would say special prayers for it and for me.

Dan also invited me to dinner at a nearby restaurant, and we engaged in additional conversation and memories of 'Nam before I checked in at Nendals Motel.

I enjoyed my time meeting Dan Carty; he was a real fine man. We planned to get together early in the morning for a hectic round of meetings and media interviews. Settling into my motel room and before bedding down for the night, I hand-washed some clothes and hung them to dry on the shower rod. Once my journal entries were recorded I laid back down onto a much-too-comfortable bed. Sleep stole over me quickly and soundly.

The next morning Dan promptly arrived, and I informed him that I would have to do something about the wet clothing I had washed the night before that had not dried. Dan solved my laundry problem by stopping at his house and tossing them into the dryer. Then we were on our way to breakfast at a local restaurant. After breakfast, we returned to Dan's house and collected my laundry. I rolled and repacked the clean clothing into the rucksack, and then we hurried off to the V.F.W. Post, arriving just minutes before the media.

Two television stations, a radio station reporter, plus The *Tri-City Herald* reporter and photographer arrived for the interview. We worked together collectively until each group was satisfied that they had their story and it was time for to me to leave. A few veterans that I had met the previous evening at the Post had gathered to witness my departure. They offered their best wishes for a safe journey and with a solid handshake from Dan Carty I was on my way.

I worked my way out of Richland toward Kennewick. Then I crossed the Yakima River and proceeded southeast along the Columbia River. I had everything I needed with me: good weather, regional media coverage, and a feeling of real strength under the weight that I carried. A good stretch of Columbia Park was part of the route, and I stopped amidst the beautiful greenery for a well-deserved break after several hours of walking.

"What are you doing in the area, dressed like that and carrying the American Flag?" a man's voice asked. I turned and saw a male Mexican American, walking his dog, as he approached me and introduced himself as Gonzales. I explained to him the purpose and intention of the mission, to which he responded with a deep sadness in his voice that his older brother had been killed in the Vietnam War. Immediately, I felt a powerful empathy for Gonzales and his loss. I simply spoke with him in terms of gains and losses. I felt a profound need to spend some time with this man and explained that although the obvious loss was his brother, significant potential for gain would exist if the surviving veterans could lead America back to grace. His brother had paid the ultimate price, but we were now in a good position to see something positive come out of that madness of Vietnam. It was important to all of us that the nation benefits from the sacrifice of lives and our veterans' loss of dignity. I assured Gonzales that the surviving veterans, such as I, were outgrowing our pain and restoring our dignity as we envisioned a purpose and a direction. Gonzales nodded his head knowingly and told me about his older brother who had been a musician and played in bands before 'Nam. It was because of his brother's talent and love of music that Gonzales followed in his brother's footsteps and became a musician in a band. There was a lot for us to discuss, but inevitably I had to travel on. I gave Gonzales an information pamphlet about the mission for a keepsake of our meeting and said goodbye. As I wandered out of his view, I thought I now had an additional reason for this mission.

Walking through Columbia Park towards the bridge, I encountered many gatherings of youths who had assembled in the warmth of the sunshine to enjoy the majestic beauty of the area. Apparently, the media had readily made an impact, as many of the youth acknowledged me and called me by name. Not one person among the gatherings I had passed along the route throughout the park was disrespectful, though I was sure many were left to wonder. I moved through the park without a break and stopped just short of the bridge for a quick lunch on a park bench, which was conveniently located by the water. After my lunch, I accessed the bridge and quickly crossed it entering the city of Pascoe. I took the first available exit off the freeway and pushed forward through the city, with the Columbia River now on my right.

I traveled at a rate of 4.5 mph to 5 mph, when a driver of a vehicle pulled up beside me and beckoned to me. I stopped and waited for him as he parked his car. He offered me a cold soda and a hearty handshake and introduced himself as Baby Huey, sergeant-at-arms for the local motorcycle club. He informed me that a lot of the guys in the club were 'Nam veterans and that they supported this mission one-hundred percent. He also told me that if I were to have any trouble anywhere in the State of Washington, I should call the number on the card that he had given to me, and they would give assistance. Baby Huey and I talked for a while about the way it came down for the guys and gals in 'Nam and at home. We talked about the way we sometimes brought it down on ourselves, too. We agreed that it was mostly because we felt ripped off and that it was not going to change for the better unless we did something about it.

I asked him to tell the boys at the Motorcycle Club that I had a good clean shot with this "Mission at Home." The rest is up to the people. It was sure nice of Baby Huey to check me out for the Club and bring me out a cold soda.

"It doesn't matter where I go in my head," I thought, "my boots are on the ground." I traveled through the residential areas of Pascoe parallel to the Columbia River. I stopped briefly at a restaurant on the outskirts and enjoyed a hot meal before I pushed onward across the Snake River. I moved with determination to walk as many miles as I could for the day. People who were impacted by the numerous media reports continued to honk their vehicle horns and wave approval as they passed by me.

When I crossed the Snake River, I noticed a park suitable to make camp for the night, but with several hours of sunlight remaining I decided to keep walking at the junction of Highway 124. I was delighted that my body had proven capable of discovering and tapping into energy reserves. I was also reminded that I am the master of my own ship. I demanded more of myself than ever before and received results. I can do so again. While I continued along for a few more miles on Highway 124, I noticed a wide-open rural area, which was heavily posted with signage indicating a bird sanctuary. I decided that this would be a suitable camping spot for the night. Keeping a wary eye out for snakes and other critters, I moved away from the road to the south until I found a comfortable little ravine and set up camp. I located the note that Dan Carty had given me with a list of Commander's names of several V.F.W. Posts, which I intended to contact within the next few days. I studied the list with my map and realized that I would meet Roy Hooney at Dayton, Lloyd 'Max' Trosper at Pomeroy and Allie Tucker at Clarkston during my last stop in Washington State.

I was especially happy to see that the V.F.W. organization was quick to get on board with their support. I couldn't help but reflect on a time not so long ago when none of the existing veteran organizations were keen on Vietnam veterans. Some of our earlier Vietnam veterans had sought camaraderie and acceptance through those same organizations only to be turned away. Those had been among some of the more acute rejections faced by our veterans. The problem arose when word got passed through the Vietnam veteran community that the senior veterans of V.F.W. only wanted to fill membership quotas and increase revenues by finally deciding to allow Vietnam veterans to join. Unfortunately, these were not-to-be-forgotten experiences. Still, I saw a unique opportunity through my mission. I would continue to research this situation on a state-by-state basis and share my good experiences with the V.F.W. Posts and promote goodwill. I decided I would seize every opportunity to watch and listen carefully to the senior veterans every time I was afforded an opportunity. I also experienced along this journey that the V.F.W. organization had developed an appreciation for Vietnam veterans. I also recognized that I would maintain my objectivity and continue to learn more while en route across the nation. I settled in for the night to a blissful sleep.

I had overslept. By the time I broke camp and got back on the road it was already past 10:00 a.m. I was walking through a hot, arid, almost desert-like area when I came upon some Mexican migrant workers, who were harvesting asparagus. I recalled my time as a job developer with the North Dakota Migrant Council, where I had worked on behalf of Mexican migrant workers. I decided to stop and speak with the workers. We spoke about their annual migrations and exchanged names of people, some of whom we mutually knew. Over time, I had come to see the migrant farm workers as America's gypsies. It was wonderful to be in their company then, as well as now. As I prepared to leave, the workers gave me some fresh asparagus and cold water for my journey.

Highway traffic was mostly uneventful since it was a quite rural route. About every other car or truck would sound its horn, so I knew I was not being taken for granted. I passed by the rural community of Eureka and hoped to make it to Prescott by sundown. Halfway between the two communities, I was stopped by a motorist who introduced himself as Tom Strycula. Tom was aware of the mission, and as we talked he offered me shelter for the night. He was on his way to the Tri-Cities and guessed that upon his return I would likely be up to his trailer home. He sure seemed nice enough, so I resolved that if he came back with the offer, I would be pleased to accept.

It was probably still two hours until sundown when a couple of the Mexican farmworkers pulled up ahead of me at a road junction. When I got up to them they gave me a cold soda, which I genuinely appreciated. They said they had timed my walking and believed I was taking approximately one-hundred-twenty steps per minute. I was amazed. I had been so engrossed in all the other elements and aspects of the mission that I had not given much thought to my rate of movement other than on a miles-per-hour basis. I stood there in the blistering sun and chatted with the farm workers. Then Tom Strycula came by again and another vehicle pulled in at the same time. "Quite the gathering," I thought.

Soon everybody was headed off in different directions. Tom took me with him to his trailer where he made me feel very much at home. He prepared some fantastic hamburgers for our dinner, and I was able to wash and dry my dirty laundry. We talked in depth about the nature of the mission, and Tom commented that I was the right man for the job. I thought it was especially nice of him. Positive reinforcement would not be wasted on me for I was indeed determined and dedicated. I had to be!

I learned that Tom worked as a machinist in the Pascoe area. Although he was not a veteran, he had a profound respect for all veterans. Tom was an all-around nice guy and just one heck of a good American. We bid each other goodnight and a restful sleep came easily to me that night. Tom woke me very early since he had to be at work by 7:30 a.m. I clasped a cup of coffee in my free hand and tossed my gear into his Volkswagen car. We headed back to the junction from where I had left off the day before to continue my journey. It was there that we said our good-byes with the morning sun barely peeking over the eastern horizon.

Once my bones and joints were loosened by a few miles of walking, I felt pretty good. I moved steadily along and soon passed through the rural community of Prescott. Many people in the community seemed aware of the mission, and I was inspired by the attention they showed. Several veterans and some media came by throughout the day. Among the veterans was Pat Manning of Dayton, who came to see what I was up to and was present when two reporters from the *Spokane Chronicle* took pictures and gathered facts for their storyline.

As I neared Waitsburg, more people and media came out to meet me, and I was very happy to see the momentum build. Media continued to do a splendid job. People were more informed; many were going out of their way to find me on the road. Some showed up just to see for themselves, while others stopped to chat. A lot of folks wanted to help in some way, and I would tell them how I thought they could help. I constantly referred offers of money to the Memorial Fund and the National League of Families.

The load of fifty to sixty pounds seemed much heavier, or perhaps it was the heat of the day that hampered my progress. I had been sweating heavily and had sweated body fluids far too quickly. My fatigues, which were clean in the morning, were now showing tell-tale streaks of excised body salt. This indicated to me that I had lost too much body salt and fluid through exertion. The walk out of the Yakima Valley, had become hilly as I started the long, gradual, arduous climb into the foothills of the Bitterroot Mountain Range.

When I finally arrived at Waitsburg, I spent my last few dollars on a cooked meal. After eating, I filled my canteens with water. I felt much better and was ready to go back on the road. I decided that I would have to go forward to Clarkston to pick up my money resupply from David. I hoped that upon my arrival, Mr. Hooney at Dayton would help me locate the Western Union Office.

As I pushed out of Waitsburg on Highway 12, I soon met a man who said he had waited for me to come by. It turned out that he was a local farmer/rancher who was quite perturbed at what he said was a concerted effort by the Federal Government to run small family farms out of business. I rested briefly while he showed me some paperwork he had, which on the surface seemed to support his allegation. When he was through talking, I told him quite simply that I had my hands full with this mission, but that I would keep an interest in the situation he had described. We shook hands and I moved back onto the road thinking that I must concentrate all my energies on this mission and not take on any other causes while en route. I recalled my studies at MACV School in Nha Trang of the Taoist Principle of Non-contention, which I interpreted to mean that one should avoid distractions and conflicts on the way to accomplishing one's goal. I decided that this would be my standard.

It didn't take long before I entered the Lewis and Clark Trail State Park. Here I found some people who worked as groundskeepers. We sat around an open fire for a short period while the sun was setting, and I explained the mission. I also told them that I had hoped to have arrived at Dayton for the night, but with twenty-nine miles done for the day and darkness setting in, my walking for the day had ended. A young lady present at this gathering of groundskeepers offered to telephone Mr. Hooney after I mentioned his name and organization. When she returned from the Parks Building she announced that Mr. Hooney was delighted that she had called and he was on his way from Dayton to take me in for the night.

Dayton was just five miles from where we stood and in no time at all Mr. Hooney arrived. As soon as we met we shook hands as though we were old friends. I had come to accept all veterans without question. A universal bond exists between veterans of all wars when they are mature enough to set aside differences and jealousies. That bond is the backbone of the military brotherhood. During the drive back to Dayton, Mr. Hooney told me that his V.F.W. Post 5549 wanted to pay for my motel room. When we arrived at the motel, I told Mr. Hooney of my resupply problem. He graciously offered to drive me to Clarkston to pick it up, but he couldn't leave until noon the next day. "No matter," I told him, "I am fortunate to have your help. Thank you."

Soon afterward, Mr. Hooney left me for the night, so I washed clothes, showered and wrote in my journal. I reflected on the mission thus far and was satisfied that support would continue to build as miles were accomplished and credibility was earned. At a personal level, I was delighted to have met so many wonderful people who were more than willing to express themselves to me concerning the issues I represented. I slept soundly.

I was well rested and ready to go when Mr. Hooney returned the next day, at noon. He explained that there were two roads to Pomeroy and one road from Pomeroy to Clarkston. Highway 12 was an indirect route, which was probably ten miles longer than Highway 126. He told me that if I was interested, he would drive to Pomeroy on Highway 126 so that I could see why most people driving to Clarkston opted for the long way around. I expressed that I was indeed interested, so at the appropriate spot we turned off Highway 12 and took Highway 126. As we drove along I paid particular attention to the terrain while Mr. Hooney warned me that this route was heavily infested with rattlesnakes and other dangerous critters. The road twisted and turned every which way. It also rolled up and down, sometimes very steeply. Roughly eight miles was not even paved, and there was a considerable walking distance between populated areas. It was a desert-like atmosphere with very few trees. However, the route was beautiful, and I decided that I would walk this way when the time arrived.

We continued to Clarkston's Post Office where I received my resupply money from David in Canada. Mr. Hooney and I stopped for a lunch on the way back before driving the long way on Highway 12. Back at the Lewis and Clark Trail State Park, I hurried to get my gear on so that I could make as many miles as possible before dark.

Mr. Hooney departed and parked his vehicle further up on the roadside to take pictures for himself and his V.F.W. Post. We hollered our best wishes at each other as I passed by. People were steadily honking their car and truck horns as they passed. Some people stopped just to shake my hand or to offer a donation of some kind. If it was food and I had the room in my rucksack, I would accept it gratefully; with money, of course, I followed procedure.

I continued through Dayton and into the rural area near the junction of Highway 12 and Highway 126 when I was stopped by fellow Vietnam veteran Mike Davis. Mike and I talked briefly, and I discovered that he had been a chopper pilot in 'Nam. Mike went on to tell me that he still flew helicopters, but he had recently injured his back in a local helicopter accident. He was delighted to meet me and gave me a media contact in Spokane. Mike also told me to call station *KREM Channel 2* and ask for Mike DeCesare. I thought it ironic that Mike Davis would fly unscathed through the hellfire of Vietnam only to receive injuries flying at home. Nonetheless, he was quite a guy and seemed to take it all in stride.

In Vietnam, the Casper Pilots who flew the support and rescue for those of us on the ground seemed to think that we were crazy to be there with the enemy just about everywhere around us. We ground troops rarely envied the guys who literally flew through 'walls of lead' to help or save us. We all thought they were crazy. Beautifully crazy!

Mike Davis departed, and I continued for a few miles before turning onto Highway 124. I scouted for an appropriate place to make camp. Most of the land was fenced on either side of the road. Since I had a real phobia about trespassing, I pitched camp between the fence and the road. I figured the location was safe enough, and hastily made a shelter. Once inside my bunk and covered by a make-shift poncho tent, I quickly fell asleep, but throughout the night I was awakened by the sound of heavy rain. In the morning, I lingered in camp and hoped the rain storm would blow over. After an hour of waiting, I gave up and broke camp. My day started in the rain for about eight miles. I walked onward with a very cool wind that added to my misery.

The rain stopped by midday, and it suddenly became very humid as the blazing sun overhead drew back the moisture from the ground. Still, I was contented since I had acclimatized to the heat-more so than to the chilling wind and rain. I moved along at a half-speed pace taking in the panoramic rugged beauty of the terrain. Very little traffic passed in either direction, and I enjoyed my brief repose from the thoroughfare. I reminded myself that this solitude could not repeat itself very often since part of my responsibility was to be highly visible along the most traveled routes. Still I enjoyed the near silence as noises of little critters scurrying here and there blended well with the rhythmic tune of my footsteps.

I stopped for a break at the Tucannon River and stripped to the waist, washed and shaved. Then I made some soup, which really hit the spot as I lay in the warmth of the sun and updated my journal. Regression visited me again, as it often did. Lying near the smooth running Tucannon River I was transported back to the banks of the waterways and rivers of Vietnam. More significantly, I remembered the An Lo River, which cut a course between two mountain ranges. Danger constantly lurked there on either side of its banks. We would run a lot of missions there and suffered a lot of losses. We were always careful to stay well back from view and camouflaged in the tree line that paralleled the river. We searched for telltale signs of enemy crossing points and trails. I was not distressed in my regressions at these times, for I knew now that this was a part of me and part of my evolution. I also realized that if those youthful efforts were in vain and no one had benefited from them, then that wasn't my fault.

Many times in Vietnam, I thought that something was missing from our program, but those things were beyond my control. Moreover, I was busy fighting for my life and the lives of my buddies, while folks back home tried to make up their minds about the whole business. In all its potentially negative capacities, the regression did not weaken me anymore because it was now a simple fact that I was a soldier who fought in a dirty war and survived. A lot of my buddies did not survive, and some are still captives, so if I am affected at all through regression, I think that it has only made me more determined to see the MIA/POW issue resolved and to witness America grow in positive ways worthy of the fallen and missing soldiers' sacrifices.

It was time to move on again, so I packed everything up and climbed back under the load. Within a quarter of a mile the pavement ended, and I started climbing uphill on a dirt road, which zigzagged its way for a few miles to the top. I noticed several rattlesnakes by the side of the road, therefore, I walked in the middle, giving the reptiles plenty of space in case of an oversight on my part. I was not anxious to hear the warning sound of the rattle anytime soon. At the top of the hill, I rested and gazed down into one of the most tranquil valleys I had ever witnessed. Again, I was reminded of the many beautiful valleys I had viewed from the mountainous areas in Vietnam. Most of our fighting soldiers who roamed the hills and valleys of that part of the world in Southeast Asia could testify to its ancient majestic beauty. Were it not for the country's ongoing wars and conflicts, the area would lend itself to certain serenity.

### Welcome to Pomeroy

I traveled quickly downhill along the dirt road when a young lady on a motorcycle passed by. She suddenly turned around and stopped. Surprised to see me, she inquired why I was walking dressed 'like that'. I smiled and briefly told her about the mission, and she seemed quite taken aback on hearing my explanation. She wished me well as she kick-started her motorcycle and then disappeared down the road. I welcomed the change in the terrain as I began to walk on level ground again. I came upon a couple of ranchers who were quite busy as they loaded livestock into a large truck. They provided me with cool water, which I accepted to replace the warm water in my canteens.

Six miles from Pomeroy, I moved onto Highway 12 and headed east at a comfortable pace. I had traveled about one mile when a vehicle traveling from the east pulled over on the opposite side of the road. With just a few more steps I caught sight of a familiar face; Ken Carlson and two other passengers from Benton City. After a hearty round of handshakes and hellos we chatted briefly, and I expressed my gratitude to him and his congregation for their kindness and generosity. I asked Ken to express my thankfulness to the people, and he assured me that he would. We bid each other a fond farewell and parted. I was still basking in the warmth of meeting Ken again when I heard a loud voice shout out, "Hey, soldier. Hold up a minute!"

I looked to see a young man, much like myself, walking towards me from a driveway. We introduced ourselves without hesitation, and it was my pleasure to meet Vietnam veteran Ron Zorza. Ron and I talked for a short time, and I explained to him that I would stop at Pomeroy for the night and contact Mr. Trosper of V.F.W. Post 2351. Ron explained that he knew Max (as he called him) very well and would be happy to contact him for me. I thanked him for his assistance, and we strolled up the driveway to his house where I was very pleased to meet Ron's family. His lovely wife, Virginia, stood in the doorway with his son, Andy (a miniature Ron), plus a very pretty little girl named Karmen. This was the Zorza family, and to me they were simply quite beautiful.

They welcomed me to their home and I felt completely at ease while we chatted and drank cold sodas. Ron called Max Trosper, who said he was eager to meet me and that he would immediately come to Ron's house. While we waited for Mr. Trosper's arrival, the family and I talked extensively about my journey. Ron and Virginia immediately suggested that I stay with them as opposed to a motel in town. I thanked them for their generosity and inquired if my arrival might cause them any disruption. They exclaimed that it certainly would not, and I was delightfully happy to accept their offer.

Max Trosper arrived, and immediately upon meeting him I sensed the presence of a strong, well-respected man. Ron, Max and I chatted liberally as though we had known each other a lifetime. Ron disclosed that he had served with the America Division in Vietnam. Max had fought in World War II as a member of Merrill's Marauders (Rangers) in Burma. My initial instinctive impulse was now explained: Max, first-generation Ranger, and me, a second-generation Ranger. We continued to chat and constantly found more common ground between us. Both Ron and Max made it clear that they felt the mission to be worthy of the public's positive acceptance and support. I was ecstatic and reassured in the company of these veterans. Max advised me that he had anticipated my arrival and had made arrangements for my accommodations in town. Then I explained that Ron and his family generously invited me to rest with their family. Max gave an understanding nod of approval and we agreed to meet early the next day.

After Max left, and while Virginia was busy preparing dinner for us, Ron told me that Max was one of the most respected gentlemen in the area. He also told me that Max was very ill with cancer. I was suddenly deeply saddened to hear of Max's poor health. I immediately reflected on the evening that Dad had died of cancer. Suddenly, I was rescued from any further distress by the littlest man of the house, Andy. He caught my attention and took me away from my sad thoughts.

I seized the opportunity to get cleaned up while Virginia and Ron put the finishing touches on dinner. In short order, we all gathered at the dining room table and shared a very wonderful meal, which I enjoyed almost as much as I enjoyed their company. After dinner, Ron, Andy and I drove into Pomeroy where I met some of Ron's friends. We stopped at the ice-cream parlor, much to young Andy's delight, and satisfied our craving before we returned home.

Later that evening, while I was seated at the dining room table writing in my journal, I was further delighted to witness a Zorza's family ritual. Ron, a gifted guitarist, played guitar for the children, who in turn were delighted by the songs he would sing for them before they went off to bed. In their pure innocence and joy, the children could not contain themselves from dancing since they were openly encouraged by the smiles and chuckles from their mother, father and a not-so-perfect stranger's appreciation of their performances. It was a totally inspirational experience. The children ended their day in merriment and laughter and went to sleep with a sense of peace and sweet dreams. "Wonderful," I thought. "Truly wonderful!"

Virginia, Ron and I talked for a short while into the evening, and during our conversation, Virginia invited me to join the family for church service since the next day was Sunday. I accepted her offer before I noticed a slight frown on Ron's face. Suddenly I remembered that he and I had talked about going fishing Sunday morning. I was somewhere between a rock and a hard place, so I said, "How about it, Ron? Want to go to church?" With no other way to go, Ron agreed to attend church service.

Sunday morning bright and early we were up and at 'em. By the time I had gotten downstairs, Ron was out of the house, down by the river fishing before breakfast. By the time, I finally caught up with him it was time to return to the house. We shared a delicious breakfast before travelling to Pomeroy to attend services at the Church of the Nazarene.

The church program was the same as it had been at Benton city: peer group Sunday school prior to the actual service. I was invited to remain with Ron and Virginia for Sunday school, and we all gathered in one room with people our age seated in a semicircle. I noticed a door open from an adjoining room as all the children walked single file into the room and formed a group in the middle of our semicircle directly in front of me. I had no idea what was to happen next. Suddenly one little girl stepped forward and reached out her little hand that held a homemade card, and all the little children spoke in unison as they said, "This is for you, for you are special."

I was stunned by their generous gift; suddenly, a stinging sensation pierced my eyes just as my throat tightened with emotions that reduced me to being speechless. I accepted the beautiful card from the child and nodded my head in appreciation and smiled at the children. But, the truth was I want to cry and cry some more. To have been the recipient of a gift of time from these children, was then and always will be an unforgettable experience. I enjoyed the combined Sunday school and Church service. I was invited to speak to the congregation, which I did, and Ron told me later that my words were very appropriate and well received. Equally rewarding was the opportunity to meet the people from the community at the church social hour before we returned to Ron and Virginia's home.

During the afternoon, Max joined us once again at Ron's house, and we enjoyed more in-depth discussions. On behalf of his Post, he had prepared a letter of support for the mission, which I gratefully accepted. Before Max left for the evening, he informed me that he would meet me in Pomeroy the next morning for breakfast. I confirmed that I certainly would be there at 0800 hours.

The rest of the evening was spent in leisure, and once again I was touched by the Zorza's family ritual. Not long after the little folks were tucked in for the night, the big folks did the same since everyone had busy plans for the next day. Ron was going back to another week's work, and I intended to start my week with a thirty-five-mile walk to Clarkston, which represented my last stop before I crossed the Snake River and entered the State of Idaho. I would soon accomplish the walk through the State of Washington.

It was sunrise when Ron woke me. We had only a few moments together before it was time to move along. I still had five miles to walk to reach Pomeroy, where I had a breakfast appointment with Max, some of his friends and the media. With a renewed strength from a good night's rest, I quickly walked the five miles and found Max and his friends seated at the restaurant.

I enjoyed the company of several civic leaders and businessmen while I made short work of my breakfast. Dan Walsh, publisher of the *East Washington*, was present and captured his story from the ongoing discussion. After breakfast, I was eager to get back to walking, the action end of business. As we parted, Max embraced me and promised to meet me on the road later in the day. I choked up a little and turned quickly to walk away. Though many years separated us, I knew Max and I were soul mates. In Max I could see my tomorrows, and I thought he quite likely saw his yesterdays in me.

**The Road to Clarkson**

I moved out of Pomeroy along Highway 12 toward the Alpowa Pass and thought of how different it was to be at an age somewhere between the children and the elders. At my age, one has lost their innocence of faith and trust as a child but has not reached the quiet knowing of an elder. I resolved that being in between these two states explained at least some of the escapism that my peers and I often employed.

Just a couple of miles outside of Pomeroy, I started to ascend, where the highway twisted and rose to the Alpowa Pass. Halfway up, I stopped for a rest. As I departed the roadside for just a few moments, I accidentally stepped on a snake, which gave a few quick movements, and I heard it snap its jaws a couple of times, but felt nothing. My mind played catch up with my body, which was already in motion backing off toward the road. Once I settled down, I realized that I had not heard a rattle. "Likely as not, it was just a non-poisonous bull snake," I thought hopefully as I checked myself all over.

I recalled the part of my training with Special Forces that had dealt with snakes and snakebites. I remembered that even the noisy rattlesnake would give little or no warning if it were completely surprised or if the snake's rattle had not grown sufficiently. I also remembered that no matter if they were poisonous or not, any snake bite was going to cause tissue damage, which would have a negative impact on my ability to perform the arduous walking requirement of this mission. I pushed onward, quite literally talking aloud to myself along the way.

Traffic was light as I walked steadily upward to the Pass. One car stopped and I talked briefly with the occupants who took pictures before leaving. I was aware that I had consumed far too much water, but I was not worried because Max and Ron informed me of a rest area at the top where I could refresh myself and replenish my water canteens. When I finally arrived at the top of Alpowa Pass, I was sorely disappointed to find there was no water running through the faucets. Still, I resolved that I would be okay since the rest of my journey to Clarkston was downhill, and I hoped to find a river or stream along the way. I wandered over to the picnic table area and dropped my gear. I set the flag staff down in such a manner that it could be easily seen from the road. I had no sooner done this and taken a seat at the table when I noticed Max driving up over the crest of the hill. He spotted me right away. Although we had just parted company a few hours earlier, I was delighted to see him again. He had brought me a light lunch and a cold soda. We talked about things which interested us most. Max kept the air conditioning on for my comfort during the whole time while we sat there and chatted.

Max showed me the article that reporter Dan Walsh had written for *East Washington,* published May 27th and titled "Trosper and traveling Vietnam vet discover they have a lot in common." Dan Walsh stated, "Max Trosper and John Blake are men of different eras and different wars. The common denominator that linked the two men can be described in a single word – Patriotism." Blake stated, "A lot of us have felt for a long time that Vietnam is unfinished business. The MIA issue must be resolved. At that point, maybe we can consider Vietnam finished."

I enjoyed this brief reunion atop Alpowa Pass with Max. I was impressed with the enthusiasm and respect that he had shown me and resolved right there and then to do something especially nice for him. I would see to it that he would have a lasting memento of the mission. I thought a little more about that while putting my gear back on and it struck me like a thunderbolt. I would send my bush cap to Max when I finished the walk. I told him that I wanted to do this for him, and he seemed genuinely pleased.

We embraced each other with a lot of caring and what naturally came so easy for us—we saluted one another. I turned on my heel to leave and heard Max driving off slowly and noticed that he was looking back at me through his mirror. I sensed that a part of him would be with me for the rest of my life. I raised my flag high and waved it from side to side as a final salute. Without looking back, I heard Max sound his car horn in response. I realized he was on his way home, and I thought, "Me too, Max—I'm going home, too."

I traveled along the top of the Pass and down over the crest of the hill. From this point to Clarkston, it would be a downhill walk. The blistering sun was just burning me up as I descended into the Snake River Canyon some twenty miles below, where I would meet the Snake River for the second time. Traffic was moderate with continual waving of hands and honking of horns. Several vehicles stopped during the afternoon, and I was constantly inspired by the driver's encouragement and offer to help.

The countryside was now rugged and mountainous with dry desert-like terrain that surrounded my every step. I felt uneasy because my water supply had run lower with every few miles. No source of resupply was presented to me until I met a young man driving a pickup truck. He offered to go forward for me and return with some water. During the short time he was gone I noticed that my skin had dried considerably, though I was still very, very hot. My body was just pouring out fluids so fast that I could hardly replace the losses quickly enough. This was a situation I dreaded. When water is in short supply and the loss of body fluids are rapid, my only recourse was to slow down the walking pace to retain fluids and slow down the loss. This situation was quite negative since I was still on the road between Pomeroy and Clarkston, and it was taking me a long time to get to Clarkston. Once more, my lessons from Vietnam reminded me that dry sweat was an early warning that my body was dangerously low on fluids. Rapid dehydration would lead to eventual heat stroke or heat exhaustion, neither of which I needed at this or any point.

The young man in the pickup came into view just in time, and I was saved from any further distress. While I alternated between filling empty canteens and a near-empty me, the young man told me that he had seen Ron Zorza earlier in the day and that Ron had asked him to keep a watch for me on the road to Clarkston. We chatted for just a few more minutes, and I thanked him profusely for the water and asked him to let Ron know that I would be okay. It was getting dark as I rested beside the Snake River. I was still about five or six miles short of my target area at V.F.W. Post 1443. I wanted to absorb the fluids I had ingested before I pushed down the homestretch of a thirty-five-mile day. It was my last full walking day in the State of Washington with one state accomplished and closer to Washington, D.C.

I looked out over the Snake River and up along the ridge lines. I imagined the sight to have been viewed quite the same through the eyes of Lewis and Clark, also Chief Joseph and the Nez Perce Indians. Here, where the Snake and Clearwater Rivers become one, there is a certain serenity of elements uniting. The high ground becomes low ground, and rock becomes water. All seemed calm in the knowledge of having born witness to man's fragile existence. All were amused, I thought, to witness man's varied determinations.

Moving on through the outskirts of Clarkston, I followed the directions Max had given me to locate the V.F.W. Post near the City Center. It was dark and seemed to take forever to make it to the Post. No one was there, so I moved on a little farther until I located a restaurant. Once inside, I ordered a sandwich and a beer. I located the pay telephone and placed a call to my Clarkston contact, Allie Tucker, who was Commander of the V.F.W. Post. We talked briefly, and Allie advised me that he was on the way to my location. I had barely finished my meal when he came through the door seemingly very excited to meet me. Allie and I went to the Skyway Motel where we met with the owner, Mrs. Luther Bailey. The V.F.W. was going to pay for my room, but Mrs. Bailey would not hear of it and donated my room, compliments of the management. She certainly seemed happy to help, since several of her family members were veterans.

Allie and I chatted briefly in my room before he had to leave. He expressed his regrets, and wished he could join me for breakfast, but he was already locked into another appointment for the morning.

Once Allie departed, I laundered my dirty clothes, bathed, and wrote in my journal. In the morning I would take care of some personal things, such as having new heels put on my boots and clearing the travel route with Idaho authorities before I crossed the Snake River and the Idaho State line.

I left my room for a few minutes to pick up a few items of junk food, which I thoroughly enjoyed eating as I watched the 'Johnny Carson Show' on television. Soon my thoughts reflected on the journey thus far. I felt encouraged as I mentally revisited the route from the Seattle coast to here and the people I had met. Satisfied that everything had gone even better than expected, I was indeed a very happy young man. My conscious thoughts were soon replaced by dreams.

The next morning, at 8:00 a.m., I had breakfast at a nearby restaurant and chatted with some people who gave me directions to the shoe repair shop. After breakfast, I walked downtown to Mel's Shoe Repair and arranged to have new heels put on my boots. Mel immediately assigned his assistant to do the work and refused to accept any payment, not even for the cost of materials. I thanked them for their support and walked back onto Main Street and headed for the Army National Guard Armory. As I entered the building I immediately met a guard person. I chatted with her briefly. She introduced me to the person in charge, Staff Sergeant (SSgt.) Atkins, a fellow Vietnam veteran who had served in the Army. We chatted for a while and hit it off just fine. Neither had heard of the Walk/Mission, but then I wasn't at all surprised. At this point, I was at the Washington/Idaho State line and outside of my previous media coverage range. I advised both Sgt. Christopher and SSgt. Atkins of my business. They agreed I would need some local media and organizational input to document the crossing of my first state line.

SSgt. Atkins telephoned Morris Bentley, Commander of the Lewiston Post of the American Legion, while Sgt. Christopher telephoned the Chief of Police at Clarkston to arrange an appointment for me to meet and speak with him. He also told me of a Vietnam veteran who lived up the valley near Orofino, Idaho. He thought that this veteran would be interested in pulling support for the mission in his area.

When SSgt. Atkins returned from lunch, I went with Sgt. Christopher to meet with the police authorities. After a brief meeting, I felt encouraged by their arrangements and confident that the Idaho authorities would be notified immediately. With peace of mind, I attended our afternoon meeting with Morris Bentley, SSgt. Atkins, and Sgt. Christopher. I instantly like Morris Bentley. He was a bright young man who was very enthusiastic when I informed him about the nature of the mission I felt pleased when he committed himself to alerting the media on the Idaho side at Lewiston. Morris suggested that a 4:00 p.m. crossing of the state line would allow enough time to alert media and coordinate an activity at his Legion Post. We all agreed, and the plans to mark the crossing of the state line were arranged. The Vietnam Veterans' *Mission at Home, 1982—One for the Boys,* would bid a fond farewell to the great State of Washington on May 25$^{th}$ , 1982.

Once I settled in my room for the evening, I was finally taken with the significance of the upcoming event: crossing the state line. There and then, I devised a simple flag ceremony that I thought would be appropriate for the event. A one-person ceremony would be performed at the center of the bridge between the two states. In the future, the same ceremony would be repeated at each appropriate point between all the other states I would cross along the way to the east coast.

My mind raced wildly as I sat quietly and watched the clock. I thought back to the preparation and planning, the relocation, and the recent reunion with David, my brother, at Seattle; the roads that led here and the many roads ahead. My mind engaged in a flip-flop routine, landing first to where words of encouragement were being heard over and over and smiling faces were visible to my mind's eye. Then it turned to the times when I was uncertain if my body and mind could perform the responsibilities of the mission. Just hanging-in-there had made me physically and spiritually strong, and I knew at that moment that I could not be turned back or stopped.

**This marks the end of John Blake's unfinished manuscript.**

## Author's notes to the Transcontinental Walk Finale

John received the same jubilant reception and appreciation throughout the many States he walked between Seattle to Washington, D.C. Although John was surprised by a grizzly bear as he hiked through Lolo Pass in Northern Idaho, and had been arrested by suspicious lawmen on at least one occasion. He knew he had witnessed more than his share of positive experiences as well.

When John passed through South Dakota he was happily surprised to meet his former Vietnam combat buddy who lived on the Rosebud Lakota Sioux tribe reservation. They had served together in Vietnam and were now reunited after fifteen years. The tribal council invited John to spend a few days at the reservation before he journeyed onward. On September 27, 1982, in South Dakota, his friend awarded John an eagle claw staff, which he mounted and carried forward to the end of the mission. During that same day, John was adopted into and made an honorary member of the Redfeather Owneeo Warrior Society. During John's visit to the Rosebud Reservation, he was blessed with an Honor Song and a Sneak-Up Dance. He was given the Lakota Sioux tribal name 'Isnala Iyanka Wieasa', when translated means 'he who walks alone'.

After seven months, and six pairs of military issue boots, each of which had been resoled at least once, John Blake's mission, *Transcontinental Walk*, which began in Seattle, Washington on May 1st, ended in Yorktown, Virginia. John felt satisfied and elated with the success of the mission. He hoped that his findings would help bridge the gap between society and Vietnam veterans, and he prayed for continuous reconciliation between the two groups.

When asked by the many supporters and media reporters along the trek if he had ever thought about giving up the mission, John's reply was honest and sincere. He stated, "I look back down the road and I think I see 'the boys'—all 55,751 that are with me on this mission. I never thought of quitting."

John was disappointed not to finish the walk in time for the dedication of the Vietnam War Memorial. He was denied access to the interstate highway system in Ohio and was driven to Lexington by a Vietnam veteran from Dayton, Ohio. John was forced to reroute the walk through the rough terrain of Kentucky, West Virginia and also the state of Virginia. But as the Memorial weekend approached, he took a short break. Through the assistance of a few Vietnam veterans, he attended the dedication ceremonies in Washington, D.C.

John believed that the national observance to honor Vietnam veterans assisted in turning around the negative attitude that many Americans held about Vietnam veterans and even some veterans against their own. He stated to a local newspaper reporter, "We were becoming a subculture in America. That's ridiculous. We are American warriors!"

After the official dedication of the memorial ceremony was completed, John secured a ride back to the mountains. John finished the transcontinental walk to Yorktown, Virginia, the site of the battlefields where America won freedom from the British. Ultimately, he arrived thirty-two hundred miles later at the Yorktown Victory Center on November 29th. On December 1, 1982, he was declared the first honorary citizen of York County, Virginia.

John believed his trip across the country also showed that Americans can pull together. During approximately one-third of the nights since John left Seattle, he was hosted by fellow veterans for a place to sleep and a warm meal. He clearly acknowledged, "It took a lot of teamwork. It's an example of what we can do when we pull together."

John had planned to write a book about his journey across the nation and the reactions he received from the people. One popular opinion that constantly drew support throughout the journey was his idea for a constitutional amendment that proposed: "America must never again enter into a conflict that it does not intend to win."

John spent five months walking and two months in non-activity walking as he visited with veterans' organizations in each town and city that he entered. He engaged in speaking forums with veterans and garnered support for the mission. He was 'checking the pulse of the nation', and determined that the nation's people were ready, willing and able to welcome home the Vietnam veterans and to tell them that their services were appreciated. He also discovered that the disgraceful attitudes and hardships directed towards the Vietnam veterans during that infamous decade after the American forces withdrew from Vietnam were genuinely regretted and sorrowfully heartfelt by the nation's people.

Lynn Mowry of Gloucester, who became John's devoted friend, summed up the mindset of the nation's people when she said, "Prior to the withdrawal of forces during the Vietnam conflict, I never did understand that war and felt 'get it over' because I didn't want anyone else to go."

Few people truly understood the Vietnam War, and perhaps not even the men and women who served. For those who believed in participatory democracy this was an opportunity to make a meaningful contribution to the lives of the oppressed coupled with the belief that America represented the only true hope for freedom. A common denominator shared by the many soldiers who served in Vietnam was the legacy that their parents, grandparents, and forefathers had served. Most served in a theatre of war from WWI to the Korea conflict. For most Vietnam veterans, it was the honorable thing to do!

Never in history did soldiers of war experience, receive, or be treated with the horrendous disrespect during repatriation as were the Vietnam veterans. Most veterans of that era experienced a vicious, horrid, unforgettable homecoming by society. The same government that sent the men and women to war simply turned the veterans loose into an unwelcoming society upon their return without debriefing or counseling, and it advised the returning veterans to behave themselves or else.

Rick, a Vietnam veteran, disclosed that his family "...looked kind of close at me. I felt like a stranger in my own home because they feared what my experience in Vietnam had done to me." Rick's observance of society and government reinforced the mindset of many Vietnam veterans when he reiterated a truth that many Vietnam veterans believed: "Stop looking at us as if we lost your war. You lost my buddies, tied our hands, and denied us a victory. When we got home we were used up and thrown away."

John felt that America was not ready in the 70's for the return of the Vietnam veterans when he stated, "Like any soldiers in any war, they were men who watched friends die in battle and who killed at their country's command. The war had cost us all too much grief at home and abroad. It was sad and difficult. The country had scorned and shunned Vietnam veterans who needed to be let 'off the hook', and the receiving society did not do that. When you have broken, even under a duty to country, a Commandment of our Lord, 'Thou Shalt Not Kill', you just need the leaders, the clergy, and the people who put you there to take you 'off the hook'. A welcome home from war is commonly perceived as a thank you for your service and that all is forgiven. Let the healing begin."

During the 70's and 80's, it is suspected that only half of the 40,000 Vietnam veterans who were Canadian volunteers returned to Canada and quietly intergraded into society without any expectation of a soldier's welcome home. Largely due to the horrendous reception the American Vietnam veterans received, the remainder like John returned or stayed in America. Today, Vietnam veterans are dedicated to ensuring that the next generation of war veterans do not return home and receive the same treatment. Never again!

In December, 1982, after a brief rest in Yorktown, Virginia, John stood true to his word and mailed Max Trosper the bush hat that he wore in Vietnam and during the *Transcontinental March*.

January 20th, 1983, reporter Dan Walsh of the Pomeroy, *East Washington* newspaper, wrote the following excerpt from the article "Trosper gets vet's hat."

> "On Christmas Eve, Trosper received a package from John Blake that proved to be his most cherished gift. On the surface it doesn't appear to be much, just a faded, well-worn camouflage military hat. To Max Trosper, however, it's much more than it

appears. It would be safe to say it is Trosper's most valued possession.

"He must have met hundreds of thousands of people on his trip," Trosper said. "That he remembered me and sent this to me is a real honor."

**Operation Backtrack Trans-Ohio March—1983**

During the months of May and June in 1983, the Vietnam Veterans of America, (VVA), Dayton, Ohio Chapter 97, worked closely with John to acknowledge the Vietnam veterans of Ohio, who had missed the opportunity in 1982 when John was forced to re-route the Transcontinental Walk.

The VVA Dayton Chapter 97 financially and physically supported 'Operation Backtrack', a trans-Ohio march from Wheeling, West Virginia, to Richmond, Indiana, a distance of 250 miles.

Dayton Chapter 97 appointed several of its Vietnam veteran members, who took over the full operation and formed a well-organized team which covered every aspect of logistic planning for the march across Ohio. This comprehensive luxury of support was absent in John's mission during the 1982 Transcontinental Walk.

The team provided the following necessities: supplies for John's attire, road support vehicle, media relations, press conferences, promotional materials, speaking engagements for John, plus garnered support from the Governor's office, State Highway Patrol and various Veterans Administration Centers in the State of Ohio.

Many Vietnam veterans still felt empty even after America memorialized their efforts with a monument in Washington, D.C. Most learned that the way to fulfillment is to contribute to the nation.

John issued the following statement in an excerpt from the press release for Operation Backtrack:

> In 1982, I, John Blake, a combat veteran of the Vietnam War, became the first pedestrian to carry the American flag across the continental United States. Impelled by a desire to promote positivism and patriotism among the American people, I

> started the walk in Seattle, Washington on May 1st. During the five-month walk, plus two-month non-walking activities, I wore full combat gear to recreate the image of the U.S. soldier during the Vietnam War.
>
> I did not solicit donations while on the road and refused to advocate the cause of any special interest group. The walk was a tribute to all Vietnam veterans.
>
> The Vietnam Veterans of America, Dayton, Ohio Chapter 97 financially supported and organized Operation Backtrack. The purpose of this year's march is to pay special tribute to Ohio's Vietnam War dead, Ohio Vietnam veterans and their families, and to appeal to all Ohioans to show solidarity with the families and friends of Ohio's MIAs and POWs.
>
> On July 5, 1983, at approximately 10:00 a.m., I, John Blake will begin a march across the state of Ohio via U.S. Route 40. The 250-mile march will commence at Wheeling, West Virginia and proceed to the destination point of Richmond, Indiana with an estimated time of arrival of July 16, 1983.

Reporter Peggy Talley from the July 12, 1983 *Ohio State Lantern* wrote the following excerpt from her article, "**GEARED-UP, Vietnam veteran hikes through Buckeye State**"

> John Blake, a Vietnam War veteran, said he was marching to pay a special tribute to Ohio's Vietnam veterans, living and dead, and to show solidarity with the families of Ohio's MIA/POWs (missing in action and prisoners of war). Behind him is a 1976 van with two American flags hanging off the back of it. Inside are two men who are also in camouflage combat fatigues. Blake's march is being sponsored by the Dayton Chapter 97 of the Vietnam Veterans of America.

**Vote John Blake for President, VVA Convention—1983**

John entertained political aspirations when he received the supportive nod of approval from the Dayton, Ohio VVA Chapter 97. John's political platform was based on reform and readiness for the future.

During that time, the VVA chapters and members were discontented, largely due to the self-proclaimed current leadership's lack of initiative and the necessary mandate and structure to promote and support the many issues that plagued the Vietnam veteran of that decade.

Dayton Chapter 97, decision to support the election of John Blake was put in a memo to the state members of all State Chapters of the Vietnam Veteran Association. Therefore:

> **B**e it resolved that John Blake, a member of the Dayton Chapter 97 of the Vietnam Veterans of America, has announced his desire and platform for the National Elections in November.
>
> **B**e it resolved that on the 15th of September the membership of the Dayton Chapter 97 of the VVA did overwhelming vote to support the election campaign of John Blake for the highest office in our national organization.
>
> **B**e it resolved that as of the above date we of the Dayton Chapter 97 will actively run a national election drive to place John Blake as the National Leader of the VVA.
>
> **B**e it resolved that we will actively solicit the delegates of the national to support the election of John Blake.

It was official that John Blake, Veterans' Advocate, had entered the race for the Presidential seat in the national organization of the Vietnam Veterans of America association. With less than two months to prepare a campaign, the push was on to organize the campaign committee with their detailed responsibilities. The democratic campaign to oppose Bobby Muller would be the first attempt in the history of the VVA. Bobby Muller was a force to be reckoned with, and he would likely not go quietly away for any opponent. To run against Muller would demand that the opponent be thick-skinned because it was a well-known fact that the fight for the Presidential seat would certainly become a tactical array of mud-slinging, in-the-gutter, vicious, personal attacks and harassment.

The organization was young with just 8,000 to 9,000 members nationwide, certainly not nearly a majority of the Vietnam veteran population. Many of the members were simply cardholders and not truly active in the organization. Therefore, the active members were mostly Bobby Muller's followers. It would become an interesting campaign, to say the least. Nevertheless, the Dayton, Ohio Chapter 97 supported John Blake and his experience as a veterans' advocate. John came out swinging and gave it his best shot.

## VIETNAM VETERANS NATIONAL PROGRAM

### THE PREAMBLE

**Produced by—John Blake, 1983**

Ten years have passed since the signing of the Paris Peace Accords and fully eight years have gone by since our nation's flag, Old Glory, was torn from flagpoles and rooftops in Saigon.

The ten and eight-year segments are only a portion of the time that had elapsed since the first wave of veterans of the Vietnam conflict arrived home to find a dispassionate American public and not-at-all-concerned government.

Plentiful are the stories of those who fought for precious life's sake alone, only to survive abroad, yet not to survive at home. The elders of the veteran population are quick to point out to the Vietnam veteran that they, too, have had to fight an ongoing battle with the Veterans Administration and various political leaders to gain and hold on to pensions, entitlements, and services.

Throughout those innumerable battles it is evident that the elder veterans were encouraged by a sense of righteousness, born out of their victory over obvious tyrannies, and a calm reassurance of knowing full well that they held the good grace of the American community at large.

Time changes most things, but in its midst some things are constant. For the Vietnam veteran community internal conflict is a constant and has been perpetuated by what seems to represent a grand design to:

1. Keep the veteran on the run and avoid any sense of social responsibility, or
2. Keep the veteran nearly totally distracted in the ongoing battle of redress for illness and injury suffered as a direct or indirect result of the Vietnam experience. Many veterans who have no entitlements are committed to the battle on behalf of those that do need redress.

Many of our most long-standing issues such as Agent Orange, POW/MIA, and PTSD have received attention. However, talented groups and individuals are in an excellent position to monitor the ongoing issues, and these people should be encouraged to do so.

The nature of the internal conflict of the Vietnam veteran community has been so intense over the years that little or no time and energy were directed *outward* to the American community at large. The Vietnam veteran has traditionally been fighting apathy, stigmatization, and downright abuse perpetually since his/her return from abroad. So intense has been this running firefight at home that few inroads have been made in some of the most important areas, i.e. relationship to the community at large, Vietnam veteran self-image, and the potential for positive impact at home.

I contend that to date not one relative plan has caught the imagination and spirit of the Vietnam veteran. What has existed and what is now being expressed is a profound desire on the part of the Vietnam veteran to:

1. Salvage something positive from the smoldering ruins of Vietnam.

2. Show by example just what participation and determination mean to our democracy.

Nobody but nobody knows better than the Vietnam veteran community that talk is cheap and action speaks louder than words. The running firefight at home continues and will be joined by the Vietnam veteran population only when the mission is defined.

There must be a national program or plan which is clear and precise as an operative order. It must challenge the Vietnam veteran's sense of caring and ongoing responsibility to and for the nation. It must be a battle cry that will adapt itself all the way from national, state, regional, local areas, and individual veterans.

Thank you for your support.

**The VVA Convention**

The Founding Convention of the Vietnam Veterans of America Association was held on November 7 in 1983, at the Shoreham Hotel, Washington, D.C. The incumbent, Bobby Muller, was successful in abating John Blake's effort to oust him from the Presidential position of the organization.

John was satisfied with his efforts in opposing Bobby Muller and recognized that he and his committees' effort made the democratic process more accountable to the organization of Vietnam Veterans of America. Ultimately, during the following decades, the organization developed into a more meaningful entity; one that today's Vietnam Veterans can proudly support.

## AMERICAN NEWSPAPERS MEDIA EXCERPTS

**"The Mission at Home 1982—One for the Boys"**
**From Idaho to Washington, D.C.**

### STANDARD, MONTANA Published June 1982
### "Vietnam vet trods on U.S. conscience" by Jim Tracey

When John Blake comes marching home next November, he wants cheering crowds to be there to welcome him.

Blake, a 33-year-old former Army Airborne Ranger, arrived in Butte Thursday afternoon on his 3,200 miles march across the country. Dressed in camouflage fatigues, full combat gear, and carrying an American flag hoisted over his shoulder, Blake said his walk across America is actually a symbolic homecoming for all Vietnam veterans.

He has greeted thousands of people with a thumbs-up since he set out from Seattle on May 1. Most of them have returned the greeting. "Ninety-nine percent of the people I've met approve of what I'm doing," Blake said.

What he's doing is calling attention to veterans who he believes have been treated unfairly by their countrymen and women. His own homecoming, after three years in the Army and 18 months of combat in Vietnam was miserable, he said. "I didn't expect much when I returned, but I did expect something," he said. "What I got was absolutely nothing. Most returning Vietnam vets were treated the same way," Blake said. "There was no real significant action to welcome the Vietnam veteran home. In fact, there was a concerted effort to make the Vietnam vet feel ashamed. But now," he said, "Americans are ready to deal with the Vietnam veteran whom they shunned 10 years ago." Blake plans to help do that. In a way, he wants to be their conscience.

He was honored last week at the state Veterans of Foreign Wars convention in Glendive. A contingent of V.F.W. members picked him up on Interstate 90 near Garrison and took him to Glendive as a guest speaker. They also gave him a new flag. He carries the flag, he said, "as a symbolic trade-off for the weapon he and others carried in Vietnam."

After a side trip to Helena to talk with Gov. Ted Schwinden, Blake returned to Garrison Tuesday to take up where he left off.

On Thursday, he was marching double-time along Interstate 15-90 near Ramsay while the highway shimmered in the afternoon sun. Truckers honked their horns at him. Other motorists waved and shouted greetings. Blake said that he walks on an average of about four miles an hour, or 25 miles a day. He said, "I'll either be in terrific shape or terrible shape when it's over."

Some nights he camps along the road. Other nights he spends in hotels as a guest of local V.F.W. chapters or with people who invite him to their homes. Except with a brief encounter with a rattlesnake near Yakima, Wash., and a scare from an elk that leaped in front of him, plus a grizzly bear encounter near Lolo Pass, the trip has been mostly pleasant, he said.

"My role will be as a symbol that the boys are coming home," he said. "America is ready for this. They want to deal with it. Now they'll have the chance to welcome home the veteran again. Let's see if we can get it right this time."

**HARDIN HERALD, MONTANA Published July 28, 1982**
**"One man's challenge" excerpt by Scott Hagel**

...Blake didn't know then that the country he was fighting for had no intention of winning the conflict in Southeast Asia. And he didn't know that the United States probably had no business being there. "But that was yesterday," he says quietly. In Blake's mind, and in the mind of so many of his compatriots, the Vietnam veterans were never allowed the relief of 'coming home' after the war. "Vietnam was the obvious exception. So we should try to be together on this thing; then we can let it go." Blake says he is not bitter toward the United States. The flag he carries 'represents the Vietnam veterans' undying faith in the nation, which should never be questioned. He is alone on his trek and asked if he ever feels lonely. "Never," he repeats,

"Sometimes, I feel the strength of 55,751 (the number of American soldiers killed in the Vietnam War as recorded in 1982). With that, he turns away and begins walking.

**GILLETTE NEWS RECORD, WYOMING, Published Aug. 10, 1982 "Vietnam vet 'heightens awareness' on long walk" excerpt by Dennis Cross**

John Blake is a Vietnam veteran who is doing something about the problem of the nation not being able to reconcile its differences with those who returned home from that unpopular war. Blake believes that given the opportunity, the nation will welcome the Vietnam vet home and tell him that his services were appreciated.

**CHARLESTON GAZETTE, WEST VIRGINIA Published Sept. 1982 "Walking for veterans" excerpt by Rick Steelhammer**

A 33-year-old former airborne ranger, John Blake, who is walking across America to raise interest in Vietnam veterans' affairs, said Thursday in Charleston that his journey has led him to believe that the nation is nearing the end of an era of apathy and negativism. Blake said, "There's a great need for us to give up on the past and go home. We are home, now. It's time to move into our communities and get to work at making things better."

**LEXINGTON HERALD-LEADER, KENTUCKY Published October 1982. "Long March Vietnam vet takes forced to detour on eastward trek" excerpt by Jim Warren**

Detoured out of Ohio, John Blake picked up his 50-pound pack and his American flag, laced up his jungle combat boots and left Lexington yesterday afternoon, walking east on Interstate 64 and bound for Washington, D.C. Articulate and soft-spoken, Blake describes himself as a 'typical Vietnam veteran'. Blake's problems in the Buckeye state were reported on 'Good Morning America' yesterday, and national wire services carried accounts of the incident. Blake was driven to Lexington yesterday morning to resume his walk after Brown's office authorized his passage through Kentucky."

**THE HERALD DISPATCH, HUNTINGTON, WEST VIRGINIA Published November 1982 "Heart and Mind: Vietnam veteran walking 'home'. John Blake had been walking the berms of roads across the nation since May 1, 1982" excerpt by Michael Johnson**

"We have been living in an era of apathy and negativism," said Blake, while drying out his rain-soaked clothes at the Huntington Vet Center, 1014 6th Ave., after speaking to a half-dozen Vietnam veterans. "That era is about to end," he said, "There's an underlying mood in America that indicates to me that we're at the dawn of a new era representing patriotism and positivism. We have to present the Vietnam veteran in his true light – as a patriot. We took the indirect route, but we're home. We're saying we're home and ready to be with you again."

**THE DAILY PRESS, WASHINGTON, D.C. Published Nov. 30, 1982 "Veteran Ends 7—Month Trek" excerpt by Ray Betzner**

John Blake believes America is on the edge of a new wave of patriotism. He ended his 3,200-mile trek Monday afternoon in Yorktown physically tired but emotionally charged. For now, Blake wants to rest and find a way back home. Blake is certain about one aspect of his return trip. "I'm not walking, that's for sure," he said.

∞

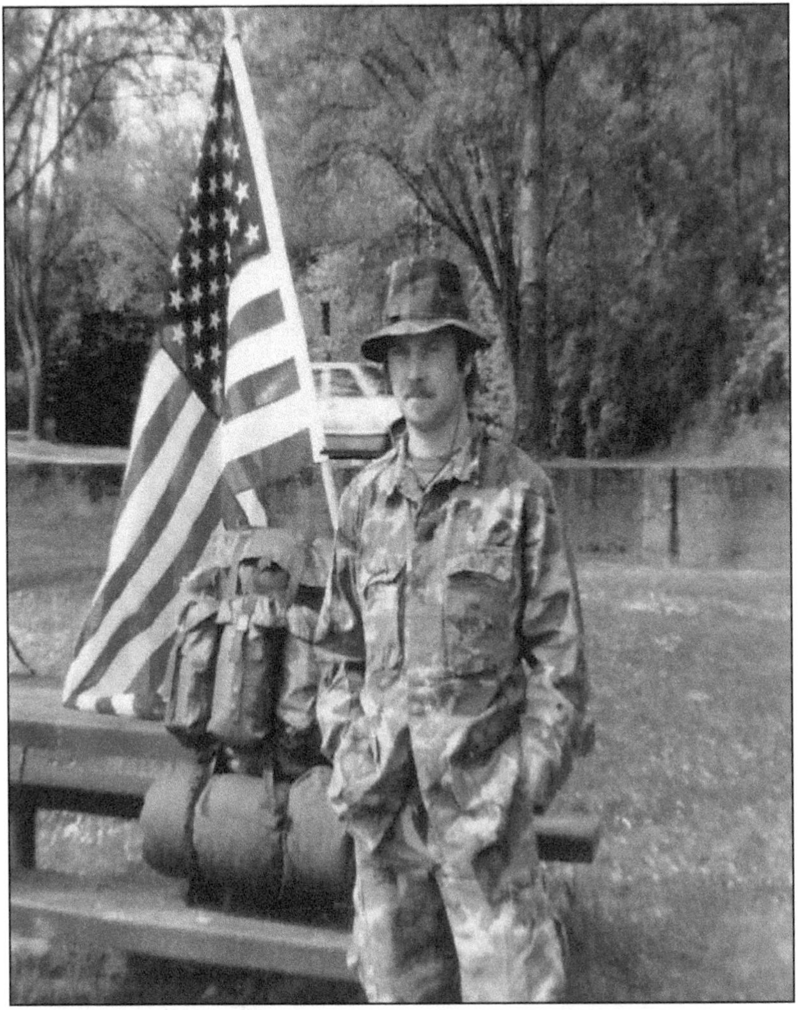

John Blake in readiness to start the Mission at Home One For The Boys transcontinental walk from Seattle, Washington (Photo courtesy of Ron Whelan)

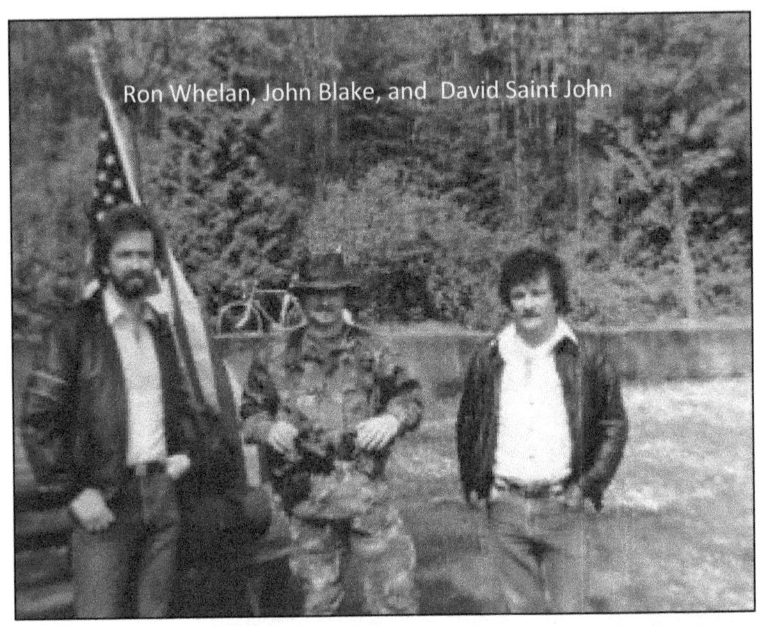
Ron Whelan, John Blake, and David Saint John

John Blake begins the first steps of a 3,200-mile walk

(Photos courtesy of Ron Whelan)

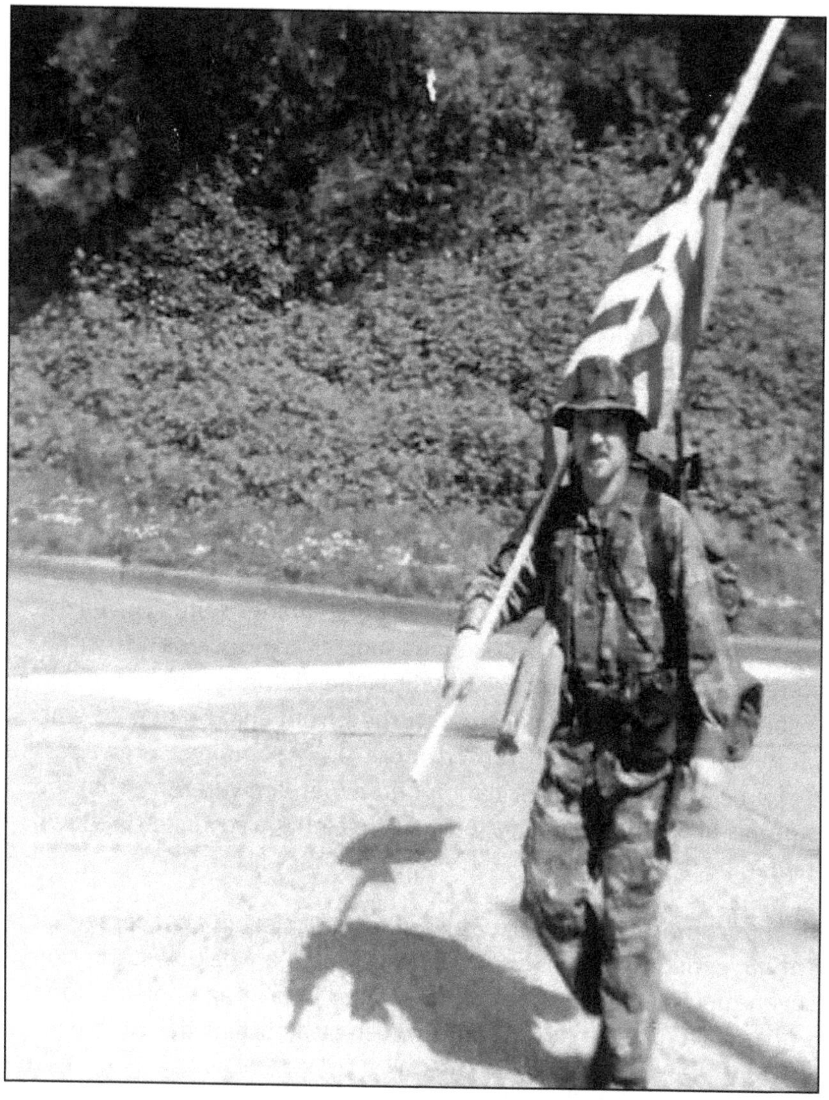

(Photo courtesy of Ron Whelan)

# Chapter 8

## The Silent Progression of John's PTSD

JOHN'S TRANSCONTINENTAL WALK ACROSS the United States soothed the demons that fueled his undiagnosed Post Traumatic Stress Disorder (PTSD) and offered him a temporary positive sense of purpose, hope, and belonging. He had been suffering a loss of identity, pride, and self-esteem ever since his return from Vietnam.

In each county and state that John walked into, he was received with interest, appreciation, acceptance and pride. The people he met reinforced the mandate of the mission and fueled John's inner-self need for acceptance, respect, and understanding. John thrived on each kind word that was spoken to him as expressions of caring, gestures of kindness and respect towards the Vietnam veterans whom he represented. The prodigal son returned from an opinionated war. He felt that he had been granted more understanding, forgiveness and appreciation for a reconciliation of the Vietnam veterans from the people he had met along the journey that now also fueled his own wounded heart and soul.

John felt compelled to walk onward and achieved an average of twenty-five miles a day for six out of seven days a week over a period of seven months, which is extraordinary for an average person. John was not an average person—he was driven by a burning desire to win.

One might question at this point, "To win what?"

Most likely, it was to win the relentless fight inside of him that pounded at his very being. It didn't have a face or a soul, but it was as real as any person or thing. It had the ability to either drive normal average people into becoming extreme high achievers or shatter them physically, mentally and emotionally. It could reduce them to that of the walking wounded as a result of their war experiences and ultimately it became a diagnosis of PTSD.

**Regression Regrets**

John spoke of regression throughout his journey across the nation. He would often retreat mentally and emotionally to former times, places and experiences that were enriching yet demoralizing, rewarding but dangerous and appreciative though sorrowful. Those retreats enabled him to focus on what he deemed to be valuable and necessary and to make right what he felt was terribly wrong in society for him and the many other Vietnam veterans who were living in their silent war at home.

When John returned from Basic Combat Training in 1969, my family and I noticed a distinct change in his personality and demeanor. We did not understand the change then, but we certainly understood it later.

The military's objective in Basic Combat Training is to transform civilian enlistees into soldiers. It reinforced four effective survival skills that are identical to the same elements of PTSD: emotional numbing and avoidance plus hyper-arousal and hyper-vigilance to increase one's ability to survive in a war zone.

Drill sergeants stressed the new recruits and established emotional numbing with constant verbal, physical and emotional harassment to sharpen the recruits' skills to function at their military jobs and dismiss distractions. Avoidance of painful emotions such as anger, grief and fear were essential in performing their military work. Why? Primarily, due to the fact that emotional distractions in a theatre of war could easily cost lives.

The military instilled exaggerated startle response as in hyper-arousal and sleepless vigilance, both instrumental in keeping new recruits alive. So was excessive rage, which is a normal response to danger and to serious threat of severe injury or possible death. In essence, the military training and experience introduced and developed the many facets that contributed to mental health stress disorders in its population.

After a few months of constant exposure to mental and physical military training elements compounded by numerous tours of duty, the emotional response network of the brain becomes rewired. The individual's emotional network has been retrained and it is highly unlikely that it can be untrained due to extreme numerous traumatic stress and direct or indirect life-threatening experiences.

Basic and advanced military training coupled with numerous life-threatening events or injuries in a theatre of war will strengthen the odds that most soldiers will develop PTSD.

**Why Me or Why Not Me**

Many veterans and civilians neither reach a cumulative point of stressors nor experience the final stressor as it relates to excessive trauma, the necessary formula to set PTSD in motion.

Stressors related to traumatic experiences will have a larger impact if caused by inhumane actions or negligence and will increase the probability that a soldier or a civilian will develop PTSD. Numerous stressors can be increased and compounded throughout early childhood and adulthood. The severity of stressors will most likely determine the degree of probability that a soldier/civilian will develop PTSD. At an unknown breaking point, it only takes one particular trauma compounded with accumulative traumas to ensure that the veteran/civilian will develop some degree of PTSD. Each person is different, as are their experiences; hence the difficulty in understanding the direct causes and effective approach necessary in addressing an individual's PTSD.

In retrospect, John's childhood was extraordinarily complex and compounded with known traumatic stressors at the age of four due to a life-threatening, traumatic fire. He experienced the sudden loss of his father and mentor during his most formative years. At the tender age of thirteen, John took the lead as the man of the house, which undoubtedly caused him additional stress and concern regarding the care and safety of his younger siblings. Consequentially, he denied himself time to deal with his grief. The question of his paternity certainly had an impact on his self-identity.

Without the necessary counseling to process severe childhood traumatic experiences, John carried his unprocessed traumas-along with additional adolescent traumas-into his adult life. Those unresolved traumatic experiences became an essential element in the foundation of his emotional mental health and disposition.

John thoroughly believed in his resolve to volunteer and enlist in the United States Army in an effort to free the oppressed in Vietnam. Volunteers respected the military training that ultimately reinforced their accumulative childhood stressors, which unknowingly defined some of them as a player in the game of PTSD Russian roulette.

John Blake earned his Green Beret with Special Forces and became a highly-skilled and respected Airborne Ranger, who performed his service in Vietnam with valor. Like many other soldiers of war, he experienced excessive traumatic stressors. The event that solidified John's breaking point and ensured that he would develop PTSD was the horrific accidental death of Sgt. George Morgan.

Soldiers and civilians re-experience their traumatic events through stressors, nightmares, flashbacks and anniversary dates of traumatic events, which ultimately places them in severe stressful mental health episodes that often haunt them for the remainder of their lives. Re-experiencing traumatic events is a symptomatic element of PTSD. These symptoms are common knowledge today, but in the 1980's it was basically an undiscovered area in mental health awareness. During that era, most medical professionals believed that the symptoms were not real until an excessive number of Vietnam veterans suddenly began to exhibit the same mental health issues and symptoms.

Military veterans, civilians, medical communities, and the Department of Veteran Affairs in North America were totally unprepared to deal with the aftermath of the Vietnam War. What transpired in the Vietnam veteran community for decades to follow was nothing less than an unnatural and inhuman massive loss of life largely due to ignorance and unpreparedness.

**Military Post War Responsibility**

The National Defense Departments in North America are experts in developing combat soldiers and service personnel to engage in warfare. What they lack is a responsible proactive mental health module designed to debrief or decompress the war experiences and traumatic events. What is needed at the end of their enlistment is an intense decompression program equivalent to the same intensified three or more months of basic training that each soldier received at the onset of their military enlistment. It is as equally necessary and relevant to survive re-entry into civilian life after the war zone as it was to stay alive in one.

Throughout history, the military has created warriors to fight and kill the enemy during wars. When the fighting is done the soldiers returned to their families forever changed. The age-old culture in the military is to 'Soldier On' the silent order is 'be tough, soldiers don't cry', but in reality they do.

Tears are a normal response to normal feelings. Soldiers are normal people with abnormal and extraordinary duties, responsibilities, and experiences. PTSD is a normal response to abnormal traumatic stressors. Life changing experiences newly define a person because the former pre-military self no longer exists.

The mission at home for families, communities, but most importantly for the individual is to learn to accept the veteran who returned as a newly defined person. He/she emerged under extraordinary circumstances. The goal in life after the war zone is to create a new beginning and learn to live in the 'now'. The veteran must love and care about who they really are today and learn to forgive themselves, the former soldier who is now a civilian. It takes time and commitment to fully re-define oneself, but it is doable.

The WWI and WWII returnees had a somewhat better opportunity to reintegrate into society, largely because they spent weeks or months together as a cohesive group engaged in self-initiated debriefing and decompressing. They supported each other during their lengthy journey home from the war. But the downside was that unless a soldier was captured or declared unfit for service he would remain at war until it ended. Due to the unusual continuous length of service and war experiences, some soldiers during that era never fully recovered from their mental wounds. Civilians were poorly educated to receive their veterans due to watching the Hollywood-style movies that depicted returnees from war struggling with mental health issues. The movies served as an indication of what families could expect from their returning men. All the support that families received was reality as depicted by actors.

The Korean veterans had a point system. After a soldier accumulated enough points, an individual could return home regardless of the progress of the war. Again, troops had the benefit of extensive travel time to rest, recover and process some of their experiences before re-entering civilian life. Still, many returnees developed mental health issues.

During the Vietnam War, American enlistees and Canadian volunteer enlistees were discharged by DEROS (date of expected return from overseas). A tour of duty was usually twelve months with an end date to look forward to. The disadvantage was that tours of duty were individual and solitary. Whole units did not travel into war or return from war together. The Vietnam soldiering experience was an individual one without continuity or cohesiveness. When the soldier's DEROS was up he was plucked from the jungles of Vietnam and ultimately placed on a commercial flight to travel home with strangers. His boots were still covered in the red mud from Vietnam. Then, less than two days later he would be sitting on a sofa in his family's living room with survivor's guilt grieving for the death of his friends. He felt the added internal conflict of leaving friends behind without his skills to help them survive. Many were confused between their soldier life and civilian life. They felt joy in seeing their family and loved ones, however the returnees suffered from the loss of belonging and struggled between two worlds, military and civilian.

Some returnees were given an administrative discharge because their immediate stress behavior became problematic for the military. Others returned to Vietnam for additional tours of duty and engaged in further traumatic experiences to complete their enlistment obligations, which ultimately compounded their unprocessed traumas. Few, if any, engaged in debriefing or decompression programs relevant to their war experiences prior to leaving the military.

Common sense should have prevailed. If it had taken several months of training to prepare the troops for warfare, then it should take at least several months of decompression to prepare troops to re-enter civilian life. When troops spend time together in a non-life-threatening environment they become more apt to discuss their experiences with each other and begin the reprocessing procedure. It is only then that military personnel trained in psychological disorders can determine which troops are exhibiting the classic signs of PTSD and other mental health issues. Early intervention is a key element in addressing symptoms of PTSD. If left unattended, undiscovered and untreated for several years, then chronic PTSD will occur.

In today's world, the universe is fully aware that there is no cure for PTSD. Early diagnoses, intervention, and education are critical in managing an individual's awareness, understanding, and acceptance. One must learn how to cope with their PTSD because life is worth living.

Yet sadly, in North America, communities plus medical and governmental systems continue to fail veterans, first responders and civilians. Lives are still being lost at an alarming rate as a result of PTSD. Why? The answer may be hidden in the fact that PTSD is an individual's mental health affliction based on that individual's experiences. No two cases are alike; therefore, a cookie-cutter approach to mental health wellness will fail. Each unique case must be addressed on its own merits, needs, and receptors.

Department of Veteran Affairs and National Defense Government departments throughout North America must give priority to its veterans' needs and take ownership in providing the necessary funding and programs. Such action is desperately required in providing mental health wellness. If not, the system will continue to fail miserably and disgracefully.

∞

# Chapter 9

## PTSD and Veteran Affairs 1984

JOHN FOUND SOLACE IN HIS VOLUNTEER WORK as an independent Vietnam veterans' advocate and assisted hundreds of Vietnam veterans filter through their Department of Veteran Affairs (DVA) benefit claim. He helped them complete the dreaded and often complicated disability claim process created by the Veterans' Affairs system. Unfortunately, ten years after the Vietnam War ended, the demand for mental health assistance grew rapidly as many more Vietnam veterans exhibited PTSD at an alarming rate.

John created a 'To Do' list titled "Important Tips in Handling Your DVA Claim" for Vietnam veterans. He floated the document, which he simply signed with a salutation of "Always One with You" marked it with an X, then signed it 'An Unknown Veteran'.

It was crucial to John that his identity remained anonymous due to his own mental health issues and intuition that it was just a matter of time before he, too, would be completing forms for his own DVA claim. He discreetly dropped off photocopies in the waiting areas of most DVA facilities and posted them in public areas where Vietnam veterans would frequent. These efforts gave him a sense of accomplishment in assisting his fellow Vietnam veterans.

John's 20-point document was filled with necessary and reliable advice, which enabled Vietnam veterans to cut through some of the bureaucracy and maintain complete and accurate personal records.

**IMPORTANT TIPS IN HANDLING YOUR DVA CLAIM**

- File claim for service and non-service connection of your condition. Do this by contacting DVA Service Officer while in the hospital.

- Give Power of Attorney to the Veterans' Service organization of your choice (DVA, V.F.W., PVA, etc.).

- Pursue all available therapy and treatment (T&T) for your condition. Keep records of T&T as best you can—always.

- Obtain appropriate Federal Government Forms and get copies of your DD214, awards, plus decorations, medical records, personal combat or service records and after-action reports (involving your unit). You can get appropriate forms from your Service Organization or Veteran Center Representative.

- Before leaving a medical treatment center always go to the Release of Information office to sign request form to have copies of your Summary Discharge Report sent to yourself, the DVA Claims Office, and your National Service Officer (NSO).

- Keep good records of all correspondence from you OR to you by photocopying everything, which has anything to do with your treatment and claim.

- Stay on top of treatment on an Inpatient or outpatient basis; do include any private treatment. Don't depend on others to move information about your treatment to your NSO or the DVA Claims Office—You do it.

- Write or have someone else write a letter, in your words, telling how or why you feel that your injuries (physical, mental or both) have complicated your life. Briefly tell a little of your life before, during and after service. Make your personal plea for recognition and support here. Head the letter To Whom It May Concern then make copies and distribute.

- Have family members and others prepare letters about you. Describing what they see you have been going through—the difficulties and the changes. If you been disowned by or rejected by your families because of your behavior then have the person or persons who made that decision do you one good turn by putting that in writing. Forward copies of these letters in support of your claim.

For a claim under Post Traumatic Stress Disorder or any other nervous condition, write in your own words and give names, dates, places, and witnesses to describe in as much detail as possible the traumatic or shocking things that happened to or around you, which have shaken you up. Explain how each continues to bother you in dreams, nightmares or flashbacks. Disclose as many incidents as you can, which can be verified or reasonably proven. These incidents are called stressors or memories, which cause you to be unwell. Create a copy-to list and forward copies to those on your copy list.

Involve your United States Senator and Congressman, or Canadian Member of Parliament, in your DVA claim when you have built a strong case. Write each of them personally, send photocopies of all your records and ask each of them to oversee your claim progress (this may help to keep the DVA honest). Make copies of all correspondence. Remember to build your claim based on truth and your personal experiences.

- File your claim for Social Security Benefits and handle the same as DVA claim.
- Always mail Certified Return Requested, of any documents from yourself to others.
- Renew each claim annually (before a year runs out).
- You have rights to appeal processes.
- Locally go to DVA Regional Board of Appeals to add new evidence.
- Washington, DC-DVA National. (In Canada—DVA Federal)
- Plus, Judicial Review-Court System Contact Lawyers' Referral--Add new evidence.

- You have the right to increased benefits if already service connected.
- DISCLOSURE—Don't run off at the mouth.
- The DVA takes a negative position on information obtained from any source / by 'any' means which suggests that you had major problems prior to your military service, and any alcohol or drug abuse before, during, or after military service.
- The DVA takes the position that you had a pre-existing condition, vicious habit, and willful misconduct; any of which will grossly affect to the negative your DVA claim, and likely, your Social Security claim.

Dear Friends;

Prepare yourselves for unreasonable disappointments, delays, additional bull s--t and frustration. It is important to stay in treatment/therapy, on medicines/medications and generate paperwork documentation. Keep your claim active, never quit, and work it hard!!!

Always one with you

An Unknown Veteran

**John's Struggle with PTSD**

John was no stranger to the mental and emotional effects of Post-Traumatic Stress Disorder compounded by his many extraordinary experiences and memories of Vietnam. From the time he departed Vietnam, he exhibited signs of depression, anxiety, sleepless nights, startled reactions, dreams, and flashbacks, plus intrusive thoughts and vigilance. John pushed all the warning signs and symptoms aside and focused on his self-designed work with and on behalf of Vietnam veterans.

John felt quite happy with his chosen interests and the company of one of the finest women he had ever met, Ms. Lynn Mowry of Gloucester. He was still frustrated at times. The pair was united in an effort to write a book from the exploits of his adventures on the *Transcontinental March of 1982*. John became more enthusiastic about where the story was going, but against good advice, John pursued advocacy interest research and validation for his story.

The pair concentrated on his advocacy work and multiple other interests. John noticed that his newly refurbished energy and enthusiasm was dissipating. Still, he continued to be self-driven in pursuit of change.

Lynn and John's veteran friends knew that something terrible had strongly affected John. Lynn took great care of John but it was evident that John had slipped way down memory lane. The war in Vietnam caught up with him. The pain, suffering, and grief that flooded his memories stole John away. He tried several times to rally back from his major depressive episode, but within a few months, he had become unraveled again at his emotional seams. More and more his war in Vietnam moved to the forefront of his mind. Whether awake or sleeping, there was an increased revisualization of real life events that had occurred in Vietnam. John broke completely. There were many more times when he felt lost and that he did not fit into the new world to which he had returned home decades ago. John constantly missed his friends who were lost in battle. Those were his most painful days. He was home in a physical sense, but in his mind he was still in Vietnam. Nothing, not a man, woman or child could equal the friendships that he had formed in Vietnam. Nothing or nobody ever came as close to him as did the Ranger brotherhood.

In the early afternoon of May 4, 1984, John experienced a severe flashback. Throughout the day he felt extremely distraught over the experience, and later that evening he made an impulsive attempt to end his life. John intentionally crashed his pick-up truck at a very high speed. He wanted to die. On that horrid night, he survived the crash with just a few bruises and scrapes. He was physically unscathed but mentally destroyed. It was on the insistence of his devoted friend, Lynn, a woman whom he loved and respected, that he agreed to be admitted to the Hampton, Virginia, Veteran Administration hospital.

During the intake interview at Hampton, VA hospital, John finally confessed that he had experienced stress disorder symptoms since 1975, which included flashbacks and nightmares that had started soon after his return from Vietnam. His initial concerns included mood controlling flashbacks, numbing of emotions, and feelings of survivor's guilt. According to John's medical records, he was officially diagnosed with Chronic Post Traumatic Stress Disorder. Bipolar Disorder was ruled out.

John wrote a letter to David on June 19, 1984, and explained a treatment plan for his recovery that the VA had recommended.

> David,
> The treatment is now set and I'll be in the hospital until about February of 1985. I'll leave here on the 23rd of July and travel to Chicago where I'll be in a special program for people with Post Traumatic Stress Disorder. I've already borrowed the money from Lynn's mother for the plane fare. Thank goodness that I'm a Vietnam vet that can get treatment at all.
>
> The doctors said that though I am very sick right now, they feel confident that I will be a new man by the end of the Chicago treatment. I really am looking forward to that time with a lot of hope.
>
> David, I'm going to be getting pensioned by the end of August. So I would appreciate you sending me a weekly allowance and maybe $100 towards the trip next month. I promise to give you $500 from my first pension in August. David, I'm fighting for my sanity down here and really need some help.
>
> On a lighter side, the doctors said that a part of the problem with PTSD is a don't give a fuck attitude, and that is where I want to be more sincere and serious. The treatment will help me to be that way. That alone would change my life for the better. All my life, since 'Nam, a lot of what I've done with me and my life is merely a result of my contempt for people, rules, and normal life standards, all because I've been sick for years. I'm looking to be reborn in a sense and if it's true what they say about Chicago VA, we will all be surprised. Please

take care. Life is going to be getting real good for me soon and I want you in it.

Love to everyone.
Always, John

David immediately shared the news with my sister and me. We, in turn, researched PTSD and realized that John would be traveling a very difficult and long road towards recovery.

We asked David to speak to John on our behalf and remain in constant contact with him. We felt that John did not need all of us inundating him with inquiries unless it was something specific. My sister and I decided that we would continue to write letters to John and show our support, plus keep him advised on positive current events regarding the family in Canada. David was never much of a letter writer, but he would be the best liaison for our family via telephone. John always spoke openly with David, whereas he constantly tried to protect his sisters from his world and often withheld vital information.

A few months after John entered Hampton (VA) hospital; he became more stabilized and was granted a day pass to visit Lynn. On that day, he received a telephone call from David, which upon his return to the hospital that evening prompted the following letter in June 1984.

David,
Sure was a lucky shot that you would telephone Lynn's house on Sunday while I was out of the hospital on a pass. I enjoyed talking with you and Ron as you both shared a bottle of wine. I still like my wine too, and probably always will though there won't be any of that for quite a while I'm afraid. Booze has not been a problem for me over the past 4 years.

No, the big thing now is this Post Traumatic Stress Disorder. I'll have to send you some literature on it so you will know what we are talking about as we go along. I don't want you to think about PTSD very much though David, because although you didn't see heavy combat, you may or may not become a victim to it. I don't want that to happen. Let's just say that I'm your brother and I'm sick. It is said that I am a very bad case so nobody f--ks around with me at all. I don't have to do anything I don't want to while awaiting my treatment at Chicago beginning July 24th. I'm heavily drugged on Lithium at 1500mg a day plus Thorazine at 200 mg for bedtime. I'm harmless, I hope.

As I mentioned over the phone, the Chicago treatment is such that I'll be in with about twelve other combat vets and we'll be taken through a six-month program. We'll be cared for by Vietnam veteran doctors and aides. The program is said to be successful by a high degree, though of course, nothing is perfect. After a while, I'll get everything sorted out with the VA over disability pensions etc.

Life in the United States is good. I'm somebody down here, whereas in Canada I'm a nobody. I've fought like crazy under Old Glory, and have a sense of belonging here.

Many thanks, David; your money order came today. Once all this treatment is passed I will be all together finally. The book can be finished in four to six months. Just having the book to work on when I get out is a good thing. That quiet and serious work will be just what I'll need while I'm finding my way back to a normal life.

I am happy that we are in touch. Remember the movie, *One Flew over the Cuckoo's Nest*. Well, that is the way it is here David. Sometimes it's funny but sometimes it's just not. I'm considered likely to hurt myself or someone else so I'm in the most disturbed category. The drugs keep me down pretty well. You didn't think the drugs were a good idea and I agree, but I gotta tell you that it's the only way they can control and trust me enough to have liberties etc. I tell you, it's a real *Catch 22* situation!

At the Veteran Administration Medical Center (VAMC) in Chicago they will begin the phase out of drugs for me and all the others participants in that program; so it goes without saying, I'm looking forward to getting there. I gotta tell ya, David, you're just a great brother and I'm lucky to have you. I'll write again soon, so be sure to take good care and to keep your cool. Don't worry about anything here they are taking pretty good care of me. If anything weird happens I'll have Lynn telephone you.

Always, John
PS: It will be okay.

John spent his time in stabilization at the VA hospital and continued with the daily recommendations of rest and medication. He responded to the many letters and cards from my sister and me. We made sure he understood that he was not forgotten and that he mattered. I had sent John some current pictures of family members that included my two young children which prompted his positive response in June 1984.

Dear Sister,
I was pleasantly surprised to get your recent letter. I especially enjoyed the pictures of your beautiful and healthy-looking children. They are really something and I'm sure they do a lot of giving towards a great feeling of self-worth and joy. And you look very well also from the one picture of you and your little daughter. Certainly, I want to thank you for thinking of me in this way.

The information you were able to pass along concerning my daughter is much appreciated. I don't really have any significant contact and really don't expect any change until she is at least grown and seeks me out herself. I am lonely for my child, it's true, but I will not interfere unnecessarily with her mother's attempt to raise her up proper.

The doctors here at the Veteran Administration Hospital have determined that for some time I have been sick with Post Traumatic Stress Disorder (delayed) which is really just saying that the war I fought has come back on me and is causing me to have rage and contempt, flashbacks, nightmares and a whole host of bizarre experiences. By the time I leave this facility I will have been here almost three months. Then I fly to another VA hospital at Chicago, Illinois where I will undergo special treatment for Vietnam combat veterans for six months. There is no cure for what is wrong with me and thousands of other combat veterans, but we will learn how to live with it. One trains for a year, fights for almost two years, and then thirteen years later somebody decides it's time to deprogram the poor bastard. Enough said.

I look forward to hearing from you.

Take care,
My love to all, John
PS: Hug the children.

John was prepared to exit the Hampton VA hospital and travel to VAMC Chicago to begin a six-month treatment for PTSD when he wrote the following letter to David on July 15, 1984, and explained the auto wreck that almost ended his life.

David,
I'm down to the last week here and next Monday I'll fly to Chicago for the six-month program and that will be it. This past three months went by very fast and I hope the others will go fast too. I don't know what to expect but they have a high success rate from what I hear.

Looking back at the auto wreck it seems that what saved me was that the truck rolled over before it crashed into the trees and pole I was shooting for. The truck was almost completely demolished but it sold for a few hundred, which was used to pay up some bills.

I'm now considered to be stable awaiting further treatment which I will get real soon. Well, it seems I was pretty bad off for a while because it took over two months just to get me stabilized. I tell you, all this shit is like a monkey on my back.

Everyone that worked on my case has been really super, the royal treatment all the way. Lynn and her Mom had to pick up all the pieces by taking care of my personal finances and shutting down my painting business.

I'm still on 1500 mg of Lithium a day but the Thorazine is down to 150 mg. All that shit keeps me pretty quiet, almost like a zombie. When I get into the new program I should be able to get off the drugs.

I'll be sure to let you know the new address and everything. I certainly hope everything is okay with you David and that you are able to enjoy the summer.

I know that having to back me financially usually means you have to go without or give something up and I just want you to know I really appreciate it. All that kindness will come back to you and more. Hang in there partner. I'll be thinking of you.

Always, John

David kept us up-to-date regarding John's condition and treatments. We were all very worried about John, and with Mom entering the early stages of Alzheimer's it was all we could manage to keep their respective medical conditions undisclosed. We each believed that it was in everyone's best interest not to tell John about Mom's condition or Mom about John's condition.

At Hampton VA Hospital in Virginia, the primary issue was to stabilize, diagnose and determine a method of treatment. The medication therapy was temporary and the effect was positive as it did relieve John's anxiety and suicidal thoughts. No therapy was conducted but the net gain was that John became stable and ready for travel to North Chicago to pursue a specialized treatment program. All travel to and from the facility at North Chicago was to be paid for by the patient. The Admissions Screening Committee at Chicago required each patient be in possession of a return travel fare in the event the patient was not accepted into the program.

Lynn arranged the travel arrangements for John and drove him to the airport. While they waited for his flight to be called Lynn and John expressed their hope, optimism, and determination. It was a sad day for the pair. She was no quitter! John felt he must not be either. Throughout his entire stay at Hampton hospital, he had treated her unfairly in a forlorn attempt to drive her away from him and away from his next journey towards psychotherapy.

John was conscious of the fact that there were several staff members at Hampton hospital who had worked on his case and consistently advised Lynn to walk away and go on with her life without John. Lynn's family also advised her to do the same. John felt he needed to protect her too from his illness. But Lynn was no fair-weather friend. Throughout his difficult experiences, she stood as the only reminder to John that there were valid reasons for a meaningful life and the potential for good work in the advocacies that they shared. If only he could just shake off the stressors, he could survive. But they would finally become overwhelming.

John traveled to VAMC in North Chicago to the Stress Disorder Treatment Unit and underwent a detoxification program from the medication that was formerly prescribed. He then engaged in group therapy, individual psychotherapy, assertiveness training, Vietnam revivification groups, goal setting groups, plus occupational and recreational therapies. Due to John's inability to master prerequisite relaxation skills, systematic desensitization was not employed. Efforts to get John to self-disclose about impacted wartime experiences were defensively warded off. He was not ready to open up and re-live the emotions of his experiences. However, John did disclose in a medical report that his first wound was on February 5, 1970, his birthday, when his unit was ambushed and he received shrapnel wounds to his right hand and arm.

During that action, the team had one killed and several others wounded. When the team had returned to the landing zone from the mission, the whole team stood down in a defiant action of disapproval of the orders issued by Command which ultimately caused the death of a team member and injuries to others. Most of the platoon was angry and retreated to the wet canteen to get drunk. John went to the base hospital and had his wounds attended to and then returned to his hootch to sleep.

Later that evening, platoon member Darryl P., drunk and disorderly, entered John's hootch while he was sleeping; threw a blanket over John's head and proceeded to viciously beat him into unconsciousness. At that moment of the attack, John was unable to protect himself. The assault left John badly beaten and traumatized by one of his own. John laid charges against the Ranger who so cowardly attacked him, but it is uncertain if any disciplinary action was administered.

The second time John was wounded was in the summer of 1970 when he received grenade shrapnel to both his front legs as a result of an ambush. When he returned to base, he went to the hospital center and had his wounds attended again.

Finally, the ultimate war tragedy in John's life happened on March 7, 1971. John was on a mountaintop with five other Rangers engaged in a radio relay mission. There was a grenade explosion. John was hit in the front left thigh with a large piece of grenade shrapnel and was medically evacuated along with one other wounded Ranger, who received a serious wound in the upper body. John's best friend and Team Leader, Sgt. George Morgan, was instantly killed by the explosion as John witnessed him being torn apart by the grenade.

Overall in Vietnam, according to John's memoirs, he was involved in 70 to 100 incidents in which he had a high probability of being killed. He participated in 84 missions and 13 combat assaults with confirmed kills. John's flashbacks and nightmares were mostly about more bazaar incidents, such as the suicide of two Americans and the overkill of local civilians.

John settled into the PTSD unit at North Chicago VAMC hospital and wrote the following hopeful and heartfelt letter to David.

North Chicago VAMC
Building 135G
PTSD unit
North Chicago, Illinoi
60064
Ph: 312-473-9877
July 28/84

Dear David;

Hope this letter finds you well and happy. Things are going well here now that I've finally arrived for the treatment program. This Post traumatic Stress program appears to be just what I need. I was accepted into the program just this past Tuesday but already I seen what the thing is all about and how it works. It's kind of like a overdue or belated de programing. They aren't trying to tell anyone of us to forget (there's no forgetting) but they are working with each of us to learn how to handle it all better than we have in the past.

The VA facility here is huge but they set aside one building for this program so we have alot of privacy. In the program there are 15 of us heavy combat vets. The staff are very sincere and dedicated to their jobs and us. I feel right now that my life is about to get influenced considerably.

Page 2

Again I gotta thank you David for sticking
by me through this. I've still got a long way to go
but it's just good to know I'm not completely alone.
The way I was feeling there for awhile I really didn't
care about anything, especially not myself. All
this time, and working with doctors and people that
really care has opened me up to ways I could really
do some good. So once I get fixed here I'm going
to finish that book and go on from there. This treatment
could go 6 months, it's hard to say right now.

It's sad under these circumstances but here
we have all these combat vets together sharing
space and time trying to undo all the damage that
was done just trying to survive and get home. We
still gotta fight together after everything, after
all that time. Everybody here's really hoping this
will make a difference.

This place will be home for awhile I'm afraid
I never lived in Illinois before but I walked across
it in '82. What some people will do just to get to
Chicago hey.

Page 3

David I gotta tell you what's going on here so that you understand. we (combat vets) saw some pretty heavy fighting and we pulled some pretty heavy stuff to stay alive and because alot of us were trying to win a war. Well there was no plan to win at all and we got pulled out without a victory and the nation dumped it in our lap for whatever happened over there. Instead of being able to think that what you did was for your country the only thing you had left was that you just did it - you were to blame. Well since that happened, over 60,000. guys decided it wasn't worth the headache so they killed themselves, tens of thousands have been in mental institutions for years and aren't getting out, tens of thousand more have been in mental institutions and are now out around drugged on medication so they won't do much of anything, hundreds of thousands more are being treated at outreach vet centers while they try to work and keep their families. Hundreds of thousands of vets are stoned most of the time on drugs and booze trying their damdest to forget. The booze and drugs got them so screwed they don't know what their problem used to be. The really lucky ones like me are getting this new treatment that didn't come soon enough to save alot of the boys.

I'm lucky David

Page 4

I did get a letter from Cathy. She sent me some pictures of herself and the children. Her letter was quite warm and friendly so I wrote back as quickly as I could. Her children certainly seem like nice enough company and I thought she must be fulfilled as a mother.

With all that's going on in my life I still get alot of time to think about you. I remember both the bad/lean times as well as the good. Now that you've taken the big step with owning property I know you're going to be okay. There was never much reason for worry about how you would do since you were always much more conservative than I - much more realistic. I came off the war experience running and I've been running ever since. Big dreams and all that were just some escape to stay on the move. Stopping meant being stoned or drunk or both. Now though David we'll see if I can pull this thing together to make it mean something. It's just a real comfort at this stage to know you are safe and away from the madness I know.

Take care until later

Yours
John Blake

PS
Send hello
Bonnie

Approximately four months of treatment had passed at North Chicago VAMC, and it was agreed that John could take a therapy break. He then turned to planning another advocacy march titled the *Living Tribute*, which he could accomplish during his time off from treatment. John set the program up quickly to commemorate and promote the scheduled turn-over ceremonies of the Vietnam Veterans Memorial complex, built by the veterans with public support funding and soon to be given freely to the nation in Washington D.C. From the point where John had ended the *Transcontinental March--of 1982* at Yorktown, Virginia, he planned to march the colors (American flag) 200 miles to Washington, as a *Living Tribute March* and present the flag to the National President of the American Gold Star Mothers.

In a letter written by John to David on September 3, 1984, John stated.

> David,
> I'm well on the mend down here. As a result of all the therapy and stuff, I have come to know myself more and can identify in some ways, where I have continually undermined even my own best efforts in life. It is not hard to imagine that I will come out of this experience with more control of myself than I've ever had. That will all get put to good use, too.
>
> There's no way to say how long I'll be here. I'll be taking off in time to carry the colors from Yorktown to Washington if it's at all possible. I really want to.
>
> If I'm not finished with the program by then I believe they'll let me take a break from therapy long enough to do that. That walk is important to me as a veteran.
>
> You told me recently that I should put all this Vietnam stuff behind me. I tried that David. I became a hippy, a husband, a father and a drunk. I can't run away from it, I have to face it head-on.
>
> I'm hopeful that soon I will be satisfied with all I have done. Soon I will know. We all will. Like it or not I have established myself as one of the foremost veterans' spokespersons in the nation and that's really worth my time. Say, I really hope

everything is going okay for you. I miss you, David. I'll be in touch brother and take care.

All is well and getting better.

Always, John

By early November, John had benefited enough from treatment that he was not considered to be suicidal nor homicidal. The frequency of intrusive recollections had decreased slightly, but the intensity still remained moderately emotionally disruptive. His self-esteem had increased, and he was deemed competent to handle his own funds.

John was released from VAMC hospital in Chicago on November 7$^{th}$ to attend the unveiling of the Three Soldier Memorial in Washington on Veterans Day. John planned to complete the last phase of his journey and mission of the *Transcontinental Walk-One for the Boys* by carrying the American flag to the final phase of the dedication of the Vietnam Veterans' Memorial. He had hoped that David would join him in Washington; unfortunately, David had commitments and was unable to attend.

For the last time in his life and during a cold, damp day in November, John Blake, The Walker, dressed in battle fatigues and proudly carried a full combat load as well as Old Glory, (a gifted flag from the Yorktown County Commission and the National Park Service.) The nation's flag whipped in the breeze while John walked his final 200 miles between Yorktown, Virginia to Washington, D.C. in honor of the Vietnam veterans, and the National Vietnam memorial site, which now included the newly unveiled Three Soldier Memorial monument. John ended the walk on Veteran's Day at the Vietnam Memorial in Washington, D.C. In a private ceremony held near the Three Soldier Statue, and just after President Reagan's speech, John presented the flag to Mrs. Lois Freeman, National President of the American Gold Star Mothers.

John extended his arms with his hands firmly clasped on the flag staff and presented the American flag, which now gently fluttered in the soft breeze, to the Gold Star Mother. Mrs. Freeman also extended her hands and accepted the flag as she listened to John say, "Dear Mother, please for you and on behalf of those sons who did not survive the fighting in Vietnam, accept these colors from one on behalf of those sons who did survive the fighting. The Vietnam veteran had no battle flag returned to America. I have known this and it has moved me to march under colors across this nation. You take this now and know that we love you and this glorious flag."

Tears stung Mrs. Freeman's eyes as she accepted the colors on behalf of all Gold Star Mothers. Her mind reflected on her own son, who was a marine and had died in the Vietnam War from a gunshot wound to the head. She held firmly to the flag staff and pulled it close to her heart and silently wept as she whispered, "Thank you. I will keep it always!"

John fought hard to hold back his own tears. Lynn stood nearby and observed the ceremony, and she was happy. John was happy! Jack Bortoli Jr., a Vietnam veteran from Michigan, who had come to Virginia to help Lynn coordinate the program, was pleased as well.

Jack and John returned Lynn to her home in Yorktown. They spent a few hours together at Yorktown battlefield where John proudly gave Jack the onsite history that regarded the Battle of Yorktown in 1781. The historical time was when General George Washington overwhelmingly defeated Lord Cornwallis's British Army and caused the surrender and end of the American Revolutionary War. They both left Lynn in good spirits, and John felt hopeful that his forthcoming return to VAMC, Chicago, might just do the trick for him. There was hope for both John and Lynn.

The men drove to Michigan where John spent a few days with Jack's family in Grand Haven (Al Capone's former rest area). John felt very good about things generally and was especially delighted to spend time with Jack's father and namesake Jack Bortoli, Sr. who, among other things, used to be Rocky Graziano's sparring partner.

John treasured the rich history of America's battles. He held great pride and faith in America and its people—especially, his Vietnam veteran brothers—when he stated, "I strongly believed that the Vietnam veterans held true to their duty and service in a troubled time. In spite of it all, the veterans and people of America grew from the experience."

## Too Much Too Soon—John Relapsed 1985

As previously arranged, John returned to VAMC, Chicago hospital to participate in the planned Therapy Program for PTSD. In very short order, his therapists launched into a no-holds-barred therapy, and all concerned were interested in getting the job done.

However, as a direct result of the "hard-push prescribed therapy," John overdosed on his return hospital stay and relapsed. The intense work triggered memories and he responded with tremendous anger. Many approaches were pursued therapeutically to break through the anger, but none were successful at that time.

Finally, John broke a hospital rule and misbehaved when he yelled at a nurse, a cardinal sin, strictly prohibited by hospital policy. Hospital authorities decided that therapy for John would abruptly cease. John declined cool-off time in the maximum security psych ward, so he was ordered to pack his belongings as he was being immediately discharged. While he packed, Lynn telephoned to get an update from John's psychiatrist and was informed of John's current circumstance.

The psychiatrist advised her, as he did each time she called, to go on with her life. Lynn was appalled, as was John, to find out that he was being discharged without any planning, medications, or funds. It was near the end of winter in North Chicago, and he had nowhere to go. It was a bad situation gone worse. John left the premises and sat outside the hospital gate in the freezing rain for seven hours. Finally, he conceded and went back into the hospital and checked himself in to be locked down in observation for one week.

While in lockdown, John proceeded to get his thinking back on track and worked several days to coordinate a discharge plan, which would see him on his way to Ohio where he would stay for a while with some veteran friends. His Vietnam veteran friends in Ohio were as equally supportive now as they were in the earlier activities of Operation Backtrack and the VVA Presidential campaign. It was decided among John's peers that he would reside with Steve Ratcliffe and his wife, who offered to share their home, a wholesome environment. He had been a helicopter crew chief in Vietnam, and they both treated each other with dignity and respect. The Ratcliffe's residence was a safe haven for John. He worked on controlling his anger without medication or therapy. John took care not to laden himself with day-to-day stressors and avoided exposure to emotionally volatile situations. He remained friendly and cooperative but avoided developing close relationships.

Within a few weeks, the Veterans Administration rated John as 100% disabled and back paid his claim. The benefit pension provided enough money for him to pay his few debts and allow him financial stability for the rest of his life.

By midsummer, John had moved back to Virginia. Lynn and John were both convinced that private psychiatry would be his only recourse to fully resolve his difficulties and attain a healthy recovery from the PTSD storm. Lynn located a private psychiatrist in Norfolk, VA, and by the fall John received regular therapy intervention. Both John and Lynn entertained a renewed hope in weathering John's mental health crisis under the watchful eye of the newly found psychiatrist.

The psychiatrist made every effort to break down John's defenses and permit the counseling sessions to rebuild John's cognitive behavior and acceptance skills. It was a form of therapy that would enable John to function more effectively in society. But after just six sessions and during a meeting with both John and Lynn, the psychiatrist broke the bad news. He spoke directly to Lynn when he said, "I can't do anything with John's PTSD at this time, because he is waging an all-out defense both internally and emotionally against the effects of the therapy. So, either he beats PTSD on his own, or it brings him to his knees. If he beats it, fine; then he can get help to keep going forward. If PTSD brings him to his knees, then I can treat him."

"Poor Lynn," John thought, as he knew she finally understood the total effect of what they were both up against. As a couple, they both knew that they would have to separate. It was the end of an era.

The psychiatrist stayed on John's case to provide crisis intervention and general referrals. By the time Christmas rolled along, John was extremely depressed and frustrated to such an extent that it was necessary for him to be referred to the local veterans' hospital for stabilization. John stayed six weeks at McGuire VAMC hospital in Richmond, VA.

## Picking up the Pieces and Moving On

Prior to discharge from McGuire VAMC, it was recommended that John should be seriously considered for intense inpatient therapy. John's attending physician at McGuire hospital put every effort into John's discharge plan for follow-up treatment. Since the Veterans Administration was in the process of incorporating the private sector initiatives of Diagnostic Regulatory Guidelines (DRG) and his stay on the acute ward already exceeded those guidelines, John would have to leave and be placed on a waiting list for inpatient therapy. The attending physicians informed John that Dr. Ryan wanted to work with him on an outpatient basis.

John felt well-rested and more stable when he was discharged from VAMC McGuire Hospital. He moved into a temporary residence located in Williamsburg, VA. Lynn's visits to Williamsburg were infrequent, but John seized the opportunity to read, meditate and take long walks. He felt ready to deal with that part of his illness that caused him to feel alienated socially. He realized he needed to take his time in becoming assimilated socially and rebuild his confidence and self-esteem. Williamsburg was steeped with history, and John had a penchant and fondness for history that he could pursue in his new environment. He now felt ready to deal with several aspects of his PTSD.

At first, John felt awkward as he spent more time in the community and responded to civilians who greeted him. John realized that he wasn't good at small talk, but he made a conscious effort to practice tolerance and patience. He practiced with people he met by leading them in general conversations, which were in no way related to military or veteran issues. He focused on their reply in order to engage in an appropriate response and generate more dialogue. The effort met with success as he tried to adapt to everyday life as a civilian. For the first time in John's life, he had to consciously focus on his communication skills.

John decided that it was time for him to try his hand at some work. He walked into a paint store across from the George Washington Hotel and offered his name and telephone number in case any of their customers might require professional painting assistance. He realized that it would have been a bit farfetched to try and resurrect his accounting skills. He reasoned that due to his PTSD, his concentration abilities had deteriorated, and he was simply not at that level of efficiency. John decided that he would first try and develop work skills and establish good habits. As it happened, a local contractor was in the paint store and inquired about John's qualifications. When he realized that John was a full journeyman painter, the contractor hired him on the spot. John was delighted and painted for the contractor at nearby Busch Gardens.

John frequently had difficulty making it to the job site, but his boss understood. John persevered and eventually worked, what he alone believed, the laziness out of himself. At first, he found it hard to keep up with the other workers on the job, but with the passage of time, that too began to improve. John started to feel good about his progress and soon realized that he had the beginnings of a somewhat normal life. Much like other people, he now had his work to complain about for small talk, and his new friends seemed to want him around to share a social beer and conversation. Pretty soon he became a part of the group and found himself invited to shoot pool on his days off with his coworkers. John's internal difficulties continued, but in-between those times he was happy.

During a long weekend, Lynn visited John to inform him that Steve in Ohio had called and said that there was a need for advocacy support for James and Dave at the Dayton Veteran Center. James was the team leader of the Vet Center Program, and Dave was a senior counselor. Both counselors were previously combat officers in Vietnam. In addition, both were well established as gifted therapists to Vietnam veterans. Each had impressive track records, especially in crisis intervention that was needed by veterans daily. They were also advocacy associates on all of John's major programs plus dear friends to both Lynn and John.

The VA was head-hunting in an early attempt to purge the Veteran Center Programs of those employees who were truly dedicated to the veterans and also those who were opposed to absorbing veteran centers into VA Hospitals. The authorities threatened not to renew James's and Dave's contracts. Moreover, the VA wanted to move the Veteran Center itself. Immediately, Lynn and John drove to Dayton, Ohio and spent the entire weekend strategizing a plan. Together they drafted a public relations campaign and wrote letters to politicians and persons of interest in the Veteran Administration. They also laid the groundwork for a Veterans Resource Center out of which James could continue his work. On their return to Virginia, the pair agreed that it was a nasty piece of business all around.

The Veterans Administration is comprised of large numbers of employees; most are good at their jobs, and others appear less so. Some are motivated by helping veterans, and then there are others who seemed to resent being there. Somewhere in the middle of that entire scenario, are individuals who use their positions to do their best for humanity while other individuals use their positions for their own career advancement. Notwithstanding, there are veterans - some legitimate and some who are not. Veterans who are being wheeled or led by the arm in various pursuits within a disparity of health services that are often insufficient.

John realized that it was all too damn agonizing and frustrating for a veteran in mental health pain or misery to be bothered with seeking help. For those who pursued help, many veterans fell through the cracks without legitimate reason. The VA was a nightmare.

Somehow, John felt he was one of the lucky ones who didn't fall through the VA cracks in the early stages of his crisis intervention. The VA saved his life and taught him about himself, educated him and stood him back up. John felt obligated to temper his criticisms with some mercy. But often he felt that the intervention he received didn't change his opinion of the pending changes in the VA. John felt that he must heal quickly and get out of the system before it destroyed the opportunity the VA gave him.

∞

# Chapter 10

## Troubling Times in 1986

JOHN LAUNCHED INTO HIS NEW WORLD of employment and attended a weekend social barbecue with his co-workers. After a few hours of socializing he felt anxious and excused himself from the barbecue social, to wash his car. His friend, Gary, ran after him and offered to help. Gary suggested that they both go and shoot some pool later, which they did.

At the pool hall, the tables were paired up with players. Gary and John were actually winning all their games. They kept winning and met some friendly people at first and then, predictably, a few not so friendly.

They each sipped on their bottle of beer while they stayed on top of their game. John soon figured out that a couple of the earlier losers now shadowed Gary and him. John became uneasy about their newly acquired audience and told Gary that they should give up the table and move on as soon as they finished the game.

Just as John expected, as soon as he and Gary exited the premises, several guys began to follow them into the parking lot and began to shout verbal insults at the pair. Gary got angry very quickly and began to shout back. John knew he was in a difficult and stressful situation when out of the blue John stepped forward, reached into his pocket and briefly flashed his Uniformed Service Identification card. Without even thinking he said, "Back up boys, CIA."

The rogues quickly froze in their tracks, and both Gary and John hastily retreated into the vehicle and left the parking lot.

They were cruising smoothly along a country road when Gary asked to see John's I.D. card, which John then took from his pocket and handed to Gary. He asked John if he had ever been an operative.

John replied, "NO!"

Gary continued talking, telling John about a firefight he was involved in down in Mexico. He was going on and on about the firefight while John worked on keeping his focus on both his driving and Gary's story. Suddenly, John had a flashback—big, fast and real! It came and went quickly, but it rocked John so strongly that he jerked the car to the roadside and slammed the driving gear into park.

Gary roared, "What the hell is wrong?"

John immediately replied, "Nothing Gary, let's get home!"

Gary offered to drive the car and John should have let him since he was a nervous wreck following the flashback, but he restarted the vehicle and immediately moved back onto the roadway.

John had never before experienced a flashback while actually driving. He attributed that to the effort required in paying attention to the demands of driving a vehicle and the eye movement that was required to watch the road and surrounding areas. Sometimes, during daytime driving, John would pull his vehicle over to the side of the road and stop because he would become fixated on the forest and tree lines. He was always alert to that tendency, and occasionally would stop and get out of the vehicle to take a short walk. The fixation had never been anything he could not handle. Flashbacks, however, were another matter. Remembering the time when he crashed his truck in a spontaneous suicide attempt, John realized that he should have allowed Gary to drive the vehicle.

It was likely the conversation with Gary that triggered the flashback. Traffic was heavy and they had not gone very far when John experienced a vision that was like a neon light, which wouldn't stop flashing.

John couldn't stop the vehicle, or turn it to the left, but he knew he had to find a way. He was scared to death. The flashing vision continued. Suddenly, he got a glimpse of what appeared to be a roadway on his right-hand side. He made a sudden turn, stopped the vehicle, slammed the shift into park and turned off the ignition. Gary was frantic, and told John that the car was sitting on the railway track. John opened the door and walked half a mile down the tracks while trying to focus his attention on the present. Gary attempted to back the vehicle off the tracks but the vehicle was hung up underneath. John had headed towards some nearby lights, and Gary began to chase after him on foot.

He caught up with John at a nearby store and tried to tell John that he could get someone to pull the vehicle off the track and back onto the roadway. John told Gary, "Higher Command has got to know about this. I got to call it in!"

Gary was frantic, saying there was no need to report it. John got upset because he couldn't remember the damn frequency or call sign. Gary didn't know what John was talking about. It didn't make sense. Gary left with a man in a pickup truck who had observed the situation and offered to help tow the vehicle.

Somehow, in his distraught mind, John called 911 for help. He felt more troubled than ever before. He saw emergency lights ahead where his car was parked, so he walked towards the lights. Help had arrived! Thank God! He felt joy when he saw the man was in uniform.

There were questions and more questions. The car was still sitting there on the railway track. John felt he had to get this taken care of and get home. He wondered what the problem was. The officer was getting angry. John was frustrated and tried to tell the officer he had to get this situation taken care of, that he was 100% disabled with PTSD, and that he had to get home. John heard the officer say the word, "arrest." John searched frantically for his ID card, which indicated his disability. He couldn't find it because Gary still had it.

John sensed a flurry of movement, a flash of something bright and a metallic click. He pushed off from the person nearby. Instantly, from a short distance, he recognized the image of a policeman, and it dawned on John that no one else was present. John felt the officer throw him down to the ground and in his own mind two words sounded over and over like a foghorn, "Don't fight."

John was secured in handcuffs and lying in the back seat of the police car, but mentally he was not. He was in a major physiological episode. In his mind, he was with his former best friend Sgt. George Morgan in Vietnam. They were sitting on top of a bunker, at the Ranger base camp, getting drunk and laughing their fool heads off. He could sense laughter throughout his body. That ended abruptly, however, when a bright light shone through the police car window and he heard a man's voice say, "The bastard is crying. I'll give him something to cry about!"

Apparently, a younger police officer with blond hair arrived with a flashlight. He had witnessed John in the back of the police vehicle crying. He jumped into the back of the police car, pinned John down across the seat and proceeded to deliver several forceful punches on the right side of John's stomach. John was aware of what was happening, but he just didn't care anymore. It was all just too much for him to process.

**Few People Understand PTSD and Even Less Care**

Deputy Smith was the first officer who responded to the vehicle that was stuck on the railway tracks. He behaved like a professional and in context with proper procedures. He tried to understand John's confusion and behavior. The second officer was a thug. He created considerable problems for John. The officer assaulted a visibly distressed person who was cuffed and unable to defend himself, and he found satisfaction in placing all the blame on John. The direct influence of that officer's actions compounded an already disturbing experience.

John was released after being charged with assault and battery. He had slapped Deputy Smith during his emotional experience the night before. John decided not to cut and run to the V.A., but rather stand ready and be responsible for his actions. He thought that no matter the complications, just maybe there would be some therapeutic gain from this experience and a forthcoming judicial kick in the butt. Lynn was very alarmed upon learning of John's recent episode. He encouraged her to spend less time worrying about him at that point; he had to find his own way. He had to determine what potential there was for his recovery and what exactly was standing in his way.

John knew he had to get busy. He rejoined the Painters Union to generate more intermittent work. Not being much of a cook, John began eating out during the evening at better restaurants with better food. He stopped reading the contemporary materials and began to revisit his study of the life and works of Emanuel Swedenborg - and one of his personal favorites—William Blake. John often attended services at several different churches in Williamsburg, but for reasons which could not be explained, he would leave the facility for risk of becoming emotionally undone. He believed that he was too distant from God to just walk back into church. Even his two favorite hymns, *Onward Christian Soldiers*, and *Youth of the World Arise*, seemed too far above him at this point in his life. He felt estranged from the very things which had kept him on track throughout his younger years. He recognized his deficiency and acknowledged that some of what he had to accomplish would take time if indeed it ever got done.

Lynn disclosed that she would be moving on with her life and that she had accepted a marriage proposal. John did his best to be supportive and encouraging. He knew it was what she had to do, and he was earnestly happy for her. John loved Lynn too much to continue to draw her into his nightmare. He had always felt hopeful that he would pull his life together to manage his PTSD to an acceptable level of functioning before she would have to save herself. Emotionally, it was a hard time.

John's judicial situation was in the hands of his lawyer, Christy. She was not certain how it would go for him, but felt that if he volunteered to work for the community it could possibly be resolved. They never found out because John was en route to the most disastrous event in his life outside of a war zone.

John felt emotionally numb and listless on a day that resembled the calm before the storm. He had made plans early in the day to rendezvous during the evening with a painter friend. But, in the interim, John needed to be doing something. He decided to go for a long drive on Highway 60 toward Richmond. That route held so much past and current history for John. Lafayette, Rochambeau and Washington marked the last leg of the *Transcontinental March in 1982*, and the first leg of *Living Tribute March in 1984*. John enjoyed his ride down memory lane and arrived back at Williamsburg in unusually good spirits.

He arrived as planned at Ada's Lounge to meet his friend. As he entered the bar, his eyes adjusted to the darkness while he listened to a group of people having an especially fun time. Instinctively, he was drawn to the bar area where the laughter was prominent and decided to have a beer as he waited.

John excused himself as he eased into a vacant seat at the bar between two people and ordered a beer. The woman sitting immediately to his left turned her attention to him, and without any fanfare she planted her lips on his and kissed him. John was taken aback by the sudden attraction and smiled at her. He was somewhat stunned, and focused his gaze toward the back of the bar. When John felt more composed he struck up a conversation with the woman who seemingly was too drunk or stoned to pronounce her name. On the third attempt, she managed to annunciate her name—Lisa. Suddenly, Lisa threw her arms around John's neck pulling him into her face and began French kissing him. John sat there at the bar for a short period of time then slipped away and purposely located a vacant table in order to escape the bar area shenanigans.

He returned to the bar to order a second beer and noticed Lisa grinning at him so he invited her to join him at the table. She became hostile and screamed, "I'm not going anywhere with you!" Then she raised both of her arms to hit John. John blocked her attempt to strike him and grabbed her wrists, one in each hand, to calm her down and avoid further assault. He stood beside her and briefly searched her face, expecting to see or hear something that could explain the situation. At that instant, John was blinded-sided when the house security guard charged into him and racked him up against the bar. John shook the guard off as the man exclaimed, "You have to leave the property!"

John didn't need to hear anymore. He quickly turned about and jogged out of the building and directly to his car. He sat in his car with the motor running and thought, "That I don't understand!"

Suddenly, John saw the house security guard and several other men approach his car. The guard confronted John in the parking lot. The security guard yelled, "Turn off the car and get out of the vehicle!"

John replied, "Forget it, bud. I'm gone!"

Suddenly, the security guard pulled the car door open and grabbed John out from behind the steering wheel, a shoving match ensued, and then a passing police vehicle stopped. Police Sergeant Samson broke up the confrontation. Everyone got bumped, fell or hurt themselves, but the result was that John was arrested and charged with four counts of assault and battery. "What a mess," thought John.

John knew he was in a lot of trouble, and his memory had blocked most of the details of the event. So he enlisted a few friends who located people who were at Ada's Lounge that evening and who had witnessed what had transpired. During the following weeks, John stayed in his apartment afraid that something else would go wrong. Ultimately, John's mental health deteriorated, and he had to be admitted to McGuire VA Hospital at Richmond where he remained for eight days to be stabilized.

Finally, word came in August that the judge wanted the five counts of assault and battery case presented. John was upset because he still did not remember enough details to make any defense. However, his lawyer, Christy, suggested that they go on through with the first hearing, and if they didn't like the outcome, they could appeal. During the court proceeding, Christy did little or nothing with cross-examination and suggested that it was John's fault for not remembering much of the events. John's lawyer proceeded directly into arguing legal technicalities and passed right over any opportunity to introduce witnesses. John just about lost his composure. No witnesses had been summoned on his behalf.

The court attempted to levy mandatory jail time for John under the new Virginia law, which had just gone into effect, but John's lawyer pointed out that the charges preceded the date of the law. Her motion that the security guards had provoked an altercation and exceeded their authority under laws applicable to them when they pursued and confronted was overruled by the court.

John took the stand, and in his own defense said that striking Deputy Smith during the first account of assault was a reflex action and an accident. He suggested, without attacking or defaming the witnesses, that he was not a complete stranger to the establishment or its patrons at Ada's lounge. Also, he testified that he did not attack anyone, but that his reaction was in self-defense.

The court informed the concerned parties that there was enough evidence to convict on all charges, and a date was set for a mitigation hearing.

The time between the trial and the mitigation hearing was a period of great misery for John. He could not keep from reflecting on his life's investment going 'down the tubes'. He was deemed a criminal. He reflected that his life had always been played out with considerable risk at high stakes. He spent all those years of war, peace and in-between, only to get to a point in life where all that he could see before him was a deep, dark socio-judicial hole. He felt that he shouldn't have sought treatment for Post Traumatic Stress Disorder as it had changed him and made him introverted, weak and blindsided. Few people understood PTSD and fewer cared.

His psychiatrist from the Veterans Administration Hospital at Richmond took the stand to testify at the mitigation hearing. The doctor took great pains to explain John's condition and PTSD. He answered some very pointed and articulated questions from John's lawyer and from the Assistant State Attorney. John was mortified at the disclosure of so much detail of his active military duty in Vietnam. He felt that the court would view him more of a threat than ever. The court was attentive to his doctor's disclosure, and John felt scared. He thought, "Were these people going to sentence John Blake or John Rambo?" John's psychiatrist was trying to save him when he stated to the court, "John will not survive incarceration."

The judge was concerned as to whether John was salvageable, and the doctor stated, "Very much so. In fact, they (VA) are not going to give up on him."

Then John took the stand and stated there was a lot he felt that he should have said and wanted to say. He just couldn't get it cognitively together as effectively as when he had been engaged in public speaking forums prior to becoming mentally ill with PTSD. However, John told the court that he and people like him needed to be thoroughly debriefed after the war instead of being told to stifle the memories and experiences. John apologized for his misbehavior in the community. He told the court that although he knew it was a serious matter of having failed to integrate or assimilate into civilian life, he wasn't going to give up. John also stated that he would continue to learn new skills and engage in continuous and new therapies that would enable him to take control of and manage his Post Traumatic Stress Disorder.

Near the end of the proceeding John was brought close to tears. In his closing remarks, the Assistant State Attorney commented on the overall situation and bluntly stated, "I just wish John Blake would get through with all of this difficulty and get on with his life!" John felt that he, too, was trying to save himself from a harsh sentencing.

When the judge rendered his findings and judgment on the case, everyone present bore witness to an example of hard justice tempered with mercy.

The judge stated, "Mr. Blake, this court finds you guilty on all five charges of assault and battery. You are to receive a sentencing of five times twelve months incarceration, to run consecutively without parole. This sentence is suspended in lieu of three years supervised probation."

Conditions of probation were discussed in detail but can be summarized that John continue with therapy at the VA and attend monthly meetings with a case worker/liaison of the court. The judge's final statement rung the loudest, "If this does not work, I will take Mr. Blake off the street for a long time!"

While John reeled under the ominous shades of that last foreboding statement, the judge added, "Mr. Blake, this court wants to thank you for your service to your country!"

John was stunned for a split second and then felt a warm glow of understanding. No words of appreciation had ever truly reached him before, and he realized it was because of the context of those proceedings that the words finally got through now. John knew that the judge meant it! He left the court building with a sense of empowerment, determined to keep his freedom no matter what the cost.

John fully recognized that PTSD is a disabling psychological condition that affects veterans and civilians in varying degrees and disrupts all areas of life experiences if not self-managed. John was armed with his own profound experiences and recognition of his PTSD, a major socio-judicial shortfall coupled with a court order in four parts plus the closing remarks of the Assistant State Attórney and the trial judge. John hit the ground running.

John arrived curiously optimistic at the Veterans Administration Hospital at Richmond for his initial out-patient treatment. He wasn't completely certain that his original psychiatrist would be taking care of his case, but it seemed reasonable. Much to John's surprise and shock, he was assigned to an oriental woman, Dr. Ki.

It just didn't add up as he thought, "How could they do this to me?" John felt that this was no time to be hit with such provocative stimuli, a pair of deep searching oriental eyes. John felt that he already had enough problems. Suddenly, he recognized that he wasn't ready for this trigger. But then he told himself, "Hey, you're going to blow yourself out of the water if you complain about the staff members. Ranger on!" Besides, he didn't want to hurt the woman's feelings. Plus, he figured that his psychiatrist was likely somehow behind the arrangement. John trusted his psychiatrist so he convinced himself that he had to try harder and do his very best. He didn't want to make any problems. But, for the record, he knew there would be days when 'oriental eyes' were going to be too much for him.

John sensed that his psychiatrist knew that, too. Still, John wondered why the doctor had set him up for 'hardball' at a time like this. He never asked him because he couldn't bring himself to pose the question aloud. He decided he would have to work with it and just hope it wouldn't cause anyone but himself a problem. Besides, he thought if he could get to where 'oriental eyes' did not faze him, even on the bad days, then that would certainly be making progress. So he went for it.

John followed through with regular meetings with his court-appointed case worker, Miss Chad. They developed an associate rapport that met their mutual concerns. John was relieved because he didn't want to get into any mind games with people. He informed Miss Chad that on occasion she would see firsthand some of what PTSD is about, and she laughed at that news. John laughed too, knowing that it wasn't a laughing matter.

Therapy at the VA became redundant despite all the work that John had accomplished in previous treatments. Dr. Ki had foregone any work on previously identified stressors or even behavior modification. Her intent was instead on walking all the way up memory lane from day one in John's life recollections to wherever. In the fall of 1986, John was leaning more on Miss Chad to listen to his gripes, frustrations, and to help him analyze his thinking.

John began to feel that the VA had dropped the ball. He continued to experience his PTSD fallout with corresponding times of being debilitated by the effects. On several occasions, he discussed situations that concerned his deep depression, anxiety, intrusive thoughts and hypervigilance with Dr. Ki. However, she simply wrote another prescription for more and stronger drugs. It was a tough time for John.

Finally, John decided that he needed to make better use of his time. He decided to move to Richmond, to be closer to the VA and his caseworker. He hoped this would give him a second chance at integration and assimilation. John felt he was in better shape this time to get on with his life.

John was aware that in nearby Washington, D.C., two Airborne Rangers, Michael Kentes, Jr., and Thomas Dineen, Jr., had put in a couple of hard years to pull together a National Association of the Airborne Rangers and Long Range Reconnaissance Patrols (LRRPs) of the Vietnam War. A convention in Alexandria was scheduled for the following Veterans Day weekend. John decided to go to Washington and see what was what. He understood that the boys were fed up with the lack of participation they had received, and the consensus was 'form up or forget it'!

John had already seen his own advocacy dreams get away from him during the VVA election, and he felt he knew something about what it would mean if these guys had to let their dreams go too. John made sure that his Ranger friends and acquaintances knew about his life struggles with PTSD and his previous run-in with the judicial system. Much to his own surprise, he came away from the convention as the first elected National Executive Director. Of fewer than thirty Rangers, he was nominated by his former Ranger friend from South Dakota. The organization had no money, internal structure or by-laws, and John didn't even own a typewriter, much less a computer, but somehow everything would come together. They each left the convention with the understanding that they would make something of the organization, more so now than ever before.

John returned to Richmond and reported the news of his elective office to everyone in his life. They seemed to be genuinely pleased. He reassured all concerned that he had not returned to full-time advocacy but was just being helpful as a public servant.

John kept up his court-manadated appointments with the caseworker and the therapist, but his therapy treatment was going nowhere. Christmas was coming and John made it a personal goal to stay out of the hospital for the first Christmas in three years, which he did.

By the end of December, John was a full-fledged resident of Richmond, Virginia. It was ironic that he would return under those circumstances to the same city that he had passed through in 1982 during the final leg of the Transcontinental March. During that year he was given the 'key to the city' of Richmond. And now, he had quietly come back to the city, all but beaten in life.

John focused his attention toward the arts and artistic pursuits and signed a lease on a very comfortable, quiet and artsy flat directly across the street from the Virginia Museum of Fine Arts. He gathered all his records and files from Lynn's residence. This would be the first time since May 1984 that he and his writings plus his research records were under the same roof. He had all the comforts of domestic service and furniture, and the location was just five miles from the VA.

Dr. Ki advised John that she would be on a three-week vacation during Christmas and that if he needed anything, he could visit the hospital for general services. John thought, "Not this year lady, I'm going to wing it!"

Four months into his judicial contracts at Williamsburg, John felt confident that he was on the right track. He decided against being a subjective, unwilling victim of PTSD because that attitude was not doing him any good. He leaned on the tools he had acquired from the VAMC in Chicago and, in particular, self-management within the limits of his comfort and acceptance of his war experiences.

There had been surprisingly few occasions during those four months when John had to cancel an appointment because of PTSD. But as time passed, life became more of a struggle than normal. John had to work harder at keeping himself together or else many more appointments would have been canceled.

One day, John's therapy session with Dr. Ki had been canceled by the V.A. at a time when he felt burnt out from intrusive thoughts. He purposely drove from Norfolk to Williamsburg, a one-hour drive, in order to show Miss Chad, his court assigned caseworker an example of what a 'stress attack' was all about. Miss Chad concurred with John's conviction that there would be times when he should not be out and about.

John believed it was one of his responsibilities to remain at home whenever these episodes struck. He felt that those devastating times were his personal and private miseries and that no one could help him. He never meant to bother, insult or garner sympathy from family, friends or professionals. He strongly believed that this was the price for each bad episode because of his earlier years in Vietnam. They were his alone to endure.

When the residual effects during the episodes had decreased in strength or when they had passed entirely, John would attempt to go on with his life and do what he was supposed to be doing. Nevertheless, he found himself verbally venting.

Recognizing stressors and understanding acute reactions are tools that make a bad situation manageable. Practicing situational preparedness was a necessary exercise for John in dealing with the unexpected triggers. Balancing daily activities with relaxation exercises were essential in coping with everyday experiences. Still, there would be many times when PTSD would lift its monstrous head and remind John that there was no cure. It was tough all around for him and self-management was critical in coping with and surviving PTSD.

On the day of his next VA appointment, John collected his vehicle from the repair shop, ate his lunch and proceeded to the hospital. He had only driven twenty miles when the vehicle broke down again, and he missed his VA appointment with Dr. Ki. As a result, John received a letter from the VA on his 38th birthday' from McGuire Hospital. Dr. Ki informed him that his treatment plan was terminated. All the alarms went off, especially, the court order. It insisted that he attend regular mental health therapy for the next three years or else he would be incarcerated for five years for noncompliance to the court agreement.

John immediately contacted and explained the situation to Miss Chad. They both had serious concerns as the action was taken without any counseling or alternative arrangements. John reminded Miss Chad that at one time his psychiatrist had commented that the way John was let go from North Chicago was 'criminal' on the part of the VA. McGuire hospital was now doing the same thing. Also, during the trial, his psychiatrist told the court at Williamsburg that they "were not going to give up on John Blake!" Why this now? John was convinced that the VA was either using some profound carrot and stick psychology, for which they were notorious, or they were truly setting up for an agency hand-off. John was furious at both possibilities. In terminating his service at the VA, they were implying that John could manage without therapy, which was not what he or Miss Chad felt was correct.

Miss Chad empathized that she had to account for John being in therapy once a week. John researched the availability of an alternative therapist. He first telephoned his psychiatrist who informed him that the Chief of Psychiatry at the VA was mad at him and probably wouldn't let him on the ward. John's psychiatrist stated, "It is time for you to talk to Dr. Dee, a Vietnam veteran at the Veteran Center and see if he can fit you in."

"What about our earlier plan for you to take me on as a case in your private practice?" John asked.

"No can do, I'm too busy here at the VA, and my private practice is booked solid, but you can call Dr. Tory," he replied. "I heard he is still taking some new patients."

John didn't waste any time. He placed a call to both Dr. Tory's private practice and Dr. Dee at the Veteran Center. After he completed his telephone calls John was confident and relieved that Dr. Tory would return his call later in the day. In the meantime, an appointment was set up for the next day with Dr. Dee, whom he had previously met in passing.

During the past years, John had spent time with Dr. Dee as a friendly acquaintance, but since becoming ill, John felt inclined to spare him any involvement with his condition. Now, John had called upon the doctor with an appeal for help.

Dr. Dee made it easier for John than it might have been had the doctor not been such a true professional. He explained that he knew a lot about John's case and would set a therapy schedule for him, which would provide for his needs, both clinically and judicially. John was elated. He immediately informed Miss Chad, and she, too, was happy. Dr. Tory returned his call that same evening, and John informed him that he felt confident that he would be in very good hands with Dr. Dee.

The following week during a team meeting at the Veteran Center, Dr. Dee assigned Jake as a therapist for John's case. Jake, also a Vietnam veteran and thoroughly briefed in John's case, interviewed John. Together they constructed a plan of attack to address John's issues.

**Hello, I Am Your Dad**

With John's permission, Dr. Dee wrote a letter to me in Newfoundland. He asked if I would contact John's former wife and persuade her to allow John to have contact with his daughter, Rachel, who was now a teenager.

Upon receipt of Dr. Dee's letter, I immediately telephoned him, and we shared a lengthy conversation. Dr. Dee realized that we dearly loved our brother John but that John's families were naive about his current health condition. John seldom shared intimate details regarding his mental health issues. I disclosed to Dr. Dee that when John returned from Vietnam he had built a wall of protection to shelter all of us from his world.

I informed Dr. Dee that I was the only remaining sibling in Newfoundland and that I had stayed near John's former wife and his daughter and also provided John with pictures and updated news of Rachel throughout the years.

Dr. Dee felt that those years lost between John and his daughter had impeded John's recovery. Perhaps now that Rachel was a teenager, she could make her own decision as to whether she wanted to develop a long- distance relationship with her father.

Dr. Dee proceeded to explain in explicit detail the many facets of John's PTSD. I advised Dr. Dee that I would do my very best to convince John's former wife to help us bridge the gap between John and Rachel. We were ultimately able to accomplish this.

A few weeks later, John received a telephone call from his former wife telling him that it would be fine for him and his daughter to get to know one another. Although John did send cards and monetary gifts yearly to Rachel for her birthday and seasonal holidays since he departed Newfoundland, it had been eleven years since they'd had any physical contact or verbal communication. The news literally brought John to his knees. He wept for the lost years they each had missed and for the joy he was about to share with Rachel.

During the following weeks, John and Rachel were reintroduced to each other by telephone. Each time they spoke John was well prepared with a list of questions to ask his daughter. He engaged her in conversation just so he could sit quietly, staring at her picture. He concentrated and listened to and memorized every nuance of personality in her voice from thousands of miles away. He had never heard her speak sentences because she was too young when he left Newfoundland. His chest felt as though it would burst with each wave of unconditional love and emotions that he had carried in his heart but was unable to entertain or share for more than a decade with his little girl.

In between telephone calls, John wrote two important letters to his daughter. He knew from that point that everything between him and Rachel would be okay and all was understood and forgiven. Dr. Dee had been correct to intervene on John's behalf. John's brother and sisters were equally happy that father and daughter were now reunited. Moreover, we were especially pleased for John's daughter and appreciative of her mother for understanding the importance of communication between John and Rachel.

One should never underestimate the power of a child. John felt more connected and happier than he had ever felt now that he and his daughter were communicating. His therapy and judicial meetings were going well, although every now and then the effects of his PTSD would surface. Some of his days were a bit too rocky for his liking, but that was par for the course.

**Hanging On**

John was committed to the newly formed National Association of the Airborne Rangers and Long Range Reconnaissance Patrols (LRRPs) of the Vietnam War (commonly referred to as the Ranger Association). He had accomplished most of his in-house tasks, which included writing a national constitution. In addition, he was busy setting up a board of directors meeting in Richmond for the first quarterly meeting.

John's weeks became hectic between therapy, judicial meetings and commitment to his work for the Ranger directors' meeting. He began re-experiencing nightmares and cold sweats due to overactivity and stress. The effects of taking on too much, too soon.

The quarterly meeting of the Ranger Association was successful. The group set an agenda and cultivated a sense of unity and direction for the board of directors. John contributed a lot of energy and some financial resources to the newly formed Ranger organization. He hoped that the organization would function well under its own steam and accomplish meaningful work in the future. And it did.

The Mayor of Richmond issued a proclamation in celebration of the Rangers' visit to the city. John was now freed up to pursue his own interests, which had fallen to the wayside. He located a part-time job to keep active and to provide some additional income, which he contributed to the care of his daughter.

Therapy sessions substantially involved John's behavioral and attitudinal shortfalls. John felt that his therapist, Jake, had pressured him too much about the assault events at Williamsburg. His immediate impression of Jake had led him to believe Jake was too much of a watchdog.

John and Jake had shared some intense therapy sessions, after which, John surmised that Jake was relieved when the session ended. John would leave to do a lot of thinking and soul-searching. He recognized those sessions as good therapy and started looking forward to each one, for the simple reason that he was getting solid feedback, and for once it felt right. It wasn't important that John like the feedback or that it be totally applicable, but that it enabled him to think beyond his own past patterns. Jake was helpful and by the end of March, John's impression was that his life was going forward in a positive manner.

All of John's immediate family members, except Mom in Canada, remained in constant communication with him. We still hadn't informed John about Mom's Alzheimer's disease. After years of distress, John's mental health was finally on the upswing largely because he had finally developed a nurturing relationship with Rachel. To upset his well-being with knowledge of Mom's disease at that time would have been cruel. We felt he needed more time to gain his mental strength. Although when Paddy, our stepfather, died on Easter Sunday that same year, we had no choice but to inform John. He took the news very poorly.

John sank into the depths of sadness over Paddy's death. He recalled his step-father's military history. Paddy had served thirty-three years with the Royal Canadian Air Force. He was deployed to a peace-keeping mission with the Canadian contingency that joined the United Nations in Cyprus to keep the peace after the Suez Crisis. John felt it was time to visit Mom and make peace with her regarding his birth certificate.

The next day, John contacted his caseworker, Miss Chad and informed her that he wanted to return to Canada to visit his mother because his stepfather had recently died. Miss Chad expressed her sorrow for John's loss, but reminded him that if he left the country it would be problematic because he had court orders to attend therapy every week. "Sorry Mom," John thought as he concluded the telephone conversation with Miss Chad.

Life went on and so did John. He had pretty much disassociated himself from the Veterans Administration, after he discovered that therapy at the Veterans Center was more effective. He continued to attend his therapy sessions, and occasionally he participated in group sessions when something interesting developed.

During one session, Jake decided to bring up John's misbehavior at Williamsburg as a subject for discussion. Jake asked John, "What could you have done to avoid or defuse either of the two conflict situations?"

John gave the question serious consideration before he replied, "Doc, there was, in each instance, a moment when I knew things were at the crossover point and something bad was going to happen. I know I was putting on my internal brakes, but I couldn't communicate. I just could not get it together. I needed a big sign to hold up that read, 'STOP'! One minute please–person with hidden disability here!" What was missing and would have been helpful was a tool to navigate through a sea of social adjustments in pursuit of wellness. The documented disabled veterans need some precise and explicit commutative medium to use when all else is failing, not a carte blanche on violence or laissez-faire on misbehavior, but a tool that would command simple respect from others and protect our own well-being. A medical alert bracelet with a card for emergency use is needed. The VA could and should do this for us. It should also develop and implement an informative general PTSD community program throughout the system directed solely at emergency responders and the general public. There're a couple of thousand guys out there just like me walking around in public. Half of them are documented right now. I am considered among the worst at 100% disabled, and I don't want any trouble with the civilians."

Jake said it was a good idea and he would submit it for approval. The other attendees felt it had merit. Jake announced during that session that he had completed his Master's Degree and would be moving on.

He asked John if he wanted to continue with group therapy. John explained that along with one-on-one therapy he found group therapy to be beneficial. Jake recommended to his supervisor that John should continue with the designated therapies and wished John to "be well" as they parted company.

John felt mental health to be a hidden disability that ranked among the cruelest pranks of nature. In the midst of all the disabilities that exist among people, PTSD behaved like a veritable evil clown that could hide in a healthy body and otherwise healthy mind. What became more ironic to John was that the person would have to be engaged in multiple life threatening traumatic experiences to acquire this particular disability. Soldiers who have become stricken with a hidden disability, been directly involved with fighting for the life and freedom of others, whereby that disability itself would then threaten one's own life and freedom for some time thereafter. It is believed by some that behind every dark cloud in life there is a hidden blessing. Does not the person without sight acutely refine the remaining four senses? It is rumored that they develop a 'sixth sense'. Does not our society take special notice and care for and about persons living without sight in the community? It was not always so in the past, but now it speaks well of society. Each profoundly physically disabled person possesses a societal recognition and provision. All except those with mental health issues.

Throughout the beginning of civilization most warriors who returned from wars discovered that they had drastically changed not only physically but mentally: Combat Psychoneurosis: nostalgia/malaise (Post civil war—endemic in South), Shell Shock (Post WW1), Combat/Battle Fatigue (Post WWII and Korea) and Post Traumatic Stress Disorder (Post South East Asia, South Vietnam, North Vietnam, Cambodia, and Laos. This would apply to all future wars throughout the world).

There is no blessing, no cure, no relative social recognition, other than academic and overt protective mechanism, and therefore, no societal provision. PTSD victims often look and act like ordinary people. As a direct consequence, they are treated as such. A problem exists, though, because the probability is that they most often will not react as would ordinary people.

The documented, treated, service-connected veteran in pursuit of wellness and conscious of his hidden disability, is not dangerous to others under the effects of Post Traumatic Stress Disorder. However, the veteran is at some risk of injuring himself. The person can be stubborn, obnoxious, easily confused and overly emotional. However, he/she is diagnostically and symptomatically defensive, plus passively aggressive in protecting oneself from harm. He/she can be socially disruptive due to profound deficits in his/her ability to communicate when emotionally upset or under duress. Some misinformed people will say, "I recognize those symptoms in basic criminal types, so there must be some correlation."

That is where the real problem rests. Post Traumatic Stress Disorder kills relationships, careers, hopes and dreams, and in many cases, its host.

**The Walking Wounded**

John struggled with PTSD throughout the remainder of his life as he searched for relief from the torment and fallout of his disability. He traveled in and out of revolving doors at VA hospitals, which for the most part were only effective in stabilizing his immediate symptoms, not the root of his problem. At times, he found temporary solace in counseling at the Veteran Center, which enhanced his ability to maintain some level of functionality. Eventually, however, a trigger or stressor would engulf him and drive him, into yet another major physiological episode. His journey was relentless—one step forward two steps back.

John bore witness to the numerous groundbreaking approaches that pertained to PTSD therapy. These were developed to resolve, understand and process the experiences and traumas associated with PTSD. Many underdeveloped forms of therapies were prescribed to patients during that era to provide some treatment and relief.

Much to John's disappointment, those newly discovered therapies during the 1980's resulted mostly in false hope for an effective recovery and the skills necessary for adjusting to civilian life. Essentially, he and numerous other veterans who lived with PTSD were ill-equipped to manage their emotional/mental health after receiving therapy. Hence, they remained the walking wounded.

During the post-Vietnam era, thousands upon thousands of Vietnam veterans began to exhibit severe symptoms of PTSD. Neither governmental departments of Veteran Affairs, nor mental health responders and physicians-much less society-were prepared to deal with the emotional and mental wounds of the Vietnam veteran. Effective treatment of PTSD would not be established until the early 1990's in the United States. It would be two decades later before the Canadian government would face its crisis with unpreparedness in the delivery of PTSD therapy for military and civilians.

In the 1980's, Vietnam veterans who sought medical intervention for their mental health needs often became the learning tool for the therapists, clinics and hospitals. Lack of experienced professional therapists who understood combat PTSD was a grave concern during the early years that followed the Vietnam War. Soldiers returned home only to continue the battle of integration into civilian life without adequate leadership, support and mental health intervention. This mostly resulted in a lose-lose situation. Conditions would not improve until the turn of the century, often too late for hundreds of thousands of veterans.

In Canada, during the 1980's, the situation for mental health support for PTSD was beyond criminal. At that time, the availability of psychological intervention or a diagnosis of PTSD was unheard of, much less treatable. Canadians who were Vietnam veterans and lived in Canada had little or no alternative but to go back over the border to the United States for mental health treatment, such as it was. Suicide rates among Vietnam veterans in North America were at a historical epidemic rate, soaring to an astronomical number of approximately 65 veterans a day!

Most veteran suicide deaths as a result of injuries pertaining to PTSD were combat veterans, but not all. Many suicidal deaths included service-related personnel who had experienced or witnessed multiple traumas or deaths, such as doctors, nurses, mortuary personnel, embalmers, pilots, field medics, chaplains, donut dollies, etc. No one who participated in the armed forces during wartime was safe from PTSD roulette.

According to John's memoirs and detailed medical records, he had engaged in nearly all available therapy programs that were offered as common practice during the 1980s by the VA. He tried Direct Therapeutic Exposure (DTE), a behavior therapy whereby stressors were vividly and safely confronted. This was often referred to as flooding or implosive therapy. That therapy was deemed better than no intervention at all and not as effective as Traumatic Incident Reduction (TIR). TIR is a regressive desensitization procedure for reducing or eliminating the negative residual impact of traumatic experiences. It is a form of exposure technique, in so far as it would assist the patient to become more aware of the traumatic event.

TIR therapy engaged the patient in repeated exposure to the trauma to desensitize said trauma. Facilitators were required to complete a series of three workshops to be qualified in TIR. These therapies were coping methods and cathartic techniques that made the patient feel better temporarily, but did not improve the person's stability. Ultimately, the root of the problem remained intact and more misguided, incomplete therapy would be forthcoming in an attempt to eliminate and address the source. Coping strategies were not a permanent solution either, as within an hour, a day or a week a stimulus would trigger the patient and result in regression to 'Ground Zero' in a heightened state of distress.

The last therapeutic breakthrough of that decade appeared in 1987 from Dr. Francine Shapiro: Eye Movement Desensitization Reprocessing (EMDR) therapy. EMDR had been introduced in its infancy and practiced without much success during the 1980's, largely due to a lack of experienced trainees. Several decades later, EMDR has shown more positive results in the treatment of addressing and quietening emotional attachments related to traumatic events for persons living with PTSD.

**John discovered a Little Knowledge is Dangerous**

In the following letter dated October 1, 1987, John disclosed facts and truths regarding his life with PTSD to prepare David for a future decision that would in all likelihood occur:

David,

I have tried to be normal, I have failed. I failed because something inside of me continuously flares up and moves me on to some greater challenge, maintaining my freedom.

I am currently spending time in the VA hospital, at Salem Virginia, which is just one step up from prison time. Over the past three years, I have spent more time in VA hospitals than in the community.

My condition is getting worse each year and I've read all the medical reports on me which say in effect the chances for recovery are poor. The end, in cases like mine, is suicide and I'm just trying to hang on to meet my daughter in person, God willing.

David, I don't see myself going down anytime soon. I still got some fight in me. My PTSD is getting to where I can't see the forest for the trees.

David, this Post Traumatic Stress Disorder is eating away at my conscious mind. I am now developing a severe personality disorder, which is currently called borderline (neurosis-self destructive) and that's what is making me less and less compatible with and for society. I've got to watch for new developments in this condition because at some point the VA will take me out of the community for all the old bullshit reasons to include 'my own good and the protection of society'. Essentially a prisoner and you know that Airborne Rangers must never get captured. That would be too much for me to handle and I'd have to exit before that happens.

You should see what they've done to some of the boys. I can't go that route. Bottom line—I will fight for my mental well-being and freedom now like never before. I am, no matter how this letter sounds, still hopeful. I don't write to upset you, but someone in the family needs to know to explain to the others if it goes down. No one need regret anything here because I've had what I needed most always, an exciting life.

The poems I write are very much appreciated by the other heavy combat veterans because I am able to speak for us as a group and raise our issues out from our combined souls. Try to understand them David, and remember that a warrior comes home bearing his shield or he can come home upon his shield. No other way is acceptable. We're not wimps—we carried that fucking war—our leaders were the wimps. We continue to fight that war every day and pay the price for their cowardice.

I am sorry David; I knew I'd have to write this letter one day and this is the time. The court battle in '84 and three years of probation thereafter took a lot of my time, energy, and mental resources. The probation period is concluded. During that period, my private psychiatrist was constantly afraid I was being pushed to the brink; ultimately, the whole process contributed to a powerful regression.

I don't know much about this new Eye Movement Desensitization Reprocessing (EMDR) therapy. But the psychiatrist at the VA wants me to participate in the therapy. If he fails to cure me he just might take it personally and make me the heavy. He's only human and I don't have much faith in miracles, much less relief from my PTSD.

Always, John

**Freedom Isn't Free**

At age 39, after several years of therapy and numerous periods of hospitalization, the Veterans Administration declared John permanently disabled and awarded him a lifetime 100% disability pension. The VA determined that all therapies administered to alleviate John's PTSD symptoms were unsuccessful. He was given a lifetime sentence of medication and a permanent pensionable income but warned to "be a good boy or else." The 'or else' meant a lifetime of incarceration in a mental health institution as a prisoner of circumstances.

∞

# Chapter 11

## Beatrice – New Lease on Life and Living

QUITE BY ACCIDENT IN THE SPRING OF 1989, John met a woman that he immediately felt was trustworthy and non-judgmental. He soon developed a fondness for Beatrice, who preferred to be called Bee. She was born with a disability, suffered abuse and had been oppressed as a child. Bee had survived her childhood by the grace of God and the wisdom of her grandmother. Bee was a gentle and understanding soul who respected John; she treated him with kindness and accepted his disability. The pair immediately bonded.

Within six months, Bee asked John to move into her home, which he did. It was the first time since John and Lynn parted that he would have the nurturing support and companionship of a woman along with a neighborhood that accepted him unconditionally.

John developed a comfort zone and was keenest in communicating with his new surroundings, especially the children. The neighborhood, commonly known as the "hood," was filled with crime and drugs, nevertheless John was not intimidated.

The neighborhood's population largely consisted of single parents, so John felt compassion for the children. He repaired bicycles for neighboring kids and often he purchased a bicycle for those children whose parent could not afford one. He even adopted a stray dog. John was behaving normally.

We were delighted when we received John's letter informing us that he had become more settled. In his previous letters, he indicated that he was all but finished with the V.A. centers No more therapy. In the event of a major depressive episode, he would return to the VA hospital for stabilization, but other than that he would be keeping his distance; more importantly, his freedom. John also provided us with a telephone number to contact him.

John was contented that he had met a nurturing lady and was satisfied with his current lifestyle. Not only did he distance himself from the veteran advocacy work, but he also resigned himself to make every effort to live a somewhat normal life. His relationship with Rachel had blossomed, and he was excited that Rachel was pregnant and he would soon become a grandfather.

We were glad there was little conversation about John writing a book. John's PTSD had weakened his cognitive abilities. Writing his story at that time would certainly have added undue pressure and stress. In the interim, it was a wise move for John not to stir up the demons that constantly lurked in his memories.

Now that John was more settled with his life, we felt the urgency to advise him of Mom's medical condition. Mom was unable to live independently and had been living with a family member for several years. It was just a matter of time until she would require a nursing home for her special needs, safety and well-being. I was nominated to telephone John immediately and explain Mom's poor health.

As I dialed his telephone number, I wondered how much stress and difficulty this next conversation would cause John. When the telephone stopped ringing, I heard a woman's voice.

"Hello."

"Hello, I said. "I am John Blake's sister, Cathy, calling from Canada. Is John there? May I speak to him, please?"

"Yes, he is—just a minute."

I could hear John's footsteps as he approached the telephone.

"Hi Cathy, this is John, good to hear from you. How are you and your children and our mother?"

"We are all doing just fine. How are you today?"

"I have my good days and not so good days. Today is a good day. As you know, it has been nine years since my diagnosis of PTSD, and I have been to hell and back many times since then. Fortunately, I am currently considered emotionally stable with the help of medication. Plus, I have the pension which is helpful—financial security. I feel lucky to be alive, as far as that goes. Have you seen my daughter lately?"

"Yes, she is doing quite well. Won't be long now, and you'll be a grandfather!"

"Imagine, Cathy. I never dreamt I would live long enough to one day expect to be a grandfather. She and I will talk tomorrow."

"That's great! John, Mom is doing well, but there is something you should know about her health. She had been diagnosed with Alzheimer disease a while ago, just after her 65th birthday, during the time when you were extremely sick. Don't be upset with us for not telling you sooner. We decided not to tell you then because you were in a critical condition."

"No, I can't be upset with you guys. I am feeling sad about Mom. Talk to me about her."

"Well, John, shortly before Paddy died, Mom started to misplace and lose things more often than usual, like cash and her pension cheque. She would hide those items in her apartment and not be able to remember where she put them. Then she would call one of us to come to her place and find the lost items. She often locked herself out her apartment without her keys in her pocket, and we would go to her aid. She would frequently become agitated and frustrated, which was out of character for Mom. We really became alarmed when Mom started cooking food every other day in extremely large quantities to feed the hungry children on television. She'd make several cooked casseroles every few days, and we'd have to go over to her place and take the food away. Finally, she started forgetting to put the yeast in her homemade bread. It was then that we knew she wasn't firing on all cylinders. We had Mom assessed by health specialists and discovered that she possessed only a small fraction of her memory. On that day the doctor told her, in front of us, that she was not to live on her own anymore. Consequently, she has not lived on her own for years. John, remember Pappy? He too had Alzheimer's disease. Mom is quite contented now, well fed and safe, but she needs constant supervision. It is just a matter of time when she will need to be moved to a facility that can offer more intensive care. But for now, all is well. John, how are you feeling now?"

"Calmer, less stressed, is there anything I can do to help?"

"Please, just continue to take good care of yourself. I know how you're feeling right now as it is difficult when there are so many miles between us. There is little we can do for you down there in the United States and often we feel helpless. But we understand that you would not have received the medical attention you needed in Canada, so understand that Mom is receiving everything she needs to provide her with comfort and care."

"Cathy, you guys shouldn't feel helpless over me because here in America I am a totally disabled veteran. In Canada, I would be quite plainly a mental patient. I could not live with that! In the United States, I rank high in the social structure because finally Vietnam veterans are respected. In the Canadian environment—well, you know, don't you?"

"Yes, John, I totally understand. Hey, we should plan to meet next year, maybe during my summer holidays. I've always want to go to New Orleans! We could meet there. What do you think about that?"

"Yea, we could do that. We'll make a plan over the coming months for your vacation next year."

"Now we have something good to look forward to. I've missed you, and we could have some fun!"

"I've missed you too," John replied.

"The children need a ride home from a birthday party. I better get going soon. John, I'll call you again in a couple of weeks. Are you still writing poems? I also do a bit of writing from time to time, too."

"Yes, I'm constantly writing poetry; it helps me to sort out my feelings and thoughts. I sent you a letter last week along with a few of my poems. Send me some of your writings."

"Will do, take care—love ya John, bye for now."

"Love ya too Cathy, bye."

We knew John would feel poorly about Mom, mostly because neither of them had taken the time to resolve the past. Now, it seemed too late. The mystery of John's surname would remain a mystery, at least for the time being.

Mom often forgot our names and the fact that we were her children. Alzheimer's had rapidly taken away most of her current memories. My siblings and I had to quickly come to terms with Mom's condition and take the role of being her friends instead of her children. It was a difficult time for all of us. We were glad that John was not living nearby to witness the heartache of Mom's disappearance into her world of Alzheimer's. It was devastating enough for us. It would have been excruciating for him.

David, my sisters and I felt more at ease concerning John's life in the United States. According to his letters, he was functioning well and seemed to be adjusted to his newly found quiet, unassuming life. We, in turn, carried on with our careers and day to day living knowing that each of us had to accept the things that we could not change. We mostly communicated by telephone with John rather than write letters. It seemed more convenient in our otherwise hectic lives.

**Family Matters**

Each day I waited with anticipation for John's response to my last correspondence. Finally, it felt like old times again prior to Vietnam when John and I were able to communicate about a common interest that we shared: an appreciation for each other's writings. I wondered if he thought my writing efforts worthy.

The following week after our telephone conversation, I received John's letter. It was too soon for a response to my written correspondence that I had recently mailed to him. Immediately, I opened the letter and read.

> Dearest Cathy and family;
>
> Hope you are all well and happy. I am sorry I don't stay in touch. It's just my way, I suppose. Some things are still difficult for me.
>
> When Dad passed away years ago and we all went through the drifting away process, well, that really rocked my world. I guess I needed the stability of his influence more than most. Then the end of an era when Mom departed from the Woodstock and we all left Newfoundland. Lastly Vietnam, that finished me off on intimacy.
>
> We are family and there is nothing I would not do for any of you. Also, the times we live in see the traditional nuclear family failing, so we are not alone. Still, I am hopeful that in our maturity we will renew the bonds if only for the sake of our children, who are apt to feel more isolated than we ever did.
>
> I've settled considerably, though all things are subject to change. My health is failing now. A few years ago, it was confirmed that I have Hepatitis C, and my liver and skin are exhibiting symptoms. The doctors recently found an ulcer in my stomach. On my most recent test for TB–I tested positive. Now I am scheduled for a complete medical workup—Agent Orange fallout.
>
> On the upside of things, as you know, Rachel made me a proud grandfather on Canada Day. My granddaughter, Sera, is beautiful and maybe I can be a better granddad than I was a dad. I believe that Rachel and I have developed a pretty good working relationship. I play a more active role in her life now. Quietly supportive, you know. She asks—she gets. Her education is secured thru my veteran benefits package, which is fortunate.

I haven't heard from our siblings but that is mostly my fault. Still, would you provide me with their current addresses so I can send them a letter?

Mother Nature is waging war on humanity these days. World politics continues to worsen and I'm glad I can finally accept that I have no influence on either.

Now maybe there is a remote chance that I can enjoy a few years before I drop. Buried another Airborne Ranger this week. He was just 41 years-of-age. He died of a heart attack! Stress kills! It has really cut me down to size. I'm so far gone that even 'good stress' is bad for me.

Write and bring me up to date; please include pictures. Give Mom a big hug for me. Don't worry for me, but do take good care of ya'll. I've enclosed a few of my poems for you to read.

All love, John

John was absolutely right in his description of our childhood without Dad. The drifting away process affected each of us. Dad's illness and subsequent death isolated our young family from the normal life and stability that we were accustomed to and desperately needed in those early years.

Vietnam changed both of my brothers forever, especially John. He encountered the most challenges in life. While each of us understood John's PTSD, it was David who readily supported John the most. He emotionally and financially assisted John to continue on until the end.

My sisters and I, even as adult women, were still being protected by our brothers. They both shielded us from the intimate, gut wrenching details of John's war with PTSD. The boys felt that some of the details would be far too disturbing. Nevertheless, we understood more than they realized, and we treated our brothers with the dignity and respect they both deserved. We understood that John did not want us to take ownership of his problem or attempt to fix it. He did not want us to feel the impact of his PTSD, as he believed, and rightly so, that it was his alone to own.

John's PTSD was the result of his experiences, and it was his to live with and adjust to. No amount of pleading or praying, screaming or crying, or abuse of him or others would change the condition. And he knew that.

John functioned for almost nine years without seeking professional help. That was a huge mistake. We often thought that if he had just gotten help sooner, then perhaps his difficulties may have been lessened. But then in the 1980's and early 1990's the quality of therapeutic intervention was deficient in its practice and delivery.

Almost eighteen years had passed since John left Newfoundland and returned to the United States. Finally, after all of his journeys, advocacy interests and life, which was filled with triumphs and defeats, John had expressed interest in returning to Canada. David received a letter in November of 1994 that disclosed John's tentative plans to return home to Newfoundland during the following year.

> Yo, David,
>
> Well, my man, we made it this far! There were many times I doubted we would. No one can say you and I played it safe. I have really missed you over the years and there were many times I could have gone to visit, but you know how it goes when you get to thinking 'leave well enough, alone'! I always seemed to worry people close to me and just as often cost them something. I was always looking for something—a reason, purpose, cause, dreams, etc. Most people just wanted to chill and be comfortable. I've lived an exciting life, David, but now the thing that has me most excited is going to Newfoundland and helping my daughter and granddaughter. I am wide open on this idea, David, and I don't expect miracles of myself or my daughter. But I believe I would like to go back to Newfoundland and find a place to grow old graciously and maybe finally set up to finish the writing. Lord knows I've plenty to write about now.
>
> I sense that here in America, there are no safe places for weak or older people. I've had all I could do to survive here being

young and strong. Don't misunderstand me, I still love this country. America is my heart, but there is nothing I can do here anymore and my physical health is failing—it's time to come home. Why not? Look at my life—I've done everything I wanted, my way, and I've given my name and life real meaning. Everything else I need to do is in Newfoundland. I'm going all the way, full circle to a vision I had of myself when I was a boy. Somehow, I knew I'd be the old man living on the mountain top, on the coast, by the sea. I am contented enough to do this now.

There is a lot for me to do here before I can leave. I'll need to negotiate with various agencies concerned with my affairs, but I do not anticipate any problems with having my pension and treatment, etcetera transferred to St. John's. David, you've always known, I never could live without a dream or a goal, so now that I have a sense of coming full circle in life I feel motivated toward these particular things. No more wars, no politics, no unnecessary competing with others, just daily tasks to provide some comfort and security for me. Mostly, to be there as an elder person and provide encouragement plus support to Rachel and Sera—when and if they need it.

Cathy is the real surprise. She has taken to writing poetry and song lyrics and she's pretty good at it to tell you the truth. I will call you soon over Christmas and we'll have a talk. Miss ya'll—take care

All love always, John

**John's Coming Home—Maybe**

David telephoned me with birthday greetings and informed me of John's plan to return home and settle in Newfoundland. He asked me to obtain a copy of John's birth certificate and send it to him in Virginia. We both felt great about the prospect of John's return.

We discussed the availability of proper medical intervention for chronic PTSD in Canada; primarily in Newfoundland. John would require assistance if he experienced a stress attack or became triggered by a stressor and developed a psychological episode. I assured David that I would certainly investigate whatever resources were here so John could make an educated decision on what was most appropriate for him.

I expressed my concerns to David regarding mental health provisions in Newfoundland. As a member of the Royal Canadian Legion, (RCL) my understanding was that there were no Canadian Vietnam veterans living in Newfoundland, and if there were any Vietnam veterans here in Newfoundland they were keeping a low profile. Also, what were the odds that our medical institutions here were even familiar with severe complex combat PTSD?

To date, Canada had only deployed peacekeepers after the Korean War. Over the past years, in Canada, there was little public awareness of PTSD. We, as John's family, often felt isolated and rarely discussed PTSD with Canadians. David agreed that this could be a problem. He mentioned that a lot of the Canadian Vietnam veterans living in Canada, specifically on the mainland, still maintained a low profile and obtained their mental health intervention from the VA personnel across the border in the United States.

Regardless of our personal concerns, I suggested to David not to mention our conversation to John. We agreed that I would do the research and provide fact-finding results according to the availability of mental health intervention for persons living with PTSD in Newfoundland. There was no sense in discouraging John's plan if it wasn't necessary.

Secretly, I hoped that my research would result in a positive outcome. After all, this was 1994, and it certainly would be wonderful to welcome my brother home. Life and living in Newfoundland and Labrador remained less complicated, less competitive and more relaxing than any other place in North America. It was a safe, nurturing and healing environment. John could do well here provided he had a safety net available in the event he required medical intervention, an essential necessity for persons living with severe chronic PTSD.

John's Christmas letter written in December 1994, arrived in the New Year posted marked with a new address: Lebanon, Pennsylvania.

Dearest Cathy,

Well, another Friday night home alone for me. I hope you are doing better. All jokes aside though I'm enjoying the peace, quiet and comfort. I'm getting to like my own cooking these days so I'm going to have to be careful not to gain too much weight—small sacrifice.

I moved to a new apartment in Pennsylvania and I'm getting settled in pretty well. Bee and I parted ways. She is a great lady, and it took a lot for me to leave her, but I felt it was time to leave the "hood" and Virginia. I expect, in the future, there will be a race war in America. It is already getting more difficult being white and living in a black neighborhood.

I'm not sure if Pennsylvania is the right place for me. It is set up as a pro-veteran state, but even that doesn't often translate Vietnam veteran from what I have experienced. Combat veterans with nervous conditions are generally unappreciated and misunderstood. I will likely move, soon—steadily movin' on.

Still, though, I sure would like to just set down in a place where I could feel safe and contented. I'm tired, so very tired! I need to rest and I need a new doctor. I need new medication. I need some decent friends. I need and need—I've never been so weak. Never! I could always keep up the good front until I could get back up and feel well. Now it's different and I don't understand. Gonna try to shake off these blues.

Now that I am on my own again, I'm going to do some serious writing. On that note, Cathy, I'm really impressed with your writing—don't stop—you have natural talent, good topics, and themes. You can only get better and it will give you more joy than anything when you hit it—get it just right. Talk about a natural high and inner peace, Lord, I'd have taken myself out a long time ago if not for the writing I do, and the children.

I've given some thought to permanently returning to Newfoundland before next winter. I've completed a claim for Canadian Disability pension, but I will need my birth certificate again before it can be processed. Can you arrange a copy and mail it to me soon?

Cathy, I'm pretty well burnt out on the fast lane of the American lifestyle. I believe I can get treatment for my nervous condition in Newfoundland because of a reciprocal agreement between Canada and the United States that provides medical treatment to all veterans living in North America regardless of citizenship or, for that matter, which country in North America they reside.

I've been thinking about your vacation for this year. Maybe you'd like to drop in at Washington, D.C. so you could see the 'Wall' and some other neat things. You wouldn't have to spend a penny while you're here—this one would be on me. We could make some memories and have some fun. Think about it okay, would be nice to see ya!

Again, I must ask you to provide current addresses for our siblings. I misplaced my address book and only just found your address from a previous letter by luck. And, as always, send more pictures of the family.

My condition is taking its toll and that is to be expected; otherwise, I am well, Cathy.

Love you and yours.

Take care, and 'Do not go gentle into that dark night'—Dylan Thomas.

Later, John

**There are no Dumb Questions**

John's letter worried me, since he had never before expressed the depth of his depression and the hopelessness that accompanied his PTSD. His condition had become progressively worse than even I had understood. It was of the utmost importance that I investigate our mental health resources in St. John's, and ensure that he would have access to proper care when he returned.

I explained my brother's condition and medical history to my own physician, who sadly shook his head and advised me that my brother would be best served by the American health providers to which he was so accustomed.

My physician qualified his statement by adding: "I regret to have to advise you that at this time, not only Newfoundland but in all of Canada, medical and government health providers, including first responders, are probably decades away from understanding and coping with chronic Post Traumatic Stress Disorder in combat veterans. It is very likely that first responders in this province and country are not trained or experienced in meeting the needs of military persons living with combat PTSD. In the event of your brother behaving inappropriately or engulfed in a mental health crisis, he and you may find that he would be locked up in a mental health institution. I doubt very much that the Veteran Affairs ward at the Miller Centre here in St. John's would be able to accommodate his needs. Plus, depending on the degree of an incident, it could be a lengthy period before he would be released. What the first responders would initially observe would be an out-of-control situation that needed to be controlled. They would probably use excessive force and not be aware of the symptoms of PTSD. I would suspect that your brother would not receive the mental health care or understanding that he is accustomed to from the health providers, the first responders or society here in St. John's. Few people would understand his situation. Obviously, your brother is receiving the best care available from the veteran hospitals and centers in the United States!"

My jaw dropped in disbelief. John would never be able to live here without proper medical support. How was I going to tell him?

First, I telephoned David and told him what my physician had disclosed. He groaned in disbelief. We both knew that John would need to be informed. The next question was who was going to tell him. David suggested that it was my duty to call John and explain the discovery. He felt that regardless of John's immediate disappointment he would understand that we had his best interest at heart if he heard the facts directly from me. David said that John was recently released from the hospital again, and that mentally, he was doing much better now.

On a lighter note, I informed David that I was in receipt of an interesting letter. An associate at my workplace had discovered a ten-year-old correspondence among some old files. The letter was from our father's niece who lived in Wales. David was amazed. We never dreamt that we had family members who still existed in Wales. The letter was written by our distant cousin, Avril, seeking information regarding the whereabouts of her great-great uncle, John Saint John, and his family. We both agreed that finding our family in Wales would be my next assignment.

We ended our conversation with the understanding that I would contact John that same day and inform him of the lack of medical support for his mental health needs in Newfoundland and Labrador.

There is never a good time for bad news, I thought as I dialed John's telephone number.

"Hello," answered John.

"Hi, John, it's Cathy. How are you today?"

"Ah, I'm good now, just got released from the hospital a few days ago."

"I received your letter, thanks for the kind words about my writings. Your birth certificate in is the mail."

"Gee, thanks. I am hoping to move to Newfoundland next year."

"Yes, that's partly why I called. I took the liberty of investigating our mental health resources here in St. John's. I have to tell you that I am deeply disappointed in what I discovered."

"Really, what did you find out?" John asked in a reserved manner.

"Well, keep in mind, while I bring you up-to-date on what I've discovered that I will always support your decisions in whatever you chose to do. Understand that I am always here for you."

"Cathy, you are the sanest person I know, I trust your judgment. What's up?"

"I felt concerned about your statement in your recent letter that you believed that you could get treatment for your nervous condition here in Newfoundland. So, I recently consulted my physician and he told me that Newfoundland and most all of Canada are decades away from understanding and coping with chronic Post Traumatic Stress Disorder in combat veterans. That alone blew me away! But then, he informed me that if you behaved inappropriately or became engulfed in a mental health crisis, the only recourse would likely be that you be detained in a mental health institution: the Waterford, which is commonly referred here by the locals as the mental. He doubted very much that the Veteran Affairs ward at the Miller Centre would be able to accommodate your needs. John, you remember those facilities, don't you? This is your decision. Do what is right for you. I will do all I can to help you."

"Christ, Cathy—that is big news!"

"I know, but I thought it would be best to inform you so that you will have all the facts before making your final decision in coming home. I am very much looking forward to seeing you in a few months. It's been almost eighteen years since I last saw you. And I am really interested in visiting the Vietnam Veteran Memorial, the 'Wall', with you in Washington."

"Yes, it will be great to see you again. Thanks for the information; I really appreciate it. I'll scope it out more before I make any drastic changes. What else is happening there?"

"Oh my God, you won't believe this bit of good news! We have family in Pontypridd, Wales."

"What! How do you know?"

"I came into receipt of a letter from Dad's great-great-niece who was searching for Dad and his family. The letter is ten years old! Dad's niece would be about my age. What do you think about that?"

"That is incredible. I think you are going to Wales."

"What? Are you serious? Maybe, in a couple of years, but my next holiday is with you in Washington."

"No—you are going to go to Wales and find your family. You can see me later. Cathy, finding your father's people is more important."

"Hmm, whatever you say. I'll go."

"Book your travel plans soon, and keep me posted."

"I will. Are you going to be okay with all this news today?"

"Yes, you've given me a lot to think about. Don't worry, I'll sort it out. Cathy, I really like your poem about the *'Starling'*. There is a difference between being in love and loving someone. Isn't there?"

"Yes John, I believe so. One can be 'in love' with a person for a period of time and never share anything more than just being in love. Still on the other hand, one can love someone forever and never be 'in love' with them. Then there are some people who fall in love and remain in love—loving and being in love with the same person throughout their lifetime. It's a rare occurrence, but I did witness that kind of love a few times between couples who were blessed with such good fortune. Doubt very much that I will ever experience such a blessing. Does that make sense?"

"Yes, that makes perfect sense."

"John, can I ask you what may seem like a dumb question."

"There are no dumb questions, what is it?"

"How exactly do you feel, when you are at your most vulnerable with your PTSD?"

"Let me put it this way, when I hear a baby cry—I cry too."

"John, thanks for sharing that with me. I appreciate your honesty."

"Cathy, before we end this conversation, I want you to know that there is a large article about your father in the Telegram and Daily News probably on microfilm. It should be easy to find. I remember reading it over and over when I was a kid. Lord, how I admired that man! He was solid as a rock! I have always been guided by the truths and strength he taught me."

You have relatives there, for sure. Good luck in your travels. Just get to Pontypridd, South Wales!"

"I will. Love ya, John. Bye for now."

"Safe journey, this is all very exciting, keep me posted Cathy. Bye for now."

My thoughts held fast to the conversation I had just shared with John. I felt sad that he constantly referred to Dad as my father and not his. Since receiving his birth certificate in Montreal during 1968, he believed that our father, John Saint John, was not his father. I recalled his reaction the day Mom refused an explanation as to why his surname was Blake and not Saint John. I constantly wondered why. We all did. Immediately, I telephoned David in British Columbia, and my twin sister in Ontario, and explained my conversation with John. They were both confident that John would sort out his plans to move to Newfoundland, based on our latest conversation. Whatever could be would be. My sister was ecstatic to learn that we had family in South Wales. She too insisted that I focus on making plans to accommodate both of my teenaged children and travel for a couple of weeks.

∞∞∞

# PART 3

# JOHN'S FINAL JOURNEY HOME

# Chapter 12

## Family Matters

THE RETURN FLIGHT TO NEWFOUNDLAND from London, England, arrived late in the wee hours of the morning. It felt good to be home.

My twin sister telephoned the following morning and was ecstatic about our newly discovered family in Pontypridd, South Wales. She informed me that she had planned a brief vacation to Newfoundland and would arrive within a few days. She wanted to hear all the details about the trip at that time. It had been ten years since her last visit home.

David was equally excited and pleased that I had found Dad's family. He looked forward to receiving a copy of my travel journal and photographs. He also informed me that John was doing quite well and that I should telephone him soon. I promised him that I would speak with John that same evening and have a lengthy conversation with him about my travels. We both knew that John would be thrilled with the news.

There was an abundance of mail to peruse since my departure, and hidden among the numerous envelopes was a letter from John dated May, 1995. The return address indicated that he was in VA Medical Center, at Lebanon, PA again.

> Dearest Cathy,
>
> Hope you are all well and happy! Love to everyone. One day, I'll see ya'll.
>
> I am back in the hospital for a while to get some necessary treatment due to my nervous condition and a change in

medication. I am planning a move to Seattle in Washington State. Can't go on thinking I have a long time left so I need to get out of the city and move to the country and enjoy the environment; developing more 'medical' problems now.

I'll be settling within 100 miles or so of David, near the British Columbia border. I've scrapped the flight to Newfoundland, maybe next year David and I will travel back there for a visit.

Enough about me—I wonder all the time how ya'll are doing. Let me know what is happening there. I hope to see you and your children one day soon.

Here are some facts I compiled about Vietnam that you might be interested in reading:

WE DID NOT LOSE IN VIETNAM, WE LEFT!

From time to time we hear or read the comment that 'America lost in Vietnam'. This statement or phrase has done much damage throughout the years, not only to Vietnam veterans but also to the entire country.

Usually, people affiliate the phrase 'losing a war' to actual defeat. In fact, Webster's Dictionary defines 'lose' as 'to undergo defeat'. When people hear the misguided statement that we lost in Vietnam, it infers that the NVA/VC beat us militarily. Nothing could be farther from the truth. In fact, we won by overwhelming odds the military victory in Vietnam. The following are facts that prove the point that the American military actually won in Vietnam.

America never lost any major battles in Vietnam. Yet the North Vietnamese lost many including the 1968 TET Offensive.

America never lost or gave up ground, yet many NVA/VC strongholds were decimated.

America lost approximately 59,000 soldiers during the Vietnam War, yet the NVA/VC lost 924,048. That is approximately 15 NVA/VC dead for every one we lost.

America had 313,616 wounded; the NVA/VC had approximately 935,000 wounded. That is approximately 3 wounded to every one of ours.

North Vietnam signed a truce on January 27, 1973, which included several agreements.

The agreements are as follows:

- That the DMZ at the 17th parallel would remain a provisional dividing line between North and South Vietnam.

- That there would be no military movement across the DMZ.

- That they would not use the force of any kind to unify the country.

Based on the Paris Peace Accord, an agreement on ending the war and restoring peace in Vietnam that North Vietnam signed on January 27, 1973, the last U.S. troops then left Vietnam on March 29, 1973. Only a small defense attaché office and a few Marines were left at the American Embassy. Saigon fell two years later, primarily because the 94th Congress rejected President Ford's plea in 1975 to honor and sustain the terms of the Paris Accord Agreement it signed in 1973. The primary provision was to provide adequate economic and military assistance to South Vietnam. Arms and ammunition they so desperately needed to win. Thirteen days after the President's plea was rejected by the 94th Congress, Cambodia fell on April 17, 1975, and South Vietnam fell on April 30, 1975.

After all the U.S. troops left Vietnam, the North Vietnamese violated the treaty and began a major offensive to overtake South Vietnam, which ended up in the fall of Saigon. There were no combat troops in Vietnam for two years prior to the fall of South Vietnam.

Cathy, these are all very important points when evaluating the fact that we actually did win militarily in Vietnam, and we left. There is a big difference between losing and leaving.

Unfortunately, due to the political problems back home, we never accomplished our objectives in South Vietnam.

If there had been a line drawn around Germany during the Second World War, and the allies were told they could not go into Germany, we would still be fighting the Second World War. If a line was drawn around Iraq during Operation Desert Storm, and the ground forces were told that they were not allowed to enter Iraq, we would still be fighting Operation Desert Storm. Consequently, in Vietnam, we were militarily limited as far as obtaining our objective because we could not cross over into North Vietnam. The American soldiers in Vietnam were subjected to some of the fiercest warfare that our country has ever experienced, and we won all the battles.

Yes, Saigon fell two years after we left, but that does not mean that we lost. It is sad that we left and did not stay there to finish it, and that we took the North Vietnamese word on the treaty. Equally sad is that the 94th Congress forced the surrender of South Vietnam and Cambodia.

If all American forces left South Korea today, and North Korea was to invade South Korea two years from now, that would not indicate that we lost the Korean War. This is the case in Vietnam. We won militarily, North Vietnam signed a truce. We left, and then they invaded South Vietnam.

We can be proud that the United States of America has never lost a war. Hopefully, there will not be any more wars that we will be involved in that we will have to win. But we can be proud of Vietnam veterans because we served our country well, and eventually our efforts stopped the flow of communism in Southeast Asia.

I am very proud for having served in Vietnam. I am also very glad that Vietnam veterans are getting back together and are experiencing the camaraderie that we experienced in Vietnam. We did a great job in Vietnam, the facts speak for themselves. We won, and then we left!

Love and miss you, John

My siblings and I cherished every letter that John wrote simply because each correspondence meant that he was hanging on to life. Still, each of us felt that one day, of his own accord, John would make it his choice to live or die. Each of us secretly hoped and prayed that day would never come. I dialed John's telephone number and tried to imagine his reaction to the good news I was about to share with him regarding my discovery in South Wales. I remembered John telling me that good stress and bad stress had the same effect on his well-being.

"Hello," said John.

"Hi John, I'm back and I found them—I found our family in Wales!"

"You didn't!"

"Yes, John, I did, I found them in Pontypridd. They are wonderful people, and they welcomed me with open arms. It was amazing. I walked where Dad would have walked in his hometown. I visited the house where he grew up, the church where he and his family prayed and also the pub where Dad probably had his first legal drink.

Our Welsh cousins and I dated our family roots back to 1847. There is just too much to describe right now. Tomorrow I will mail you and David a copy of my travel journal, which is quite detailed with photographs; it will explain everything. You should receive a package within the week."

"Cathy, this is brilliant news! I knew there had to be family in Wales. Tell me how you actually found them, and about the first moment you met them."

"To make a long story short, I was in Cardiff on Sunday, May 21$^{st}$. My intent was to attend church and listen to a Welsh choir, but instead I boarded a train to Pontypridd. Once in Pontypridd, I located the street address that was on the letter and knocked on the door. I discovered that Avril, our cousin, had moved, but I was directed to ask the lady across the street who might remember Avril's family. Luckily, she did remember them and telephoned Avril's mother, Moria. Everyone was surprised, most especially me. Avril's sister, Adele collected me, and we drove just a few streets away to their mother's home. John, it was the most remarkable experience in my life to be welcomed with open arms into Dad's family. All the details are in the journal. Once you read the story, we will chat again about Wales."

"Cathy, you were meant to find them. I can hardly wait to read your journal."

"John, don't be spooked by what you read, but I truly felt Dad's presence with me the whole time while I traveled, except on the return journey home."

"I believe you did. He was very protective over you girls. I do not doubt for a minute that he watched over you."

"John, I like to think that I brought Dad's spirit back to his homeland. I could not feel his presence with me on the return trip to Newfoundland."

"Perhaps you did indeed bring him home."

"How have you been lately?" I inquired.

"I just spent a few weeks in the V.A. hospital. I am more stabilized now with a change in medication—again. Overall, I just try and keep a low profile in society and mostly read a lot of books. I have decided to move again soon. Maybe, I'll settle in Seattle, Washington, for a while near David."

"Sounds like a plan. Oh, by the way, our kid sister is coming home this weekend. I'll mail that package to you today. You take good care of yourself and we'll talk again very soon."

"Yes, indeed. I am looking forward to receiving that package."

"Goodbye, for now, John."

"Bye Cathy, and thanks for calling."

**The Family Secret Revealed**

I waited at the airport for my sister's flight to arrive from Ontario. I was anxious to see her again; maybe she could help me shed some light on the origin of the Blake name that had tormented us for so many years. I knew then that I would bring up the subject when the time was right.

Her flight arrived on time, and we were soon reunited. We stopped at a local restaurant and enjoyed a meal of fish and chips. Finally, we settled down at my home and discussed the trip to Wales. My sister was impressed with the letters Dad had written and the many photographs I captured on my journey. She was delighted that we had family in Wales. I informed her that I really wanted to resolve the mystery of the Blake name. She agreed. We both knew it was too late in life to question Mom. She had already forgotten that we were her children—much less what transpired in 1949, the year John was born.

Then my sister had a brilliant idea: Why not talk to Nanny about our concerns? I thought about that idea and decided the time was right. Nanny would understand our need to know the truth since Mom wasn't able to clarify the issue.

The next day we hurried over to our uncle's house where Nanny lived. "Nanny!" we both cried as we entered her bedroom. She stopped crocheting, looked up and gave both of us a big, happy smile.

"My, oh my! I haven't seen both of you together in a very long time," said Nanny.

"We thought that you might be able to help us with a few questions we have about our past." I said.

"I'll try," replied Nanny. "What is on your mind?"

"Well Nan," I asked, "is Wayne—who now calls himself John Blake—our full-blood brother? He believes he is not John Saint John's son. Years ago he discovered that his last name was recorded on his birth certificate as John Wayne Blake."

"Yes child, of course he is your brother," said Nanny. "Wayne was born several months before your father and mother married. Your parents became a couple in early 1948. They were always together. John Saint John was proud as a peacock when his first son, Wayne, was born in 1949. It was your mother who wanted to wait until after the child was born until she regained her figure before they had a wedding celebration."

"Nanny, did Mom really marry an officer named Johnny Blake while she was in the Navy, and did he die of malaria?" I asked. "At least that is the story we heard. I have seen the surname, 'Blake' on John's birth certificate and on Mom and Dad's wedding certificate, but the surname did not show up on the other three birth certificates. However, Mom's maiden name did."

"You girls must have a good reason for asking all these questions today. Why do you need to know about your mother's past?" Nanny asked. "It was a long time ago."

"Nanny, we need to know because we both remember the day when Wayne or John, whichever you want to call him—received his birth certificate from the Newfoundland government and discovered that his last name was not recorded as Saint John." I stated. "He was devastated, and stopped believing that our father was his father, too. He asked Mom why his birth certificate indicated a different last name than David's birth certificate. Mom's only reply to him was, 'You figure it out'."

"Nanny, there is a secret in our family that is hurting all of us." I said. "Nothing you say can change the love we all have for Mom. But, if she knew that her secret had caused so much despair for each of us over the years, then she would surely tell us. But it's too late now; Mom is basically lost in her Alzheimer's world. Nanny, we need to know. Please tell us the truth."

"Yes, you are right girls; it is time for the truth. Your mother never married Johnny Blake. She came home from the Navy pregnant, and in those times, it was a social disgrace to be an unwed mother. She told a lie to protect herself and her daughter, Annette. No one questioned the situation, and the lie was forgotten. Your mother was known as Mrs. Blake. After the war, the father of her child, Officer Johnny Blake, returned to England and his family.

"Your mother and father fell in love and she became pregnant with your brother. Then a few months after his birth, they married. That is why Wayne's birth certificate bears the surname, Blake, as did your mother's on their marriage certificate. It wasn't until a few years after their marriage, when she was pregnant with David, that your mother confessed to your father that she was never married to Johnny Blake.

To your parents, it wasn't an issue. I know that your father meant to have the name changed on Wayne's birth certificate, but the Woodstock burnt down, and life was hectic until the new house was built. Then you two girls arrived, and I guess he must have forgotten to take care of that detail. But I'll tell you right here and now, as God is my witness, John Blake is Wayne Saint John, and his father is John Saint John. And I'll tell you another thing, if there was any doubt that Wayne was not his son, John Saint John would have never have married your mother. I don't know why your mother couldn't tell her son the truth. All I can say is that it must have been foolish, selfish pride that stood in her way." Stated Nanny.

"Nanny, we certainly appreciate you telling us the truth about the past. This information will mean the world to Wayne/John. Perhaps it may even bring him some peace." I said.

"Is he still troubled by that war?" Nanny asked.

"Sometimes he is," I responded. There was no use in trying to explain to Nanny about Post Traumatic Stress Disorder or the fact that the past fifteen years of John's life was spent in and out of VA hospitals in America. Nanny would be heartbroken if she heard the details of his troubled life. We only told Nanny about the good things that occurred in his life. I recalled her being extremely proud of John when we showed her the newspaper clippings of his march across the United States in 1982. He made history then, and she was proud and delighted with his accomplishment.

"Cathy, go to the kitchen and make us some tea and bring back some of those Purity Jam-Jam cookies that are in the cookie tin." Nanny asked. I was happy to comply.

We sipped our tea while we chatted about old times. We did a lot of laughing about our earlier years. It was a good day.

I decided that I would not wait another day to tell John the truth regarding his surname. For quick reference, I sorted the birth and marriage certificates on the kitchen table. Armed with the historical documents and the conversation with Nanny, I dialed John's telephone number.

"Hello," responded John.

"Good evening, John, did I wake you up?"

"Hey Cathy, no, I wasn't sleeping. I'll catch a nap later. I seldom sleep at night."

"Why don't you sleep at night?"

"Because sleep comes with a regular visit to 'nightmare alley', so I mostly just take naps. What's up? Two calls in the same week. Are you two girls scrapping already?"

"No, I wanted to call you and share some good news. We visited Nanny today, and she is doing just fine. But, she told us something that you will find interesting."

"What's that?"

"First, I have proof that you are indeed John Saint John's son."

"Yeah—really, tell me everything," John replied cautiously.

"When I returned home from Wales, I immediately obtained all our birth certificates plus Mom and Dad's marriage certificate. I have them right here in front of me. Those certificates indicate that you were born six months before the wedding. Mom used the name, Blake, on your birth certificate and on her and Dad's marriage certificate. But, on the other three birth certificates, she used her maiden name."

"Why would she switch from the Blake name to her maiden name? She was previously married."

"That's the question I had, too—until earlier today when we visited Nanny. We asked her to tell us if Mom had really married Johnny Blake during 1946 and if he had indeed died. She confirmed that Mom was never married in 1946, the year she returned home pregnant from the Navy. And Johnny Blake never died in 1946. After the war, he returned to his family in England. It was a story that Mom fabricated; a lie to protect herself and her unborn child from social disgrace. She carried on using that fictitious name. You were born and acquired the name, Blake," simply because Mom and Dad were not yet married. They married six months after you were born. Before David and us girls arrived, she had acknowledged to Dad that she was never married before and that is why her maiden name is recorded on David's and our (the twins) birth certificates. Are you still following me?"

"Yes, but why didn't they change my birth certificate?" John emotionally asked.

"Well, I asked that question, too. Nanny said that Dad had full intentions in doing just that. It made no difference to them as a couple that she had lied about a prior marriage. He understood the circumstances, and he loved her child, Annette. What mattered was that he had a son—you. But, another child arrived two years later and then the old Woodstock burned down. Life became hectic, with Dad having to find temporary accommodations and rebuild a new home for his family. Then we arrived—the twins. Imagine the chaos in their lives! Annette was seven and you were four, plus David was just two years of age when two infants arrived. It was an oversight that your birth certificate was not corrected."

"Okay, why didn't Mom tell me that when we were living in Montreal before I joined the United States Forces?" John asked with hurt and anger in his voice.

"John, I remember that day in Montreal, and it was a devastating time for you and us, your brother and sisters. We shared your pain and confusion. Nanny felt that foolish, selfish pride stood in the way of her telling you and the rest of us the truth. I'm so sorry she did that to us. But now we have the truth. You are John Saint John's son; there is no doubt in my mind. Nanny also said that Mom and Dad were inseparable. John Saint John would never have married her if there was any doubt in his mind that the child she was carrying was not his child. Today, there is no doubt that you are John Wayne Saint John. And, you can take back your name anytime you want."

I could hear John choking back a sob of relief that caused my eyes to sting with tears as he paused and cleared his throat. Then he stated, "Cathy, this really is great news and it explains a lot of unanswered questions. My only regret is that it is now too late for me to let Mom know that all is okay. Thank you for your effort in finding the truth. Now, don't misunderstand me, but I made this name John Wayne Blake, what it is today, and this is the name that I will take to the grave."

More tears rolled down my cheeks as I listened to John's voice quiver under the stress of our conversation. "I completely understand your reasoning; I am just very proud that you are my brother. Dismiss and forgive any regrets that you may feel between yourself and Mom. I am confident that she would have eventually told us. It's just that her memory faded too soon. Now, I have one small request."

"What would that be?" John said softly.

"In the future, when we talk about Dad, please don't refer to Dad as your father when addressing me or our siblings because he was our father. Okay?"

"Right on, Sis!" John exclaimed cheerfully.

"Perfect Bro, now go and enjoy a restful nap," I replied.

"Will do, and Cathy, thank you for the good news. You know what this means to me."

"Yes, John, I felt that knowing the truth would help in healing some of the past. We, your family, felt your pain over that issue throughout the years. Now that you are armed with the truth, no more doubts. Believe!"

"Now I believe!" He chuckled.

"Good, I must call David and advise him of our conversation. You take care. Bye for now."

"Yes, do that. Say hello to our brother for me, okay? Bye for now."

I knew in my heart that John was as pleased as he could be that he was indeed John Saint John's son. John was right in his affirmation that he was and would remain to be John Blake. Knowing for a fact that John Saint John was his father was just one less heartache that needed mending.

I thought, God love Nanny for being so wise and understanding. I felt grateful for our family. David needed to be informed. I quickly dialed his telephone number and waited for him to answer.

"Hello," said David.

"Hi there, just wanted to speak to you before you went to work for the day."

"What's happening?"

"I just had a lengthy conversation with John. He said to say 'hello' to you. But, more importantly, we both wanted you to know that there is absolutely no doubt that our father is his father. Nanny resolved our doubts today. Plus, I discovered other pertinent information that leaves no doubt whatsoever and confirmed the truth."

"Wow, that is great news! Listen, I must leave for work, but we'll talk later. How is John feeling about the news?" David asked.

"I believe that he is happy in his own way and much relieved. I know that he will take comfort that his mentor was indeed his father. We discussed all the information very thoroughly, and he seemed genuinely pleased. I couldn't be happier for him!"

"Me too! This is wonderful. Thanks for letting me know. I'll get all the details later. Bye for now."

"Yes, speak with you later. Bye."

David and I continued our conversation later that evening, and he, too, was relieved that finally the truth had been revealed. My sister's visit on the island passed too quickly, and before we knew it we were both back at the airport saying goodbye.

The following week, I received a postcard from John that stated he had thoroughly enjoyed my travel journal with the photos and that our last telephone conversation was something truly special. It seemed as though it was shaping up to be a good year for the whole family.

∞

## OUR DAD

**Pvt. John Saint John**
**WWI Newfoundland Regiment #673**
**originally from Pontypridd, Wales**
**1889-1962**

*Right:* Dad, as we knew him was indeed the kindest of all people. The wonderful memories we shared were never enough.

## Chapter 13

## A Brief Visit to Canada and Goodbye

THE SUMMER OF 1995 WAS PEACEFUL and uneventful. My brothers and sisters also enjoyed their summer. In early August, John suddenly decided to visit David and his wife in British Columbia. It was the first time he had returned to Canada in approximately twenty years.

Thirteen years had passed since John and David spent any face-to-face time together. Many years of letters and telephone conversations had ensured that the pair still shared a very strong bond. The boys' last reunion was in Seattle, Washington in 1982 during the launch of the Transcontinental March. Neither time nor distance could make a difference in their relationship.

John arrived in Vancouver, and the visit marked his first meeting with David's wife who he immediately admired. She was a kind and generous woman and made him feel accepted and welcomed in their home. John felt she was certainly the right woman for David. It was obvious to John that they were both happily married, and he felt his love strengthen for them.

John and David reminisced about the good old days they had spent together before Vietnam and the lean and hard times they shared after Vietnam. David witnessed for the first time the effect that PTSD had on John's personality, and it saddened him. The brother whom he loved and followed throughout their lifetime was now reduced to a mere shadow of himself. David felt helpless as he witnessed and—perhaps for the first time—fully understood the impact of John's illness. He clearly understood that most people who had been traumatized by combat or any other life-threatening events were extremely prone to PTSD. It was a warning to David to keep a close watch on his own health issues.

John carried his undiagnosed PTSD for thirteen years after his return from Vietnam. The consequence of delayed intervention ensured that he would pay the supreme price for the rest of his life. When he did acknowledge that he needed mental health assistance, the resources were underdeveloped and unproven to warrant a good recovery.

Official records pertaining to veteran suicides were practically non-existent prior to 2005. However, there were unofficial statistics among the Vietnam veterans that suggested approximately 30 to 33 deaths a day between the years of 1965 to 1995, the number of estimated suicides among Vietnam veterans was approximately 350,000 souls. Veteran groups expect that number to triple over the next twenty years as the veteran population discover their delayed chronic PTSD. North America's governmental agencies and mental health professionals will continue to learn tragic lessons, well into the next century, through the lives of veterans suffering from chronic PTSD.

John planned to travel to Newfoundland while he was in Canada and visit the rest of his family. He desperately wanted to see his daughter and meet his granddaughter. Unfortunately, his visit to Canada was cut short when he realized that he required hospital stabilization for his disorder. David arranged transportation, and John returned to Portland, Oregon, where he immediately checked himself into a VA hospital for several weeks. As soon as he was released he wrote the following letter in September 1995.

> Dearest David and family,
>
> Just a few lines to say hello; hope ya'll are well and happy!
>
> Boy, that Portland VA is no place for Vietnam veterans. I came away more upset than when I went in. I like Oregon pretty well but I'm still gonna scat to Hawaii next Saturday or Sunday. I will likely live in or around a town named Kailua, which is just twelve miles from Honolulu on a different coast. Veterans' hospital right there for my out-patient treatment and stuff. No winter for me this year, ha-ha. I still plan to visit

Newfoundland around May next year. Maybe David and I can go back there together. I'm stuck in a rough part of town here where I am, but I stay in at night so as nothing else will go wrong. I have been reading a lot of books just to pass the time away. No need to worry about me now for a while. I know how close I am to trouble all the time. So since I want to be winter-free this year, I will be careful. I've got to get away from these crowds. Too much going on; it's like a carnival. The people are nicer in Oregon. It wouldn't be a bad place for me except further down state near the ocean is supposed to be a decent VA in White City on the California Line. Have to remember that!

I get out each day and take in the surroundings by bus. They have an excellent bus system here. While I was in the hospital I got mad at the VA, and since I had met another ex-Special Forces patient who was getting fucked over by the FEDs. I wrote a page of notes and had him take one for himself then I passed out about twenty more. That's all I could think of to handle the anger, which built up inside of me while I was at that place. The main thing I know now for sure is that the government is definitely getting the VA hospitals ready to open up to the general public. This is a brand spanking new VA facility and they treat combat veterans like dirt. Young guys and gals with alcohol and drug problems are getting all the attention. They are not even supposed to be in there. It's over man! I've got to make some long-lasting plans for my treatment; private insurances and private psychiatry to stay out of trouble and keep my pensions and freedom. Times are changing!

I will call Saturday around noon. Love ya'll,

Always, John

PS: With thoughts to the end of my story. Soon I will go home.

'To those who have fought for it;<br>
Freedom has a taste the protected shall never know'

**"...but, what can you do..."**

It's not about how long; it's about how well you live
About how much you'll take, about how much you'll give
You are special in your ways, as you must always be
The only thing that matters, you must be free

From all forms of Tyranny. Free—Totally.

John W. Blake©1995

**Hawaii—October 1995**

John arrived in Honolulu, Hawaii, by mid-October. He located a hostel and settled into the tropical environment, which we believed he thoroughly enjoyed. It was a place where he found the simplest things pleasing.

He walked along the beach for a couple of miles each day and watched the ocean roll in and out, plus he would swim twice a day. He had visited the Hickam Air Force Base and shopped at the BX (Base Exchange) where he purchased cheap groceries and cigarettes. He planned to go camping up in the Kaneohe Bay area where it was quiet and away from the general population. He felt as though he had died and gone to heaven.

John registered with the Honolulu Veteran Center and was assigned to Marlene, a counselor. He spoke fondly of Marlene in his letters, and remarked that she was a real sharp lady with a straight forward approach. No bullshit. She took herself and her work very seriously, and John decided straight away that he would take her seriously and follow her advice to the letter.

Marlene ensured that John was registered in the Hawaiian VA computer system for veteran services and he immediately received his new Hawaiian VA card. He visited a doctor there at the VA hospital and received a one-month supply of medication. As far as the VA was concerned, John was a full-time Hawaiian.

The hard-core veterans like John loved and enjoyed Hilo, the big island. The VA forwarded John's file to Hilo, to ensure that when John arrived there they would be familiar with his needs. He was really pleased with the idea that he could expect efficient service and care when he arrived at Hilo in early November. Hilo had a laid-back attitude, which was why the veterans liked it—no hassles.

John needed and welcomed the remoteness; he needed solitude. Especially in the age of advanced communication technology, he felt perfectly safe and contented living away from mainstream civilization. Being isolated or alone in Hawaii was not the same as during 1982 when he walked across the United States without any communication equipment or companions. During the Transcontinental Walk, he had felt totally removed and remote without a cell phone, or any other communication equipment that was linked to a satellite. Technology had progressed, and it was a good thing.

John felt it was good to be alive and under fifty years of age, but—more importantly—to be free. He also knew that if there was ever a tomorrow when he could not function acceptably by societal standards, then it would become imperative that he remove himself from mainstream society.

Reluctantly, John agreed to complete a VA survey at the veteran's center, which he found emotionally troubling, but he managed to get through the work with the assistance of the staff. The VA referred John for an eight to ten-week stress therapy program. The staff advised him that since 1984 through 1985, a lot of new therapies had been refined and promised improvement in the quality of life for patients living with chronic combat PTSD.

John felt he was truly in Paradise. He felt certain that if he dropped dead at any time, one thing he could be sure of is that he would go down happy. Sadly John had stopped being happy when he received the news that his dearest friend from his teenaged years in Newfoundland had died. She had married and moved to the United States then died in a vehicle accident during the summer of 1969, while he was training in Special Forces. He tried to make a comeback several times and develop a happy life but never succeeded.

The media announcement that America was going to send troops to Bosnia angered John. He felt it was absolutely, deadly wrong to send troops there. In John's opinion, the Serbs were going to start more 'bullshit' and that they were not worth the loss of one American life.

He also felt that the Serbs had been fighting for territory for a couple of hundred years or more and that they started WWI, which set the stage for everything else in that century. And, now they wanted to influence the twentieth century. He was infuriated.

Telephone conversations with John in Hawaii were impossible, because he did not obtain a cell phone. We had to rely on letters from him, which arrived without a return address. John would write bits and pieces every day, and once he had a dozen pages he would photocopy the document and mail a copy to each of us in Canada. Occasionally, he would telephone David. John assured us that he would arrange a P.O. Box when he arrived in Hilo, but he didn't.

In one particular document he mailed to us, he provided contact information for Marlene, in the event we did not hear from him in a couple of weeks. But he told us not to worry because he always carried a few pieces of identification and constantly wore his military identification tags.

John mentioned that Marlene gently warned him to tread carefully through the Inpatient Stress Program because it could do more damage than good. She was not talking about anything specific, except to say that the people who provided the treatment were young, enthusiastic recent graduates or even students who meant well. But, sometimes they were just testing their new skills and researching thesis material.

John believed that Marlene felt he was fair game and cared enough to suggest that he be alerted and objective. John's condition was very advanced and chronic. He had learned how to maintain and maybe that was the best he could hope for. He would have to be careful, whatever he decided. He had a trusted counselor in Marlene, and he was confident she would set him straight if necessary.

Bellows Air Force base is located in Honolulu County, and John felt it was the right place on planet earth for him to relax and enjoy the sun. He would set up a small camp and enjoy his quiet surroundings without any fuss or tourists. At the military store, John purchased an Army two-man pup tent, a poncho liner, a half-size machete and a few other camping items. The attendants at the military store also recommended that John camp out at Bellow's Airbase. It was a secured area, and nobody would mess with his camping gear when he was not on site at the camp. It also had a nice beach where he could snorkel and frolic in the water with a boogie board. He was living the childhood he never had by camping in the forest and playing in the ocean. Little wonder he felt the euphoria of Paradise.

John spent several weeks out on Bellows. On one occasion, he had an accident while surfing with the boogie board. He crashed and went face down onto some jagged rocks and fractured his ribs and jaw. The injuries, which were painful and noticeably severe, kept him from any further activities in the ocean. John collected his belongings and moved to Hilo, where he expected to experience a more tranquil life.

When John arrived at Hilo, he immediately checked in at the Veteran Center. The people there convinced John that the injury to his face had to be fixed. He had already developed a serious infection in his mouth due to a wound that had not healed. He was sent to the Tripler Army Hospital in Honolulu and was admitted. During the several weeks of hospitalization, John wrote a letter dated November 18, 1995 to David and informed him of his situation.

> Dearest David and family,
>
> All is well. Tripler is quite the place. Better than any VA Hospital, but I don't think I'll stay here very long.
>
> The staffs here don't know what to make of me and I'm not sure I understand them, but I'm using my time to calm down and heal my face and ribs a bit. I should have been stitched up inside and outside of my mouth and that is my only regret.
>
> The people over here say "Fuck it. You're tough—deal with it and by the way—Why do you need psych time?"
>
> Fuck ya'll for causing me to worry about bullshit and then try to explain it. All this shit is easy; fuck the pain—physical pain. It's nothing compared to what's going on inside.
>
> I'm not downing anyone for trying to be caring or helpful, but I strongly advise the care providers and ya'll don't start 'caring' more than I do and I simply don't care much at all. For the record, David!

But, I am healing from my recent surfing injury and I've met some veterans from Hilo, the big island, and they are great with providing information. I'm getting a good idea about how to pace myself in getting settled. I don't want to spend much time in the populated areas so I'll probably find a spot where I can set-up without anyone fucking with me or my head. I've got to get on with this thing so that neither I nor the government gets me off track. I'm in the right place on 'Planet Earth'—there's no doubt.

There is stuff (drugs) going on here like everywhere else, but here I can avoid trash and have a chance. Simple as that! The veterans around me here are trying to draw me into their issues and, of course, I'm inclined to be involved. God help me. I've got to stay focused on what I'm supposed to be doing.

It appears that staffs at this facility are a combination of active duty people and civilians. It seems like a pretty good setup since they balance each other a bit and maybe keep each other honest. I mean, no one on active duty is going to play many games or take unnecessary chances with the veterans. Regular DVA staffs do whatever they want. Almost like no one is in charge. I never did like that. Never will!

Perhaps some good will come out of this situation as long as I calm down enough before I'm discharged. When I am released it will be straight to Hilo, the big island because Oahu is too fast for me.

There are many problems here with the locals being upset, but I'm going to try real hard to get along wherever I set down and get on good terms with those around me.

The veterans in the bush; I'll have to avoid at first because from all I've discovered they are for real and dangerous. Hate to go down on a cheap shot or the boys not taking the time to know me. You know they are going to be suspicious. My plan is to stay out of where they are and let time pass.

I have no personal involvement and the few women I have talked with are all about 'partying' so I just move on. There's a

> large problem with crime and drugs here, like everywhere, but I do believe I can slip around it pretty well.
>
> All else is routine. I hope the Feds get back to work soon or there'll be no checks in December. Boy, watch the hospitals and jails fill up quick. Aha!
>
> Not me, I'll go camping. I don't care what they all do. I cannot lose my cool.
>
> All love, Always! John

David immediately informed my sister and me of John's last letter. We felt concerned when he moved from a familiar community in Washington near David and traveled to Hawaii. We felt that the stress alone from moving to a new area without any real friends in his new surroundings would become problematic for him. It appeared, once again, that John had isolated himself from all the people who cared about him. Without a fixed address or a direct telephone number, John's family members were left without any avenue of communication. We each felt his deliberate isolation from us, his family. It was a warning of something more serious to follow. We each felt uneasy as we waited for the next correspondence from John.

The next month passed without any additional letters from John. He'd often telephoned David every few weeks just to stay in touch. As Christmas day approached there was no communication from John. We all knew that this was his worst time of the year. Holidays and anniversaries of traumatic events constantly triggered an episode of deep depression and anger. This was the most likely time that he would seek mental health assistance to stabilize his PTSD. In early February 1996, David finally received a telephone call from John. It was just as we expected, John had been hospitalized since Christmas. David telephoned me.

"Hey Cathy," he said when I answered.

"Hi, how are you?"

"Good. John finally called a few days ago. He's not doing really well."

"I sensed the holidays would cause him a lot of grief. Did he admit himself into the hospital?"

"Yes. He spent six weeks there and was released a few days ago. But, he sounded different this time—confused and low keyed, almost beaten." David sadly replied.

"David, that is so disappointing to hear," I said. "I hope he will be alright."

"Me too, I'll let you know the next time he calls," promised David.

"Thanks. That will be great."

Attempting to lighten the conversation, David noted, "Valentine's Day is next week. Do you have any plans?" He asked.

"Yes, I plan to be at a reading of poetry by local artists."

"Sounds good...have a great evening. Bye."

"Thanks, David, take care. Bye for now."

∞

# Chapter 14

## Broken Hearts on Valentine's Day, 1996

VALENTINE'S DAY IS A TRADITIONAL DAY filled with romantic overtures sweetened with an unusual amount of specialty candies, pungent roses, and romantic love songs. Never in our wildest dreams did we, the family, anticipate that Valentine's Day would be anything different from previous years.

After a busy day, at work. I attended the Writer's Alliance Valentine Decadent Chocolate event. I arrived at the Curling Club and immediately settled in for an evening that promised a glorious rendition of artistic readings delivered by original authors. It was to be a delightful evening.

As I listened to the poetry readings, I experienced a familiar uneasy emotional wave of devastation wash over me. I felt alarmed. I tried to focus on the author who read her lovely poem filled with affection. But I lost my concentration, and once again, an ominous feeling blanketed me. Suddenly, I had an urgency to leave. I knew that I had to return home. Something was desperately wrong.

I stood up just as the author finished her last words, and I bolted for the door. I just knew that something was terribly wrong at home, but what could be so very wrong? I felt everyone's eyes follow me out the door, questioning my sudden exit.

Within ten minutes, I burst through the front door of my home. My daughter stood in the kitchen, surprised and grateful that I had arrived. She informed me that John's former wife had called and that she was upset and crying. She left a message to call immediately, it was urgent!

I dialed the number and heard the sad tone in her voice as she answered the telephone. Upon hearing my voice, she burst into tears and cried, "Something terrible has happened to your brother, John, in Hawaii. Two Royal Newfoundland Constabulary officers have just left Rachel's apartment. They gave her a contact number for the Hilo Police Department. Please go to her. I just know he's dead!"

Stunned with disbelief, I informed my daughter that something very serious may have happened to John, and that I had to leave immediately and go to Rachel. I asked her to try not to worry and told her that I would return home within an hour.

**Tears on Our Pillows**

My heart beat rapidly, and my thoughts raced as I drove the short distance to Rachel's apartment. Despite my feelings of disbelief, I considered what might have happened. I drove my car along Topsail Road barely aware I was driving. I chanted aloud, "He can't be dead, he can't be dead, not our John. There must be some mistake!"

Rachel met me at the door. Her beautiful eyes swollen from crying now brimmed again with tears. Fearfully I asked, "What happened to your father? What's going on?"

"Two police officers were here just a half hour ago," said Rachel, stifling a sob. They told me to call the Hilo Police Department in Hawaii for details regarding an urgent matter concerning Dad."

"Have you called?"

"I can't," she said, handing me a scrap of paper with the telephone number.

With each number I dialed, I dug deeper for all the inner strength I could muster. I listened to the ringing of the telephone line, waiting for someone to answer. I braced myself for the worst and prayed, "Dear God, no, no, not John." With that thought, the call stopped ringing.

"Hilo Police Department, Officer Burien," said the soft-spoken officer in a Hawaiian accent.

"Hello, my name is Cathy Saint John. I am John Blake's sister. I'm calling you from St. John's, Newfoundland, Canada. Has something happened to my brother, John?" I asked, eased myself down to the floor and braced myself for his reply.

"Ms. Saint John, I'm sorry to inform you that your brother is dead."

"Dead? Are you sure it is John Blake?" I whispered in shock.

"Yes." Officer Burien quietly replied.

I looked directly at John's daughter and gently nodded my head while my tears flowed freely, confirming the fact that our John was indeed dead. His daughter cried softly numbed by the realization that her father was gone. Hope was now shattered; a reunion that would never occur.

"Please tell me how, when and where did he die?" I asked.

"He died last evening, February 13th. He was found by a custodian checking the premises at the Federal Post Office."

"Found where—at the Post Office?"

"On the ground," he quietly replied.

"What do you mean? Did someone push him off a building? How did John die?" It was becoming increasingly obvious to me that my inquiries had become emotionally difficult for Officer Burien. What was he holding back?

"Ms. Saint John, I'm sorry to inform you that your brother committed suicide."

His words struck me. It felt as though a ton of bricks had fallen on my chest. I could feel the tightness in my throat, and my body trembled as I quietly asked, "Suicide, are you sure?"

"Yes, we are sure, he left a note. We are absolutely certain. I am the Officer in charge of this case. I was called to the scene. Ms. Saint John, I am very sorry," stated Officer Burien with deep emotion.

"Your brother's remains are at Hilo Hospital morgue awaiting an autopsy. You will need to contact a funeral home here at Hilo. The police report will take a couple of months to prepare, and you may request a copy of the report in writing at that time. Is there anything else, Ms. Saint John?"

"No, nothing else," I said. "Thank you for your assistance. Good-bye."

I stood up and immediately saw the look of shock on Rachel's beautiful young face. I knew she was devastated. She was the face and eyes of her father when he was her age. When John was her age, he had already lived a lifetime. Two tours of combat in Vietnam had taken its toll. My heart was broken, but this wasn't the time for my tears. I knew I had to contact our other Vietnam veteran brother, David, in British Columbia.

I left Rachel in the hands of her close friend who gave me the assurance that he would take good care of her, especially over the coming days. The urgency now was to contact David and my twin sister. Poor Mom was fortunately or unfortunately in the second last stage of her Alzheimer's disease. She had forgotten a few years prior that she even had children. Blessed was she today not to know or suffer the loss of her first son. Mom's loss would be felt threefold by her remaining children.

Driving home in the rain, my thoughts were with David. How was I going to tell him that John was dead, much less tell him that he died by his own hand? I searched my heart, and I knew there wasn't going to be an easy way. This was going to hurt David immensely. I prayed for strength for my family. Our loss was going to take considerable time to heal for it was only our family who fully understood the magnitude of the loss from our fallen soldier.

The telephone was ringing as I entered my home; the display indicated that it was David calling. I picked up the call and spoke his name.

"David."

"Cathy," He replied. I could sense the deep sadness in his voice echoing his pain, suffering and helplessness. I immediately sensed that he already knew about John.

"David, oh David, we've lost John. I can hardly believe what has happened! I wasn't expecting this today. How are you doing?"

"Jesus, Cathy. I don't know how I'm doing. John called last night and said he was going to take himself out. I told him to check into the hospital so he would get help there. John said that he was tired of fighting the demons; he stated that he has lived with his PTSD condition and Agent Orange contaminants for almost thirteen years. He believed that it was just a matter of time before the authorities captured and confined him. He was weary of 'dogging' the authorities. Enough was enough. He just wanted peace. John claimed that was why he went to Hawaii, and he had hoped that his last visit to British Columbia had prepared me for this day. I told him not to do it, but he warned me that if I contacted any authorities, he would take them out, too. I can't believe he did it."

"I know, David, it's a big shock. But you knew John better than any of us. He was always a man of his word. God forgive me for saying this, but you did the right thing by allowing John to die with the dignity he deserved. We both know that he would have ended up in some veterans' hospital or institution, dying of cancer from Agent Orange. If not that, he would have lost control of his life, only to be incarcerated for his remaining years due to his PTSD. Time was running out for John. That alone would have made him a prisoner of war—in his mind. David, you knew that, too."

"Yes Cathy, I knew that. But why now?"

"David, if it wasn't now, then when? Remember this: John was trained by the elite Special Forces of the United States Army not to be taken alive. There wasn't anything any of us could have done to stop what happened. I only wish he had given me a clue that this was what he intended. I would have respected his right to die, but there was just so much more I wanted to tell him before he left us. I wanted to see him again, just one more time, and now, it's too late.

David, I only just found out a half hour ago after speaking to the Hilo Police. How did you find out? Have you spoken to our sisters? Do they know about John?"

"A family member of John's former wife now living here in British Columbia just called me and told me John that was dead. I'll call our sisters when we are finished speaking. Cathy, I want you to take care of the details. Can you do that?"

"Yes." I quietly responded. "It's time John came home. We'll bring him home to Newfoundland. He always wanted to come home, remember."

"Yeah, it's too bad it had to be like this."

"I know, but it's the right thing to do. I'll call Hawaii tomorrow and get things moving. If this can't be done by phone in a timely manner, then I'll take the next flight to Hawaii."

"Good girl, I knew I could count on you!"

"David, what time did John call you last night?"

"It must have been about 8:45 p.m. Hawaiian time. Why?"

"Just wondering, that's all."

"Listen, get some rest now. You have a lot to do tomorrow. I'll call you tomorrow night."

"Okay, but David, you have got to promise me that you'll take good care of yourself."

"Promise, don't worry, I love you. Good night, Cathy"

"I love you too. Goodnight."

**Bringing John Home to Rest in Peace**

Hawaiian time is six and a half hours behind Newfoundland time. This meant that I had to wait until 3 p.m. local time before I could establish an 8:30 a.m. contact in Honolulu with Marlene, John's former counselor at the veteran center.

Meanwhile, my focus turned to Rachel. I wanted to check on her and disclose the conversation I'd had with David last evening. I drove to her apartment and informed her that David asked me to handle everything that was required and to obtain further information about John's death. I told her I would also make the arrangements for John's remains to be shipped home. I explained the time difference and that I would contact Honolulu later in the day. I also advised her that I would drop in daily to visit her and that it would probably be at least a month before John's funeral took place. I reminded Rachel that there were a lot of details to handle, and family members needed time to get past the shock of last evening and plan their return to Newfoundland. She knew that if she needed anything, I was just three streets or a telephone call away.

John had spoken kindly in his letters about Marlene, and I remembered that he mentioned if anything tragic happened, we could contact her. He praised her as an intelligent, no-nonsense individual who was very kind. I searched the container where I kept John's letters and found his first letter from Hawaii, which contained Marlene's contact information.

The veterans center in Honolulu placed my call on hold for a few minutes before transferring me to Marlene. It was quite evident that she was equally as devastated as we were that John was dead. When I asked for details of John's death, she avoided my question.

Marlene stated that she had met John a couple of times and immediately liked him. He had shared some of his writings with her, and she was quite impressed by his intelligence and sensitivity. I explained to her that John also felt a deep respect for her professionalism. I confessed to Marlene that my family was in shock and I needed some direction. We needed answers as to what transpired in Hilo the previous evening. I explained that the police did not release any details. Who could assist us in arranging the return of John's ashes and belongings? I also advised Marlene that if I didn't have answers that day, I would be on a flight to Hilo the next morning.

Marlene was aware of our needs and requested three hours to cut through the red tape, at which time she would provide me with a contact in Hilo. When our conversation ended, I wondered why Marlene was reluctant to discuss the details of John's death. I sensed the same avoidance that I'd experienced last evening with Officer Burien. Why?

Exhausted, I laid down to rest, but was unsuccessful. Attempting to function without sleep for two days had begun to take its toll. My mind wandered back to an evening during 1976 when John left Newfoundland. I recalled the moments before he boarded that flight and the premonition that warned me then that we would never see each other again. And we didn't.

The ringing of the telephone stole me away from my thoughts. True to her word, it was Marlene. She called within the three-hour time limit. She instructed me to telephone the veteran center in Hilo and contact Jim Morrow. He was a Vietnam veteran and therapist who specialized in counseling trauma victims. Marlene assured me that Jim would be the best person to discuss the expedition of John's remains, which would be cremated. His personal belongings would also be returned. She advised me against traveling to Hawaii. Marlene wished me and my family well and offered her heartfelt sympathy. "We will all miss John," she stated. "He was indeed a very special person."

I thanked Marlene and promised her that I would not travel to Hawaii unless the situation required it.

I retreated to my office with a heavy heart knowing that the next conversation would be the most challenging. The room was illuminated by a small table lamp. I sat on the floor with the telephone beside me in the corner of the room while I mustered up the courage to dial the telephone number. Finally, I did.

"Hilo veteran center, Vernon speaking."

"Hello, this is Cathy Saint John. May I speak to Mr. Jim Morrow, please?"

"Yes, just a second, he's expecting your call."

Within a few seconds, I heard a man's voice gently announce, "Jim Morrow speaking."

"Mr. Morrow, I'm John Blake's sister, Cathy," I whispered, attempting to relax what had become an all too familiar tightening sensation in my throat. My tears streamed uncontrollably down my face as I choked out the question, "Can you tell me what happened to John?" I covered the mouthpiece of the telephone to stifle the sound of my sobs and then regained my composure as I listened to his voice.

"Cathy, call me Jim," he requested in a deep soothing voice; a voice that commanded peace and spiritual comfort. Immediately, I felt calmer and more assured that I was communicating with a person who fully understood my gut-wrenching, emotional pain, but more importantly a person who was capable of sharing his expertise and experience.

I nodded my head in confirmation to his request, sucked in a deep breath and asked, "Jim, please tell me what you know about John's death."

"John apparently visited the veterans center late that afternoon and requested a couple of envelopes. Kristen was on duty and gave John the envelopes. He took the envelopes and immediately left. About 9:30 that evening we were called by Hilo police with the news that your brother was found dead on the premises at the Federal Post Office. We responded to the call, and upon arrival we immediately saw John. The custodian said he had seen John walking about the Post Office building around 8:15. Therefore, we estimated time of death at about 8:30. The FBI was called to the scene because the death occurred on Federal property. We believe John was sending a message."

"What do you mean a message?"

"Well, veterans, in general, don't have a lot of tolerance when it comes to the Federal authorities. The consensus around here was a 'thumbs up' for John. He had gotten the 'Federal boys' out to work after hours."

"Jim, last night, I spoke to David, our brother who lives in British Columbia. He stated that John had called him at 8:45 p.m. Hawaiian time. They spoke for about five minutes. It must have been shortly after that when John took his life."

"Then his time of death must have occurred at nine o'clock, taps."

"What do you mean, taps?"

"That's military time. taps are played at dusk and military funerals. It means 'lights out go to sleep'."

"Jim, exactly how did John take his life? I have some idea, but I must know the details. The family needs to know today. It will be months before the police and autopsy reports are released."

"What do you know?" Jim asked in an uneasy tone, wondering how much he would have to explain.

I hesitated to answer. The concern in his voice confirmed my suspicions that everyone, including Officer Burien, Marlene and Jim were all traumatized by John's death. Why?

Jim repeated his question with authority. "Cathy, what do you know?"

"Jim, I don't know how true this is, but my brother, David, was advised that John's throat was ruthlessly cut open with a machete. Is that true?"

"Not exactly, Cathy. John did use a half size machete and very skillfully performed a cutting wound. The result was he quickly bled to death peacefully and painlessly," Jim gently stated.

I listened to Jim describe John's death in detail. It wasn't difficult to comprehend what he had described. John had taken himself out military style and immediately died from self-inflicted cutting wounds. Somehow, I wasn't totally surprised or shocked.

"Cathy, are you alright? Tell me what you're thinking." Jim asked.

"Jim, he died all alone on a slab of concrete. Why?"

"Have you ever been to Hawaii?"

"No, and right now I don't believe I will ever go there."

"One day you'll change your mind, but for now I will tell you this. The last sight your brother viewed is why John came to Hawaii to end his life. Hawaii resembles Vietnam, mountainous with lush green foliage. The weather is much the same: monsoon and heat. A lot of Vietnam veterans come here. It reminds them of the 'Nam. They don't mix with the tourists, and live in the countryside.

John's final view was of well-kept grounds, flowers, shrubs and a spouting water fountain. Beyond that is a crystal-clear body of blue water framed by magnificent mountains. Actually, Hawaii is quite beautiful and peaceful."

"Jim, you make this all sound so comforting, but I don't understand. We recently received letters which indicated that John seemed busy and content. The postcards I received indicated he was finally happy. He had found a piece of heaven for himself. He was truly ecstatic. Why would he suddenly end his own life?"

"Cathy, I understand your confusion," he continued. "I've seen what you've just described many times in Vietnam veterans. They reach euphoria once they have accepted their decision of death. Many Vietnam veterans who are deeply troubled with PTSD such as John live in tremendous torment, deep depression and constant despair. It is only when they come to terms with their decision to end their pain and suffering do they reach an acceptance of their chosen destiny," stated Jim.

"Another important item in understanding the Vietnam veteran is a date or anniversary," he stated. "The 13th or the number '13' must have meant something to John. Keep in mind, it wasn't a decision hastily made. John obviously had taken tremendous time and effort in coming to terms with his decision to leave this world. The how, when, and where have been answered, and the 'why' will unfold as time goes on. Remember, John sent a message. When the pain of his death passes, you will fully understand."

"Jim, where do I go from here, and how do I proceed in having John's cremains and belongings transported home?" I asked. "I understand from John's Living Will that his final request was to be buried in a Military Cemetery. There is one such cemetery here in Newfoundland, just a few streets away from my home. Lately, John had expressed interest in returning home to Newfoundland. However, the mental health services available here were essentially non-existent for persons suffering from chronic combat PTSD. Regardless, the Will stated that his personal belongings be returned to his daughter along with the American Flag, Old Glory."

Jim replied, "First, contact a funeral establishment in your hometown and have them contact the funeral home and arrange for the cremation here in Hilo," instructed Jim. "The funeral home here will send documents for you to sign and that will be sufficient for the United States Government to release John's remains into your custody.

"Incidentally, John's belongings were neatly packed and waiting in his hotel room when the police picked them up," he continued. "The police will hold these until they inventory the items; then they'll release them to a designated party.

"We at the veterans centre can assist you with that, but we will require a faxed consent from you giving us permission to take custody of John's belongings. When the police department has finished their report, we will pick up his things. That will take a couple of weeks."

"Jim, thank you for your assistance, I could never manage all of this without you—and the help from the veteran center." Then I asked, "Is there anything else about John's death that I should know?"

"There is one other thing," he acknowledged. "John had secured on his person a banner and it read: LEAD, FOLLOW OR GET THE HELL OUT OF THE WAY!"

"I wonder what he meant."

"I'm not sure, but knowing your brother, I'm sure it was part of his message."

"Jim, thank you again, you've been very patient, understanding and a comfort to speak with I realize this must be difficult for you, too, reliving our tragedy."

"Cathy, you probably don't realize it, but you have been a help to me, too. It's necessary to talk out traumas. It's the only way that traumatic incidents can begin to heal. So, thank you."

"Jim, may I telephone you again if I need to discuss things over the next few weeks?"

"Certainly, that's what I'm here for...to assist veterans and their families."

"Bless you, Jim, I have a feeling you're heaven-sent."

"Take care of yourself, Cathy. You still have a trying time ahead."

"I will. Just one last thing," I said. "I understand from the police that John left a note. Did you see the note?"

"Yes, I did," said Jim. As he paused, I could hear him taking a breath and then his voice cracked as he said, "John wrote, 'I apologize to the staff at the veterans center for putting each of you through this, but I've always been wondering where the boys went—I think I'll go looking for them now'."

A minute of silence passed and then I asked, "Jim, did he mean that he was going to look for his friends who died in Vietnam?"

"Yes, that's exactly what he meant. He went to Ranger Heaven looking for the boys."

"I understand now. Thank you again."

"You're welcome."

**John's Final Journey**

A funeral home in Hilo, Hawaii, was contacted and arrangements were put into place. A local funeral home in St. John's, Newfoundland would receive John's cremains. The expedition documents were faxed, signed and returned with a heavy heart. Our families' deep sadness was just settling into reality. The days that followed were extremely difficult. I didn't understand the feelings that had overtaken my well-being, and I sought advice and contacted Jim Morrow in Hilo.

"Hello, Hilo veteran center, Jim Morrow speaking."

"Hello Jim, this is Cathy. Do you have a few minutes to speak with me? Have I called at a busy time?"

"Yes, Cathy, we can speak. Is there something wrong?"

"Jim, I'm experiencing a reaction of sorts that is very unfamiliar to me. I don't sleep at night, and I am not able to eat much, but I expected that under the circumstances. I constantly find myself thinking about John in the morgue and I'm cold—so very cold. It's like my blood is running cold. My flesh feels warm, but inside I'm deathly cold. I'm constantly trembling. Are you familiar with this type of reaction?"

"Yes, you're experiencing shock. It's not uncommon. John's death was sudden and traumatic to you. Now, your body has reacted to the trauma. There are five stages of grieving: denial, anger, bargaining, depression, and acceptance. It is important that you allow yourself to flow through each stage. The most difficult stage is depression. You don't want to stay there. It is very dark there, very dark. It's important to move through that stage as quickly as possible to avoid depression getting a grip on your well-being. You'll need to pace yourself to feel well. You've been given a difficult task to deal with. I'll help you all I can. Have you made the arrangements yet in expediting John's remains home?"

"Yes, I have. A funeral home in Hilo is taking care of the cremation. I need to make arrangements to have John's belongings returned."

"Fax me authorization. We at the veterans center, will pick up John's belongings from the police station and arrange to have them sent to your home."

"Thank you, Jim, that is very kind of you. I certainly appreciate your assistance."

"It's important to take care of yourself, and let me remind you we are only too happy to assist you and your family in any way that we possibly can. Remember, it also helps us to get through this difficult time."

"Jim, thank you for listening, I appreciate your advice."

"It's a pleasure to help you. Remember, take care of yourself. You're welcome to call anytime."

When we said goodbye, I knew I had a better understanding of what was happening. I sent the fax that gave Jim the authorization he had requested. I felt relieved that soon John's belongings would be returned to Newfoundland. I felt appreciative that people like Jim Morrow existed and that he was there when our family needed him.

My family was in grief. Each member, in his or her own way, sought relief from their pain and sorrow. During the days and weeks to follow, each of us turned to one another for support and comfort. We prayed for peace and tranquility to fill our despairing souls and ease the pain of our loss.

Unfortunately, there was precious little time for me to grieve. I remembered Jim's advice to work through the process, but with so much on my plate, I neglected my grief.

Each day I felt I had to do whatever it took to ease the stress and emotional load for my siblings. More importantly, it was my responsibility to bring John home and fulfill his final request. Business first, grieve later.

Many people on the Avalon Peninsula of Newfoundland would remember John—likely by the name Wayne Saint John. He had spent his early years in Newfoundland and attended school, dated girls and worked a part-time job prior to our family's departure in 1966.

I knew that an announcement needed to be placed in the local newspaper regarding John's passing. After consulting with David and Rachel, I wrote an article with their approval and prepared to submit it the editor of the local newspaper. Perhaps we were biased, but we felt that his story would be of interest to the public. We naively thought that the editor would publish the article or write one of their own regarding our brother, a Newfoundlander of numerous achievements finally coming home to rest in peace.

I presented the article to the receptionist at the newspaper office, and the receptionist, immediately showed it to a manager. The manager returned to the counter with the article in hand and informed me that he was sorry for our loss, but the article wasn't a story that they were interested in publishing. They did, however, offer me a discount rate should I want to publish it. Of course, I did! The following article was subsequently published.

**FOR THIS SOLDIER THE WAR HAS FINALLY ENDED**
**JOHN W. SAINT JOHN—BLAKE**
**February 5, 1949—February 13, 1996**

John W. Saint John-Blake died suddenly on February 13, 1996, in Hilo, Hawaii. John was affectionately known as Wayne Saint John; son of Pearl and the late John Saint John (WWI), a businessman of Topsail Hill, Conception Bay, Newfoundland. John attended Bishop Field and Foxtrap High School during the mid-1960s.

In 1968, John joined the United States Army during the Vietnam era. He completed Special Forces training earned the 'Green Beret,' then ultimately served as an Airborne Ranger. John completed two tours of duty in Vietnam. He returned to Newfoundland, married and settled into family life. After several years of undiagnosed mental health difficulty and turmoil, John returned to the United States and was eventually diagnosed with Post Traumatic Stress Disorder (PTSD). It was there he received treatment and an understanding of the disorder.

During his years in the United States, John devoted his life and writing skills to assist other Vietnam veterans navigate the bureaucracy in government under the pen name 'Mr. X'. John was a gifted writer and poet. He found tranquility in the many pages of writings he produced during thirty years of writing. He was a character of the cause. This alone was all the incentive he needed to be there-for the plight of others.

In 1982 John walked 3,200 miles across the United States of America, and carried the American flag to bring awareness of the Vietnam veterans, POWs, and MIAs in an effort to 'check the pulse of America'. The walk coincided with the unveiling of the Vietnam Veteran War Memorial in Washington, D.C.

John fought a long, hard battle with PTSD, and it was not without the battle cry 'don't let the enemy get you,' did he

> fight his last battle on February 13th. John died a triumphant soldier and freed himself from an enemy that had consumed his life for the past thirteen years. John W. Saint John—Blake devoted his life to the tranquility and freedom of others.
>
> For this soldier, the war finally ended. May he now rest in peace.

Immediately after the article was published, my telephone constantly rang. Being the only 'Saint John' in the local telephone book, my number was easily located. I wasn't surprised; our family was well known during the 1960's. Many of his school buddies and friends telephoned. They were shocked and saddened that he had died as a result of his injuries pertaining to PTSD.

What was more ironic was the reporter who called from the local newspaper. He said, "I'm sorry to be calling you during this difficult time. But I remember a story about that guy who walked across the United States. It must be difficult when a guy is shell-shocked. I'd like to do a story about him for the newspaper."

I couldn't believe what I had heard. 'Shell-shocked' was a term used post WWI for soldiers suffering from severe nervousness. I told him I would get back to him.

Later in the evening, I received another unusual telephone call from a man who I immediately recognized by name. He told me that he was calling from Markham, Ontario. He was fascinated by my brother's story and the fact that he was Newfoundland's only 'Green Beret' and 'Airborne Ranger' who served two tours in Vietnam. He was aware that John had walked 3,200 miles across the United States carrying the American flag and that he was Canadian. The caller boasted that our John was indeed a hero and a true Newfoundlander. The caller wanted my approval to erect a monument in newfoundland in honour of John's memory. I couldn't believe what I was hearing. I almost laughed out loud, and that was something I hadn't been able to do in weeks. He then asked me if I would agree to a monument being placed in St. John's prestigious Bowring Park.

I gathered my thoughts and calmly replied, "Let me first explain who my brother was. He was John Saint John's son. He was the child that accidently burned down the former Woodstock Cottage Club in the early 1950's. I recognize your name as my father's former business partner who failed to provide insurance coverage on the Woodstock Cottage Club in Topsail, during that era." The caller immediately disconnected the call.

I telephoned David and advised him of the conversation with Dad's former business partner, and a reporter from the newspaper. David moaned in disbelief. The reporter's comments were more concerning than Dad's former business partner. We decided we would be very selective over who we would permit to write articles that concerned our fallen soldier. David suggested I contact the reporter and offer to write the article subject to editorial approval.

A few days later, I contacted the same reporter and said. "My family and I have concluded that you, Sir, don't understand PTSD, but an article about John's life could be provided to you subject to editorial approval if you are still interested."

I heard an impatient puff of breath when he grunted his response, "No thank you," and immediately hung up.

The local funeral home called to notify me that the cremation had taken place in Hilo. John's remains and Old Glory were in transit to Newfoundland. The funeral director suggested I visit his office and discuss the service and other details that concerned burial. He also suggested that I contact the local Royal Canadian Legionnaires and American Post Padre to perform the military portion of the service. It was at that point when the funeral director advised me that I would need to contact Department of Veterans Affairs (DVA), Canada, and obtain authorization for John's cremains to be interred in the military section of Mt. Pleasant Cemetery, commonly known as the Field of Honour.

Mt. Pleasant Cemetery is a public cemetery with a small section reserved for veterans of WWI, WWII and Korea. There are Canadian and American soldiers buried in the DVA departmental plots and even some civilians without any military connection. The funeral director and I did not anticipate any difficulty in my family purchasing a small burial plot for John's cremains. We each felt that a veteran is a veteran.

I began to feel confident that within a few weeks my family could bring closure to our loss. The memorial service was scheduled for the middle of March. This would allow enough time for my sisters and David to travel home. It was beginning to look hopeful that very soon our family could pick up the broken pieces, pull ourselves together and carry on with life just as John would want.

We were extremely aware of John's triumphs and struggles in life. We knew in our hearts that he would not want us to be deeply troubled by his sudden death or to be grief-stricken for any length of time. He would never want any one of us to live a minute of our lives anywhere near the darkness that had encompassed his own life.

John's death was to be a celebration of freedom from the darkness that engulfed his life, free from the demons that preyed on his mind and free to come home and rest in peace with the other soldiers. The only remaining aspect of his funeral was a 'farewell salute'.

**Outside the Fence**

Mr. Tom Strong, Sub-Regional Director of Veterans Affairs, Newfoundland, Canada, was given the dubious task of handling the family's burial request. We were seeking permission to purchase a small burial plot in the local Field of Honour, the only military cemetery in St. John's Newfoundland.

My first impression of Mr. Strong revealed a man whom I felt was sincerely concerned with assisting the family. He asked several questions concerning John's military past related to any history within the Canadian Forces/Reserves. He asked if John had been a recipient of any disability pension.

My response was that John was in the Canadian Cadets when he was a young teenager, but the family had left Newfoundland in 1966. John had joined the American Forces in 1968, at the age of nineteen and received an honorable discharge in 1971. I informed Mr. Strong that the Vietnam War had a devastating effect on John. In 1984, he was declared one hundred percent disabled and received a U.S. permanent disability pension. I also advised him that in 1995, John was approved for—and received—a Canadian disability pension. Mr. Strong, armed with John's history, proceeded to investigate John's eligibility for burial in the Field of Honour, the military section of Mt. Pleasant Cemetery. Within a few days, Mr. Strong responded with an answer.

"Ms. Saint John, I am sorry to inform you that, under the Canadian DVA, guidelines, we are unable to grant you permission to purchase a plot for your brother's remains. His military background does not meet departmental criteria."

"You can't be serious," I replied taken aback. "John was a veteran who served in the elite forces of the United States Army, our allies, and was honorably discharged. John maintained his Canadian citizenship, for God sake! John died a decorated veteran and a Canadian. His cremains are now en route to St. John's with the intent that his ashes be interred in the only military cemetery here in St. John's, Mt. Pleasant Cemetery. This is outrageous! There must be a way! John's memorial service is scheduled for the 16th of March. Please take another look at this case! I pleaded.

"I'll make some more inquiries for you, but it doesn't look promising," advised Mr. Strong.

"Yes please, try again. This is unbelievable," I insisted.

Mr. Strong would eventually make three additional attempts to achieve a positive answer, but his efforts were of no avail. The Canadian Federal government constantly repeated their answer, "NO." We needed to bring closure to our loss. More importantly, we had to fulfill John's final request, which was to come home and rest in peace in a military cemetery.

During our final conversation, Mr. Strong reiterated the Federal Government's position concerning the matter. "The Canadian Vietnam Veterans are not accepted nor recognized as war veterans by the Department of Veterans Affairs, Canada," he reported. This information would be met by total disbelief and shock from our family.

"Mr. Strong," I replied, "on behalf of my family, we appreciate your efforts and understand our Federal Government's position. But, we will not accept or allow the Government of Canada to shun the

Canadian Vietnam veterans. This issue will become public knowledge in the near future. Hold onto your chair, because we're all going for a rough ride!"

Reverend Tilley and American Post Padre Mr. Riddle met with me to discuss details pertaining to the memorial service. I informed them that burial for John's cremains would be delayed until DVA Canada changed their policy or made an exception for John's interment in the military cemetery at Mt. Pleasant. I explained that the Field of Honour is the only military cemetery in eastern Newfoundland, and according to DVA Canada it is not available to Vietnam veterans. I also advised them that although the Field of Honour at Mt. Pleasant is not one of the four official "Fields of Honour" in Canada, however, it is titled a Field of Honour that contains DVA departmental plots. All parties involved were in disbelief except, of course, our Federal Government. Was this really happening in Canada?

"Ms. Saint John," said Mr. Riddle, "let me make some inquiries. Perhaps there is a way."

"Thank you for asking, but DVA said there is no way possible, at least not now. We are going to take this issue to the media, as this is madness."

"Just let me give it a try. Give me one day to try," pleaded Mr. Riddle.

"I can assure you, Mr. Riddle, I don't believe they are about to change their minds, but if you feel you must, then so be it. Yes, go ahead and give it another try. We do appreciate your effort."

The meeting was concluded after we selected the hymns and prayers. We confirmed the details of the honour guard, which would be performed by Mr. Riddle and members of the local American Post. RCL Branch No. 1, was also invited to participate in the service. Everything was in order; everything except the burial.

I felt bewildered as I sat in my parked car and wondered what this world had become. It was inconceivable to me that an honorably discharged, decorated-for-valor, Vietnam veteran who was a Canadian and the son of a WWI veteran—would be denied burial in a Canadian military cemetery. It was a cruel injustice to a Canadian family of a soldier who had honorably served in the United States Army, Canada's ally.

I was entrusted with my dear brother's final request, yet was about to fail him and my family shamefully. John's cremains could have been buried at Arlington, the most renowned cemetery in North America. Our country had rejected John's final request and denied closure for his family.

Tears stung my eyes as I thought about how much John had given to this world and how little he'd received in return. And now, his homeland had denied him his request to rest in peace there. I reflected on my brother's youth, a boy of thirteen who suddenly became the man of the house by acclamation after Dad's death, to a soldier of barely twenty years old who served two tours in Vietnam. Tours of duty in Vietnam that destroyed the brother we knew and understood. He gave endless assistance to countless U.S. Vietnam veterans, men who gave him reason to 'hang-on' and keep fighting. He walked 3,200 miles for the 'boys'. He sacrificed spending time with his family in order to protect each loved one from the heartache and madness of his PTSD. We had lived and loved him from a distance through telephone calls and letters. In the end, John relinquished his life. He had given up so much and expected so little. He sought only to have his final request respected.

The next day, Mr. Riddle telephoned me at home and informed me that he had tried his best, but the result was still negative. DVA Canada decision was firm, and had suggested that there was a nice plot just outside of the fence alongside the military section of the Field of Honour. DVA's recommendation was deemed unsuitable.

Shaking my head in further disbelief I gently replied, "With all due respect, Mr. Riddle, John had been outside of the fence most of his life, but not this time. This time he's coming home, and he will be respected." I thanked Mr. Riddle for his good intentions, and confirmed the time of service. I advised him that burial for John would be delayed indefinitely due to our country's unjust policy. I told him that the family would be initiating a public campaign in the days to follow. We said our goodbyes and immediately after I had hung up the telephone it rang.

David had called to say that he had just received a letter in the mail from John, which was mailed the evening he died in Hawaii. He read it to me and we both sobbed. I asked him to fax me the letter, which he did.

John's last correspondence from Hilo, Hawaii prior to his death.

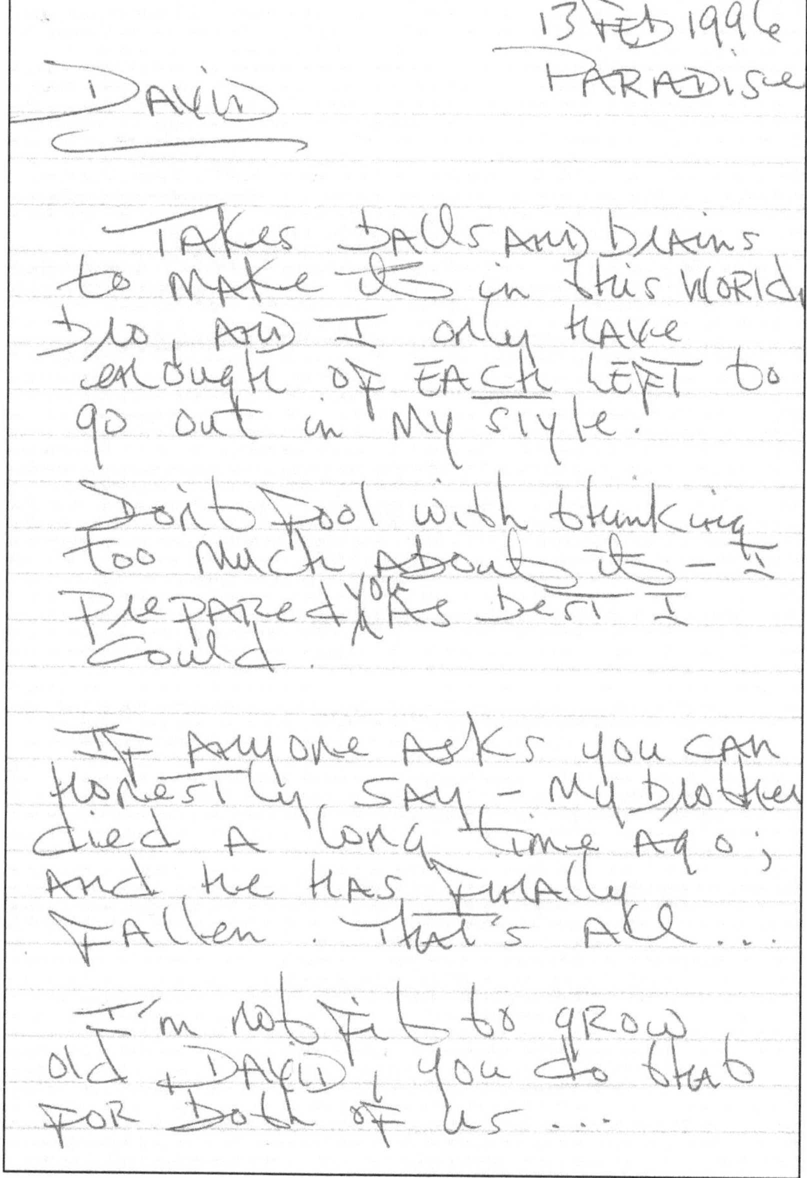

13 FEB 1996
PARADISE

DAVID

TAKES BALLS AND BRAINS to MAKE IT in this WORLD, BRO, AND I ONLY HAVE ENOUGH OF EACH LEFT to go out in MY STYLE!

Don't fool with thinking too much about it - I PREPARED YOU AS BEST I Could.

IF ANYONE ASKS YOU CAN HONESTLY SAY - MY BROTHER died A LONG time AGO; AND HE HAS FINALLY FALLEN. THAT'S ALL...

I'm not fit to grow old, DAVID, you do that FOR BOTH of us...

**John's Final Return Home**

John's cremains finally arrived home. The funeral director called and requested a meeting to finalize the details. When I arrived at the funeral home, I was greeted by the director, who escorted me to his office. I sat down with a heavy heart. Directly in front of me on a mahogany desk laid a small shipping carton from Hawaii. The director gently opened the package and revealed what was left of our dear, sweet brother. A small plastic bag contained John's grey, sooty ashes accompanied by a small brown envelope. I opened the envelope that contained John's metal service identification tag, strung on a rawhide rope. It was the same identification tag he had worn in Vietnam over twenty-five years ago. Our soldier boy had finally come home to rest.

I felt alone in the office, and perhaps I was. I held John's military 'dog tag' and gently touched each letter of his name: BLAKE, JOHN W., identification number, blood type, and religion. I remembered the time when his name was John Wayne Saint John, the boy whom I had lovingly called Wayne.

I reflected on the lifetime of sacrifice, pain and suffering that had transformed Wayne Saint John into John W. Blake, Mom and Dad's first son. I remembered John telling me, quite frankly and without malice, that he had made his name what it was and that was the name he would one day take to his grave. And now, that day had arrived.

I departed the funeral establishment with the sight of John's ashes embedded in my memory and his military tag firmly gripped in my hand. During the silent drive home I recalled a particular family story from John's youth. It was one that gave me a peaceful, happy feeling.

Apparently, John was quite the character, even at the tender age of two and a half. I smiled half-heartedly as I visualized him as a little boy with a thick mop of dark, curly hair and green eyes that sparkled with pride and mischief whenever he escaped the nursemaid.

It was a time long ago, before the big fire that burned down the former Woodstock Cottage Club. The dining room was exquisite, and many of St. John's finest ladies and gentlemen would gather there for afternoon tea. Whenever John escaped the nursemaid, he would make a beeline to the dining room and entertain the patrons. Mom would often be busy in the kitchen supervising the staff and organizing the food orders when suddenly the air would be filled with young John's rendition of "Beautiful Brown Eyes." "Beautiful, beautiful brown eyes," he'd sing. "...I'll never love blue eyes again." Horrified, Mom summoned the nursemaid to catch young John and return him to their living quarters upstairs. In the meantime, John continued singing and collecting coins as gratuity for his performance before being gingerly captured and swept away by the unnerved nursemaid.

Once I parked my vehicle, a deep sadness swept over me again as I studied John's military tag beneath the moonlight. I tucked it in my pocket, entered the house. Once my family settled down for the evening, I reached for John's tag to hold once again. It was then I noticed the discoloration in the rawhide rope. I examined it more closely and decided to wash the rope before giving the military tag to Rachel in the morning.

Warm water flowed softly from the tap as I massaged the stiffness from the strand of rawhide. At first, clear water drained into the white sink while I gently ran my fingers over the rawhide. Soon the water in the sink became discolored, first brown, then crimson red and finally pink. I realized this would be the closest I would ever come to touching what remained of my brother. Twenty minutes passed as John's blood mixed freely with my tears, which dropped between my fingers. I caressed the strand of rawhide and whispered, "I'm sorry your life was so very difficult. I wish I could have done something more for you, but wishing doesn't change anything. Does it, John? I'm going to miss you. All those years we could have had are now gone. Never again will we share our interest in poetry or exchange our thoughts, words of wisdom or sibling advice. No, we will never again laugh about the foolish things that filled the years of our early childhood in Topsail, Newfoundland. It's all gone now. But most importantly, did you know you mattered and that I loved you? Did you know that I needed you? I needed to know that you would always be there as you promised in your letters from Vietnam."

I wiped away my tears and gently patted dry the strand of rawhide with a towel. I left it draped over the cabinet door handle to air dry overnight. I promised myself that I would take John's military tag to Rachel in the morning. I knew it would initially bring her sadness, but I also felt that it would eventually bring her comfort and peace.

The next morning, I visited Rachel. She was both happy and sad when I placed John's identification tag in her hand. She instinctively slipped the strand of rawhide around her neck. The tag rested gently on her heart. She pressed her hand over it and vowed never to take it off.

The letter arrived from Tom Strong, Sub-Regional Director of Veterans Affairs, Newfoundland and Labrador, Canada. The official written response explained why DVA Canada would not permit the burial of our late brother in the Field of Honour at Mt. Pleasant Cemetery. Finally, DVA's position was stated as large as life in black and white. Our Canadian Government's position claimed that Canada was not involved in the Vietnam War. Our family—and most Canadians—certainly knew that was a falsehood.

The frigid Atlantic coast March air that blew a bitter gale that day could not have made me feel any colder than Mr. Strong's letter. I was numbed and revolted that there would not be any closure in John's death for the foreseeable future. I was sickened that the Canadian Vietnam veterans (CVV's) were not accepted as veterans in Canada. I now fully understood the rejection evident during the 'bad' years that followed the Vietnam War in America. The very same or worse rejection that soldiers experienced in the 1970's was now being felt by our family here in Canada, twenty-five years later.

Time had not changed my country's attitude. The ignorance, fear and misguided pride that DVA Canada projected in their response could not have been more dishonorable or despicable. The explanation of Canada's non-involvement was the turning point for my family. We knew the difference. Canada was indeed involved in Vietnam, and we were not about to go quietly away. Nor would we accept the disgraceful attitude presented by the Canadian Government's state of amnesia concerning their participation in the American war effort during the Vietnam War.

The first of many public media interviews occurred that very day, in my home. Canadian Broadcasting Corporation (CBC), *Here and Now* local news aired the first interview, and the media clip went national that evening. During that first interview, with tears in my eyes, I vowed that no matter what it took, this country would respect John Blake, a Canadian Vietnam veteran in Canada. The fight was on!

Once the reporter and her crew left my home, I retreated to the privacy of my bedroom, threw myself on the bed and cried. My heart had been broken by the abandonment of our government at the very time our family needed it to be respectful and forthcoming. The next day, I made a promise in John's memory that my family and I would fight hard for what was right and just. We would carry the load for the next five years, if necessary. It was our intent to bring awareness of our family's plight for John's final request to the nation to be honoured. We would have 'one more for the boys'—our Canadian boys.

Later the next day, my family and I discussed the CBC interview and the official letter from the DVA in Canada. We all agreed that we would plan our course of action after the memorial service and bring additional national attention to our government's atrocious decision.

When I arrived home from a meeting later in the afternoon, there was a delivery slip attached to my front door. I had missed the delivery of John's belongings, which were sent from Hawaii. I contacted the courier, and they assured me delivery before noon on the following day. There was also an unusual phone message. A male caller from Ontario stated that he had viewed the story of my family's plight concerning John Blake's burial on CBC national news. He said that he, too, was a Vietnam veteran in Canada and was very sorry for our troubles. He stated with conviction, "Never give up! And don't ever let them see you cry again!"

That was my turning point. I recognized that there were people out there, rough and ready, strong and willing, to listen and help. All I had to do was stay strong, take the lead and they would both follow and guide me. I knew then I was not alone. I also knew that those politicians in Ottawa would never ever witness me in a delicate state again. This was my time to toughen up and stand strong! Perhaps this was part of John's message. In bringing John home, I had to lead and supporters would follow. Maybe then the politicians who were in denial would get the hell out of the way. Time would tell.

David telephoned and confirmed that his flight to Newfoundland would connect in Toronto with our sister's flight. I felt grateful that they would travel together on their journey home. I advised David that John's belongings had arrived. We agreed that after the memorial service we would open the boxes that contained John's personal items together with Rachel. I wished him a safe journey home and confirmed that I would be at St. John's airport the next day at midnight for their arrival.

The next day, the courier arrived with John's belongings as promised. Shortly after, I left the house to run errands. When I returned home, there were several messages. One in particular was from a man who indicated that he was a Canadian Vietnam Veteran (CVV) who lived in Winnipeg. He had also watched the interview on CBC national evening news the night before and expressed his heartfelt sympathy. He requested a return telephone call at my earliest convenience. I noted his name and number and I knew I would return his call before the weekend, after the memorial service.

My brother and sister's flight arrived on time, and we were relieved to finally see each other. John's sudden death had taken its toll on each of us. Now together, we could lend support to one another and progress through this difficult time.

The next day, we shared a light brunch and prepared to attend John's memorial service. Each of us knew that there would be no "rest in peace" for John today.

With heavy hearts, we entered the chapel. Side by side, we walked down the aisle to the chapel's altar table. John's enlistment picture stood beside the funeral urn, which contained his cremains. The United States flag, Old Glory, stood as a reminder to all of us that John was a Vietnam Veteran of the United States Army. And we were proud of it. A picture of John during his *Transcontinental Walk* was displayed, a distinct reminder of his dedication in 1982. The floral arrangement that Rachel and I had created rested nearby on a pedestal. The Canadian flag stood in reverence as a reminder to all that John and his family were Canadian citizens.

Members of the clergy, veterans, family, and friends from our childhood were seated in the chapel. Prayers, hymns, and a military honour ceremony were offered in a Christian memorial service as we celebrated and reflected on John's life. For one blessed hour, I almost forgot that our country—specifically, a few misguided people in our government—had denied our fallen soldier the honor to rest in peace.

Our family placed a message on the last page of the Memorial Service pamphlet. It stated that DVA's decision against inurnment of John Blake's cremains in the military section of Mt. Pleasant cemetery was unacceptable.

> "Burial for John, our native Newfoundlander, proud Canadian and Vietnam veteran, in the Field of Honour at Mt. Pleasant will be delayed indefinitely.
>
> The policy of the Department of Veteran Affairs in Canada has dictated that Canadian Vietnam veterans are neither accepted nor recognized as veterans eligible for burial in the Field of Honour in St. John's, NL. This government policy can only be changed by the voice of the people. The time has come to right this wrong.
>
> Your support in this matter would be greatly appreciated, so please voice your disapproval of their decision to your Provincial and Federal Government members both locally in Newfoundland and Labrador, and nationally in Ottawa.
>
> Thank you for attending this service. Your presence today will always be remembered."
>
> The Blake – Saint John families

After the memorial service, we placed John's cremains in safekeeping. Our immediate family congregated at my home. We were relieved that this part of John's journey had been completed. Then we braced ourselves for the battle that lay ahead of us with our Canadian government.

∞∞∞

# PART 4
# OUR MISSION AT HOME FOR JOHN

# Chapter 15

## Not Without Honour

OUR GRIEF-STRICKEN AND DEVASTATED FAMILY reflected on John's life and journey home to rest in peace. It was unthinkable that we would ever consider burial for John without the honour he so rightly earned and deserved. We felt that our government had done John and us an injustice. We reiterated our position to stand strong for each other in our quest to fulfill John's final burial request.

We converged on the few boxes that had arrived from Hilo, Hawaii. It was emotionally difficult to sort through John's treasured belongings. We viewed the few items he had cherished and carried to Hawaii. His belongings spoke volumes about his decision to minimize his life.

The boxes contained some of his written memoirs, pictures of family members, plus a few personal belongings. We decided that all documents needed to be photocopied, plus a copy his memoirs, poetry, journals and medical documentations would remain with me in the event one day his story would be told. Once the photocopying was completed, John's original documents were given to Rachel.

Before my siblings returned to their homes, we discussed our campaign plan of action. We recognized the need for a website, petition and campaign material. Communication was of the utmost importance. Each family member had taken exception to Mr. Strong's response, especially when he stated, "...Canada never declared formal hostile intentions against the Republic of Vietnam." This indicated just how little our appointed governmental representative understood about the Vietnam War and Canada's involvement. The force used by the Democratic Republic of Vietnam (North Vietnam) in support of the Viet Cong rebels against the Republic of Vietnam (South Vietnam) was the People's Army of Vietnam, also referred to as NVA (North

Vietnamese Army). The United States of America, our ally and neighbor, participated in the Vietnam War to assist the Republic of Vietnam (which is South Vietnam) against the NVA.

Living on an island off the most easterly coast of Canada often fostered isolation at the best of times. Now more than ever, we recognized that we would need tremendous grassroots support across Canada if we were to create awareness of our plight. If we failed in this effort, our family could easily be forgotten within a few weeks due to our isolation. We recognized the need to generate national media coverage and maintain our momentum. Metaphorically speaking, we needed to take a page out of John Blake's life story and make it happen, just as he did with the Transcontinental Walk in 1982.

David indicated that he would have a website created for the campaign when he returned to British Columbia. He also expressed that since John believed me to be a "pretty good writer," I would be responsible for communications. We also agreed that we needed to locate and gain support from the Vietnam veterans in Canada.

Up until this point, my only first-hand knowledge of Vietnam veterans came from my brothers' experiences. David confirmed that he would contact the Vietnam Veterans of Canada Association (VVIC) located in British Columbia. He was confident that the association would utilize their network and open up a channel of communication among the Vietnam veterans across Canada to assist in our campaign. We had our work cut out for us. Nevertheless, we accepted our duty to our late brother. We felt determined to leave no rock unturned in our quest to bring about a positive outcome to a negative decision by the Canadian government.

On March 18$^{th}$, the "Not Without Honour" campaign was initiated and launched. Within a week, I had participated in several CBC radio interviews locally and nationally. The interviews were arranged by CBC "On the Go" radio host, Jeff Gilhooly, who took a keen interested in our campaign.

On March 22$^{nd}$, I interviewed with Michael Enright, host of the *"As It Happens"* CBC National Radio Show. The interview was primarily driven by the host seeking my brother's war experiences in Vietnam. I skirted around any discussions regarding war stories from Vietnam simply because I was not qualified to discuss questions of that nature. Our family was involved in our own war with our own country; that was the issue. I deflected his questions and spoke only about the campaign at home. I needed to advise him and the public that the real issue was a less known important fact that Canada's Department of Veterans Affairs and the United States Veteran Affairs shared a Reciprocal Agreement Treaty of 1988. The agreement stated that any American or Canadian veteran who served in WWI, WWII, Korea or Vietnam, living in either Canada or the United States could seek medical care and aid from either country at any time. The country which the veteran had served would reimburse the country that provided the care. The major drawback in the Treaty that we encountered was the specific lack of burial prevision for Vietnam veterans in Canada. Due of the treaty's deficiency only WWI, WWII and Korea veterans are accepted for burial in departmental military plots in Canada, not Vietnam veterans. I explained that, as it stood, the CVVs would have to go back over the border one last time for a soldiers' final honour to be buried in a departmental military plot, if their homeland was Newfoundland. It was my intention to remind the public that our family wanted to purchase a burial plot for our deceased brother in the veterans' Field of Honour. There would be no cost to Canada. During the interview, however, I did not have an opportunity to thoroughly address the reciprocal agreement.

On March 26th my first of many letters to the Canadian Government was sent to David Collenette, Minister of National Defense and Veterans Affairs. The letter referred to an age-old departmental policy that stated Vietnam veterans were neither accepted nor recognized as eligible veterans for burial in the Field of Honour. I insisted that this dilemma could be rectified if Canada would negotiate with the United States under the Treaty of 1988. It was time to right the wrong.

**Building Campaign Support**

We created a petition to bring public awareness to our plight with a request for Canadians to write their Members of Parliament in Ottawa. The petition basically stated: "Department of Veterans Affairs Canada will not accept nor recognize Canadian Vietnam veterans as eligible veterans for burial in a Field of Honour. A gentle wind of change has begun to swirl softly and swiftly across this country and will continue until Canada recognizes and accepts those Canadians who had chosen to be soldiers during the Vietnam War as readily as she accepted the Americans who chose not to be soldiers. Write today; you can make the difference!"

Initially, our intent was to cover the area within a sixty-mile radius outside greater St. John's. Then, if necessary, redirect the petition across Canada. Not one establishment refused to accept the petition.

We then focused on and recruited the Vietnam veteran organizations throughout Canada from a contact list that was provided to us by the Vietnam Veterans in Canada (VVIC) located in British Columbia.

Each organization we contacted was more than willing to help. They each received a faxed copy of the petition, and then they printed additional copies and circulated them in their location as an effort to garner national support. I felt that in a matter of a few weeks the petition would extend from coast to coast, which it did. More importantly, each veteran organization educated me about Vietnam veterans in Canada. Moreover, they offered substantial connections to people who would be supportive of our mission. By the end of the week, I had over one hundred new contacts, none of whom I had ever met. But I knew if they would listen, I would talk!

Since my father was a former WWI veteran, I was entitled to an Associate membership with my neighborhood Royal Canadian Legion Branch (RCL) No 1. The members and veterans accepted me without hesitation. Many of the legionnaires had followed our story in the newspapers and on CBC Television/Radio. The vast majority of members' sympathies were heartfelt. They were deeply disturbed regarding the way our veteran brother had been treated by the Canadian government. I wrote an official letter to the RCL Newfoundland and Labrador's Provincial Command requesting their support of our campaign. A quick response confirmed RCL Provincial support for the burial of John Blake in the Field of Honour, at Mt. Pleasant cemetery.

We then designed a cover letter and distributed an informative package to each RCL Branch and Provincial Command in Canada regarding our late brother and subsequent campaign. The response was overwhelming. My comrades at the Legion advised me that the

Dominion Command President, Chuck Murphy, was visiting St. John's for just one day regarding Legion business. This would become my first contact with the national entity of the RCLs. I seized the opportunity and quickly prepared an information package that detailed our difficulties with DVA and hand-delivered the correspondence to the hotel reception desk where he was registered. A few weeks later, we received confirmation that the matter would be given serious consideration. Our goal was to bring all the Legions across Canada on board, one by one if necessary.

Every day we received an abundance of faxes from people who expressed their interest in helping our family. We also received copies of letters from people across Canada who had written letters in support of our campaign to their local Minister of the House of Assembly Canada (MHA) in Ottawa and DVA. We were encouraged by the amount of support that had grown in just two weeks.

The mail delivery at my home increased tremendously in volume. Packages arrived from Canadian Vietnam Veterans Associations (CVVA) across Canada. These included gifts of caps and tee-shirts sporting their logo and branch. Letters from civilians and Vietnam veterans wished us success, and some offered advice. Many veterans even shared their own stories of discrimination. These deliveries arrived on a regular basis, and we responded to all their letters.

One letter was from Mike Madigan, a band member from the well-known local musical trio, 'The Sharecroppers.' Mike stated that he had read the article which appeared in the *Evening Telegram*. He said that he was shocked to read about a policy dictated by the DVA: "Canadian Vietnam Veterans—Not accepted nor recognized as eligible veterans for burial in the Field of Honour."

Mike asked that I accept on his behalf a complimentary cassette from his trio group, which contained a very special song titled 'The Legionnaires Song...Lest We Forget' written by the Sharecroppers for the Canadian veterans who attended the November 11$^{th}$ Remembrance Day celebration each year. The Sharecroppers had received an acknowledgment letter from Prime Minister Jean Chretien that commended the musical group for paying homage to the RCL.

Mike stated that the following song lyric, *But with each passing memory and each new sunset, all must tell their story, 'Lest, Lest We Forget*, was equally meant for our precious brother, John, as it was for anyone else who fought for freedom of the oppressed. I listened to the Sharecropper's cassette, especially the Legionnaires Song. The song did bring me comfort and inspiration; so much so, that I immediately wrote the song that ultimately became our campaign song. The following lyric is an excerpt from the original song: *A soldier is a soldier and this, what remains, the mutual respect, understanding and pain; one look in their eye and the story is told of a time spent a long time ago.*

I telephoned Mike and thanked him for his letter, music and inspiration. I explained to him that I had been deeply inspired by his kindness and had just written a song for our campaign. He asked if I had written the musical chords. With a chuckle I explained that I was not musically talented, but that I had a tune for the song stuck in my head. He immediately offered to record the song pro bono with a musical arrangement solely for purposes of the campaign. Mike asked me to record the lyrics and tune onto a cassette tape. I felt overwhelmed by his offer and agreed to his suggestion. At that moment, I forewarned Mike that I was not a good singer either. We laughed.

Each day brought new acquaintances into the campaign; people who were willing to take time out of their busy lives to help make a difference. The Vietnam veteran associations throughout Canada became my lifeline. Every conversation was an education.

I was instructed by the CVVA Quebec to obtain the book, *Quiet Complicity,* written by Victor Levant. His extremely well-researched book proved to be a treasure that provided an authentically documented account of Canada's involvement in Vietnam. Mr. Levant's research proved without a doubt that Canada was indeed a willing participant in the Vietnam War. Through declassified documents, mostly from the United States, Levant clearly showed exactly how and why Canada supported the United States and South Vietnam's effort during the Vietnam War. Canada was an eager and willing participant and supported the South Vietnamese conflict against the North Vietnamese Army. I read that book three times before I grasped the magnitude of our Canadian government's involvement in Vietnam. Eventually, I shared several conversations with Mr. Levant, who then lived in Montreal. Mr. Levant was gracious and patient as he ensured that I fully understood Canada's complicity in the Vietnam War. He also informed me that during the writing and research his mail had been constantly opened. On several occasions, the contents of packages shipped from the United States that should have contained declassified United States government documents were at some point prior to delivery replaced with old newspapers. I gleaned from his conversation that I should not be surprised if I, too, experience some difficulties with mail deliveries.

Senator Jack Marshall had received a Canadian Forces Decoration (CD), plus a Canadian Order of Merit (CM). A Newfoundlander from Corner Brook and a strong supporter of the CVVs, instantly became our most trusted ally in Ottawa. I first learned of Senator Jack Marshall through the CVVA Ontario. They informed me that it was he who presented the resolution that passed in the House of Commons during June 1994, urging the Government of Canada to provide an appropriate site for the CVVs National Memorial. Senator Marshall was quoted at that time as stating, "It is time to accept that Canadian Vietnam War Veterans are a part of our history. They cannot, and should not, be ignored or forgotten any longer. I felt those were great words by a great man!

Senator Marshall and I shared several telephone conversations throughout the campaign. I took comfort in knowing that he, too, was in support of our family's issue regarding DVA. He was instrumental and provided a complete mailing list of all Members of Parliament (MP), Ministers and Senators in Ottawa. Plus, he provided me with his personal telephone numbers in Canada and Florida in the event I required his advice. I admired Senator Marshall and his tenacity at a time when our Canadian government ceased to return any telephone calls to me or my family, much less provide any mailing addresses. Nevertheless, I was armed with 450 addresses for the MPs, so each received a postage-free package regarding the Not Without Honour campaign.

True to his word, Mike Madigan and the Sharecroppers did a wonderful musical arrangement and vocal production of our tribute campaign song. Mike expressed how good he felt about the end product and that it was an honour to have done this for my family and our late brother. He now felt more connected to the whole issue concerning the Canadians who fought in the Vietnam War. Mike hoped that our campaign song would make its impact and deliver an understanding to all who struggled to see why my brother's remains were not resting in the Field of Honour. I listened to the final production and felt very grateful and appreciative for Mike's friendship, which had made our campaign song possible.

I immediately distributed copies of the song to several local radio stations. All but one agreed to air the song on a regular basis. I was invited to speak on-air in person and via telephone, with open-line hosts regarding our family's campaign, which had grown rapidly from coast to coast in Newfoundland and Labrador. People continued to sign the petition at a steady rate. Support increased constantly.

**First Official Response from the Elected in Ottawa**

Finally, Lawrence MacAulay, Secretary of State for Veterans, responded to our campaign letter sent to Minister Collenette on March 26th.

Secretary of State positions in the Canadian Federal Government are occupied by elected members of parliament, who are assigned to assist Cabinet Ministers of State. However, unlike Ministers of State, they are not members of the Cabinet. Secretaries of State are considered potential ministers in training.

Lawrence MacAulay's letter was revolting. In the final paragraph of his letter, he reminded me that the Canadian government did not recognize the Vietnam War as a military engagement in which Canada had participated. Canada never declared formal hostile intentions against the Republic of Vietnam, and Canadian troops never participated in the Vietnam War under the Canadian flag.

Our family fired back on June 18th with the first of what would become numerous written responses to Lawrence MacAulay.

Mr. MacAulay,

With all due respect, you certainly have missed the boat concerning this issue, rendering your response redundant. This issue is not about the Vietnam War. It is about humanity, dignity, and honour. The time has come for Canada to morally embrace her Canadian sons and daughters who served our allies in a war, against communism.

Your effort to address my letter was a blatant attempt to avoid the issue, conscientiously and morally. Your departmental statement concerning Canada's alliance with the United States leaves the impression that this is a union of convenience rather than one of commitment. Fortunately, this is not the consensus of the people.

We, as Canadians, must not forget that the United States was and still is our closest and most dependable ally. As in any relationship or union, morality and respectfulness strengthen the bond of friendship.

Your comparison of operations in the United States Forces concerning Vietnam to that of Grenada and Panama was embarrassing and intolerable. Vietnam was a conflict that lasted seventeen years, and an estimated 40,000 Canadians volunteered and joined the American Armed Forces, many of whom served in Vietnam.

During the Sixties, Canada capitalized on and profited from American operations in Vietnam to the tune of 68 billion dollars—blood money! That's a lot of nonparticipation.

Canada's involvement consisted of manufacturing ammunition and bombs in Ontario, destination South Vietnam. Canada tested and developed the formula 'Agent Orange' a chemical spray in Gage Town, New Brunswick, destination Vietnam. Canada also issued Canadian Passports for the purpose of providing a false identity for American Intelligence Agents posing as Canadian reporters. And Canada exchanged Canadian officers of the Third Royal Canadian Regiment 'on loan' to the U.S. Army 2nd Infantry as training officers to train the United States and Canadian enlistees. Some of those Canadian officers actually served in Vietnam 'on loan' from Canada.

Last, but not least, Canada received American civilians (draft dodgers and deserters), then proceeded to employ and educate the same. Consciously and morally Canada participated in the Vietnam operations, as did the Canadian civilians.

As stated by Senator Jack Marshall, *The legitimacy of the Vietnam war is irrelevant. The Canadians who enlisted in the American forces believed that the principle of freedom was in jeopardy and they were prepared to die for it. Ultimately, that is all that matters*. Senator Marshall's statement personifies why the late John W. Blake and tens of thousands of other Canadian boys joined the American forces and served in Vietnam.

John W. Blake's mentor was his father, John Saint John, who served as a soldier in the Newfoundland Regiment during WWI. Our mother served as a 'Wren' in the Women's Royal Canadian Navy during WWII. We, as a Canadian family, understood firsthand the meaning of freedom, a privilege which many take for granted. Accordingly, it was not without a conscientious, moral commitment that our Canadian civilians, brothers and sons, joined the forces of the United States during the Vietnam War. They served our neighboring country as openly and readily as did the American civilians who served Canada during WWI, prior to the sinking of the Lusitania, and during WWII before the bombing of Pearl Harbor.

In our opinion, it is veterans such as these who deserve the title 'Honourable', for they are the ones who have earned it. Persons who use that title following federal election must have a conscientious and moral obligation to uphold that privilege.

Canada's contentious denial of involvement in the Vietnam War and the DVA's lack of interest and respect for Canadians who are Vietnam veterans are immoral and an inhumane tragedy against her own sons.

We are requesting that you and your department immediately develop and execute an amendment to the Treaty of 1988, the Reciprocal Agreement between Canada and the United States to provide burial in departmental plots and military cemeteries. The United States will cover he expense for those veterans eligible under Veteran Benefit Guidelines.

As you know, this will eliminate any burial costs to the Canadian government and/or Canadian taxpayer. Keep in mind that our family has consistently advised that we will absorb all costs for burial of our late brother's cremains.

We trust you understand that we are most serious and that you will give this matter your fullest attention.

Thank you and Godspeed.

The Saint John—Blake families

Naturally, all correspondences from DVA freely circulated among our supporters.

At the end of June, a local reporter advised me that the Honourable Jean J. Charest would be attending an event at the Newfoundland Hotel, which enabled me to provide him with a campaign package.

During late August, I received a copy of Jean Charest's letter, to Lawrence MacAulay. An excerpt from his letter stated:

"I am forwarding a copy of a letter I received from Ms. Cathy Saint John and her family regarding the burial of her brother in the Field of Honour section of Mt. Pleasant Cemetery in St. John's."

"For humanitarian reasons, I hope you will consider Ms. Saint John's request to have John W. Blake buried in the Field of Honour."

## Curious Discrepancies in the Field of Honour at Mt. Pleasant Cemetery

Meanwhile, we focused our attention on the several obvious burial discrepancies in the Field of Honour at Mt. Pleasant cemetery. I brought my concerns to a few members of the local Legion, hoping they could shed some light on the discovery. I was informed that they too questioned the authenticity for those particular burials. This led me down a path of further research and discovery.

I contacted Tom Strong at the Provincial DVA office and disclosed that I had discovered two American veterans who served in WWII under American colours and a Canadian force serviceman—who did not serve in a theatre of war buried in that same Field of Honour. The burials had occurred after the military cemetery was designated a "Field of Honour" in 1983, but yet to be listed as one of the official four "Fields of Honour" in Canada. Mr. Strong had not been aware of those discrepancies and was surprised. He noted the details of each person that I had researched and promised to return my call.

True to his promise, Mr. Strong called within a few days and confirmed each person had departmental approval to be buried in the Field of Honour. I was delighted to hear that news. I suddenly felt hopeful. Since exceptions had been made in the past for a non-veteran plus two American veteran burials in this military cemetery, then why not a burial for John Blake's cremains?

"Mr. Strong, under the circumstances, if exceptions have been made in the past then the department must make an exception for John Blake."

"No, the department will not make an exception for your brother."

"Why? Is it because he died by his own hand?"

"No."

"Is it because he is a Vietnam veteran?"

The department has responded to your request. There is nothing else I can say—goodbye."

I suddenly realized that there was more to this situation than what initially met the eye. I knew I had struck a nerve with Mr. Strong. I also realized that we required more information. Moreover, we needed to know where the other deceased CVVs were buried in Canada. How many, if any, Vietnam veterans were buried in Fields of Honour DVA governmental military plot facilities across the country?

I asked each of our CVVAs throughout Canada to search as many military cemeteries as possible, especially Fields of Honour, and report back with photos of any interesting findings. David gathered Vietnam veteran burial information in British Columbia. The CVVAs throughout Canada planned to search graveyards in their provinces and provide a list of Vietnam veteran graves, documented by photographs by mid-fall. Maybe, by some remote chance, some Vietnam veterans were already buried in military cemeteries designated Government of Canada departmental burial plots in the Fields of Honour.

This was a huge challenge, and we knew it would take a few months to complete. But everyone was willing to investigate their area throughout Canada. We had nothing to lose and everything to gain if—by some remote chance—we located a Vietnam veteran buried in a Field of Honour in Canada. Meanwhile, the Vietnam veterans assisting this effort felt that they would likely find some of their deceased buddies, so it was a win-win situation.

Through the initiatives of the VVIC and CVVAs in Canada, our story was linked on their websites and also distributed within monthly newsletters to their members. Many of the United States of America Veteran Associations and associated organizations became aware of our situation and showed a tremendous amount of interest in our family's campaign. This resulted in more contacts being directed towards us. Our contact base continued to grow, and we appreciated everyone's efforts.

Judging by the numerous support letters that were faxed to us it became obvious that an extreme amount were sent to DVA Canada too. It was equally evident that the authors of the support letters received the same generic letter that we received from MacAulay.

DVA, Ottawa continued to ignore us. But, somebody in Ottawa was still interested, because within weeks of my response to MacAulay's letter, it became quite apparent that some of my mail from outside of Canada had been perused, or otherwise not received as expected. Somehow, I was not surprised.

**Sorry to Inform You—John is Gone**

During the late evenings and early mornings, I'd spend time reading John's memoirs and constructed several lists of contacts comprised solely of his Vietnam veteran friends and civilian acquaintances in America. I created a separate list of names including telephone numbers that I had become familiar with through John's letters.

I telephoned Lynn Mowry, one of John's most trusted friends in Virginia during the mid-eighties. When she answered my call, I explained that I was John's sister and that he had recently died. As expected, Lynn was deeply saddened by his death. We spoke for an hour when she informed me that she and John had started to write his book regarding the *Transcontinental Walk*. Lynn had held onto the manuscript for over ten years. She spoke fondly of John and knew exactly why she had kept his writings. Now, she wanted me to have the manuscript. "Perhaps, one day you might finish his story?" she asked sadly.

"Maybe, one day I will." I said quietly. But, for now, Lynn fully understood the challenges that laid ahead for my family and me. We both understood the value of John's unfinished manuscript simply because no other form of John's notes or journals existed. The only items I possessed of the 'Walk' were newspaper clippings that documented his journey across the nation and a few photographs.

Next, I called Steve Radcliffe in Ohio. He was equally saddened by John's sudden death. Steve told me that he and several other Dayton, Ohio, veterans had assisted John during *Operation Backtrack* in Ohio. The same veterans had also assisted in his run for president of the Vietnam Veterans of America Association's Founding Convention in 1983. It was the first I had heard of those events. Steve advised me that he, too, had held onto much of the written material regarding those events and would be pleased to mail the documents to me. Steve expressed his fondness and respect for John. Then he advised me about John's difficulty with the VAMC hospital in Chicago. It was Steve who had arranged for John to come and live at his home in Ohio during that difficult time. The dots were beginning to connect regarding John's time spent in the United States with friends he considered family.

Steve asked me to contact another friend of his and John's from *Operation Backtrack*, and VVA Convention era. A former reporter named Lynn Schultz, had captured on cassette tapes several hours of an audio interview with John. Steve kindly provided me with her contact information and insisted that I contact her, as soon as possible. Steve offered me his assistance to our family's campaign. I was delighted to welcome him aboard the team and promised to fax him a campaign package. I assured Steve that we would talk again very soon.

As per Steve's advice, I contacted Lynn, that same evening. She, too, was deeply saddened by the news. She advised me that she still had the cassette tapes. I was astounded. Lynn had kept those tapes stored in a dresser drawer for years not wanting to share John's words with just anyone. Lynn stated, "The Vietnam experience caused deep wounds to the spirit, including those of us more passively affected. John was a healer of those wounds." I didn't know that!

Lynn told me that John and her family had shared a relaxing evening meal and that after dinner John had shown her young adolescent son, Andy, some pretty sharp soccer moves. Andy, who by 1996 was twenty years of age, still recalled meeting John. Lynn wanted me to have the audio tapes. I was deliriously thrilled that John's voice, beliefs and convictions had been recorded and kept in safe-keeping. I thanked her profusely for the conversation and knowledge of the taped interview.

A part of me resented that John did not educate me about his beliefs and work. I felt that the more I discovered about John, the more I wished he had trusted me and other family members and allowed us to be a bigger part of his life. Then maybe he would still be alive. I recognized then that a bargaining part of my grief was taking over my thoughts. John never wanted us near the dark side of his world. When he did want us, it was too late. Canada was ill-prepared to assist persons living with PTSD.

Before sleep overtook me, I wrote a 1,200-word article for the Downhomer Magazine. The piece was scheduled to be published in the September issue.

The Downhomer Magazine had a large following and was the most popular locally produced magazine in Newfoundland and Labrador. I knew our article would be exposed to a few hundred thousand readers throughout our province, plus subscribers in Canada and the United States.

David called and informed me that the VVIC in British Columbia was planning their annual Firebase Weekend event in Maple Ridge, B.C., during the last weekend of August. It was a reunion that brought Vietnam veterans together to remember their fallen comrades and socialize with their brotherhood. A few Veteran Affairs officials from the United States would be on site to inform veterans of services and benefits that were available to those who suffered from the effects of the war.

Firebase Weekend was going to be dedicated to the memory of John W. Blake. David told me to make plans to be there and to bring plenty of printed materials such as flyers, posters, business cards and audio tapes of the campaign song.

**Firebase—Maple Ridge, British Columbia**

It was wonderful to see David again when he met me at Vancouver Airport on August 28th. We were scheduled to be at the Firebase throughout the weekend. I looked forward to finally putting a face to the voice of the many people who were assisting us with our campaign in western Canada.

The community of Maple Ridge was just a thirty-minute drive from David's home. We arrived on site in the afternoon. The Firebase event marked the first time that I would come face-to-face with Vietnam veterans other than my immediate brothers. Before the weekend ended, I gained a new understanding of who my brothers really were and what they sacrificed for our freedom.

I had never felt more naive and out of my element than I did on that first evening at the Firebase. Naturally, David fit in, but I was like a fish-out-of-water. I was a civilian. They were veterans. The veterans' wives and children lived the lifestyle of their veteran. What to do? How was I going to fit into this environment?

"Cathy, are you okay? You look scared to death," said David.

"Yes, I'm okay. And no, I am not scared - just concerned."

"What do you mean?"

"I am wondering how to communicate with Vietnam veterans. I have just realized that my culture as a Canadian civilian is inadequate, plus I am the only civilian here. These veterans and their families share a veteran's culture, one in which I am not experienced. You and John sheltered us from your reality."

"Don't worry, stay close to me and observe. Once these good folks hear your Newfie accent they'll want to keep you chatting. Seriously, give them time to trust you. Remember, these veterans feel our loss. More importantly, they still carry the loss of their buddies who never returned from Vietnam, and they always will. Look beyond the surface of what you see here and keep an open mind. We are Vietnam veterans, some of the roughest, toughest, bad-ass soldiers in North America. Most of us live with the effects of the war and with PTSD. Before this weekend is over, you will realize that some veterans have deeper wounds than others. We've been to hell and back too many times since Vietnam. It's not about what people say that matters to us; it's about what they do."

"Okay, I get it. I'll follow your lead. Eyes wide open and mouth shut."

"Believe me, Cathy, once these boys understand and trust your intentions, they will help you. Most of the veterans coming here this weekend are former Green Berets, Marines and Rangers from the 173rd Airborne, 'the herd'. Oh, by the way, heads-up; some of the Rolling Thunder bikers will roar in here later tonight too."

I nodded my head. Still, I stayed close to David for the remainder of the evening. I felt like a youngster clinging onto her parent's shirttail in fear of the unknown or becoming lost in a crowd of strangers.

As the veterans arrived, they quickly joined in with those who were already settled and engaged in hearty conversations. I sat among everyone to listen and observe the interaction. After an hour, one of the veterans nodded towards me and asked David, "Does she speak?"

Both David and I laughed when he replied, "Does she ever! She's my sister from Newfoundland!"

Then another veteran stated, "My father was stationed in Argentia during WWII. That is where he met my mother, and after the war they returned to the United States."

"Yes b'y small world aye. Throughout the years, Newfoundland and Labrador have shared an interesting history with the American Forces," I said. "I still hear stories about when the Yanks came to Newfoundland and left with the prettiest girls," I stated as I deliberately thickened my accent in jest. David laughed at me.

The ice was broken, and the boys began to chat with me. We spoke about everything from my accent to their stories from Vietnam. Soon, we were all in harmony. The veterans began to understand why I had traveled from Newfoundland to be with them at their Firebase Reunion. They immediately accepted me as a sister into their brotherhood. I felt humbled.

David and I had not intended to sleep at the reunion site since we were only a half an hour drive away from his home. But, as the evening progressed. He had a couple of beers with the boys and decided that we should not drive home until morning. Since we didn't have any accommodations arranged, our only alternative was to sleep in his car. David settled in the front seat with his feet stuck out the passenger's window, and I settled in the back seat, curled up with his jacket as a pillow.

It was quite the experience when twenty or more bikers rode in on their Harleys at two o'clock in the morning. They passed right alongside us where we slept. I immediately bolted into an upright position as the motorcycles roared by us. I tried to wake David, but he couldn't hear me over the thunder of the bikes. Then I laughed at myself, laid back down and fell asleep.

It was dawn when I crawled out of the vehicle and left David there to sleep for another hour. I felt as though I had not slept at all, but at the same time, I felt exhilarated. I knew it was an honour just to be there with those Vietnam veterans. I stood alone on the deck of the chalet that overlooked the camping grounds adjacent to a lake surrounded by tall mountains. Then I noticed Stan, a former marine Vietnam veteran who I had spoken with the previous evening. I had given him a cassette copy of the campaign song. He was sitting alone on the tailgate of his truck smoking a cigarette. I could hear our campaign song *Not Without Honour* as it played softly.

The Sharecroppers harmonious voices gently told the story of our family's plight, which echoed throughout the stillness in the valley. Stan played the song three more times as the morning birds awakened. I felt privileged just to be there at that moment and quietly share the familiar lyrics I had written, *Honour all soldiers for freedom they fought—they lived and died in Vietnam*.

I believed that the previous evening had been an absolute education and a growing experience for me. I realized that our family's effort and the Not Without Honour campaign was really about all the CVVs, not just John W. Blake. I felt this was the way John would have wanted it to be: one more for the boys.

When David awoke, we decided to retreat to his house to shower and eat breakfast. We quickly returned to the Firebase and spent additional time with the veterans before the scheduled events of the day. I set up an information booth with printed materials and a picture of John. The campaign song played continuously for those who wanted to listen, and they did.

A burly Vietnam veteran, one of the bikers, who had arrived under the cloak of darkness, stood nearby. He motioned to his buddy to be quiet as he listened to our campaign song. Tears streamed down his rugged face. He was deeply saddened by the message in the song. I immediately remembered what John had told me about how it felt to live with PTSD. I now understood just how wounded a soul can be when the depth of emotion and delayed grief are compounded with rejection and abandonment. I reached out my hand to him, and he quickly clasped mine. Instinctively, he knew that I understood.

I spoke with the veterans and their families and several committed to assisting us with the campaign. Their assistance would prove to be invaluable. Soon large groups of attendees were called to order to begin the Honour Guard ceremony.

The Honor Guard members from the US formed up and carried the colors while the piper played *Amazing Grace*. Prayers of remembrance for the fallen warriors and their families were expressed. The Honor Guard performed a three-volley rifle salute in honour of the late John W. Blake, their brother and ours. Then the bugler sounded the military 'taps'. The American flag was carefully folded 13 times into the symbolic tricornered shape so only the blue field with white stars remained. An Airborne Ranger Vietnam veteran accepted the flag from the honour guard and marched toward me. The veteran stood before me and extended the folded American flag. His voice slightly quivered when he stated, "This flag is presented on behalf of a grateful nation and the United States Army as a token of appreciation for your loved one's honorable and faithful service." I placed my hands on the flag when he asked, "Please accept this flag in honour of United States Army, Special Forces, Airborne Ranger Sgt. John Blake's service to the United States of America."

I accepted the flag just as tears escaped beyond the edge of my sunglasses. It was then I realized the heavy price my brother paid for his service and our freedom. It was a solemn occasion. The formal ceremonies were completed when the colors were marched off. One of the veterans picked up an expelled shell casing and placed it in my hand. My new friends, Iva and Wayne approached and embraced me in a group hug. I welcomed their gesture of friendship.

The veterans and families gathered together for a barbecue social. I spent the entire day speaking with the wives and children of veterans, gaining valuable insight into their lives. I quickly learned and understood how they each balanced their lives and how each woman and child understood and accepted their Vietnam veteran.

Members of the 'Herd', 173rd Airborne, listened to our family's issue and the difficulties we experienced in dealing with the Canadian Department of Veteran Affairs burial policy. The American Vietnam veterans shook their heads in disbelief that Canada would deny one of their ally veterans a final request to be buried in a military plot on his home soil. We discussed the many issues that they, too, had experienced after Vietnam. At the end of our conversation, the members of the 'Herd' committed to bringing our story to the national level of the 173rd Airborne Organization in America. John was one of them, so no further discussion was needed. Mission accomplished. I felt blessed.

One of my many observations at the Firebase was that Canadian Vietnam veterans were still decades behind emotionally in coping with and healing from their war experience as compared to their American Vietnam veteran brothers.

During the flight home to St. John's, Newfoundland, I reflected on the weekend spent at the Firebase and understood why John felt it was his mission to shelter us from his PTSD. At the same time, I discovered that it was a mistake for John to have distanced his family from his life and experiences. It was evident that the Vietnam veterans whom I had recently met at the Firebase were successful in living with their experiences largely due to the trusted, tangible support and acceptance of their families.

Some veterans had returned from the war, married their childhood sweethearts and began a new life together. Other veterans married people who never knew them prior to Vietnam. I witnessed a rare, unconditional love and commitment between the couples. Some of the childhood sweetheart wives disclosed that although their partners had changed because of their war experience, the wives resolved to acknowledge their grief and to mourn the change. Over time, they also recovered from their grief and fell in love again with their war veteran spouse. Some ladies confessed that living with a veteran was not always a bed of roses, but as time passed they educated themselves to their spouse's experiences and needs. The ladies I had met at the Firebase had succeeded. I gleaned from our many conversations that they were as flexible as British Columbia Douglas Fir trees. When difficult times blew hard, as it often does in relationships, those ladies learned to bend and maintain their resilience without breaking. As time passed, togetherness, understanding and trust assisted many a family in reinforcing their veteran's need for love, acceptance and forgiveness at home.

## Campaign Gains Momentum

After a long day of travel from coast to coast in Canada, the next morning I approached my office half-heartedly, still feeling totally jet lagged. As suspected, during my absence fax messages continued to spill onto the floor in a continuous strand of paper three feet high in the middle of the office. It was a welcomed sight.

With regard to mail I had received, I recognized a letter from Department of Veterans Affairs and tore it open only to read more nonsensical rhetoric from Lawrence MacAulay. My response would wait.

It became obvious to me that I would need to collect information from the veterans who were roaming around the military cemeteries in Canada before responding to MacAulay's letter. We desperately needed new information in order to make further arguments. In addition, it was important to speak with a representative of Arlington National Cemetery in Washington, D.C. I had a gut feeling that something was not quite right about the rhetoric that our Canadian government was expecting us to accept.

Meanwhile, Ida Tuttle from British Columbia had sent a package to me that contained the book, *Recovering from the War: A Woman's Guide to Helping Your Vietnam Veteran, Your Family, and Yourself*. The package also contained a few monthly newsletters, all written by author Patience H. C. Mason. I welcomed the gift as there were no books available in Canada concerning veterans and families living with PTSD. It was quite an informative read.

In addition to Victor Levant's *Quiet Complicity*, the Canadian Vietnam veterans recommended that I read author Fred Gaffen's books, *Cross-Border Warriors* and *Unknown Warriors.* Fred Gaffen shared many experiences of Canadian Vietnam veterans plus the social rejection and isolation they experienced when they returned home to Canada. Gaffen's books proved to be an informative description of Canada's involvement and the Canadian men who served in the Vietnam War.

Twenty-five years after Vietnam, in 1996, Tracey Arial authored *I Volunteered*. The most vivid illustration of Canadian volunteers in the Vietnam War, Arial's book depicted the many obstacles that our

Canadian Vietnam veterans had to overcome since their return to Canada. Most of the Vietnam veterans mentioned in her book became supporters and a large part of our campaign effort.

It was not until I took a brief vacation to the United States that I was able to purchase non-fiction novels written by American Vietnam veterans, especially Airborne Rangers. It was then I gained some insight about the type of work my brother engaged in during Vietnam as a LRRP member of the 75th November Airborne Rangers. I purchased a copy of every novel that was available at the bookstore and stuffed my suitcase with approximately thirty new books depicting the Vietnam War and its warriors.

I read each novel and became familiar with the logistics and dynamics of jungle warfare in Vietnam. But my questions were still largely unanswered. Ironically, I searched every picture that was published in those novels in hope that I would find a picture of my brother's face as a soldier. There were none.

I was not able to resolve the many intimate questions I possessed regarding the kind of soldier my brother was and his time spent in Vietnam. John's diary was informative, but left many questions unanswered. His poetry spoke of the brotherhood and camaraderie that the Rangers shared, but my knowledge was still incomplete. My need for understanding of John's specific experiences and life in Vietnam would not be resolved until two decades later.

Each conversation with a Vietnam veteran became a lesson learned. They taught me how to read and understand John's military records, especially his DD214. They deciphered the military jargon. I would often hear military buzz words or slang that would require definition. The veterans were patient and kind as they assisted me, a civilian, get a handle on their culture. This offered me a better understanding of the Canadian Vietnam veterans' world. Those lessons proved invaluable.

Bob Bolduc, a Massachusetts Vietnam veteran, was highly recommended to me by the CVVA in Quebec. When I contacted him, Bob had already been briefed by the CVVA Quebec members regarding our campaign and had expected my call. He had prepared letters on behalf of the campaign to several senators of the United

States Congress. He suggested that since my brother John knew Senator Tom Daschle personally, I should write to the Senator. I did.

Bob was anxious to assist us with our campaign in the United States. He volunteered to handle the circulation of the petition in Massachusetts. He was willing to do as I had done in Canada: actively recruit the support of national veteran associations, especially the VVA, V.F.W., and the American Legion. The Not Without Honour campaign became an international campaign.

Bob advised me about his friend, Joe Murphy, a devoted member of the American Legion. Bob described him as a little man with a big heart who was a strong advocate and dedicated friend of the Canadian Vietnam veterans. He wanted to help us, too. Throughout the course of the campaign, Joe wrote approximately fifty correspondences to me that explained his continuous effort in our campaign. His letters were always a welcomed sight.

Rob Purvis, a Canadian Vietnam veteran and a former Airborne Ranger, assigned to 'K' Company, 75$^{th}$ Airborne Rangers, spearheaded the first CVV reunion at the Vietnam Memorial Wall in Washington, D.C. during 1986. The event was a tremendous success and the catalyst for many more public events for the CVVs. Moreover, it was an awakening to Canada regarding the role that Canadians played in the Vietnam War. Fortunately for us, Rob became our contact in Winnipeg, Manitoba, and a strong supporter of our campaign. Although both he and John served as Airborne Rangers in Vietnam during 1969, they had never met each other or worked together on any missions. Each was stationed at a different location in Vietnam.

CBC Radio host, Jeff Gilhooly, informed me in June that approximately two hundred renowned national and international journalists, TV anchors and Radio hosts, plus reporters throughout North America were due in St. John's within a few days to attend a convention at the Radisson Hotel. My best opportunity to distribute our campaign pamphlet to each attendee would be on their first day of the conference. I was determined to do this at 9 a.m. as they entered through the main door of the conference room. I thanked Jeff profusely and promised him that I would be there.

Tracey Arial, a writer in Montreal, had faxed me the mailing addresses and contact information for all major newspapers in Canada. She advised me how to handle a press release, which would basically guarantee that they would print the article. Bless them all.

A couple from Ontario, whom I had met at the reunion in British Columbia, confirmed that they were very successful in bringing support onboard from Dominion Command of the Army, Navy, and Air Force Clubs throughout Canada. The Clubs committed to circulating the petition throughout their organization and writing letters to DVA officials in Ottawa. Great news!

Iva and Wayne were equally successful in bringing our issue to the media in British Columbia. The radio show was well received. We could expect a lot of support from British Columbia. Iva confirmed that her husband, also a Vietnam veteran, successfully solicited the support of the 173rd Airborne Society in America. Perfect!

**Vietnam Veterans Buried in Canada**

Our search throughout local graveyards indicated several dozen Vietnam veterans were buried in Vancouver, Winnipeg, Ontario, Montreal and the Maritime Regions. The CVVs, as expected, came through in fine style. The most interesting discovery for our campaign was the burial site of SP/4 Larry R. Collins, United States Army, located at the Brookside Cemetery in a non-official Field of Honour in Winnipeg.

Larry Collins was killed after eleven months in Vietnam on May 1, 1969, at 22 years of age. Less than a month shy of his DEROS. He was buried in a Canadian Government burial plot with full Military Honors. A United States Military Color Guard was deployed from North Dakota for his funeral service and burial. Sgt. Larry Collins' resting place is among WWII and Korea veterans.

Rob Purvis, Vietnam veteran from Winnipeg, stated, "Larry Collins, Bill and Gerald Buffie and I were childhood friends. We had all grown up together in the same neighborhood and attended grade school together. It was the summer of 1968, and we were each fresh out of high school. After watching the Vietnam War on the news every evening in Winnipeg, we decided to go to the United States and enlist in the US Army at Fargo, North Dakota."

The boyhood friends remained together throughout Basic Training in Fort Lewis, Washington. After basic training, they shook hands, wished each other luck, split-up and went their separate ways. That was the last time Rob Purvis saw Larry Collins. Rob and his family make regular visits to Larry's gravesite to ensure that his friend's headstone is in good order and to remember times they had shared years earlier.

**Fields of Honour in Canada**

Winnipeg's Brookside Cemetery is one of the largest and oldest military interment sites and home to the only Commonwealth War Graves Commission Stone of Remembrance in Canada. The cemetery also includes other important military monuments, including the Last Post Fund Columbaria, the first of its kind in Canada. It is also the only military cemetery in the city of Winnipeg, the same as Mt. Pleasant in the city of St. John's, just larger and older. Brookside is the resting place of over 12,000 veterans, service men and women, war heroes who are interred alongside each other. All interments are marked by the military grey Barrie granite upright monument, mounted in the familiar beam style. The burial site is a splendid display of remembrance, dignity and respect for the men and women who served not only Canada but Canada's allies in all theatres of war, including Vietnam.

The Last Post Fund is a Canadian non-profit organization established in 1909, whose mandate is to assist in facilitating a dignified funeral and burial for veterans on behalf of Veteran Affairs Canada. Arrangements for interment or purchase of a niche are arranged through the Fund.

In 1996, the criteria for one full interment in the Field of Honour stipulates that the deceased is a veteran, service man or woman plus one only additional cremated remains of either a spouse, child, sibling, parent or grandparent.(www.winnipeg.ca/ppd/cemetery_brooksideFOH.stm)

DVA Canada shares the same departmental relationship with the 4.5 acreages at Brookside Cemetery in Winnipeg, Manitoba, as it does with the single acreage at Mt. Pleasant Cemetery in St. John's, Newfoundland. The only difference between the two is that in the mid 1990's, Veterans Affairs Canada provided Brookside Cemetery with 5 million dollars for military ground improvements, whereas Veterans Affairs' monetary contribution to date to Mt. Pleasant was slightly under $500,000.

In 1996, the year my brother died, neither Mt. Pleasant nor Brookside Cemetery were officially Canada's Fields of Honour. However, DVA held departmental burial plots in both cemeteries.

The four Canadian "Fields of Honour" that were considered official at that time were respectively located in British Columbia, Ontario, Quebec and Nova Scotia. Those findings would become pertinent in developing support for our family's issue with DVA Canada.

**Arlington National Cemetery**

Bob Bolduc advised me to contact Mr. T. Sherlock, Military Cemetery Archivist at Arlington National Cemetery. I did so, and discovered a few amazing facts. Mr. Sherlock indicated that four former Canadian Forces personnel were buried in Arlington National Cemetery prior to 1948, and he faxed his findings with supportive documentation.

**Veteran #1**—William Strong Jr., a Canadian citizen and former Canadian Army Lieutenant, volunteered and served in the Canadian Forces during WWI, died December 1919, and was buried at Arlington National cemetery.

**Veteran #2**—Thomas Henry Dalton, a Canadian citizen, served with the Sapper Canadian Engineers during WWI, died November 1923, and was buried at Arlington cemetery.

**Veteran #**3—Robert J. Watt, a Canadian citizen who served with the 8th Field Ambulance Co., 26th Battalion during WWI, died July 24, 1947, and was buried at Arlington cemetery.

**Veteran #4**—Franklin Leroy Cash Jr., was an American citizen recruited on behalf of Canada and served as a Leading Aircraftman in the Canadian Army during WWII prior to 1941. This was a direct violation of the United States law. He died on September 13, 1942. On September 16, 1942, he was buried at Arlington National Cemetery.

His burial was authorized one day after his death. He had served in a foreign war with Canada during WWII, prior to the United States entering WWII after the bombing of Pearl Harbor.

**Veterans one, two and three** volunteered and served in the Canadian Forces during WWI shortly after Canada entered combat during December 1914. All were Canadian citizens, and all served under Canadian colors. All three are buried in the United States at the world-renowned Arlington National Cemetery.

The United States entered the war on April 6, 1917, after the sinking of the Lusitania. Prior to that event, the United States remained neutral in the foreign war effort, much like Canada during Vietnam. The United States became an important supplier to Britain and other allied powers, also identical to Canada during Vietnam. Prior to 1917, the prime goal of the United States during WWI was to foster peace. That was also true for Canada during the Vietnam War, with the exception that Canada played an active role and provided assistance to both the United States and South Vietnamese forces against North Vietnam.

**The fourth veteran,** an American citizen who was recruited on behalf of Canada and served under Canadian colors in a foreign war, was a pilot during WWII prior to 1941 in direct violation of United States law.

**Historical Similarities—Allies**

In 1939, WWII was considered a foreign war by the United States until two years later after the bombing of Pearl Harbor.

Similarly, in WWI and WWII, American civilians were welcomed into the Canadian Forces and fought in both wars under Canada's colors in what the United States of America considered, at the time, a foreign war.

During the 1960's, Canadian civilians were welcomed into the United States armed forces and fought in a foreign war under America's colors in the Vietnam War, which Canada considered a foreign war.

Canada readily made it possible for our Canadian male population to serve with the United States Forces in Vietnam without any repercussions or consequences. It was deemed appropriate for Canadians to join the Americans in wars and vice versa. It was the natural thing to do according to our military history.

Whereas Canada condoned the Canadian volunteer action during the Vietnam War, it would seem morally responsible that the Government of Canada show respect and appreciation to Canadians who are Vietnam veterans who served in a war with our neighboring ally, the United States of America.

Still, the Secretary of State (Veterans) in Canada and the Minister of Veterans Affairs continued to desperately try and convince me, plus several hundred thousand supporters, that Canada was not an ally of the United States during the Vietnam War.

**Campaign Solid Support Nationwide**

In early October during a telephone conversation with Mr. MacAulay, Secretary of State, (Veterans) I reiterated that prior to 1983, the Field of Honour at Mt. Pleasant Cemetery was indeed a military cemetery and absolutely no different than any other military cemetery in Canada.

I reminded him that just recently the Dominion Command of the Royal Canadian Legion had passed a resolution stating: Vietnam veterans have Ordinary Membership status, meaning a veteran is a veteran!

I informed him that I was in possession of 15,000 signatures and approximately 500 letters and faxes that supported the petition and campaign, representing only my personal effort. The same petition that circulated throughout Canada was at that time uncounted.

One thing was quite clear. The vast cross-section of local signatures indicated that citizens, military personnel, veterans of WWII and Korea, plus a very special veteran who was a Canadian former POW, agreed with my family. A positive resolve to the issue of burial for John W. Blake in Newfoundland, Canada, from the Government of Canada was not only necessary but mandatory.

I respectfully urged MacAulay to re-think the position that he had taken thus far. I personally did not want to cause disgrace to DVA, Canada nor openly shame my country.

I informed MacAulay that since early September, John's burial issue had filtered into the United States with responses from individuals, groups and Government officials in both Canada and the United States. Communications from the factions who supported our issue continued to arrive daily at an overwhelming rate. I advised him I would be participating in a Nationwide Press Release and Radio/TV Talk Shows in both Canada and the United States.

I expressed my hopefulness that a positive solution could be found whereby all concerned would find satisfaction. But first I needed to share with MacAulay a few observations that I discovered during the Firebase reunion in Vancouver, B.C.

I hoped he'd listen when I told him that the unique society of CVVs and their families in Canada continue to endure sacrifices, specifically loss of pride, respect and dignity due to the Canadian Government's absence of acceptance and acknowledgement. Throughout the years, the Canadian Government has shown more respect for the seals off the east coast of Canada than for the brave warriors of Canada. The difference between a veteran and a soldier is that a veteran finds peace. Canadian Vietnam veterans are still soldiers and will remain so until elected people do something.

I entertained the hope that he might understand why a change in his decision was necessary. I asked Mr. MacAulay to please rethink his former decision, not because I personally had made the request but simply because thousands of Canadian veterans and civilians from all walks of life and wars believed it necessary.

I reminded Mr. MacAulay that I was not a politician, nor was I the president of any association. I was simply John Blake's sister, a proud Canadian and a member of a Canadian Vietnam veteran family.

Mr. MacAulay heard my argument and reiterated his negative decision. It became more and more unlikely that he would change his position, regardless of our pleas or any additional factual information that we might discover.

**Ottawa's Revolving Door**

MacAulay's response was no surprise. If anything, it empowered the campaign and its supporters to continue the fight. Figuratively speaking, the gloves were off, and everyone rolled up their sleeves and settled in for the long haul. My family and I recognized that there was little value in any additional communication with Mr. MacAulay. Therefore, I wrote a letter to the Prime Minister of Canada, The Honourable Jean Chrétien, and explained our family's dilemma.

The letter informed the Prime Minister of Canada about a Canadian family from Newfoundland with modest means, and an endless devotion to each other's beliefs, principles, love and respect. Our beliefs and dedication to each other could not be broken by the passing of time nor distance. I explained that the nationwide campaign, Not Without Honour, was in its eighth month. I informed him that the campaign had gained the respect and support from Canadians (veterans and civilians) throughout Canada and the United States. Then I specifically asked Prime Minister Chrétien for his leadership to bring closure to our tragedy in a dignified manner. I requested he alleviate the unfairness and indignity which our family had endured since February 13, 1996, regarding our late brother's death and burial.

I informed the Prime Minister that the current decision by the Secretary of State (Veterans) was unconstitutional and violated the Charter of Rights and Freedoms, as the late John W. Blake had been denied a birthright: to be buried in a military cemetery on home soil. I reminded him that this was a service that is readily available throughout Canada for all veterans with respect to the province of origin, but not in Newfoundland—solely because John Blake was a Vietnam veteran. Notwithstanding, a precedent was established in 1969, when a Vietnam veteran who was also a Canadian citizen was buried in a DVA burial plot at the Field of Honour, at Brookside Cemetery in Winnipeg, Manitoba.

I reiterated that we, as a family, wanted only to bury our brother with the respect and dignity he justly deserved. We wanted to avoid a media circus and further disgrace to our country. I respectively asked for a timely response to ward off an imminent international campaign media release.

Finally, on my birthday I received a response from the Office of the Prime Minister. The official letter indicated that my comments had been given careful consideration and that the Secretary of State (Veterans), Lawrence MacAulay would want to reply to me directly. The Prime Minister's Office deliberately and shamefully shoved me out through Ottawa's political revolving door.

**Memorable Excerpts from Support Letters**

To David Collenette, Minister of Veteran Affairs

...On April 7, 1996, an edition of the Evening Telegram with an article entitled, "Not Without Honour" caught my eye. As I began reading I was saddened by the death of John W. Blake, even though I didn't know him. Then my feelings turned to sympathy for his family and friends for their loss. As I read on, I felt pride for our fellow Newfoundlander (and Canadian) for his courage during battle, his personal accomplishments after and his fight for his beliefs and for his fellow veterans.

I felt he, like all veterans, deserved the honour. As I neared the end of the article, I felt angered as I read that the late John W. Blake was DENIED burial at Mt. Pleasant Cemetery's Field of Honour. Anger turned to sadness and sadness to shame. Ashamed to say I'm Canadian. I always thought Canadians respected veterans, ALL veterans.

For the Love of God, the Pride of Country, and the Respect of the Dead, let John W. Blake rest in peace where he deserves to be laid, in Mt. Pleasant's Field of Honour, with all the other veterans who deserve this honour, no matter where they fought or when or for whom. No such policy should exist.

Sincerely,
Mrs. Fowler, St. John's, NL
To David Collenette, Minister of Veteran Affairs, August 21, 1996.

...Mr. Macaulay, John Blake deserves to be buried as a true veteran. Throughout his military service in the USA and fight for recognition for himself and his war colleagues, he maintained his Canadian identity and ties to his family and home in Newfoundland. Therefore,

I ask that you review your department's decision to deny him a proper burial and allow him to rest in the Field of Honour.

Yours, sincerely,
Member of Parliament, House of Commons, Canada -St. John's, NL

To David Collenette, Minister of Veteran Affairs

...I read with a heavy heart the article about John W. Blake being denied burial in the Field of Honour in his native homeland because he fought in the Vietnam War and Canada does not recognize that War as their own, but John W. Blake was your own and he was ours.

The war for these men did not end because they came home and it did not end for the families of those who did not come home. The suffering for John is over now, but it will continue for his family as it does for all the families of veterans.

By denying John the rightful honor of being buried where he belongs because of a Canadian policy, you are only adding to and continuing the suffering of his family.

Help heal this pain and bury John with others that sacrificed so much and amend the Treaty of 1988 to allow his burial in the Field of Honor. his rightful place. Haven't we all suffered enough.

Sincerely,
Mrs. Wilson, Vietnam Widow
Albany, Oregon

To Lawrence MacAulay, Secretary of State (Veterans)

...I do not know the Saint-John family but I cannot help but sympathize with their anguish over this situation. For my own part, my late father was a veteran of World War II, having served with the Royal Navy in numerous campaigns between 1940 and 1945 and suffered the indignity of the Japanese prisoner of war camps for a period during the war. I also know of the post-traumatic stress he suffered in later years as a result of the horrors he endured during his service. I am sure he would feel as I do now that Mr. Blake is deserving of some recognition by his own country for his years of service and that his burial in the FIELD OF HONOUR will allow his memory to be kept with pride and dignity by his family. Surely there must be some way your department can reconsider its policy in this matter. It will be a shame on Newfoundland and Canada to deprive him and other deserving Canadians of this final honour.

Yours truly,
Ms. Boggan, Mt. Pearl, NL

To David Collenette, Minister of Veteran Affairs Sept. 18, 1996

....My constituent relates in the case of Mr. John Wayne Blake, a Canadian from Newfoundland who enlisted in the US Army during the Vietnam conflict and served for a year and a half during that war. Mr. Blake recently passed away. His family attempted to have him buried at the National Defense Cemetery in St. John's, Newfoundland. Unfortunately, permission to do so was denied by the Government of Canada. My constituent also informed me that in my riding (district) a Vietnam veteran is apparently buried in a Canadian Military Plot (Atikokan, Ontario). In light of this information, I would appreciate if you might provide me with an explanation as to why this Canadian was denied access to the National Defense Cemetery in St. John's Newfoundland.

Yours truly,
Member of Parliament, House of Commons, Canada
Thunder Bay, Ontario

To David Collenette, Minister of Veteran Affairs
...I was greatly saddened earlier this year to learn that my dear friend John W. Blake had died. I knew him in the years that he was conducting his walks, making speeches, and writing as an advocate for Vietnam veterans. My grief has been increased to hear that present policy bans the remains of Canadian Vietnam veterans from being buried in the Field of Honour.

I hope that the Department of Veteran Affairs will have the wisdom to change this policy and permit John's remains, and those of all other Canadian Vietnam veterans, to be buried in the Field of Honour. John's death has been a terrible blow to those of us who cared about him. This pain is worsened because the present policy is delaying his burial indefinitely.

John advocated reconciliation and healing from the deep bitterness engendered by the war in Vietnam. In this spirit, Canadian Vietnam veterans should be accepted into the Field of Honour as their final place of peace.

Sincerely,
Ms. Mowry,
Achilles, Virginia

To David Collenette, Minister of Veteran Affairs

...The Canadian Government speaks about National Unity and two thoughts come to mind: one is that we could learn from our French Canadian countrymen/women about loyalty, and the second is that a policy that denies a Canadian citizen John W. Blake burial at Mt. Pleasant Cemetery's FIELD OF HONOUR is an insult not only to JOHN BLAKE and his family but to the people of Canada.

In closing, I feel in my heart I have to say that it is not the people who do not know what Patriotism is but some of those we have elected.

Respectively Yours,
D. Miller,
St. John's, NL

**Public call for Lawrence MacAulay's Resignation**

On the seventh of November local legionnaires and media members stood silently together at the Field of Honour on that frosty morning engaged in a pre-remembrance ceremony offered by DVA. As a Legionnaire, I too stood there among numerous RCL comrades who supported our family's actions in anticipation of a pending press release that called for the resignation of Secretary of State (Veterans) Lawrence MacAulay.

Prior to the ceremony, I had faxed a press release to all national media contacts across Canada. Simultaneously, my brother, David, also engaged media in Vancouver, and we communicated the following press release:

**Not Without Honour Press Release**

Nine months have passed since John Blake's cremains arrived home for burial in St. John's, NL, from Hilo, Hawaii. Today, my family sadly reports that burial of our fallen hero has yet to occur due to the continuous unfairness displayed by DVA Secretary of State (Veterans), Mr. Lawrence MacAulay.

Blake's final request was to be buried in a military cemetery. Had his family left his cremains in the United States, his final wish would certainly have been immediately honoured. But in expediting their beloved brother's cremains home to St. John's, NL, for burial in the military section at Mt. Pleasant Cemetery, the family has continued to encounter major opposition from Mr. Lawrence MacAulay, who refuses Blake's final request.

The Government of Canada, specifically the DVA, has blocked the family's effort to purchase a burial plot in the only military cemetery in St. John's.

The nationwide campaign, Not Without Honour, was created for the sole issue of burial for John Blake in the military cemetery commonly known as the Field of Honour. This campaign has gained the respect and support of hundreds of thousands Canadians - veterans and civilians alike. Organizations such as the RCL (NL) Provincial Command, the Army, Air Force, Navy Clubs and the American Legions throughout Canada. Also, people in both Canada and the United States support the family's campaign.

It is of the utmost importance to the family, friends and supporters of the late John Blake that his cremains be placed among his peers and comrades. A veteran is a veteran, for whom the mutual respect, understanding and pain require no explanation. This campaign will continue until this matter is resolved in a positive manner.

John Blake's family members have exhausted all avenues of effective communication with Lawrence MacAulay concerning the issue and DVA Canada has become dictatorial and self-serving. The veterans and people of Newfoundland and Labrador (NL) have indicated a strong support for the family's issue, but Lawrence MacAulay has blatantly ignored the people of NL and Canada in their quest to resolve this issue.

The issue of the Vietnam War is irrelevant. What is relevant are the veterans of that War. The Government of Canada must discontinue displaying wild excuses and denying involvement in that war. Canadians are not naïve; we know exactly what Canada's involvement was in Vietnam. It cannot be denied. The facts are real. Canada was indeed involved in formulating and testing Agent Orange in Gagetown, NB; it manufactured munitions in Ontario; plus Canada reaped billions of dollars as profits from that War - the one in which we were supposedly not involved. Can we forget? Hardly!

The Government of Canada must cease the attitude that Canada was not involved in the Vietnam War and the mind stay that it cannot recognize or allow itself to remember John Blake or any other CVVs in Canada. It mattered little to the Government of Canada that approximately 40,000 Canadian families were directly affected by that war. It is also immaterial to the Canadian Government that all costs, medical, pensions and burial needs are the responsibility of the United States Government Reciprocal Agreement Treaty of 1988. A treaty, which insured that the cost and care for Vietnam veterans will never cost Canada or Canadians one bloody cent.

Lawrence MacAulay, an elected official, has continued to insist that we must not show respect or dignity for these veterans because we were not a combatant nor was our flag flown.

The Canadian flag was flown unofficially by many young Canadians who volunteered and served our closest ally in Vietnam. An imprint of the Canadian flag was stamped on every piece of ammunition that was manufactured in Canada that ultimately found its way into the body of a North Vietnamese soldier.

As Remembrance Day draws near, let us not forget the famous words of John McCrae's poem *In Flanders Field*; "The torch be yours to hold it high if ye break faith with us who die, we shall not sleep, though poppies grow in Flanders Field."

We must never forget the men and women of this country, who fought the fight against communism and dictatorship in order to champion democracy.

Lawrence MacAulay has failed the veterans and people of this country, most especially the people of Newfoundland and Labrador. He must resign immediately!

**Remembrance Day Service in St. John, NL 1996**

On Remembrance Day, the weather was bitterly cold as dignitaries, veterans, legionnaires, and civilians laid wreaths in remembrance of all wars at the National War Memorial in downtown St. John's. Approximately two thousand people attended.

The buses from the DVA hospital pavilion arrived at the War Memorial Cenotaph with a dozen or more elderly war veterans in wheelchairs. We legionnaires greeted them and placed the wheelchair veterans in the front row on the right side of the memorial across from the dignitaries.

After I wrapped a warm blanket around the first elderly veteran, I took my place directly behind his wheelchair. Jim, a legion comrade, gave me a copy of the new agenda and pointed out that at the last minute my name was removed at the request of a federal government presenter. Jim shook his head in disgust and advised me to follow the last presenter as previously arranged. I confirmed that I certainly would.

During the ceremony, I stood among my fellow legionnaires proudly wearing my late brother's war medals and awards tightly fastened to the right side of my legion blazer. I also wore my father's WWI medals, which were attached to a small homemade cushion and worn as a wristband.

It is illegal for Canadian Legionnaires to attach and wear family members' Canadian war medals from WWI, WWII or Korea on their legion uniform. It is acceptable, however, for a family member to wear a deceased family member's war medals/awards from another country. It was proper etiquette for me to wear my late brother's war medals and the wristband with my father's war medals during Remembrance Day.

I had prepared a wreath in honour of all war veterans but most especially the Canadian Vietnam veterans. The wreath was draped in a black ribbon to signify mourning and loss. The laying of that wreath would mark the first time in Newfoundland's history that a wreath was laid in honour of Canadians who served and/or died in the Vietnam War.

During the onset of the memorial ceremony, a federal government member quietly stepped up beside me and whispered abruptly that I could lay the wreath in my possession after the official ceremonies closed and only when the officials had departed. I whispered back to him that I was supposed to be on the program as the last presenter on the official list. He squeezed my arm at the elbow and insisted, "Not today."

I fixed my eyes on the dignitaries and reflected on the turmoil into which my family was thrust following John's death. I felt certain our late father and each of these wonderful veterans from WWII and Korea would never oppose the burial of John among their fellow veterans. I knew exactly where the opposition lay, and I knew that I would be remiss to myself and all involved if I allowed myself to be intimidated. I would not allow them to strip this time of reverence away. I waited my turn during the ceremonies with full intent to lay the wreath of remembrance according to my conscience.

The last presenter stepped forward with his assistant and both stood centered to the memorial as they began their presentation of a wreath. I picked up the wreath and held it close as they stepped back from the monument, they turned and walked toward their original position alongside the official dignitaries.

Suddenly, I stepped out from behind the veterans who were seated in wheelchairs just before the Master of Ceremony moved toward the microphone. Immediately, he noticed my movements and stopped as I walked to the center area of the Cenotaph. With a quick right turn I stood directly in front of the monument and bowed my head. Slowly, I walked forward five paces and positioned the wreath among the other wreaths. I then backed off five paces, followed by a quick right turn, and assumed my former position behind the veterans and legionnaires who had discreetly smiled and winked their approval.

When I gazed across the vast space that separated the veterans from the dignitaries, I noticed a few hard looks directed at me. More importantly, I recognized several of our provincial dignitaries who had smiled and nodded in approval. I did the right thing at the right time.

**A Blatant Display of Governmental Ignorance**

On November 12, CBC Radio show, *"On The Go"* with host Jeff Gilhooly, engaged Lawrence MacAulay in a fifteen-minute telephone interview regarding the issue of denial of burial for John Blake's cremains in the local Field of Honour in St. John, Newfoundland.

Jeff stated that the telephone interview was in response to a call for Mr. MacAulay to resign as requested by Ms. Saint John, sister of the late John Blake, CVV. He continued to say that the family's campaign had the support of the RCL in NL and that veterans in NL believe that the policy should be changed to include soldiers like John Blake. In an excerpt from the interview, Jeff asked, "Mr. MacAulay, why can't John Blake be buried there?"

Mr. MacAulay stated, "John Blake was a veteran of a foreign war from a foreign country, and that is the reason why he cannot!"

Jeff questioned why the policy could not be changed.

MacAulay responded, "Well, if you change or make an exception for one person, then the Field of Honour is not for Canadian veterans who fought for Canada and, in fact, is why that restriction is in place – to make sure that the Field of Honour is for Canadian veterans. If you make an exception for this, then the Field of Honour is open for anybody who fought anywhere or whatever way you wish to open it. If you open it, then, it is not a Field of Honour for Canadian veterans of the First World War, Second World War and the Korean War. Now anybody can have a military cemetery, but Fields of Honour are reserved for this type of thing. If I was to make an exception, then it would not be a Field of Honour for the First World War, Second World War and Korean War veterans, and, in fact, **I would diminish their honour!**"

**Campaign Reaction from CBC Interview November 12th**

Metaphorically, moans of disbelief and disgust could be heard as they echoed from the Field of Honour at Mt. Pleasant cemetery clear across Canada from coast to coast and throughout the United States and as far away as Down Under in Australia because of MacAulay's statement. The reaction from the people concerned was the same as our family's—total disgust that an elected person could be so blatantly ignorant and disrespectful. Yet he held the delirious belief that he was right to do so. DVA Canada's mandate is to serve its veterans, in this case the mandate seemed to have been conveniently forgotten.

Privately, our family felt deeply hurt by the government's stand - due solely to its elected non-veteran representatives who continued to deny our brother his final resting place. Few people witnessed the tears we shed or the anger we felt due to our government's vulgar display of misguided lack of dignity, honour and respect for veterans. Our grief was compounded by the continuous falsehoods camouflaged as existing policies that were directed at us and our campaign supporters by our Canadian government.

As a former Canadian military family, we were appalled that an elected civilian would devalue the sacrifice of the many constituents who rightly earned the title of 'war veteran' This official proceeded to interpret his own bureaucratic meaning of honour without having ever actually experienced the sacrifice and courage exhibited by those for whom the honour is so deserved. We never dreamt that an elected civilian would deliberately disregard the voice of several hundred thousand Canadian civilians and veterans. After all, these were the very people who gave him the opportunity and responsibility to listen to and speak for the people, not against them.

David and I discussed the events that occurred over the past few days. The family's campaign had grown in leaps and bounds during nine months from a local issue into an international campaign across Canada and the United States. We knew there would be a federal election in 1997, along with a postal strike. The current federal government had ceased communication with us, but we still held onto the hope that there could be some interesting developments should the federal government experience a change in power after the next election. We continued to discuss strategy and development for additional support and awareness. We felt blessed to have met so many extraordinary people who were now a part of our campaign. Before David ended our telephone conversation, he said, "Don't give up, Cathy."

"I won't give up!" I replied. "Although, it is hard to fathom that this year will end without any closure to John's death. Christmas is just a month away. It's time to lay down the campaign's rucksack and set it in the corner till next year. It's family time now. I'll send a Christmas message to our supporters and let them know that we are breaking camp for a couple of months and thank them for their continuous support. We'll wait and see what 1997 brings!"

"Thanks, Cathy, I'll talk to you soon," said David. "Love you."

I told him that I loved him, too, and hung up.

**Happy New Year 1997—Maybe**

While waiting to have some blood work done at St. Clare's Hospital, I noticed the cover of a Salvation Army magazine that showcased a story titled, *The Lone Woman in Dieppe's Military Cemetery*. Naturally, I had to read the curious article, and I asked the receptionist to photocopy the page for me, which she did.

The story indicated that on May 20, 1940, during WWII, Mrs. Mary Janet Climpson (a Lieutenant in the British Salvation Army and wife of Brigadier General Herbert Climpson) plus Brigadier Kenneth Nutty and an additional female passenger escaped Arras, France, by car and traveled to Dieppe. On the Saint Pol Road the trio had joined a convoy of military vehicles escaping the advancing German Army when the convoy was attacked by German planes. The drivers stopped the convoy vehicles, and all the occupants dove for cover into the adjacent ditches, where they remained until after the Germany aircraft had departed.

The occupants of the convoy exited the ditches one by one, except for Mrs. Mary Janet Climpson. A large piece of shrapnel had pierced her back. She was instantly killed. Her husband and travel companions wrapped her body in a blanket and continued their journey onward to Dieppe. When they arrived in Dieppe, the harbor was in chaos as it too had been badly bombed. The next day, British soldiers prepared a grave with a marker, and Mrs. Climpson, still wrapped in the blanket, was buried in a shallow grave at Dieppe.

In 1949, the Canadian Government created the first Dieppe Canadian War cemetery near Dieppe, in France at Hautot-Sur-Mer. It is commonly known as the World War II Commonwealth War Cemetery.

Under the jurisdiction of the DVA Canada and out of respect, Mrs. Mary Janet Climpson's remains were relocated to the Canadian War cemetery. On the cemetery index, her grave is listed under miscellaneous with a footnote, *Salvation Army*, since she was a Canadian civilian and not an armed forces member.

Mrs. Climpson is the only civilian woman and the eldest person buried in the Canadian War cemetery among the 943 men of the British and Allied Armed Forces who died in and around Dieppe, France, during World War II. The cemetery contains nearly 700 Canadian burials and over 200 British, with small numbers of Australian, New Zealanders and Indian. Canada did not have to inter her body in that particular cemetery since there were numerous war cemeteries in Dieppe. Canada chose to do so.

The article gave me a sense of pride knowing that in 1949, someone at DVA in the Canadian Liberal Government had the good sense to recognize that Mrs. Climpson, a civilian casualty of war, was honoured. An exception to both the Canadian and Commonwealth military burial guidelines was exercised in 1949. Indeed, it was the honourable thing to do. I wondered why members of the current Liberal government lacked the wisdom of their forefathers. Then I thought: "How much more time would pass before someone with a conscience and authority at DVA Canada grew a spine and did the honourable thing for Sgt. John Blake, Canadian Vietnam veteran?"

**Strategic Planning 1997**

February was an emotionally difficult time for my family and me. We were deeply affected by the first anniversary of John's death, and we felt as we did the night we received the news that he died: stunned and heartbroken! What compounded our grief most on that anniversary was our Canadian government and its elected civilian officials' insane, continuous bullying. Regardless of our difficulties, we knew we would continue the campaign.

Finally, by mid-March, we pulled out of from under our state of sadness and focused on the campaign's strategic planning for the coming months. After several discussions with our first-line contacts across Canada and the United States, I felt regenerated and ready to continue the mission. Armed with an in-depth contact list that contained information for the national Vietnam Veterans Associations in the United States, Australia, and South Vietnam, we forged ahead.

Our good friend, Senator Marshall, advised that in light of MacAulay's outrageous statements last November I should try just one more time to contact the Prime Minister's Office before I released the updated campaign material to our contacts in the United States and beyond. He half-jokingly said, "Give them one last opportunity to reconsider and redeem themselves." I confirmed with Senator Marshall that I would try again. He also advised me that the federal election was scheduled for June and that if the issue was not resolved at that time, then it might be to the campaign's advantage to try and oust MacAulay from his Prince Edward Island federal seat in Parliament. It was possible but not probable. Nevertheless, nothing ventured, nothing gained. I assured him that, if necessary, I would give every option my best shot.

Senator Jack Marshall was a veteran of WWII and a retired member of the Progressive Conservative Party. He told me that in 1968, he was elected as Newfoundland's Member of Parliament from Humber—St. George's—St. Barbe district and served from 1968 to 1978. Then he moved onward to the upper house of Parliament, the Senate, from 1978 to 1994. In March, during the late 1960's, he almost brought the Liberal government down over a better deal for veterans regarding the *Veterans' Land Act* deadline. In its time, it was quite the kafuffle. I admired Senator Jack Marshall and valued every word of his shared advice. He completely understood veteran issues and their needs.

As recommended by Senator Marshall, I wrote one last letter to Prime Minister Chrétien and received an official response on May 1, which stated, "I regret to inform you that this office (Office of the Prime Minister) is unable to intervene in this matter." This seemed a cowardly response! But to tell the truth, we honestly did not expect anything much better, so it was no surprise.

Locally, the petition had gained enormous support. Within the first year of the campaign, we reached 25,000 signatures, largely from the greater St. John's, Southern Shore and Conception Bay areas. Our website and supporting websites were constantly updated with the latest statements. Vietnam Veterans were writing their own articles regarding our campaign for their newsletters based upon descriptive website material we posted. Letters of support for the campaign that were sent to our government in Ottawa were continuously copied to our fax line. The response to the campaign supporters from the Government of Canada DVA was the same dismal generic letter.

Members of the local RCL remained extremely supportive and generous with their advice. Since the previous Remembrance Day, several of the veterans/legionnaires suggested that when the next grave at the Field of Honour was opened for a burial, I should just go there and spread John's ashes into the gravesite. I explained that I could not do that simply because I would never be able to acknowledge his grave with a memorial marker.

Much to my surprise, a WWII veteran approached me one afternoon at the RCL Branch #1 and asked me to sit with him in the lounge. We were seated in the far corner of the members' room when he quietly told me that he was recently diagnosed with a terminal illness and that he did not have long to live. He stated that he and his wife had divorced years ago and that when his time came he would be the only person to occupy a plot at the Field of Honour. I felt tears well up and sting my eyes and the muscles in my throat tighten when he said, "There'll be plenty of room for me and your brother; let him rest with me. He'll be in good company, and so will I."

I took a deep breath and stifled any chance that my tears might escape when I reached across the small table, covered his hand with mine and replied, "God love you. You are so very thoughtful to think of my brother and our family. Thank you for your kindness and generous offer. John would certainly have admired you and your courage. Must I give you an answer today? Can we talk again in the coming weeks?"

"Yes, of course, you can telephone me anytime. I am just glad that I saw you today. I also want to tell you that almost everyone here and throughout the island believes that your brother has every right to be buried in that Field of Honour. And don't let any of those shaggin' elected civilians tell you anything different. It is time for me to return home. This is my telephone number. Call me when you have decided," he stated. Then he stood up and handed me his card. We shook hands and said goodbye. We never spoke again.

I knew that it would be impossible for John's cremains to be buried with this gracious veteran. DVA would oppose the veteran's request. DVA's guidelines indicated that the second burial in an existing plot had to be occupied by the veteran or the spouse or a child of the marriage who was under the legal age; provided that the spouse waived their right for burial in the plot. DVA would never give approval. I also knew that I did not have the heart to inform the WWII veteran of the policy at that time. He felt that he had brought me a solution to John's burial, and it was obvious to me that my family's plight weighed heavily on his heart and mind. He died in his sleep a week later. I attended his wake and tucked a message into the pocket of his legion jacket. After his funeral, I watched as they lowered him into his final resting place at the Field of Honour. I will never forget him.

A few weeks later, I received a fax from a Mr. Orr, who lived in central Canada. His message stated, "During a recent trip to the USA, I located my grandfather's military papers. He is a Canadian WWI veteran and came from Sydney Mines, Nova Scotia. I have family in Cape Briton and Newfoundland. I could request to have my grandfather's remains moved and placed in the Field of Honour there in Newfoundland, and then you could place your brother in my grandfather's prearranged gravesite. Would this be acceptable to you and your family? Let me know as I am returning to the USA soon, and I will get the documents and start the process." He signed the fax, "Orr, DMZ '69," which indicated to me that he, too, was a Vietnam veteran. I immediately responded to Mr. Orr and thanked him for his heartfelt offer and consideration. I explained to him as I had explained to the many others who had reached out to us in a similar manner. We would never be permitted to acknowledge that John Blake's remains rested in the grave. In our family's opinion, that would be an action that we could not accept.

A few Legion members suggested that I have my WWI father's remains exhumed from his resting place alongside his first wife in Topsail and bury both John and Dad together at the Field of Honour since Dad was a

WWI veteran. In our family's opinion, it was an unspeakable thing to do. Dad's wish was to be buried alongside his first wife, and our Mom honoured his final request.

The hundreds of thousands of courageous people who supported our efforts to fulfill John Blake's final burial request were equally hurt and angry with MacAulay's comments and decision. If for one minute the Secretary of State, (Veterans) Lawrence MacAulay entertained any thoughts that his comments and actions would silence our family—and consequentially our supporters—then he was gravely mistaken. His decision and actions continued to add fuel to the fire, which ignited a deeper awareness and validated the grief, pain and anger that every veteran and civilian supporter felt throughout North America and beyond toward governments who lacked respect for veterans.

**Rolling Thunder X- Washington, DC 'Run to the Wall' 1998**

After several discussions with both the CVVA in Quebec and Ontario, plus our counterparts in America, we decided that I should attend the Memorial Day Weekend in Washington, DC. Ironically, it was the same location that I had hoped to experience with John, just one year prior to his death. He had insisted that I go to South Wales and find our Welsh family. In doing so, I forfeited my only opportunity to spend time with him My only consolation was the memory of John's excitement when I informed him of finding our Welsh family coupled with the proof that our father was his father too.

Due to the numerous postal annoyances that I experienced regarding my mail not arriving at its destination both to and from the United States, I realized that it was advantageous to include the campaign materials in my luggage. I packed an additional large suitcase, which I filled with several thousand campaign flyers and business cards—valuable information that we would distribute at the Washington Memorial. The CVVA in Ontario arranged a speaking engagement for me at the memorial site through the coordinators of Rolling Thunder Inc. I was scheduled to speak as the third and last speaker at the renowned Lincoln Memorial Reflecting Pool. The first speaker was a congressman, followed by former prisoner of war (POW), Bobby Garwood.

Charlie, a CVV from Ontario, and his wife met me at the airport upon my arrival in Washington. We attended a meet-and-greet event, which gave me an opportunity to speak with several dozen CVVs who made the journey by motorcycle to participate in the Rolling Thunder Ride to the Wall. It was arranged that I would meet with the Canadian veterans the following morning at the Pentagon parking lot and ride in with the bikers.

The next morning, due to many street detours, the taxi driver stopped his vehicle a couple of blocks from the Pentagon. The driver instructed me to walk along the roadside and over the embankment onto the parking lot. The Rolling Thunder-Ride to the Wall would officially begin when all motorcycle groups and riders silently wait in the Pentagon parking lot and form-up. When I gazed into the enormous parking lot, I viewed at least 100,000 motorcycles and riders. I wondered, "How am I going to find the Canadian Vietnam veterans?"

Some of these individuals looked slightly bewildered as they turned and watched me creep down the embankment like a nanny-goat. I did not want to slip and roll out of control onto the paved parking lot. Once on solid ground, I threw my shoulders back, took a deep breath and approached a group heavily dressed in leather attire and asked, "Do you know where the Canadian Vietnam veterans are parked?" They looked at me as though I had two heads. Eventually, I was directed to a man with a walkie-talkie who pointed me in the right direction. After weaving for twenty minutes through the parking lot filled with bikers and their motorcycles, mostly Harleys, I was relieved to see the familiar faces of the Canadian contingency. Dennis, Vietnam veteran and President of the London, Ontario Association, assigned me to be a passenger on his son's motorcycle. I informed his son that this would be my first ride on a motorcycle in twenty-five years. He smiled and assured me that the ride would be memorable. It was.

At 12 noon, the bikers simultaneously started their motorcycle engines in one huge, thunderous rumble, which was obviously heard throughout the city of Washington, D.C. It would soon be felt and seen along Thunder Alley as the progression of motorcycles and riders began their official Run to the Wall journey in honour of those who never returned from the war, men and women whose names were etched on the Vietnam Memorial Wall. Throughout the parade route, people had gathered to view the riders and show their support. I could sense an abundance of pride and acceptance for the Vietnam veterans. The sidewalks were lined six rows deep with spectators who waved and cheered for the riders who cruised toward the Memorial grounds. At one point, the parade of motorcycles slowed to a crawl, and a group of spectators noticed the small Canadian flag, which I held in my right hand as it fluttered in the breeze. Suddenly, I heard them excitingly announce, "The Canadian Vietnam veterans are here!" My heart swelled with pride for our boys. I smiled and waved at the patriotic crowd as we moved forward toward the parking area.

The Vietnam Veteran Memorial 'Wall' was dedicated in 1982 to honour the courage, sacrifice and devotion to duty and country of all who answered the call to serve, including the Canadians. It was the longest war effort in U.S. history prior to 9/11 and the Afghanistan war which began in 2001.

The 'Wall' stood entrenched in solitude and reverence. For many it was a heartbreaking journey, for others it was a point of healing, but for me it was a time to walk where my brother had walked.

During John's historic walks, he had been to this site several times. In the past, he had wanted to bring me here to see and understand why his work in America was so important. I could easily imagine John standing there in 1984 by the newly unveiled statue of The Three Soldiers, commonly known today as the Three Servicemen Salute, as he presented the American flag to Gold Star Mother, Mrs. Freeman. With that thought, I could feel John's presence and pride tempered by sadness and grief for his friends and the many thousands of soldiers who never returned from Vietnam.

The veterans and I continued our journey to the entrance of the Wall. As we approached the cornerstone of the Memorial, it felt as through the Wall had risen up from the ground until it towered over us. It mesmerized us and commanded our attention and respect. Carved in the reflective black granite were over sixty thousand names of the men and women who had given their lives for the freedom of others. Included were the names of those soldiers who were missing in action. We located the many names of John's fallen friends, especially George Morgan and Roberto Patino, which he had recorded in his journal from Vietnam. These were soldiers whose deaths had made a huge impact on John's life. The CVVs captured the etchings of each name directly from the wall in remembrance of their sacrifice. I felt privileged and honored to stand among the gallant veterans who continue to this day to pay the price for our freedom.

It was time to gather at the end of the Reflecting Pool and present a speech. The CVVs positioned themselves strategically with our campaign materials throughout the 200,000 plus veterans and civilians. People either stood or sat on the green lawns and concrete steps of the Lincoln Memorial site. They waited to hear the speakers of the day. The small stage and podium were positioned with the Reflecting Pool behind the stage and the Lincoln Memorial and grounds directly in front. I waited in the speakers' holding area with two CVVs, while Bobby Garwood and his veteran support group stood nearby. At that point, I did not fully understand the story of Bobby Garwood, nor the impact it had on his life. The participating congressman was already on stage speaking about veterans' benefits. He suggested that each veteran should take full advantage of their earned benefits. The crowd listened somewhat attentively, but it was obvious that it was Bobby Garwood that they wanted to hear. I believe the congressman sensed their lack of interest and kept his speech short, due largely to the continuous chant of "Bobby, Bobby, Bobby."

Next Bobby Garwood took his position on stage. The crowd whistled and clapped in support. When Bobby began to speak, everyone fell silent and listened intensely as he struggled to speak of his life as a prisoner of war in Vietnam. He had spent nineteen years as a POW. Finally, he was released but treated as a traitor in his own country until the truth was discovered. It was quite evident that he was a broken man, riveted with heavy complex PTSD. The crowd encouraged him to take his time to deliver his message. They offered their understanding, support and blessings plus words of encouragement, acceptance and love.

I listened to Bobby's every word and felt that our John, in his last years, had been equally as wounded and broken as Bobby. I observed the veterans seated nearby and realized, too, that John would have been their age had he lived. For a moment I imagined my brother sitting there among the veterans giving me the thumbs-up and smiling. My emotions were running high at that point. I felt a brotherly love for each and every one of those veterans. Conversely, I harbored a passionate dislike for my government due to Canada's constant denial of involvement in

Vietnam. My additional bitterness was the result of the Canadian government's shameful disrespect towards our boys who served in Vietnam with Canada's approval.

Bobby Garwood finished his story and left the stage surrounded by his support people. As he passed nearby me he paused and looked curiously at me. He noticed the large enlistment picture of John Blake, which I held in readiness to take to the podium. I acknowledge him with a gentle smile and nod that indicated I respectfully understood his pain.

The master-of-ceremonies introduced me as I hurried onto the stage. When I gazed across the sea of people, my knees went to jelly. They sat quietly waiting for me to speak. Immediately, I held up the large photograph of John Blake and move it from side to side for all to see and spoke the following five sentences into the microphone.

"This is a picture of my brother, John Blake, a Canadian Vietnam veteran and a Canadian citizen, who served two tours in Vietnam, and he was your brother too. In 1982, prior to the unveiling of the Wall, John walked across America and carried your flag to 'Check the Pulse of America', and he did this for you. John died last year, in Hilo Hawaii as a result of PTSD and I repatriated his cremains home to St. John's, Newfoundland, Canada; for burial on home soil. But my Country denied me permission to purchase a burial plot in our only military cemetery because he is a Vietnam veteran; my country's decision is unacceptable and I need your help. Will you help me?"

A thunderous roar echoed from the crowd and broke the silence with an astounding, **"YES!"**

I informed the people that the Vietnam veterans holding up white flyers were CVVs and that those flyers and business cards contained all the necessary information they would need to help us make a difference. I thanked everyone for their consideration and left the stage as they applauded.

Bobby Garwood was standing at the bottom of the steps. He had taken the time to listen, too. My boys gathered around me and we shared a much-needed hug. Then Charlie, a CVV, had returned with news that all of the campaign materials had been distributed and that he'd just purchased the book, *Spite House—The Last Secret of the War in*

*Vietnam*, the true story of Bobby Garwood, written by Monika Jensen-Stevenson. Charlie asked Bobby to sign the book as a gift for me. Bobby and I discussed John's service in the United States Army and our family's campaign in Canada. Then he quietly said, "Your brother loved you." I gently nodded my head in agreement and replied softly, "You are loved too."

It had been a long and emotional day, and we returned to the hotel and prepared for our last meal together. Bobby Garwood and his team joined us, too. It was wonderful to sit back after dinner and watch the camaraderie of the Vietnam veterans. The Americans and Canadians were all alike. They were the 'boys', the Brotherhood of Vietnam veterans.

A poster copy of John's photo was passed around the dinner tables, and everyone signed a message. It immediately became one of my most cherished treasures from the campaign. My flight was scheduled to leave by noon the next day, and as we sat around the table I knew that I would most likely never see these veterans again. But what we accomplished that Memorial weekend would be forever remembered. The campaign had been publicly and officially launched to the American people. I felt that John would have approved.

**Back on the Home Front**

The 36$^{th}$ Canadian Federal Election was called for on the second of June. We entertained a glimmer of hope that if the Federal government changed political parties, then we stood a better chance in attaining approval to purchase a burial plot for John's cremains in the Field of Honour.

During the interim, I contacted Progressive Conservative candidate Dan Hughes, the strongest opponent of Lawrence MacAulay in the federal election. After a lengthy discussion I provided him with hard copies of all pertinent details of our campaign and MacAulay's responses. Mr. Hughes was genuinely astounded and equally disgusted by our government's official stance. He also advised me that he would certainly challenge MacAulay on the subject during the election campaign.

We continued to move forward in our campaign and generated additional support from Australian Vietnam veterans. Carey McQuillan, a member of the Down Under Chapter X of the International Society of the 173rd Airborne Brigade wrote, "As a citizen of the world, I find the matter intolerable. As an Australian Vietnam veteran, I am totally outraged. That pompous ass has obviously neither put himself before his country on a Field of Honour nor endured all which that honorable action entails. For him to state, 'to make an exception, then it would not be a Field of Honour for the First World War, Second World War and Korea War Vets. And, in fact, I would diminish their honour' is not an acceptable comment from one that has not earned the right to make such a judgment. His presumption is that to include Vietnam veterans in such a Field of Honour is dishonorable. Good God! I, too, can hear the moans of disbelief coming from that Field of Honour to here. I will forward your correspondence to our Vietnam Veterans Federation here in Sydney and also to the Vietnam Veterans Association in Australia." Carey assured me that his fellow veterans would be incensed to learn of the matter and the disgraceful treatment meted out to 'one of their own', a member of the 173rd Airborne.

David Keall, an Australian Vietnam veteran wrote to me and included a copy of his four-page letter to Canada's DVA. An excerpt from his letter duly noted Canada's participation in the Vietnam War. He wrote: "The facts indicate to me that whilst not admitting involvement in this conflict, the Canadian Government was quite willing to sit back and reap the rewards, and reward without effort is thievery. Why is the Canadian Veteran Affairs Department taking such a strong stance against John W. Blake and his family? Is it because he was a Vietnam veteran? It is quite obvious that Mr. MacAulay had no relationship with any veterans because anyone who understands veterans would not treat them this way. Some of the facts Mr. MacAulay stated on the radio interview have now been proven to be falsehoods. What is his problem? A veteran is a veteran. Canada, like Australia, is a large country with a relatively small population. I believe the Government of Canada is elected by the people under the Westminster system. Quite often, MP's (Members of Parliament) once elected tend to forget the people they represent."

Also, included in our rapidly growing list of new supporters was the Society of the Vietnamese Airborne, the *Red Hats,* who were one of the most elite fighting forces in the ARVN and stood as a reserve unit alongside the South Vietnamese Marine Division. *Red Hat* representative, Roy from Germantown, Tennessee, was instrumental in writing to Lawrence MacAulay and wrote an article in the monthly *Static Line* newspaper, which is dedicated and devoted to paratroopers from all wars and from all countries.

On the second of June, we watched the election results on CBC television with great anticipation. Many constituents in Canada hoped for a change in government, but none were more hopeful than we. By the end of the election results, the Liberal party had lost a lot of federal seats but was still able to form a majority government for the next four years.

What was rather interesting to our campaign regarding the election was the electoral riding of Cardigan on Prince Edward Island. Lawrence MacAulay's federal seat, was almost lost by a difference of .5% or 100 votes. The golden boy of Prince Edward Island had been taken down a few pegs by his opponents and more specifically by Dan Hughes. In comparison to previous elections, MacAulay's popularity had dropped significantly from plus 10.01% of the vote in 1993 to a downward slide of minus 16.59% of the vote in 1997.

I like to think that MacAulay's attitude towards the burial of Canadian Vietnam veterans in the Field of Honour and my family, in particular, was a contributing factor to his substantial loss of popularity. Perhaps the message was becoming a bit louder and clearer. The people of this country needed a more positive response and resolve to Veterans and their issues, including the John Blake issue!

Within a few weeks a Federal Cabinet shuffle occurred and Fred Mifflin, originally from Bonavista Bay, Newfoundland, and a former Retired Rear Admiral of the Royal Canadian Navy, was appointed as the new Minister of Veterans Affairs. He took over from the previous Ministers of Veteran Affairs, David Collenette, Doug Young and the Secretary of State Lawrence MacAulay. In addition to becoming Minister of Veteran Affairs, Fred Mifflin held two additional ministerial positions: Minister of Fisheries and Oceans, plus Minister for Atlantic Canada Opportunities Agencies (ACOA). The cabinet shuffle provided us a hopeful resolution to our cause, especially with a fellow Newfoundlander sitting at the helm. Perhaps he would steer a course towards a more positive outcome for our family and supporters. Time would tell.

The 75th Ranger Regiment Association, made up solely of United States Airborne Rangers, contacted us and provided their utmost support for our family's campaign. The letter that they wrote to DVA Canada spoke volumes to the long history of the Rangers and included a strong reference to the never-ending relationship shared between Canada and the United States. An excerpt on behalf of the 75th Ranger Association by then president Richard Ehrler and Vice-President Terry B. Roderick stated:

> It is distressing for our Association to think that one of our own is not able to be buried with honor on his home soil. Ranger Blake served two tours in Vietnam when many of our own citizens would not make the sacrifice requested of them by our government. To deprive him of being buried on his home soil seems unfair indeed. The fact that Ranger Blake served in some of the most elite fighting units in the Vietnam War is not the issue here. Any ground where soldiers are buried is hallowed ground, and he certainly fills the bill and deserves to be buried with those who have fought for freedom and peace for others less able to do so. Anything less is an injustice.
>
> The 75th Ranger Regiment Association fully supports the cause his family has taken on to have Ranger Blake buried in the Field of Honour, located at Mt. Pleasant Cemetery, St. John's Newfoundland, Canada. We ask that the previous decision made to prevent this from occurring be reconsidered—and bear in mind that our world is one of constant change when things or ideas do not seem fair to all involved. Hopefully, this issue of justice and equality will be cleared up shortly and Ranger Blake will be able to take his rightful place among others of his like. Then his family will be able to rest, knowing their family member is laid to rest in a place deserving of his service to others. Anything less will be unfair and unsatisfactory to all who have fought for freedom, justice and equality for all.
>
> Ranger Blake's record speaks volumes for itself, but it should be known that he was not an everyday soldier. He was one of the best any country might have to offer and a member of the most elite soldier group in the world, The U.S. Army Rangers. RANGERS LEAD THE WAY!!!

In August 1997, Steve Radcliffe from Dayton, Ohio, and members from the Connecticut Rolling Flags Inc. presented a resolution at the National Vietnam Veteran Association (VVA) Convention in Kansas City, Missouri on behalf of the VVA Miami Valley Chapter 97.

The content of the resolution was much like the resolution that we drafted for the RCL Convention scheduled for the following year. We revised some of the text to meet the Vietnam Veterans of America criteria.

During the presentation, Steve stated:

> John Blake passed away on February 13, 1996. Our Chapter became aware of his death and the campaign to dignify and honour our Canadian brothers.
>
> I have been to every National Convention of the VVA and have watched our organization evolve over the years and grow into one of the most respected and effective groups, including not only the politicians but also the Vietnam Veterans. John spoke about them at the First VVA National Convention, where he was once a candidate for the National Presidency.
>
> A few months after the convention, John became aware of his PTSD and was declared 100 percent disabled. John struggled with his demons for many years until his death. I, our Chapter and others have supported John in his efforts to bring awareness to all our brothers and sisters through his *Transcontinental Walk across America, Operation Backtrack, and Living Tribute March* his final 200 miles from Yorktown to Washington, D.C., and his presidential efforts at our First VVA Convention. We need your support to bring this Resolution to the floor and get it passed. Let's get this done so John and our Canadian brothers and sisters can rest with dignity and honor.

On August 8, the resolution passed unanimously by the 600 delegates in attendance. This meant that the issue of John Blake's burial would now officially become the business of the VVA National Committee. Roland Nichols, President, Vietnam Veterans of America, Chapter 664, was instrumental in contacting Senators Paul D. Coverdell and Max Cleland, and the Office of the Vice President in Washington. Senator

Cleland contacted the American Consulate in Toronto, Ontario, to review the issues and provide a report. Our family was not privy to the report. Mr. Nichols also ensured that our issue in Canada reached the approximately 60,000 members, of the Vietnam Veterans of America Association.

Several months after the Federal Election, in November 1997, the newly appointed Minister of Veteran Affairs, Fred Mifflin, replied to the numerous letters that had accumulated in support of the late John Blake. Naturally, we continued to receive copies of correspondence from our supporters.

It came as a disappointment, plus a bit of a surprise, that Mifflin's response was redundant and more sugar-coated than MacAulay's. Unfortunately, it revealed the same misguided rhetoric. Nevertheless, I admired Fred Mifflin and his illustrious military career. He was a well accomplished naval commander and a Newfoundlander. Nearly everyone on the Island admired him. He was one of ours. Still, it infuriated us that he continued to tow the political Liberal parliamentary party line. In his response to Cdr. R. J. Winder of the American Legion, Ontario, Mifflin stated, "...Turning then to the question of the burial of a Vietnam veteran in a plot and cemetery primarily dedicated to Canadian veterans of the First World War, Second World War and Korean War, there is the obvious answer that the existing regulations would not permit such a burial. More than that, however, is the reality that there is no such thing as an exception in the area of service eligibility. The veteran either served Canada in our war and peacekeeping operations or the veteran did not. This is why, notwithstanding all the reasons for which several or even numerous individual cases may recommend themselves as exceptions to the rule, the service criteria must be respected. Once those criteria are stretched, there is no turning back..."

At that point, I reminded myself to send Mr. Mifflin a report of the numerous exceptions at the Field of Honour, with which his fellow predecessors were quite familiar. Moreover, a Vietnam veteran had already been buried in a Winnipeg's Field of Honour in 1969. We felt positive that he was quite familiar with the numerous burial exceptions. Nevertheless, reinforcement was warranted. And so, the campaign continued.

## Campaign Broadens in Preparation for the 1998 RCL Convention

Our campaign continued its focus and secured enormous support, one by one, from the RCL Provincial Commands and Branches throughout Canada.

The resolution which would be tabled at the next convention in Winnipeg, Manitoba in 1998 was mailed to approximately 1500 branches of the RCLs throughout Canada. When the resolution was addressed on the floor of the upcoming convention it would either be passed or struck down based on each Provincial Command's final decision.

During the months prior to the convention, I personally telephoned the Presidents of every provincial RCL Provincial Command and discussed the issue. Each Command President was genuinely supportive and confirmed that they would give the pending resolution thorough consideration during their next provincial meeting. They all confirmed that they would advise me prior to September or earlier of their decision following their scheduled Provincial Command Annual meetings and selection of delegates to the National Convention.

During our local RCL Branch #1 Annual Meeting, I was nominated and gained delegate status with eligibility to attend the scheduled National Convention the following year. This action guaranteed me access to all delegates at the convention, a venue to garner the RCL's full support across Canada and the opportunity to sway any undecided delegates at the convention. Members of the RCL Branch #180, Ontario, also presented the same resolution #310 to Dominion Command in the assurance that at least one of the proposed resolutions presented would be accepted. But in order to be successful at the convention, it was imperative that resolution #310 gained full support from both Alberta and Ontario RCL Dominion Commands, whose combined effort held 51% of the national delegates' votes prior to the National Convention. And we did.

### Resolution#310: Burial—Canadian Vietnam Veterans

**WHEREAS** the Armed Forces of the United States recruited and/or accepted approximately 40,000 Canadian civilians as volunteers during the war in Southeast Asia to serve Canada's ally the United

States of America and whereby Canada waived the law of traitorous and permitted Canadian civilians to serve America in Southeast Asia, in a war against Communism, without fear of being charged and/or prosecuted under the governing laws of Canada, plus the many facts concerning Canada's involvement have become public knowledge through declassified documents; and

**WHEREAS** a reciprocal agreement between Canada and the United States in 1956, amended in 1988 to include Vietnam Veterans states—'any Veteran who served in WWII, Korea or Vietnam can and will receive medical attention and/or aid in either country and the country for whom the veteran served will pay the cost'. The agreement made no provision for burial; and

**WHEREAS** Canada's claim, "We were not involved in that war" continues the denial in acknowledging the Vietnam Veterans in Canada as Canadian-born Vietnam Veterans who served an allied force and therefore will not permit burial of any Vietnam Veteran in its 'Field of Honour'. As no other Military Cemetery site is available in Newfoundland, this constitutes discrimination and dictatorship, which is not acceptable; and

**WHEREAS** The Royal Canadian Legion, Dominion Command, accepted Vietnam Veterans as true Veterans in 1995, extending membership status as Veterans, stating 'A Veteran is a Veteran':

**THEREFORE BE IT RESOLVED** that the Royal Canadian Legion, Branch #1, St. John's Newfoundland, do hereby submit this resolution, with its mandate to strongly encourage the Government of Canada to reconsider Canada's negative decision concerning burial privileges of our Canadian Vietnam Veterans, with respect to Canada's involvement during the Vietnam era and accept the Canadian Volunteer Vietnam Veterans, who served the Armed Forces of the United States with honour and dignity, in a war against Communism, by granting them burial privilege in the Field of Honour, providing there is no alternate Military Cemetery within the deceased Veterans' birthplace, this being the Veterans' desire. All such requests are subject to proof of military service via form DD214, proving an honourable discharge or an ordinary discharge, also all costs for burial are the responsibility of the family and/or the United States of America, as stated in the Veterans Benefit Guidelines, provided by the Department of Veteran Affairs, U.S.A.

Since the recent Federal Election, letters of support for our campaign continued to flow into the office of DVA from RCLs across the country and from individuals throughout North America. Each received the same misguided negative response. I also wrote to Mr. Mifflin but did not receive a response from the newly appointed Minister.

When we were ready to move ahead with our petition to the House of Commons in Canada, I spoke with Mr. Mifflin's Deputy Assistant and asked, "To whom shall I send the Not Without Honour petition that contained 25,000 plus signatures?"

The Deputy Minister informed me to keep them as a souvenir. Once again, the door to DVA had been slammed shut not only in my face but in the faces of 25,000 local people in Newfoundland who had signed the petition. There was not going to be any forthcoming cooperation from Mr. Mifflin or his office staff.

Certainly, nothing surprised me anymore, and although I was not personally familiar with the newly appointed Minister of Veteran Affairs, both my family and I expected more than what we received. We became disheartened that a fellow Newfoundlander who was quite politically capable and who often supported Newfoundland and Labrador's issues, especially our fishery, had refused to make right what was absolutely wrong at Veterans Affairs. But we quickly recovered, picked ourselves up, dusted ourselves off and dug-in again for the long term.

Before long, it came to my attention from a local member of the Legion that Mr. Mifflin believed that it was just a few local legionnaires who supported our issue and that he was not going to be bothered with our family's plight. That belief could not have been further from the truth, as he would soon discover at the RCL National Convention.

**Royal Canadian Legion National Convention, 1998 Winnipeg, Manitoba**

David did not have delegate status at the convention; nevertheless, he joined me in Winnipeg. Together again, and two years after John's death our hearts were still heavy with grief when we met, but we focused on the task ahead.

Several Canadian Vietnam veteran legionaries held delegate status, which mutually lent support to our endeavors. The supportive presidents and delegates from Legion branches in Alberta and Ontario guaranteed their support when they met with David and me. Before the first day of the convention ended, we knew we had a solid fifty-one percent of the possible votes. My duty the next day, was to visit and speak as scheduled with each provincial legion delegation in their perspective conference rooms.

On the third and final day, the delegates gathered in the main ballroom at the hotel for a full day and proceeded through the many resolutions that would be voted upon. Once a resolution was passed it became the duty of the RCL Dominion Command to forward the resolution to DVA for action.

After lunch, our campaign resolution #310 was tabled and discussed on the floor of the convention. Suddenly, two members of the RCL Newfoundland Provincial Command who held powerful committee seats within the infrastructure of the RCL Dominion Command walked over to where I was seated and sat down beside me. I thought it strange simply because from the beginning of our campaign neither one of those persons ever visibly acknowledged support for our family's issue. Suddenly I was flanked by two of the most powerful people in the Dominion Command. Why the sudden display of support? I sensed a couple of 'foxes in the chicken coop,' but I dismissed the thought and focused on the discussion.

At exactly 3:15 p.m. on June 17$^{th}$, resolution #310 was accepted and passed with an astounding ninety-five percent of the delegations' vote, which overall represented 600,000 legionnaires in Canada. As soon as the vote was confirmed the two powerful legionnaires who sat with me suddenly stood up and walked away without so much as a farewell. David and I were thrilled with the victory. What, if anything, could go wrong now?

Later that evening, the delegates and their guests were invited to attend a posh gala hosted by DVA Minister of State, the Honourable Fred Mifflin. This would be the first and only time that my brother and I would meet Mr. Fred Mifflin face to face. We proceeded through the reception line and our names were announced: "Cathy Saint John of Newfoundland and David Saint John of Vancouver." We politely shook Mr. Mifflin's hand. However, I will never forget the surprised look on his face when he suddenly realized that we were the family of the late John Blake. At that point, it felt as though it should have been a time of reckoning. Instead I felt terribly sad for the man who now held my hand as I looked questioning, into his eyes without speaking. I offered a familiar Newfoundland nod that he would clearly understand suggested. *Why have you forsaken us*? He released my hand as if he knew exactly what I was thinking and glanced shamefully to the ground.

The next day, David and I returned to our respective homes on alternate coasts in Canada. We were elated that this milestone had been accomplished; we received tremendous valuable support from the RCLs throughout Canada. Legionnaires supported burials of Vietnam veterans in the Fields of Honour. Our issue and support were now well documented, so much so that DVA Canada was now officially mandated by the veterans to act upon the resolution. We hoped they would respond positively.

The convention proved it was not just the support of a few local legionnaires and veterans as Mifflin may have entertained. It was a clear majority of Canada's legionnaires and veterans in Canada. We also recognized that it would be late October before any official decision would be forthcoming from DVA. At this point, our campaign had the support of approximately two million people throughout North America. (Note: Facebook would not be established until 2004)

During the flight home, I pondered if this would be a good time to take a low profile and recharge my batteries while we waited for the response. It had been an extreme two and a half years of both physical and emotional campaigning for the right to bury John's remains at home in a military cemetery. After spending time with

David, I recognized that neither he nor I had resolved our grief. I knew that it would be necessary for us to find a way to do so for our own future mental and physical health.

Since the campaign was gearing down I used my spare time to inform several of our key supporters throughout North America and beyond of the RCL's National Convention results. All were thrilled and relieved with the news. We felt confident that it was just a matter of time when we would finally bring closure to our loss and spiritually bring John 'home'. In the interim, I availed of the following few months to continue writing John's story, which I had begun shortly after he died. I was disappointed that throughout those past few years I still had not discovered the answer to my question. Who was Sgt. John Blake, the Airborne Ranger? I desperately needed to locate and meet some of his Ranger brothers who worked alongside him in Vietnam. I needed to learn more about John Blake, the November 75$^{th}$ Ranger.

DVA responded four months after the RCL National Convention. James, a legion friend, telephoned and advised me prior to the publication of the Convention Report exactly what DVA stated in their comment to resolution #310. James quoted DVA when he said: "Veterans Affairs has refused the submission on the basis of a moral commitment to honour the dead of WWI, WWII and Korea, and that to open the Field of Honour to others would lessen the honour and commitment made to the Canadian war dead." I felt as though someone had literally torn the heart out of my body and stomped on it.

"James, what the hell has happened? The resolution had the consensus of the RCL members across Canada. Refusal of the resolution is based on a moral commitment! Who's moral commitment? Certainly not the people of Canada or its veterans. DVA has the mandate to listen and act upon the democratic recommendations by the veterans and members of the RCL. A moral commitment is not a policy or a law. What kind of political bullshit is this?" I stated, totally exasperated.

"Cathy, I am equally disgusted as you are by this decision, and our RCL members will be gob-smacked when they receive the Convention Report next week. Veteran Affairs is still spinning you through that revolving door in Ottawa. I am so sorry and ashamed of what they are doing to you and your family. They are morons without morals!"

"James, thank you, we appreciate your continuous support. Obviously, I am feeling gutted and disappointed not just for my family, but more so for the hundreds of thousands of Legion members who stepped up to the plate, as warriors, only to be oppressed by a few misguided governmental fools. What to do now? The fight continues, and we will not stop until every stone has been turned over in search of a positive solution."

"That's our girl! I knew you wouldn't quit! That crowd in the federal government DVA will not listen to you or for that matter any constituent in the country regarding your family's issue. If I were you, I'd seek the assistance of our provincial government. There has to be a king-maker somewhere in the political wood pile. The Legion convention proved your support across the country; it may be worth a try."

"Yes, indeed James, you're right. I will do exactly that! I have tried to deal directly with the federal government because of its jurisdiction, but now it is basically over between us. Thank you for your support and advice. Feel free to let the 'boys' at the legion know that I will be OK."

"You're welcome. I only wish I had the power to do more."

"I understand how you feel. I'll keep fighting. Goodnight James."

"Goodnight and good luck Cathy."

Before I retired for the evening, I contacted David, as well as our key frontline supporters in Canada and the United States. I discussed DVAs' decision concerning resolution #310, and my intent to approach and involve our provincial government.

Under the circumstance, our supporters' response was predictable as was their continuous support. We each agreed that we would continue onward with our campaign until there was no further hope or until the family had reached their internal five-year mandate, whichever came first.

**Campaign Continued into 1999**

During a chance meeting in downtown St. John's on Canada Day, July 1st, I spoke with Newfoundland and Labrador's Premier Brian Tobin. I briefly introduced myself and explained our family's issue. He acknowledged that he was quite familiar with our story. He also stated that he was highly interested and informed me to contact his assistant and schedule a meeting, which I did.

In the interim, I contact familiar members of the provincial opposition party who in turn generated many letters to DVA. During November, a meeting with Premier Tobin transpired, and we discussed the issue for an hour. He confirmed that he would discuss the matter with his counterparts in Ottawa. Nothing changed as a result of his effort however.

The only thing that did ultimately change was that in August 1999, Federal Cabinet Minister Fred Mifflin retired. And a Newfoundlander, George Baker was appointed as Minister of Veterans Affairs until October 2000. By that time, former Premier Brian Tobin had retired from Provincial politics and returned to Ottawa, on the Hill, in readiness for the next Federal Election in 2000.

I approached George Baker concerning our family's issue and received the same dismal response. After the 2000 Federal Election, Baker was removed from the Federal Cabinet primarily to make room for the newly elected Brian Tobin. Ultimately, Baker would be appointed to the Senate in 2002.

The VVIC associate Doug Marsh, Chief of Staff and a Vietnam veteran wrote a five-page compelling letter to DVA, which proved to be extremely interesting. In an excerpt from his letter he said, "Because we believe in the morality of our war, the Vietnam War, in combating an ideology that was a threat to the freedoms that our democratic country favors; and, because John Blake, and other Canadians were soldiers of the democratic community, as were the brave warriors of World War I and World War II and Korea; and, where together, democratic warriors fought and continue to fight, and together they died and continue to die; we believe that so, too, should all democratic soldiers 'Rest in Peace' together. The Vietnam Veterans in Canada are, therefore, requesting a reconsideration of your decision, which excludes Canadian Vietnam Veterans from Canada's Fields of Honour. Cathy Saint John, John Blake's sister, has presented her reasons to you. We have reviewed them and concur with her."

Doug Marsh indicated that John Blake was an active member of their organization and that they found that his warring experiences were the same as any combat soldier—blazing idealism, heroism, disillusionment, fear, pain, innocent youth and betrayal. His only variation from the Great Wars and Korea veterans was the era.

Marsh addressed the fact that the Field of Honour 'rule' needed to be reassessed when he said, "How does the Canadian government intend to honour their Canadian Peace Keeping Forces, the Canadian Gulf War Veterans, and the Spanish Civil War volunteers, whose actions were treated as illegal, and who were recognized and honoured as veterans on June 7, 1995. What is an honour? Shakespeare noted in Julius Caesar that 'Honour wears different coats to different eyes'. The Canadian-Spanish Civil War volunteers exemplify his definition: Criminals yesterday, heroes today. What happened? Certainly time, social and political circumstances evolved. Will this take place for the Canadian Vietnam War volunteers? In time and in more befitting social and political circumstances, will we too be seen under 'different eyes'? Will we, be honoured? We believe so. In fact, the winds have begun to shift."

He also continued to question, "Is it any wonder that the United States and Canada are such close allies? Is it any wonder that Americans enlisted in Canada's armed forces during the Great Wars, prior to their country's entry? Is it any wonder that Canadians joined the American forces in their War effort in Vietnam? Americans and Canadians share a moral citizenship. The morality of their men and women and ours should be judged, not by our consequences, but rather by our motivation. Their and our intentions were good; we acted from a duty. In fact, Immanuel Kant, the German philosopher stated, 'Act as if the principle on which your action is based were to become by your will a universal law of nature.' We Canadian volunteers acted, as did the American volunteers, under the universal principle of the right to self-determination. We ask what Shakespeare asked in the *Tempest*: "We are such stuff as dreams are made on, and our little life is rounded with sleep. All soldiers are as one, let us sleep together."

**DVA Criteria Stretched Far Beyond Any Reason at Field of Honour**

During my last walk through our local Field of Honour, I accidently tripped over a veteran's memorial marker and landed directly in front of the gravesite of civilian Ms. E., age 38, who had been buried among the veterans nearby the Columbaria. I was shocked at what I had discovered and noted the information from her grave marker. The research disclosed that her inurnment took place in 1998, two years later to the day when the late John W. Blake's burial was placed on hold and still being denied permission for inurnment by DVA Canada.

One can only imagine the distress that discovery created. My family and I did not hold any contempt or grudges for the six individuals who were awarded special consideration status and who were indiscriminately buried at the Field of Honour. However, we certainly felt disgusted with DVA for not granting a special consideration for our brother, John Blake.

I telephoned Mr. Strong and asked how and why any civilian could be buried in a single inurnment plot in the Field of Honour? He simply stated, "The family's request was given special consideration."

Apparently, Ms. E's father was a WWII Veteran and was buried several plots away from his daughter's cremains. I then asked if the wife had waived her right to be buried with her veteran husband. Mr. Strong replied, "No, she can be buried there, too."

I reminded Mr. Strong that DVA's criteria insisted that a veteran and/or a wife or child may be buried but not both, and the child had to be under the age of 18. I asked Mr. Strong if it was normal to include an adult child of 38 years without the surviving spouse forfeiting her right to burial in the Field of Honour. Mr. Strong stated, "Yes, but the cost is borne by the family."

Cost! My family and I knew only too well the monetary cost of managing our campaign for almost five years. Yet, our emotional and mental costs far exceeded any possible monetary costs that could occur. The cost for a burial for our late brother would have been a blessing if DVA would just make an exception for our family's needs, too.

During our campaign, between the years of 1996 to 2001, we had corresponded and dealt with five DVA Ministers and one Secretary of State (Veterans). Each federal official constantly stated in their correspondence to our family and supporters that, "To open the Field of Honour to others would lessen the honour and commitment made to the Canadian war dead and the service criteria must be respected. Once those criteria are stretched, there is no turning back."

We strongly believed that the criterion had been stretched far beyond any rhyme or reason and that there was definitely no turning back.

DVA not only disgraced themselves in their refusal to sell our family a burial plot for John Blake, Vietnam veteran, in our local Field of Honour; moreover, those DVA Ministers, throughout the duration of our campaign had disgraced Canada, and that was disgustingly outrageous!

We felt it was obscene and morally criminal that elected government officials had bullied our grief-stricken family, blatantly told us falsehoods and withheld vital information. Then, once confronted, they hid behind policies and regulations that did not exist. The audacity of those politicians who, when once confronted with the information that a Vietnam veteran was indeed buried in 1969 in a Field of Honour in Winnipeg simply stood in deafness and oblivious of the truth. They continued to disgracefully practice noncompliance of DVAs' guidelines to those who neither met the criteria nor earned the honour, while they continued to deny us and John Blake. Part of my heart and soul that loved and respected the institution of Canada, my country, became terminally broken. At the same time, I cherished and valued its people. Well, most of them.

David and I shared a lengthy conversation that concerned the most recent discoveries, and we came to a consensus with John's daughter, Rachel, to bury John's remains in a strictly military cemetery in British Columbia, within six months, during the spring of 2001. We agreed that John had found some solitude and peace on the west coast of Canada before his difficult years developed. That thought brought us some comfort in our decision, but the reality was that it was going to take considerable time, if ever, to find forgiveness towards those who stood in our family's way to bring John home.

## An End to Our Honourable Campaign 2001

It was heartbreaking to advise our key supporter that we had reached the end of our mandate. After the most recent discovery at our local Field of Honour, it was unanimous to the family that John Blake's memory and the well-being of his family deserved peace. The good fight was over. The Field of Honour at Mt. Pleasant had lost its credibility as a strictly military cemetery for veterans by none other than Department of Veterans Affairs Canada itself.

With the assistance of those involved, we wrote the final correspondence that would be filtered internationally throughout each association who supported our campaign and hopefully offer the readers some closure. The message stated:

> To all supporters of the International Campaign, Not Without Honour, please accept our heartfelt thank you for all of your courageous efforts and support throughout the years.
>
> Five years have passed since John Blake's cremated remains arrived home for burial in St. John's, NL, Canada, from Hilo, Hawaii. At that time, a request to DVA Canada was initiated to purchase a small burial plot in the only local military cemetery commonly known as the Field of Honour. A gentle enough request, but not a gentle response.
>
> DVA Canada denied Blake's family's request largely due to ignorance and discrimination; specifically, John W. Blake was a Canadian Vietnam veteran.
>
> In short form, Blake's family launched the Not Without Honour campaign. With the assistance of over two million veterans and civilian supporters throughout Canada, USA, Australia, Britain and Saigon, we continued a relentless and gallant effort to overcome all the tangible and intangible obstacles that DVA Canada placed before us. We worked very hard, and what a famous team we made. We won all the battles but not the war.

Unfortunately, we were unsuccessful in dissolving the ignorance and discrimination of those who were elected to listen. Now the time has come to bring closure to our family tragedy

Finding peace in our heart is a difficult thing, but forgiving others for their ignorance is a start. I truly believe they never understood what they were dealing with, and the fear of the unknown overruled their good judgment and common sense. It is a far greater being to whom they will answer...

Blake's final request was to be buried in a military cemetery at home. The aforementioned Field of Honour cemetery in St. John's, Newfoundland no longer meets that criterion. The Field of Honour has been lessened by none other than DVA Canada who chose to override its own regulations and guidelines, even after John's family made the initial request.

To date, DVA approved several non-veterans who were neither eligible nor entitled to burial privileges in the departmental reserved burial plots for veterans at the Field of Honour.

On Saturday, April 7, 2001, at 2p.m./1400 hours, John Blake's remains will be buried in the strictly veteran military section at Forest Lawn Ocean View Memorial Park cemetery in Burnaby, British Columbia, Canada with honours. An Honor Guard will be dispatched from Ft. Lewis, Washington.

Our family recognizes that this honour is fundamentally reserved for fallen soldiers during a theatre of war. We are deeply honoured and appreciative that the United States Army has so graciously chosen to honour our brother in Canada on their own accord.

All are welcome to join us. If for any reason you cannot join us, don't despair. Kindly visit another veteran's gravesite from any war at that time and offer a 'Farewell Salute.' Blake would have liked that—you were his real brothers; we know that he loved you, and we do, too.

This now concludes the Not Without Honour International Campaign. We wish to extend our heartfelt appreciation to all veterans and civilians who assisted us in any manner. We will forever remember your hard work, countless letters of support on our behalf to DVA Canada and to our family, plus the numerous telephone conversations of encouragement, which kept us going forward. You are our extended family, and you will always have a special place in our heart.

Welcome home and thank you for our freedom.

**Rest in Peace Special Forces Airborne Ranger, Sgt. John W. Blake, CVV**

On April 7, 2001, family, friends and the general public of St. John's and surrounding areas gathered at St. Thomas Church in St. John's, Newfoundland, and engaged in a burial service without the remains.

Simultaneously, in Burnaby, BC, our brother David stood alongside John's remains surrounded by Vietnam veterans, family and friends from British Columbia, Ontario, Quebec, and the United States for the official graveside service.

Throughout the United States, many supporting associations organized and held services in their perspective time zones that coincided with the original service in British Columbia, as a remembrance to their brother, Airborne Ranger, Sgt. John W. Blake, 'The Walker'.

The following is the same brief message that was read at each memorial service throughout North America, while I spoke to the congregation in St. John's:

> Today will mark a new beginning in many people's lives throughout North America, especially the Canadian Vietnam Veterans in Canada and most certainly the Saint John - Blake families.
>
> Few people truly knew John Blake as well as his immediate family, but many people respected and believed in him and his ability to make sense out of what was deemed senseless.
>
> John's solo walk across America in 1982 spoke volumes about his love and respect for his fellow Vietnam veterans. He aided in the

> healing of Vietnam Veterans and society. That healing now holds a better understanding and a newfound respect for Vietnam veterans. Our only regret is that he could not heal himself.
>
> John's sudden death five years ago sparked a rude awakening in Canada, one that jolted his family and friends into disbelief and then action. Throughout those years, a strong network of support grew to bring over two million supporters, veterans from all wars and civilians from five countries together to forge an alliance, which now signals a 'Welcome Home' to the Canadian Vietnam Veterans. This is a very good day, one that we can be proud of. The boys are home in heart, mind and soul. Let this revelation bring you peace as you know that each of you played a large part in completing John's labor of love, the continuation of respect and acceptance for his fellow Vietnam Veterans in Canada. This is the legacy of John W. Blake's troubled life and final request.
>
> On behalf of the Saint John—Blake family, we wish to extend our heartfelt gratitude for your support, understanding and kindness. You gave us the strength to take it all the way, and we did. Let this day mark a new beginning for all of us.
>
> May God speed forgiveness and tranquility to all of us toward those who could not understand.

Throughout the weeks that followed, many Veteran associations sent cards and messages of expressed remembrance in their final salute to our fallen soldier. Steve Ratcliffe in Ohio sent a video of the memorial service that was held on the seventh of April in John's honour at Dayton, Ohio, which recorded the audio of both a twenty-one-gun salute and the military Taps. The videotape also captured personal messages from Steve and several other Vietnam veterans. Included was a newspaper article written by Dale Huffman, a reporter with the *Dayton Daily News*, who covered the event.

**Canadian DVA from Bad to Worse—Update 2005**

In 2005, unknown to the public and without proper discussion or public notice, Department of Veterans Affairs Canada changed its official Fields of Honour list to include St. John's, NL, and Winnipeg, MB. The official Fields of Honour in Canada are as follows:

St. John's, NL—Mt. Pleasant Cemetery
Halifax, Nova Scotia—Fairview Lawn Cemetery
Brampton, Ontario—Meadowvale Cemetery
Pointe-Claire, Quebec—Lakeview Cemetery and the
Pointe-Claire, Quebec—The National Field of Honour
Winnipeg, Manitoba—Brookside Cemetery

This currently leaves the capital of not only one but two provinces in Canada without access to military burial plots for Canadians who are Vietnam veterans. This was a deliberate attempt to exclude the large population of Vietnam veterans who live in Winnipeg burial access to the one and only military cemetery in their city, despite the fact that there was a Vietnam veteran already buried at Brookside Cemetery in Winnipeg in 1969. The decision to exclude Vietnam veterans from burial in the only military cemetery in two provinces within Canada was executed purposely and with malice. Unfortunately, this was another shameful attribute of some Canadian politicians.

Perhaps it should be mandatory that Ministers of DVA Canada must have served in a theatre of war. A true veteran of a war would certainly understand that all Canadians who are veterans and who served our allies in a war against communism and freedom of the oppressed are equally deserving of honor and dignity as those who fought and served in any war under Canadian, Commonwealth or NATO colors.

Isn't it time the Canadian government demonstrated respect for its citizens and acknowledged the Canadians who volunteered and are Vietnam veterans in Canada? Twenty-two years have passed since John Blake's death, and DVA Canada elected members are still behaving shamefully.

No family should ever have to experience burial discrimination for a war veteran as did the John Blake family. It should not happen in Canada or anywhere!

∞

# Chapter 16

## Discovering Sgt. John W. Blake, N/75th Ranger

ON SEVERAL OCCASIONS since John's burial in 2001, many unsuccessful attempts were made via the internet to locate John's Ranger brothers in an attempt to learn about John's life as an Airborne Ranger.

Fast forward ten years to 2011. I suddenly felt driven to search the internet again and seek out the N/75$^{th}$ Rangers to locate familiar names that had been mentioned in John's diary. Once I located the 75$^{th}$ Ranger Regiment internet site I posted a message, and within a week I received an email from SF Airborne Ranger Rudy Teodosio. He recommended that I contact the November Company Rangers 75$^{th}$ Infantry, Unit Director Robert Henriksen, which I did.

Subsequently, Robert communicated throughout his Ranger network the news that John Blake's sister required assistance in finishing a book she had written about John's life. He informed the Rangers that I was quite knowledgeable about PTSD and even more knowledgeable regarding Vietnam veterans. He informed them that my education in these areas was the direct result of the five years I had spent campaigning on behalf of my Ranger brother, who had died in 1996.

Robert stated that my dilemma in finishing the book resulted in the lack of knowledge of my brother's work and the brotherhood he shared with the Airborne Rangers during Vietnam. He asked the membership to help me finish his story and provided my contact information in the email. Ranger Henriksen connected me with numerous Airborne Rangers who had run missions with my brother in Vietnam.

Within a few days, pictures and comments began to flow freely from the N/75$^{th}$Rangers. Each Ranger who emailed me provided a story from Vietnam or photographs, which became valuable treasures to our family. The outstanding assistance that was extended to me and my family by the November Company Rangers made me feel deliriously positive!

Ranger Sven Henriksen, Robert's brother, wrote: "I can tell you that when Morgan (John's Ranger buddy) died, it had a tremendous effect on John. As you may be aware, John wrote several poems dedicated to Morgan and a few other soldiers who had died. Also, I remember reading that the VVA had again forwarded a petition to the Canadian Government to have John buried in that Military Cemetery in Newfoundland. I remember it well because it brought back a lot of sad memories of when I learned of John's death years after leaving the Army."

In February, I received an email from Ranger John Bryant and was surprised that he referred to John Blake as Wayne Saint John when he wrote:

"When I met your brother, so many years ago, we were not friends. There was a misunderstanding of attitudes and personalities while out on a mission that went ugly during a Typhoon."

"This was my first mission, and the first rule for new guys on a mission is to keep your mouth shut and do what you've been told. I was paired with an experienced Ranger, and although I questioned his technique of building a sandbag bunker and I secretly named it the 'temple of doom', all of my 'are you sure' questions were met with 'I know what I am doing'.

"While the weather was perfect the first day, on the second day the wind started to blow, and we finished building the radio-relay shack. The rest of the day we zeroed our weapons, and John Blake entertained us with his ability to handle the M60 belt-fed machine gun. Watching John with his M60 was impressive; he would call shots that he was going to take. The targets were nearly 400 yards away. After he ran out of tracers, the verification of the rounds hitting the rocks were the exploding dust particles as each round struck its target. Then he called a shot on a crow flying by. He shouldered the M60 like it was a .22-gauge rifle and took his shot. The striking round struck its target in flight. There has never been a better man with the M60 than Ranger John Blake.

"That night the wind got stronger, and I left the 'temple of doom' and went to the radio-relay shack within minutes of my departure the 'bunker of doom' collapsed. The Ranger who was assigned to train me had been crushed by cascading sandbags. He was pretty messed up with approximately six hundred pounds on him, so we moved him to the communication shack. I grabbed my poncho and found a large rock to hunker down behind to get out of the wind and stay warm.

"The next morning a chopper flew in to extract him for medical care. The wind was picking up and John Blake, our Alternate Team Leader, told me to put my shelter in one place, although I had chosen another place, which started a bitter exchange of words. This became my misunderstanding and conflict with John Blake; i.e., breaking the new guy's rule 'keep mouth shut and do as told'.

"On day five, the rain was relentless and the gusty wind howled. We would remain without resupply and incoming choppers for the day. On day six, a thick fog bank took the place of rain, and we ran out of food. By the ninth day, we were still socked in with fog. Our spirits were low, and it was our third day without food. There was plenty of water in the mud puddles that we could purify. We communicated with higher command and vowed that if we could not get a chopper by the following day, then we would march back to the rear and kill anything that stood between us and food.

"On the tenth day, we got word that a pick-up chopper would extract us. We stayed there as ordered, but no one really believed that a chopper would come. The fog was still very thick. Visibility was only ten feet. Suddenly, the radio crackled with the signal from an incoming chopper. We talked the pilot into our location and bounced pen flares off the chopper to convince the pilot that we were directly below him as the pilot gentle landed the chopper.

"Once we arrived at LZ English, we stored our gear, tore off our wet and muddy clothes, showered and dressed in clean fatigues and headed for the mess hall. We packed our trays with food. But our stomachs were so shrunken from not eating for four days that we were only able to eat a third of what we had taken. We were disappointed that we could not eat more.

"The next morning it was business as usual, except for the contention between John Blake and me. These differences caused me to fight John twice and each time I started both fights. Each fight ended the same way, with me waking up thinking that a tank ran over me! After the second time, John kicked my butt and beat my face into an unrecognizable state. John asked if we could put aside our differences and be friends and I gladly accepted his offer. We shook hands and became the best of friends. John, Limey and I would often hang out together.

"If I'd known that John had a 'fight card', I would never have challenged him. In case you don't know, a 'fight card' is what professional boxers have that records their win/loss record and who their opponents were, basically the history of the boxer.

"I remember the 'flag' incident as though it was yesterday. Our First Sergeant mentally hurt John as much as the war did. We were having a Field grade or General grade inspection. Our command feared a negative inspection and acted like fools. The day before inspection our command had a mock inspection. John's standard for his area was constantly 'squared away and standing tall'. John loved and respected Canada. He had a Canadian Flag on his wall. It had been there for a very long time with no problems. When our First Sergeant inspected John's hooch, he walked in and told John to take that 'rag' off his wall! That hurt John worse than the beatings he gave me. John volunteered to fight for our country and accepted the roughest assignments and was a mentor of men. For our First Sergeant to call the flag of his country a 'rag' was like being pierced in the gut with a bullet. John and I spoke about this often.

"When I got back from 'Nam, I ran from the Army and anything green. However, I did talk to John a few years after my return. A couple of years ago the Ranger Association contacted me, and I started remembering old friends and the brotherly love we shared with each other. I am saddened by the death of John.

"I had to write and tell you how much your brother meant to me. He was a great soldier and a very dear friend. He loved Canada as much as any American loves the USA. We saw and lived through some of the same atrocities of war. He was a great man!

"Occasionally, I would show a friend the scar under my nose that John Blake gave me. Well, he didn't give it to me; I had to fight him twice to get it! I have always considered it a badge of pride.

"I do want to say that John loved his family and his country. I will always remember Wayne Saint John."

Our family deeply valued and appreciated what Ranger Bryant said about our brother, and I constantly chuckled at the thought that he believed that John was a professional boxer. Our Dad must have taught John well years ago. The real surprise was that he referred to John Blake as Wayne Saint John. That discovery spoke volumes to me that my brother deep down inside believed and acknowledged to his friends that he was Wayne Saint John. Ranger Bryant's openness about the flag issue clarified why John stood down from the Rangers after the incident with the First Sergeant.

Rangers Herbert Baugh and Chuck Moseby were both on Hill 606 when Sgt. George Morgan died. I contacted them, and we shared several lengthy telephone conversations which clarified the accident that physically ended George Morgan's life and spiritually ended our brother's life. Herbert and Chuck assisted me in understanding the life and work of the N/75$^{th}$ Ranger in Vietnam. We discussed the "Ranger Rendezvous" at the end of July, and I immediately booked my flight and accommodations for Columbus, Georgia. I knew that I would do my best to attend and once again walk where John had walked. In Fort Benning, Georgia—the very place where he had completed his airborne training in 1969.

At first Ranger Mike Swisley and I made contact by email. We exchanged telephone numbers, and I was thrilled when we shared several telephone conversations. He remarked that speaking with me reminded him of John. Perhaps it was the Newfoundland accent or maybe it was a family likeness in our passion toward similar matters. John and Mike had been great friends in Vietnam. Mike disclosed that no matter how bad it got in Vietnam, John was always ready to go to work the next morning. He was a good soldier.

Mike emailed several photos that included himself, John, Patino and Morgan during their time together in Vietnam. Then he said, “I am really excited to be a part of John’s family. I truly believe he was trying to find and help all of us on his journey across the US, and I am so sorry I didn’t know it was John. I want you to know that your brother meant a lot to me, and he wanted to be the biggest hero in the outfit. We all competed for that recognition. However, he stands alone in the fact that he was a special person and everybody liked him. Your brother was all about honor, and that is something I admired about him. He was a man before his time.”

My family and I were overwhelmed with the photos because we had never viewed any pictures of John during his time in Vietnam. Now, the pieces were coming together, and soon I would totally understand John Blake, the Ranger. And so, our healing began.

Through social media I contacted Ranger Jeff Horne. He immediately replied. “Glad to hear from you” he messaged. “John took me under ‘his wing’ early in my time in Vietnam and was a most trusted friend. I owe him more than I could have ever repaid, so I spent my career trying to be as good a leader to my soldiers as he was to me. I’ve always considered it an honor and a blessing to have been able to soldier with him. He was a true hero and a rare soldier in a very small and rare Army community. I can’t say enough about his impact on me.”

When I read Jeff’s message, I felt that John had earned endless respect and friendship from many of his teammates. Jeff was the Ranger who received John’s M60, which John had noted in his journal from Vietnam.

The Rangers described in John’s memoirs were all very young men when they served in Vietnam, and it was an honor for me that we were finally in contact. This gave me a better insight into the Ranger brotherhood, and I was immediately welcomed into the Ranger family.

Nothing or nobody could ever erase the sadness in our hearts, or keep us from missing John, or dismiss the mental anguish that our country inflicted on us during those years after his death. But the joy in locating and communicating with John’s Ranger family generated a heartfelt kindness and understanding that offered peace and healing to my family and me. Indeed, we felt blessed.

**Ranger Rendezvous**

Murphy's Law struck within a few weeks prior to the Ranger Rendezvous in Columbus, Georgia. I developed a serious viral infection that presented as congestive heart failure. Suddenly, I was sharing a room with a few other ladies on the cardiac ward of the Health Science Complex in St. John's.

After several days of investigation and monitoring, it was determined that I did not have a heart condition. I was lucky. The fluid that had collected in my chest cavity due to the viral infection was pushed off with drugs. Ultimately, it took several months for me to make a full recovery from the infection.

Travel was out of the question, and due to the lengthy recovery it was inevitable that I would miss my golden opportunity to meet the 'boys', John's Ranger brothers in Columbus, Georgia.

In an email to Robert, I asked him to kindly forward my email to the Ranger Reunion members with my sincere apologies. I stated:

> I regret that I cannot attend the Ranger Rendezvous due to sudden medical reasons. I am deeply saddened that I had to cancel my plans to travel to Georgia and miss the opportunity to meet the November 75th Airborne Rangers.
>
> It is still and always will remain very important to me that I meet as many of the 'boys' who served in Vietnam, between January 1969—August 1971, with my brother John Blake—not just to share the experiences and knowledge, but to share and extend the friendships that were created decades ago. Friendships that are timeless.
>
> I wish you and your families a most enjoyable reunion for 2011. I hope to meet many of you at the Mini Reunion next spring in Las Vegas.
>
> Warmest personal regards.

Robert informed me that I would be missed and that when they made the scheduled skydiving jump, in which I was to participate, they would send me pictures. He also told me that he had arranged for a life-size vinyl poster of my brother dressed in combat gear holding his M-60 for the attendees to autograph. He would send that, too.

Mike Swisley and his wife, Jeanette, immediately telephoned and expressed an urgency to come to Newfoundland and meet me. Mike said, "Now that we found John Blake's' family, you are family to us, and we are anxious to meet you. We'll check for flights and try to arrange a visit to Newfoundland within a few weeks."

Jeanette, Mike's wife, explained, "Mike wants to see where John came from and where he was raised—it means a lot to him. We are sincerely concerned for your health and are happy that you're doing well! If for any reason you need help, please call us. Mike would be there in a minute. We understand that the Rangers are working on a Las Vegas Mini-Reunion in early June, 2012, and we have volunteered to help Ranger Ron Thomas accomplish it. We would hope that you will be able to attend. We think it will be a larger event than it was two years ago."

During the telephone conversation with Mike and Jeanette, I expressed that traveling to Newfoundland from California would be a marathon for just a one-week visit. Although I would certainly welcome their visit, I hoped that they would be able to stay for at least two weeks. There was so much to see and experience on our island. But, since there was no further difficulty with my health, I suggested that we should relax and make plans to meet at the mini-reunion in Las Vegas. I was committed to attend. Mike and Jeanette felt comfortable with my explanation and agreed to wait and visit Newfoundland later.

All the same, it meant the world to me and spoke volumes of the brotherhood that they would even consider coming to Newfoundland simply to meet John's sister. I assured Mike and Jeanette that when they did arrive, they would never find a warmer welcome anywhere else in the world than right here in Newfoundland.

**Las Vegas, Ranger Mini Reunion 2012**

Come hell or high water, it was my intent to be in Las Vegas for the mini reunion. Nothing was going to stop me this time. Finally, the dates were released for the get together. After consulting with the boys, I booked my flight and hotels reservations. I felt extremely excited that this time we would certainly meet.

Within a couple of days, an email arrived that announced the mini-reunion was canceled. I felt heartbroken. Nevertheless, I responded to the email and advised that I still intended on traveling to Las Vegas and if anyone wanted to join me there, then we would have a get-together of our own.

Ranger Herbert Baugh was the first to respond by email when he said, "OK, let's just do it. It's our party, so we will do what we want. I'll bring the BBQ, Cathy can bring the lobster and Mike can bring the beer. If anyone else wants to join us—great, if not, we will have fun without them. I will need to leave by the 9th. Tad (Patrick Tadina) always said: "It only takes two to have a reunion." Mike tell Jeanette that we have a date to see the Saxophone man, the same place we always meet. You can come also, Mike...or maybe not!"

Mike quickly responded by email and said, "OK, we have a date; we will be there, and we'll bring the beer. We will need to leave by the 8th. We will book a room at the Golden Nugget as it is a wonderful place to be. Can't wait to see the Saxophone man, and there is no way I would leave you alone with my wife! Most of all, I look forward to seeing Cathy and you, too!"

It was a done deal! I would finally meet some of the Rangers who ran missions with John in Vietnam. Mike, Herbert, and Ron were instrumental in spreading the word that we were meeting in Vegas, and the list of attendees grew. Ranger Carl Millinder plus his wife and daughter planned to attend. Ranger Rudy Teodosio, my first contact with the N/75th Rangers, confirmed his attendance with the understanding that many more planned to join us.

**Golden Nugget, Las Vegas**

Standing in the vast hallway at the Golden Nugget directly in view of the reception desk, I searched the crowd looking for familiar faces that I could identify from previously emailed photographs. Then suddenly, I heard a Texan accent calling my name. It was Herbert Baugh. He and several other Rangers were seated at the lounge directly in front of the shark tank pool.

I turned, then ran and threw myself directly into his arms and gave him a big hug. Laughing with excitement, I burst into chatter about how wonderful it was to finally meet him as I wiped away a tear that threatened to escape. Herb quickly introduced me to Rudy. It was a great pleasure and honour to finally meet him, too. Rudy reached into his pocket and handed me a Ranger medallion that represented the Rangers' brotherhood. I admired the medallion and listened attentively to a story associated with the coin. Then I tucked it into the corner of my passport folder, knowing that it was in safekeeping and would always be close by me.

I inquired about Mike and Jeanette. Herb told me that they had arrived late the night before and that they should be downstairs shortly. He also told me that Carl Millinder and family would arrive by noon and Ron Thomas would join us later that day. Herb said that he expected at least a dozen or more Rangers to arrive throughout the day. I felt ecstatic that so many others would be joining our unofficial mini-reunion. It was a strong indication to me just how deep the 'brotherhood' ran.

I excused myself from the group and promised to return within twenty minutes. Meeting Herbert and Rudy was emotionally powerful. The degree to which I missed my brother after sixteen years since his death was still overwhelming. I also knew that during the days to follow, I would have to be vigilant in keeping my own emotions under control. In 1997, shortly after the shock of John's death, I was diagnosed with delayed PTSD. I had recovered my own childhood traumatic events that had been buried for decades. I recognized that it would be wise for me to take time-out periodically throughout the coming days to mentally and emotionally process new information about John, the Ranger. John had told me in the past, good stress and bad stress had the same effect on persons living with

PTSD. The impact of meeting his 'brothers' was astounding. This get together was going to be an emotionally tough journey, but it would also be a beautiful time for all of us.

I retreated to the Casino and located a semi-quiet area near the entrance. This allowed me to process my thoughts while I mindlessly pressed the play button on a dollar slot machine. Ultimately, that one and only spot in the Casino would become my go-to place whenever I felt emotionally overwhelmed. The barmaid worked the floor, and as she passed by the players I requested a bottle of water. Within ten minutes she returned with the water, but not before my investment of twenty dollars had generated three hundred dollars. I checked out the winnings, sat there and sipped the water. I felt ready to return to the Rangers.

When I approached the group, I asked Herb if Mike and Jeanette had arrived. Much to my surprise the man standing next to me turned and looked directly into my eyes. Instinctively, I called him "Mike!" We embraced each other as though we were hugging someone else we both had loved, John Blake. We clung to each other knowing that this was the closest either one of us would ever come to spirituality holding our fallen brother. It was then I realized that the Rangers needed me, a remembrance of John Blake, as much as I needed them. I felt Mike's shoulders tremble with emotion as we buried our faces into each other's neck, just holding on not wanting to let go of the moment. Reluctantly, we stood back from each other and wiped away our tears. Jeanette reached out and embraced both her husband and me. It was wonderful to finally meet Mike Swisley, John's close friend in Vietnam.

Mike stared at me and said, "You have your brother's green eyes. I will never forget them or him." I smiled and then squeezed his hand and said, "You are right! John and I are the only two in our family with green eyes, as the rest of our crowd have blue!"

Herb got us all laughing when he commented on my accent. Then, with his Texas drawl, he asked me to annunciate, "out and about." I joyfully played along and spoke the requested words. Everyone in our group laughed. The scene was set for a joyous event.

The open area bar where we first met became our main rendezvous point for the duration of our visit. It was there that we discussed the Rangers' many memories, and I viewed several photo albums that recorded their time in Vietnam. I listened attentively to every story and experience that was shared. Occasionally, I drifted away to my spot at the casino and processed my new-found knowledge and emotions. I completely understood why my brother had loved Mike Swisley and the Rangers.

Mike's wife, Jeanette, was a godsend. She was a lady of tiny proportion with enormous insight and ability. She provided me guidance in understanding the many facets regarding the Vietnam veteran Rangers. Mike and Jeanette had attended school together but never dated throughout their school years. Then, when Mike returned from Vietnam, they began dating and shortly after were married. They settled down together, and within a couple of years started their family.

Meeting Mike and Jeanette reinforced what I had discovered at the Firebase in 1996. A successful transition from a theatre of war and continued success into civilian life largely depended on the women who embraced their spouse's life with complete acceptance, understanding, and pride in their partner's war experiences. It did not depend solely on the person who went to war but the person who returned, and those to whom the person returned. Unfortunately, not everyone who returned from a theatre of war was as fortunate in life as Mike and Jeanette. It was a complicated journey, but for those who did succeed in the transition, life became most rewarding.

Our first evening together was spent 'out and about' on the renowned Fremont Street with its unique and bizarre attractions. The Saxophone man lived up to Herb's accolades and played a memorable performance of the blues. It was quite the experience. We laughed and carried on like long lost friends. When we returned to the Golden Nugget for the evening, everyone retreated to their rooms. I returned to my spot at the Casino. This time I placed sixty dollars into the same slot machine, set the machine on a maximum bet of three dollars and tapped the play button, but I was oblivious of what transpired on the screen. My mind was in rewind mode as I recalled the many conversations and observations of the day. I checked my watch and suddenly realized that I had been sitting there for an hour. I noticed that the winnings had accumulated to a thousand dollars! I cashed out and returned to my room totally exhausted after an exuberating day. I contributed my good fortune to the Ranger medallion and closed my eyes to a most welcomed sleep.

One by one, we gathered for breakfast, and I spent the morning chatting over coffee with Mark Carter, Jim Crossbuck, Carl Millinder, Richard Baker, Jerry Herrera and many others. Ron arrived and informed us that the whole group would be honoured guests of the local VVA branch that evening. They planned a barbecue for us with some of their members. We were delighted.

During our morning conversations, I suddenly remembered the tidy winnings of last evening and told Rudy that I believed he had given me a lucky medallion. Jokingly, he asked for it back. Herb was very interested in swapping his medallion with mine. Mike just shook his head and laughed when he said, "It's unbelievable, and you are so much like your brother."

Mike, Jeanette, and I had pre-arranged a daytime helicopter ride with Sundance Tours over the Vegas strip and the Grand Canyon. For me, it was an excursion of a lifetime. I had always wanted to ride in a helicopter. The limousine picked us up at noon, and we had a fantastic afternoon. We returned to the hotel just in time to meet up with everyone and attend the barbecue.

Several of the Rangers who drove to the get-together reunion provided transportation for those of us who traveled by air. We squeezed into vehicles and arrived at the V.F.W. Post together. Ron arranged for each of the attendees to have a black ball cap with the 173rd Airborne patch on the front and an inscription that simply stated "Vegas 2012" on the side. Jeanette and I were the only women in attendance, and Ron provided pink caps for us.

Before I left Newfoundland, I had purchased four dozen 50 ml bottles of Newfoundland Screech (Dark Rum), and I felt that the BBQ would be the right place to share the small gifts from home. As soon I arrived, I placed a half a dozen tiny bottles in the center of each table. The boys certainly appreciated the thought!

After dinner, each veteran stood up and gave their name, rank and military statistics. Some told a story from their experiences in Vietnam. Each veteran was remarkable. One introduction created an unprecedented response. A former soldier stood up and told a story of when he was a medic assigned to a medivac chopper. The event he described was challenging and heroic. The former medic's voice quivered with emotion when he said, "I worked real hard on that Ranger, and I wish I knew if he had survived. There is always one experience that stays with you forever and he was my 'one'."

Suddenly, from a nearby table, a chair shuffled, and a visibly shaken veteran stood up and cried, "It was you who saved my life!" Then he proceeded to identify himself and began to tell exactly where the action had taken place with a full description of his life-threatening injuries. It was a privilege to have witnessed that bone-chilling event that had spontaneously transpired. Right there in that room, almost forty-two years later, two Vietnam veterans were reunited. It was an astounding moment. The two veterans embraced each other, shook hands and saluted each other. The rest of us completely lost it—tears fell everywhere.

Once we regained our composure, the introductions continued. Ron shared a few words with us and then introduced me and asked me to speak to the group. I was unprepared. I didn't expect to make a speech. But I knew I would feel regretful if I did not tell these wonderful people how important it was that I meet the Rangers and how much I appreciated their assistance and support to my family and me.

I thanked Ron for the introduction and said, "I have traveled here from Newfoundland, Canada, primarily to learn about my brother's life as a Ranger in Vietnam. Some of his team members are here, too. They have traveled from many different locations across America to help me 'get it right' as I write my brother's story, so he will be never be forgotten."

"You see, my brother was a Canadian who volunteered in the United States Army in 1969. He served two tours in Vietnam with the 173$^{rd}$ Airborne. He was Special Forces and served as an Airborne Ranger with the N/75$^{th}$ Rangers. When he returned home to Canada, he didn't find the peace he was searching for, so he returned to the

United States in 1976. That was the last time I saw him, and I was just twenty-three years old then. That was thirty-six years ago."

"In 1982, he walked across your country, boots on the ground, dressed in full combat gear with a load of fifty pounds on his back as he carried the American flag to bring awareness of the Vietnam veteran. He was also a veterans' advocate and helped thousands of veterans deal with the VA system. He died in 1996 because of his injuries pertaining to PTSD. Our family completely understands why."

"From his memoirs, I was unable to fully understand his life in Vietnam. Since arriving here and connecting with his Ranger brothers I have gained a tremendous amount of knowledge. I want to thank each of you for letting me 'Run with the Herd' this week. It has been an honour and a privilege."

The 'Herd' responded with tears in their eyes and an astounding "HOOAH!"

The formalities were completed, and everyone settled into viewing the many veterans' photo albums that were available. We took advantage of the opportunity for a few additional group photographs.

I felt especially happy to meet Rudy since it was he who had led me to Robert, the unit director, and from there to actually meeting the Rangers. Rudy had previously informed me that he had never run missions nor was he familiar with John. As I viewed his photo album, it never ceased to amaze me how very young all the Rangers were when they served in Vietnam. When I turned the next page, I saw a poem, '*You Are, To Me This*!' and as I read the first few lines, I recognized the writer. I smiled and asked Rudy if he knew who had written the poem, and he replied that he did not know because the poem was distributed throughout Ranger Hill on LZ English.

"Rudy, this poem was written by John Blake after he stood down from fighting the war because of the Canadian 'flag' incident," I said.

"Are you sure?" asked Rudy.

"Absolutely, I have read this poem many times over the past fifteen years. So, now you really do know John Blake!" Rudy smiled as he nodded affirmation.

It was getting late and those of us who were staying at the Golden Nugget expressed our heartfelt appreciation for the invitation to the barbecue. We then bid farewell to the host and local veterans. During our return to the hotel, we continued to discuss the amazing reunion that we were privileged to have witnessed between the two veterans. Once we arrived at the Golden Nugget, everyone else retired to their rooms for the evening. Again, I found myself sitting alone in my old familiar spot at the casino, processing all the activities and conversations of the day. I felt extremely blessed and fortunate to be right there, at that moment, learning from the Rangers.

The cocktail waitress passed by and I ordered a glass of white wine. This time I inserted a hundred-dollar bill into the same dollar machine, set it on max and automatically pressed the play button periodically while I reflected on the day. Time went by quickly, and I was completely engulfed in my thoughts and did not notice an unusual 'click, click, click' sound. Suddenly, bells sounded and lights started flashing on top of the machine. Strangers stopped to say congratulations. I had unknowingly hit the jackpot and was completely surprised by all the commotion!

Two casino attendants approached me at the slot machine and turned off the noisy alarm. They collected my Canadian passport and driver's license. Within ten minutes the attendants returned with my identification and a tax receipt worth fifteen hundred dollars. A mandatory thirty percent was normally withheld from single winnings over twelve hundred dollars, but the attendant explained that non-residents simply had to file an out-of-country tax form to collect the withheld amount. Then they asked me to hold out my hand as one person watched and the other person counted the cash winnings. The attendant ultimately placed thirty-seven one hundred-dollar bills in my hand. The total winning jackpot was just over five thousand dollars. All this happened within an hour of leaving the barbecue. The funniest thing about the whole event was that I was completely alone without any of my Ranger brothers nearby to celebrate and say, "Hurray or Hooah!"

I sat in front of the lucky machine for an additional ten minutes somewhat concerned about leaving and getting into an elevator unescorted. Then, I saw Herbert Baugh walking nearby and rushed over to meet him.

"Herb, you are not going to believe this...but I just won five thousand dollars!"

"WHAT?"

"Yes, it's true. Would you please escort me to my room? I really do not want to get into an elevator or walk down those long corridors by myself."

"Hell yes! Come on girl, Rangers lead the way!" We both burst into laughter when the elevator doors closed. We could easily imagine Rudy's expression and the other folks' reactions regarding my sudden winnings. Tomorrow, our last day together, was certainly going to be a fun and exciting day!

I was still in total disbelief the next morning and giggled with delight as I hurried downstairs to join the Rangers for breakfast.

Good news travels fast. Just as I turned the corner towards the restaurant, the 'boys' saw me approaching and began cheering. Herb was sitting there grinning with delight, probably because he had been the first to know. Rudy look amazed as he shook his head in disbelief. There were many offers to purchase the lucky medallion. But, it was all in good fun.

The group and I enjoyed breakfast. I suggested that I wanted everyone in our group who was available to join me for dinner at Vic & Anthony's restaurant. I asked Herb to obtain a head count by 2 pm, but in the interim, I would make a reservation for at least a dozen people for 5:30. It was my treat, compliments of the Golden Nugget. During the remainder of the day, the boys spent their time together in a cabana overlooking the swimming pool with music and cold beer. We all had a great day and a memorable dinner.

Throughout that last day of our reunion, I reflected on what I had learned from the Rangers. They were indeed a unique brotherhood, remarkably caring and devoted. I felt grateful that they had taken me under their wing and made sure that I fully understood the magnitude of my brother's life as a Ranger in Vietnam.

Parting was going to be difficult, but I recognized that most of us would meet again in the future. Holding onto that thought was little comfort when we finally parted. We never did say 'good-bye'. We simply said, "See you at the next reunion in Columbus, Georgia."

Most of the Rangers slipped away during the very early morning the next day, and the few who had later departures were subdued. But the most difficult farewell was saying goodbye to Mike and Jeanette Swisley.

Time spent with these Rangers was both enchanting and bittersweet. I often reflected on our loss of John to PTSD, and from time to time during my visit with his Ranger brothers I envisioned my brother as if he had lived, aging as gracefully as the Rangers who had made the journey to Las Vegas. Those wonderful, amazing Rangers made it their mission and traveled from all corners of America to welcome Ranger John Blake's sister into the Ranger family. That effort personified the brotherhood: Leave no one behind!

**Ranger Rendezvous—Columbus, Georgia 2013**

Twenty four months overdue, I finally made the journey to the annual Ranger Rendezvous in Georgia. Flights were delayed due to thunderstorms in the mid-central United States. I arrived three hours late into Atlanta with approximately a two-hour drive ahead of me before I reached Columbus later that night. I didn't expect Ranger Robert Henriksen to wait for me at the airport, but he did.

Once I cleared the secured area and proceeded into the waiting population, I heard a familiar voice shout out my name in drill sergeant fashion. "Cathy, where is your Ranger hat?" We had previously agreed upon this identification clue so that he would know for sure it was me in case he was unable to pick me out of a crowd of travelers just from a photo.

"Robert, I didn't expect you to wait for me because of the flight delay, so I took my hat off," I replied as we embraced. It had been two years since Robert and I met by telephone, and now we stood face to face. "I telephoned your wife while in transit and told her about the delay. Didn't you get the message?"

"Yes, I did. But I decided to run a mission and ensure that you made it safely to Columbus."

"You're amazing; all the Rangers are amazing! Bless your heart and thank you."

The ride into Columbus was exhilarating. Robert did not stop talking, nor did I. And I knew the next day would be unbelievable. I would finally meet three more renowned Rangers who had run missions with John Blake: Patrick Tadina, Chuck Moseby, and Jeff Horne. Plus, I would be reunited with my new-found family of Rangers and their spouses who had attended the get-together in Vegas.

I learned in Las Vegas that standard interviewing techniques were not acceptable when pursuing information or conversations with the Rangers. It was more effective to leave the voice recorder in my room, simply listen and observe the Rangers and then later make notes in a journal.

Robert made sure I understood the history of Fort Benning, especially the Ranger Memorial. But first on his agenda, he made doubly sure that I met everyone who may have known my brother, John.

First and foremost, Robert introduced me to Patrick Tadina (Tad). Tad impressed me as a gracious and humble man who contributed his personal well-being and continued existence to the "Big Ranger in the sky." His renowned military reputation and history preceded our meeting. John mentioned him several times in his memoirs, and there was a time in the past when John traveled to Hawaii in hope of finding Tad. Sadly, all he found was his own death.

Tad remained in the military after Vietnam and engaged in covert operations until he retired. There I was standing next to the man for whom my brother had searched for so long ago. During the following three days, Tad and I shared many conversations about his life and time spent in Vietnam and the men who served beside him.

Then Robert introduced me to Chuck Moseby. This was Chuck's first ranger reunion at Columbus, Georgia. The discovery of old friends and memories was tremendously rewarding and equally painful. I hugged Chuck as soon as we met. We had shared several conversations and I knew this reunion would be emotionally difficult for both of us. Chuck was also on Hill 606 when Morgan died. He spoke respectfully and caringly about John as a Ranger and as a brother. He totally understood the magnitude of PTSD. All the Rangers and their spouses fully understood PTSD.

During the second day, I finally met retired, Army Command Sergeant Major Jeff Horne. He was soft spoken and exhibited tremendous kindness and respect. Jeff told me of the time during John's second and last tour when John took him under his wing shortly after Jeff arrived in Vietnam. John shared information and guidance that assisted in Jeff's safe return from many dangerous missions. I was constantly impressed by the unconditional brotherly love that the Rangers shared with each other.

I suspected that Jeff felt that all too familiar feeling, similar to what I experienced when I first met Mike Swisley. Jeff likely felt in meeting me that he had reconnected with a part of John, and once again I felt as though I had shared time with my brother. Perhaps it was so.

At the hotel, the veterans gathered in a large convention room and the camaraderie surfaced as vigorously as it did in Las Vegas but on a larger scale. Numerous stories and photo albums were shared from time spent long ago. It was the go-to place to meet and listen.

Late one evening, several of us gathered in the conference room, and a veteran who I had just met sat with us. He was visibly upset due to his untreated PTSD; moreover, he was visibly fuming with anger that obviously continued to plague his life. Chuck stepped up to assist him as he was becoming extremely upset and agitated. It was obvious to all of us that he was in a PTSD stress episode. With tears in his eyes, the veteran passionately asked Chuck, "When does it fucking stop? Does it ever fucking stop?"

Chuck clasped the veterans head between both of his hands, pressed his own forehead against the distressed veteran's forehead and then spoke with conviction as he said in a low voice, "It never stops, every second of every minute of every hour in every day I think about the war and the things that happened back then." Then Chuck stood back and looked the man directly in his eyes and said, "We have a life to live right here and now! The VA can help you manage your PTSD;

treatments and supports are a lot better today than they were thirty or forty years ago. Get the help you need. You will get through your delayed PTSD and this crisis, but you will never forget your experiences, nor should you."

After further discussion from those of us who sat at the table, the veteran who was in despair accepted what Chuck and others said, and he calmed down to a point where he was no longer severely distressed. The veteran's PTSD stress episode was skillfully reduced after a few hours of discussion with the Rangers. He realized that his reactions were normal because of his experiences and that there was good medical treatment available if he would just visit the Veteran Affairs hospital in his area and ask for assistance. He understood that they were there to help veterans with PTSD process their experiences and traumas. One can only hope that he found the help he needed.

I had the privilege to meet numerous other Rangers who remembered our brother in Vietnam. One Ranger in particular was Don Bazadi, a Navajo Elder whose nickname was Chief. I enjoyed his conversation, especially when he said that he had met John in Vietnam. He told me that he went into John's hooch looking for another Ranger when he saw the Canadian flag pinned on the wall over John's bunk. John was there writing a letter. He realized that John was Canadian and asked him, "What are you doing in my war? You don't have to be here." Chief said that John replied, "Thought you might need a little help in stopping the threat of communism." Chief admitted that he instantly liked John.

Robert Henriksen told me a story later that evening of a time when several teams returned from a mission and headed to the chow line at the mess hall. My brother and a few of the boys were positioned about ten people behind the start of the line. In third place was an African American Ranger (Robert referred to as, "a black Ranger.") While both black and white Rangers plus other ethnic military personnel began to pour into the mess hall, all the black Rangers walked up to their friend who was third in place in line and jumped the line. That action really pissed off the rest of the boys. Robert said, "Your brother walked up to the first one in the group who had jumped the line and asked him and his buddies to kindly go to the end of the line. First, they just looked down at Blake like he was nuts. Each one of those black Rangers was a big husky guy, and each towered over Blake in height. We figured there was going to be a racket at any minute. One of the black Rangers whispered something to the Ranger to whom Blake first spoke to, and within a few seconds the Ranger said, 'No problem man.' And the group moved to the end of the line."

Robert said he and his team members were really impressed. "We figured we were gonna have to fight for our dinner. Anyway, I found out later that the guy who whispered into the black Ranger's ear had said, 'Don't mix it up with him; he's a Golden Glove Boxer.'"

I immediately burst into laughter.

Mike Swisley arrived at the table and asked what was so funny. So, Robert told him. Then I informed the boys that John was not a Golden Glove Boxer or a Canadian Light Weight Boxing Champion. He was simply very skilled at boxing as our Dad had taught him well when he was a young teenager. After Dad died, John attained the rest of his fighting skills during the local Friday night community dances on the Conception Bay Shore in Newfoundland. Many a Friday night he would arrive home with the collar torn off his new shirt.

However, neither Robert nor Mike accepted my explanation. Mike said to Robert, "You remember that bell outside of our hooch?" Robert nodded affirmatively.

"Whenever someone rang that bell and your brother was sleeping, John would jump out of the bunk and land on his feet holding his fists up, poised in a boxing stance ready to take a smack at someone—anyone," Mike said.

"OK boys, I am not going to argue with you two," I said. "Believe what you want. You've been told." I knew that to the Rangers, John Blake would always be a champion.

Upon the wall in the far left corner of the Ranger conference room, hung a life-size poster of John dressed in combat gear and holding his M60 in readiness for a mission. It was an impressive sight and the same poster that Robert prepared for the previous Georgia reunion, which I missed. He brought it back for this reunion.

The veterans signed the poster, noting their years of service. Each time I entered the room, I viewed the poster and thought, "If only you had survived long enough to find and reunite with your Ranger brothers, you would certainly be alive today."

**Fort Benning, Georgia 2013**

I sat next to James, a Vietnam veteran during the drive to the airborne base at Fort Benning. He asked if I knew how many Vietnam veterans had died by suicide since the Vietnam War ended. I really had no idea when I replied, "three hundred thousand?"

"Almost a million," he sadly said.

I fell silent and shook my head in disbelief. I certainly believed the veteran. Who really knew for sure? Accurate records did not exist, and there was no process to accurately record the number of suicides in the military during the Vietnam era Still, no one doubted there was indeed an epidemic of suicide deaths as it related to the approximate 3.2 million military personnel who actually served in the Vietnam Theatre and the overall approximate 9.1 million enlistments into the United States forces during the Vietnam era. I remembered John sending me information that 60 veterans a day, epidemic portions, were dying as a result of suicide since 1973 after most of the troops returned from Vietnam. (*Today, we are reminded that 22 Afghanistan veterans a day are dying as a result of suicide due to their war experience injuries pertaining to PTSD.*)

Robert parked the VIP vehicle, which held Tad, James, his wife and me. We attended the 21st Annual Ranger Hall of Fame presentation where sixteen inductees were honoured. The impressive facility was populated by everyone who attended the Ranger Rendezvous and the current on base Ranger Regiment. The young Rangers were quite impressive, extremely muscular, polite and attentive.

When the formalities were completed, the reunion participants retreated to the Ranger Memorial. The vast entrance to the memorial was paved with granite bricks that bore the names and units of Airborne Rangers, dead or alive. Robert helped me locate my brother's paving brick, and when I looked down at his name on the brick, my heart skipped a beat. A sudden sadness washed over me, and my tears dropped down upon the brick between my feet. John Blake's paving brick was set in perpetuity directly above George Morgan's. Perhaps it was coincidental, perhaps not. I suddenly remembered John's journal from Vietnam and realized with certainty that the moment George Morgan died on Hill 606, John did too. He just had not yet fallen.

I recognized that it was right and fitting that their paving stones were placed together. Those who remembered the tragic deaths of Ranger Blake in 1996 and Ranger Morgan in 1971 would immediately recognize that the memory of two best friends rested together on that hallowed ground. I felt honoured for both my late brother and his comrade.

Once inside the Memorial area, we read the familiar names of the Rangers who were inducted into the Hall of Fame. I even recognized several names from John's memoirs. Then we gathered for a photo opportunity to capture the moment.

Robert acted as a host and guide throughout the whole reunion. He pointed out many areas of great interest. He pointed out the barracks enlistees of the Vietnam era had called home. They spent three weeks at basic airborne training, which included the parachute practice towers. My brothers, John and David, were there during the spring of 1969. It was a humbling experience to walk where they had both walked together.

Fort Benning is steeped in history, and the museum was an excellent experience; especially with the renowned Patrick 'Tad' Tadina, Hall of Fame member, as part of our entourage. We had enormous fun when Tad was recognized at the museum by civilians. It was at that moment Tad exclaimed, while pointing at his Hall of Fame display, "That was when I had hair!"

The museum was a state-of-the-art facility with Huey helicopters suspended overhead by a rigging in the ceiling, numerous weapons and a reality walk through a corridor designed to give the visitor the experience of walking into a jungle in Vietnam. Initially, there was just a single layer of foliage overhead and then a double layer until finally a triple layered canopy of thick foliage blackened any penetrating light. The sound effects of artillery added to the ambiance. Tad commented that if felt real, and I certainly had no doubt that he was right. The experience was terrifying. I imagined John in that type of environment and partly felt the reality of his experiences. We spent only five minutes in the corridor and I was equally glad to be out of the jungle.

John, like all the other Airborne Rangers, spent days upon days in that type of environment where tremendous danger lurked. Tad and I shared many enriching conversations during the reunion. I was thrilled to have finally met him, the warrior who shared his military expertise with my brother and many others LRRP's several decades ago in Vietnam.

The Rangers are a strong, courageous and riveting force reinforced by their silent partners, the women. The ladies who stand alongside their Rangers are the force behind their veteran's strength and success since the war. They work endlessly to promote understanding, compassion and remembrance for the brave men who answered the call of duty. I marvel at their sisterhood.

During the Vietnam War, there were only three Canadian volunteers who became members of the Special Forces and Airborne N/75th Rangers. Two trained together in Fort Bragg, North Carolina: Sgt. John Kelly from Ontario, KIA, and Sgt. John Blake from Newfoundland. There was one other who remains unidentified. In total, there were approximately ten Canadian volunteers who became Special Forces Airborne Rangers and were assigned to alternate companies of the 75th Ranger Regiment. Each was an elite soldier in the American Army. Never again in history will a Canadian ever become an American Airborne Ranger or a Green Beret. Current United States Army regulations now specify that an Airborne Ranger or a Green Beret must be an American Citizen. As a Canadian, I was deeply honored and privileged to have attended the 75th Ranger Reunions and to be so readily accepted as their Canadian sister.

The privilege of meeting so many warriors, many of whom my brother wrote about in his journal of Vietnam, was a dream come true. The endless conversations that we shared and their affirmations that my brother was a 'skilled and caring warrior' was inspirational. The life-sized poster of John in combat readiness that hung on display and readily signed by his Ranger bothers during the reunion remains my most priceless possession. I am forever grateful to the N/75th Rangers for opening their hearts to me and my family. Reunions are healing and highly therapeutic. I recommend all veterans attend them each year to stay connected. Unfortunately, John became disconnected from his family, his veteran brothers and the world.

Today, North American medical intervention has made significant advances in treating PTSD. Numerous treatment options have been refined since the late 1990's. People who live with Post-Traumatic Stress Disorder need to learn the necessary skills that will help them to face the emotional aspect of their experiences. Those who have made a successful transition can help. Most importantly, those persons who choose to end their lives and end their emotional pain need to fully understand that the moment they lay down their pain, it will be carried and felt tenfold by their surviving loved ones. That is the ultimate tragedy of PTSD.

During the Ranger reunions, I felt privileged to witness the resiliency of the bond shared by the brotherhood that was forged in Vietnam by the veterans. It appeared to be tempered with pride, strength, mutual respect, understanding and love. Once a Ranger always a Ranger! I constantly thought that John would certainly have been extremely proud of his Vietnam veteran brothers' success and progress in healing their collective war experiences during the past decades. John's mission in life for his veteran brothers and society had come full circle. They had made it through the difficult years. I couldn't help but feel that if only John had survived, the rewards would have been endless.

∞∞∞

## GLOSSARY

**ARVN**--Army of the Republic of Vietnam
**Cherry**--American military slang for a new arrival
**Claymore**--Anti-personnel mine used in the Vietnam War
**CO**--Command Officer or 'Old Man'
**CONUS**--Continental United States
**CVV**--Canadian Vietnam Veteran
**CVVA**--Canadian Vietnam Veteran Association
**DEROS**--Date of expected return from overseas
**DRV**--Democratic Republic of Vietnam
**Dust Off**--Flight out
**DVA**--Department of Veteran Affairs
**Frag**--Fragmentation grenade
**FSB**--Fire Support Base
**Gooks**--Derogatory term for Vietcong or NVA
**Gunships/ Dust Off and Slick**--Informal name for Huey helicopter
**Herd**--Military Slang for 173rd Airborne Brigade
**HG**--Hand Grenade
**Humbug**--An event that should never had happened
**KIA**--Killed in action
**Kit Carson Scout**--North Vietnamese Regulars who defected and acted as scouts for US troops
**LZ English**--Landing zone base
**Medivac**--Chopper for the injured/sick
**MG and M60**--Machine Gun
**N.C.O. Club**--Non-Commissioned Officer Club
**NL**--Newfoundland and Labrador
**NLF**--National Liberation Front
**NVC**--North Vietnamese Cong
**PAVN**--People's Army of Vietnam
**P.E.I.**--Prince Edward Island
**PX**--Post Exchange
**RCL**--Royal Canadian Legion
**S-5--**Civil Affairs
**SFC**--Sergeant First Class
**SSG**--Staff Sergeant
**V.F.W.**--Veterans of Foreign Wars
**VMAC**--Veteran Administrative Medical Center
**V.R.**--Visual Reconnaissance
**VVA**--Vietnam Veteran Association
**VVIC--**Vietnam Veterans in Canada
**WACO--**Military slang for a Psychiatrist
**Widow maker**--Euphemism for an American set booby trap
**Yes b'y**--Newfoundland slang for 'yes boy'

## EPILOGUE

Trying to avoid bad memories, shutting out feelings and people, or always staying 'on alert' may seem reasonable to persons suffering with Post Traumatic Stress Disorder. However, these behaviors do not work because trauma can and will control the survivor's life. Traumatic memories cannot be erased, but the emotional stress they cause can be healed and managed. Taking ownership of and responsibility for one's PTSD is vital to the affected and their family's survival. Understanding how the brain works under the influence of PTSD is important.

To simplify the matter, the emotional function of the brain has changed and the safeguards that were noticeable and functioning prior to the traumatic experiences are now misfiring information and responding in a non-acceptable mode. Can this be changed? Yes, with proper therapy and emotional safeguards in place and with the sacrifice of personal time and effort, part of the brain that addresses emotions can be retrained. Under the guidance and knowledge of mental health professionals, a person living with PTSD can learn how to retrain their brain to function in an emotionally acceptable manner. It will take time, but with patience and perseverance, relief from anger, fear and aggression this can be achieved. Adjusting to and living with PTSD takes resiliency, strength, knowledge, compassion and a clear understanding of the disorder.

The following information is derived from numerous internet searches, and personal experience and may provide an understanding of how the brain functions in PTSD mode. It is not intended as an alternative for professional assistance. The author strongly urges persons living with injuries pertaining to PTSD to seek professional medical assistance. The following are some interesting findings:

- The amygdala [uh-mig-duh-luh] is a part of the brain's limbic system, which makes rapid judgments about safety or danger without reasoning or cognitive function and is involved in emotions of fear and aggression.

- The hippocampus [hip-uh-kam-pus], also a part of the limbic system, regulates emotions associated mainly with transforming information into long-term memory and memory recall.

- The hippocampus records the emotional reaction to normal experiences, not abnormal experiences.
- The amygdala and hippocampus brain elements generally function together without any duress. When memories are stored with numerous abnormal traumatic experiences and life-threatening events, such as in PTSD, then abnormal emotions attached to abnormal memories are also stored.
- The hippocampus cannot process abnormal emotional information associated with trauma. The result is the amygdala becomes emotionally impaired. Therefore, when persons with PTSD suffer surges of abnormal anxiety their brain cannot emotionally distinguish between a real or imagined threat of danger.
- Duress begins when all emotional communication between the amygdala and the hippocampus become distorted and confused. The amygdala goes into over-drive and communicates to the hippocampus that danger is evident, whether it is real or not, and overrides the stored safeguards and reasoning. Suddenly, the emotional part of the brain accelerates without a handbrake.
- Next, the anxiety rises, anger ensues, and emotional control is absent. At this point, the person with PTSD is experiencing total emotional loss of control and is headed for a train wreck—(flight or fight mode is enabled) if safeguards are not implemented and exercised.

Recognizing personal stress levels and breaking point is the first key step in taking charge of fear and anger. Educating caregivers, family and friends before a full-blown episode occurs is an initial step in developing personal understanding and safe-zones.

Develop, exercise and practice safe-zones regularly before you need to rely on them in an emotional emergency. Create a tranquil place in your memory where you can focus your thoughts away from any current triggers and practice relaxation techniques to immediately reduce stress levels.

Most importantly, in the heat of an argument, shout-out a pre-arranged warning word that is familiar to you and your loved ones as a warning that whatever is happening must immediately stop, and those involved must turn and walk away. The PTSD owner must initiate his/her mental retreat to their safe-zone. Don't resume the conversation until everyone concerned is more emotionally stable.

Living with an individual who has PTSD does not automatically cause PTSD, but it can produce vicarious or secondary traumatization, which is almost like having PTSD. Recipients of vicarious PTSD should also seek mental health counseling. Be supportive and understanding to your veteran or civilian loved one, and validate their feelings without being condescending or overbearing.

Educate yourself, your friends and family members as a proactive approach to daily living with the diagnoses of PTSD of a family member. Be open with the people in your community so that they, too, can and will facilitate a smoother transition. Under no circumstance take ownership of the veteran's or family member's PTSD. The key to living with a person who has PTSD is 'do not try and fix it'. It is not yours to fix; it belongs to the owner. Only those with PTSD can learn to process and manage their emotional self. Be understanding and knowledgeable. It is a tough but manageable journey. Family and friends can aid in the recovery by being supportive and listening without rendering judgment or poor advice.

Most people think that veterans of war or adult men and women do not cry and are desensitized by their horrific experience. That is not true! Being emotionally devastated by traumas and shedding tears is acceptable and a normal response to their traumatic experiences. Veterans and civilians who smother their negative feelings may smother all feelings of joy, love, peace and serenity. To get those feelings back and begin to feel contented and happy, the person must release unrealistic ideas of how they should be feeling and go through the process of grieving their many losses, their fear and anger. They need to accept without fault the experiences they cannot change.

The goal is to learn to accept who they are now more than whom they were before the war or the traumatic experience. Working through emotional pain is, surprisingly, learning how to live. Survivors come to accept that they have been to hell and back too often, and it hurts.

Later in life, it will hurt again, but at a lesser degree. Processing traumatic memories in a safe environment with a professional therapist leads to healing. Processing memories alone is regressive and non-effective.

Both veterans and civilians need to step up and get the professional and community help they need to survive. The using of medications and therapies with open discussions brings families closer together in the healing process. Service dogs are lifesaving, but if there is a lengthy waiting period for a service dog then adopt a dog or raise a puppy. Either way is a win-win solution.

Together as a community and a nation, people can end the war on death because of injuries pertaining to PTSD. Stay strong and open the lines of communication. Get involved and work together with veterans and civilian from the community level to the provincial level to the national level.

Leave no one behind, and reach out to one another, Veterans and civilians who suffer and live with PTSD need to identify themselves to others in the community so that they can share understanding and lend support to you and your families. Together we can help break down the barriers and stigma that inhibits people from seeking help.

You are never alone

**CANADA WIDE**

The new Canada Suicide Prevention Service (CSPS), by Crisis Services Canada, enables callers anywhere in Canada to access crisis support using the technology of their choice (phone, text or chat), in French or English:
Phone: toll-free 1-833-456-4566
Text: 45645
Chat: crisisservicescanada.ca
(https://thelifelinecanada.ca)

**UNITED STATES OF AMERICA**

National Hotline& Chat
1-800-SUICIDE -- 1-800-784-2433
1-800-TALK -- 1-800-273-8255
TTY – 1-880-799-4TTY -- 1-800-799-4889
(http://suicidehotlines.com/national.htm)

## Rangers Oath

Recognizing that I volunteered as a Ranger, fully knowing the hazards of my chosen profession, I will always endeavor to uphold the prestige, honor, and high esprit de corps of the Rangers.

Acknowledging the fact that a Ranger is a more elite soldier who arrives at the cutting edge of battle by land, sea, or air, I accept the fact that as a Ranger my country expects me to move further, faster and fight harder than any other soldier.

Never shall I fail my comrades. I will always keep myself mentally alert, physically strong and morally straight and I will shoulder more than my share of the task whatever it may be, one-hundred-percent and then some.

Gallantly will I show the world that I am a specially selected and well-trained soldier. My courtesy to superior officers, neatness of dress and care of equipment shall set the example for others to follow.

Energetically will I meet the enemies of my country. I shall defeat them on the field of battle for I am better trained and will fight with all my might. Surrender is not a Ranger word. I will never leave a fallen comrade to fall into the hands of the enemy and under no circumstances will I ever embarrass my country.

Readily will I display the intestinal fortitude required to fight on to the Ranger objective and complete the mission though I be the lone survivor. Rangers Lead The Way!!!

(Handbook SH 21-76)

## "Ragbag"

My mind is burdened! I'm heavy of heart!
As I look at the picture I hold, of you,
I remember you, Ragbag, though we're apart,
You're with me now; and the others, too.

With me! But in a different way,
For I can't see you, anywhere,
Things are catching my eye—each day,
Reminding me, still, you are here!

I remember also the times we'd talk,
How we'd laugh and raise such hell,
Along with the days, we each would stalk
The Gooks! Hey Pat, it sure was swell!

Today, with your picture, it all is clear,
Why you should go ahead of me,
You never knew the end was near,
So you kept going! You wanted to see!

To see what, Pat, what have you done?
Didn't you know you'd hurt us too?
The days aren't nearly so much fun,
As when I'd walk and talk with you.

Things are different! Yes, I know!
Though, still, sometimes, I talk to you,
It all will pass, and time will go,
I wish I knew what I was going to!

I remember now, the way you fought,
The way you felt, and the way you cared,
In life you've passed a lesson, well taught,
The end you found wasn't what you feared!

Things will go on, and me, somehow,
Will join you somewhere, by and by!

I'll keep on fooling around for now,
Remembering you, Pat, you didn't die!

Didn't die? No! Because I remember!
The way you were, when you were here,
Nothing in the future could ever dismember
My memory of that—is very clear!

With honest pride in having known Sgt. Roberto L. Patino, N/75$^{th}$ Ranger as comrade and a good friend—John W. Blake©1971

**Author's note:**

Roberto Patino's son and namesake, Roberto, contacted the N/75$^{th}$ Rangers in 2014 at which time he first read the poem *"Ragbag"*.

Golf Team Leader, Sgt. Patino's self-imposed nickname, *"Ragbag,"* was a respectful collection of miscellaneous attributes that held a special meaning to himself, Assistant Golf Team Leader, Sgt. George Morgan and to John Blake.

The following poem was written by John Blake while in Vietnam at the end of his first tour of duty. John was beginning to lose faith with the American people who were not in support of their troops in Vietnam

## "A Soldier, Is a Lonely Man"

What about the human side of this war?
Is it really that bad; that hard to endure?
Does a man feel the loneliness in many ways?
Will his memory still drift to happier days?

No one talks about these things,
As in most cases, it often brings,
Sadness to the life of each lonely man,
Hindering his capacity to understand.

Time for thought has proven to be,
A handicap for many a soldier, like me!
Each problem keeps flowing, through every thought,
Destroying one's interest! Starting the rot!

Take a problem sent from home!
Sent to a soldier all alone!
Let him play with it in his mind!
And watch as he becomes entwined!

Entwined, with problems greater still,
So great they may destroy his will,
Understand me, if you can,
A Soldier is a lonely man.

John W. Blake©1970

## "Yesterday"

Yesterday, Morgan! Where did you go?
Whatever happened to our routine?
Can you find some way to let me know?
So I don't blow the whole damn scene.

Yesterday is gone! I know that now.
I can't see you, anymore.
There's a brand new wrinkle on my brow,
As I go on with this half-assed war.

I'll not forget, the friend you were.
The many ways you cared about us all.
Sometimes I know I will refer,
To you and yesterday, if I should fall!

Yes! You're gone now Morg! I know that well!
For I was there to watch you go.
Today the fools want me to tell,
How it was! For it seems, they missed the show.

I know you'd laugh if you were here!
Laugh so much—you couldn't speak!
Go to the cooler and get us a beer,
Open them, asking me," Why so weak?"

Horrible, stupid and selfish emotions!
Why can't I just say, "What to hell?"
Cast my weakness, onto the oceans,
And, say, "Well Morg, it sure was swell!"

In my heart, I know what I must do.
Get up and go meet tomorrow! Someway!
As to how successful, I shall be,
Is something, we'll have to wait, to see!

John W. Blake ©1971

## "My Little Man—Michael"

I want to be there, at his side!
To talk with him and see his pride,
In me, his Dad! His very own!
I hate to have left him, all alone.

To look in the eyes of my little man,
Watch as he grows, to understand;
That he is what I need in life!
Along with, of course, his mother; my wife!

She gave me Michael, and to be sure!
I never could ask for very much more,
My little man! A man of might!
Shall fill each lonely day and night!

All alone, without his Dad!
I fear he'll forget he ever had,
A father who loved him every day;
Who hated to go, yet, was taken away.

Away from what – What did I gain?
Except the agony and the pain,
Of missing my son! My wife! Our ways!
And living a life of endless days!

Michael! One day, you'll learn, as I!
That man will war! And men will die!
You'll see, as I, the agony too!
And then you'll feel the way I do.

I cannot tell you what is right!
But, I hope, my son, you'll never fight!
Somehow, I know you shall one day.
Pick-up a gun, go on your way.

How can a father, such as I,
Feel so much hurt' so want to cry?
Not be able to let it show,
In fear, you'll see and start to know.

## "My Little Man—Michael" continued

Know that, contrary, to what I thought,
The ends I've reached weren't those I sought.
This life I lead is just no good!
I'd protect you from it if I could!

Protect you from it, so say I!
In hope that one day, by and by
You'll look at me and understand,
You are my life! My little man!

Dad's little man will grow, as he!
There's nothing he can't have, or be!
I'll live the best part of my life,
For you, and Mom! My son! My wife!

One day, I'm hoping, we shall be,
In a place of love and serenity!
Where boys can grow up to be men,
And never have to fight again.

Michael! Read this, when you can!
And give your Dad a helping hand!
Try to learn something, here, from me!
Grow into the man, I hope you'll be!

Don't worry, my son, I'll soon be home!
And you won't have to learn on your own.
You'll walk at my side and never see,
How important you are, in this life, to me!

With Sincerity and understanding,
John W. Blake©1971

**Footnote:** When Cpl. John Ormiston returned from Vietnam, his life was difficult. The war had followed him home and like so many others he, too, lived with undiagnosed PTSD. The years that passed took its toll. In 2001, John was engaged in months of contractual clean-up work in New York that entailed the removing of debris and asbestos dust that followed the collapse of the Twin Towers. On July 9, 2007, John Ormiston died on his birthday as a result of cancer caused by asbestos dust. His son, Michael, read the above poem for the first time in 2015.

## THE CAMPAIGN SONG

## NOT WITHOUT HONOUR

Dear John, your death, a mission did bring,
A call to Canadians from sea to sea,
We brought you home to the soil of your land,
But your country denied you. Was it God's given plan?

To rest with the soldiers who believed just as you,
They fought for freedom with our Allies, too.
They gave of themselves and prayed that there'd be,
No more war for eternity. (Repeat once)

Chorus: Ye Vietnam heroes, Welcome home,
With tormented souls and tales untold,
It's never too late to heal the torn,
And we'll turn our backs no more.
No, we'll turn our backs no more!

Honour all soldiers for freedom they fought,
They lived and died—in Vietnam,
Let not us forget nor turn our backs,
On the Canadian Vietnam Vets. (Repeat once)

A soldier is a soldier and this, what remains,
The mutual respect, understanding, and pain,
One look in their eye and the story is told,
Of a time spent a long time ago. (Repeat once)

Chorus: once

Let not us forget nor turn our backs,
On, the Canadian Vietnam Vets. (Repeat once)

(Sound of bugle ending music with fading military taps)
Cathy Saint John©1996

## John W. Blake—Biography

No state in the USA can claim credit for being the home of John Blake. He was born and raised in Topsail, Newfoundland, February 5, 1949. He lived almost half of his life in Canada and the remaining years in the United States.

John W. Blake was nineteen years old and a Canadian volunteer when he was inducted into the United States Army on January 13, 1969. He is the first native of Newfoundland and Labrador, Canada, to earn the renowned Green Beret of the United States Special Forces. He is also the first Newfoundlander to proudly wear the "Black Beret" of the United States 173rd Airborne Rangers in a foreign war.

On the eighth of January, 1970, John was deployed to Vietnam. He was honorably discharged from the United States Army on August 17, 1971. He was awarded One Bronze Star for valor, two Army Commendation Medals (ARCOMS), and a MACV Recondo certificate and patch. He declined three Purple Heart awards. By September, he returned to Newfoundland, Canada, and studied accounting at Memorial University.

In 1976, John left Newfoundland and returned to the United States and gained more understanding of his condition. He had developed symptoms of Post Traumatic Stress Disorder (PTSD), and without professional assistance, he struggled undiagnosed for two decades. Mostly, he felt alone and out of step with everything around him. To say that he marched to the beat of his own drum would be an understatement.

In 1982, John Blake, a combat veteran of the Vietnam War, became the first pedestrian to carry the American flag (in exchange for his M60) across the Continental United States. Impelled by a desire to promote positivism and patriotism among the American people, Blake started his *Transcontinental Walk* in Seattle, Washington on May 1,

1982. During the five-month walk plus two months of non-walking activities, Blake wore full combat gear to recreate the image of the United States soldier during the Vietnam War. The walk was a tribute to all Vietnam veterans.

After 3,200 miles and six pairs of Army boots, John arrived at the Yorktown Victory Center in November 1982. On December 1, 1982, he was declared the first honorary citizen of York County, Virginia. These events were well documented by media during 1982. On the fifth of July 1983, hosted by the Vietnam Veterans of America Dayton, Ohio Chapter 97, John once again dressed in full combat gear and proudly carried the American flag when he paid special tribute, by walking 250 miles across Ohio during *Operation Backtrack*, to honour Ohio's Vietnam War dead. He appealed to Vietnam veterans and their families and to all Ohioans to show solidarity with the families and friends of Ohio's MIAs and POWs.

In September 1983, John Blake, the Veterans' Advocate, entered a race for the Presidential position of the first National Election of Vietnam Veterans of America (VVA). One year later, John organized and accomplished a trans-state walk across the State of Virginia as a *Living Tribute March* in honour of America's 'Gold Star Mothers'.

During 1984, John continued his veterans' advocacy work and was very familiar with the VA system. He was no stranger to the injuries and mental effects and exhibited all the signs of Post Traumatic Stress Disorder Since his return from the war, John pushed all the warning signs and symptoms aside and focused on his advocacy work with the Vietnam veterans. John's untreated PTSD progressed until, ultimately, he was declared 100% disabled in 1984. Time and the lack of state-of-the-art therapy during that era—and deficiencies of the VA system—added injury to the complex disorder.

John W. Blake died February 13, 1996. He spiritually discharged himself from the United States Army.

"Memories are happy and smiling faces."

John W. Blake

# THE AUTHOR

During the past three decades, Cathy Saint John, the author, has written numerous articles of local interest for the *Evening Telegram*, *The Downhomer*, and *The Newfoundland Bride* magazine. She is an avid reader and writer of poetry and songs.

This is her first published book, a labor of love that has taken her two decades of research and numerous rewrites to complete. She is humbled and honoured to have completed her brother's unfinished manuscript, not only for her family but for the general public. May all remember the now-silenced voices like John Blake's.

In sharing John's experiences, the author is hopeful that her brother's story will assist other persons living with PTSD—as well as their families to fully understand the many facets and devastating depth of living and struggling with the injuries of Post Traumatic Stress Disorder.

Hopefully, this story highlights the urgency to end the war at home for veterans, civilians, and their families who struggle with the challenges and effects of PTSD. Cathy feels that societies needs to be better educated and more proactive in accepting and understanding people who suffer from PTSD as a result of their extraordinary traumatic experiences. She is equally hopeful that communities and government agencies will strive to gain a greater insight into the hidden world of persons living with the injuries of Post Traumatic Stress Disorder.

In turn, Cathy believes this will foster an understanding and acceptance of persons living with mental health illnesses and assist in reducing the stigma attached to mental health issues.

She was born and raised in Topsail, Newfoundland until 1966 and later lived in various parts of Canada. She returned to Newfoundland in 1973.

Cathy can be contacted by email:johnblake.thewalker@gmail.com

## Memorable Photos

*Above:* Our family in 1969 when John *(left)* and David *(right)* returned home to Montreal from Basic Training

*Above:* John, Cathy and David

*Above:* Cathy at St. John's, NL cenotaph during Remembrance Day 1996

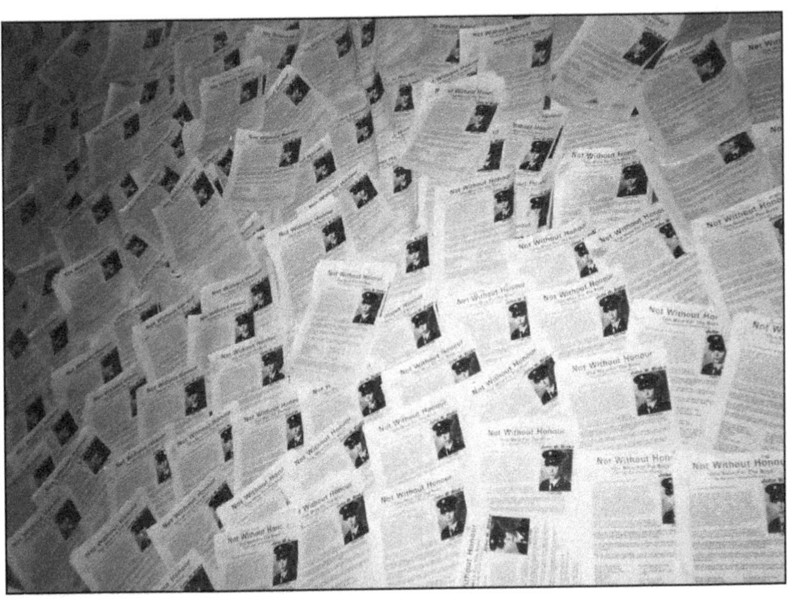


*Above:* Petitions reflecting the Not Without Honour Campaign 1996

*Above:* Firebase, Maple Ridge, B.C., 1996 tribute to Sgt. John W. Blake

*Above:* Presentation of the United States' flag and military taps Firebase, Maple Ridge, B.C. 1996

*Above:* Rolling Thunder, Washington, D.C. 1997
Pentagon parking lot

*Above:* Rolling Thunder, 1997, Cathy is the passenger on motorcycle on the right

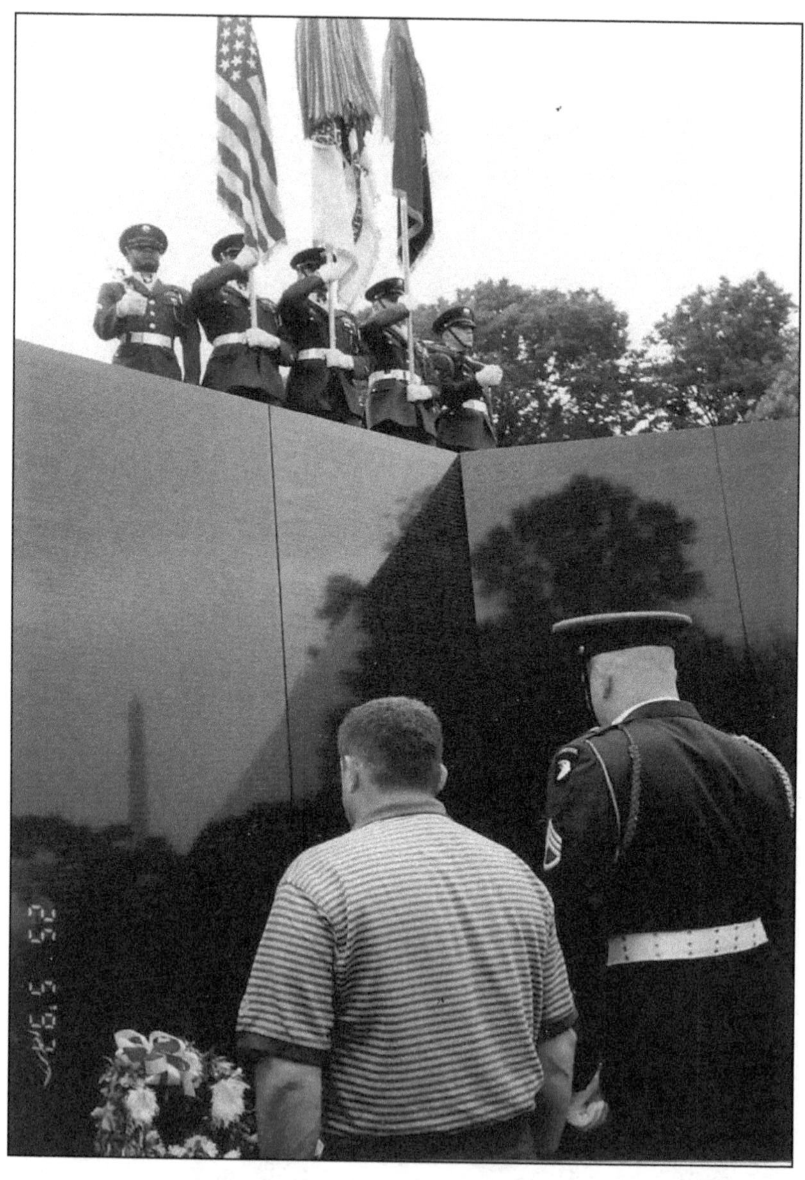

*Above:* The Honor Guard at the Vietnam War Memorial, Washington, D.C. 1997

*Above on the left:* The Vietnam Memorial Wall and Cathy pointing to George Morgan's name 1997

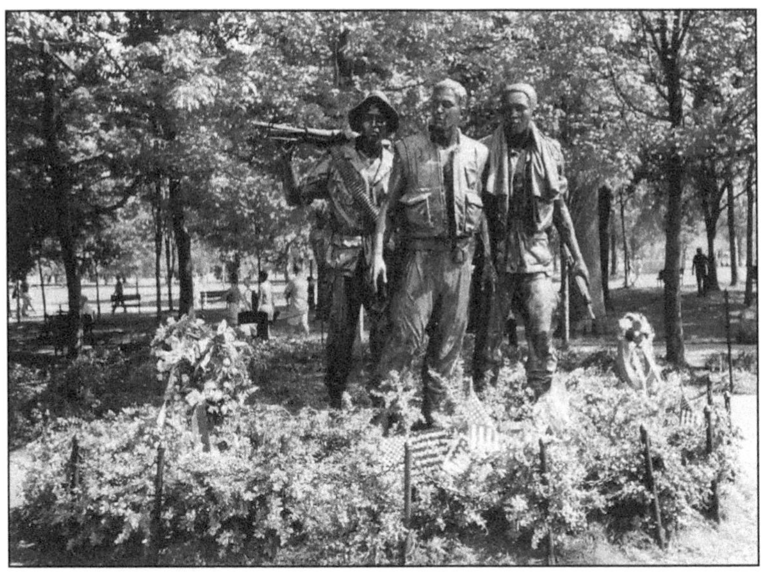

*Above:* The Three Servicemen Vietnam Memorial site where John presented the American flag to a Gold Star mother in 1984

Veterans and civilians listening to the guest speakers, Washington, D.C. 1997

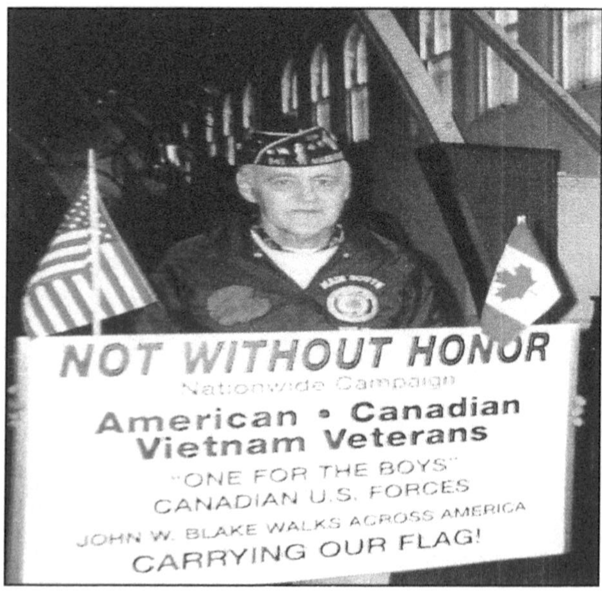


*Above:* Joe Murphy, one of many Americans who dedicated their time and effort to our family's campaign

*Right:* Larry R. Collins, Canadian KIA in Vietnam during May 1969. His remains are buried among Canadian WWII and Korea veterans in a Canadian departmental plot own and serviced by DVA, Canada.

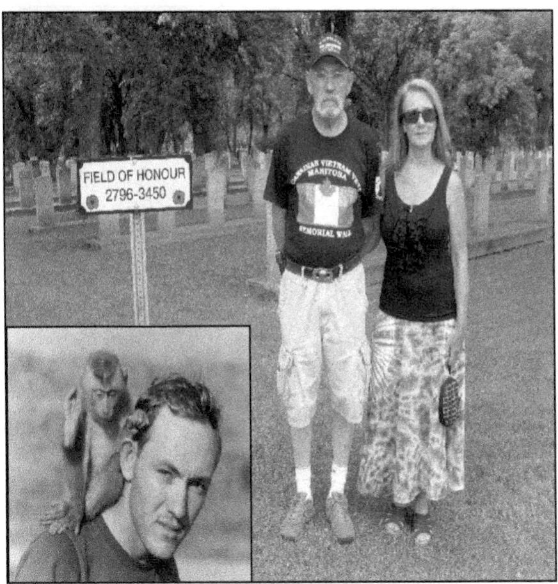


*Above:* Rob Purvis, Vietnam Veteran (Canadian) and his wife Shirley, visiting their friend Larry Collins at the Field of Honour at Brookside Cemetery, Winnipeg, Manitoba, Canada
*Photo insert:* Airborne Ranger Rob Purvis in Vietnam

*Above:* United States Army Honor Guard from Ft. Lewis, WA deployed to British Columbia, Canada to honor one of their own Sgt. John W. Blake. David Saint John accepting the US flag.(Photos courtesy of 70th Regional Support Command, Seattle, WA)

Sgt. John W. Blake burial service April 7, 2001 at Forest Lawn Ocean View Memorial Park, Normandy Section among Canadian veterans in a strictly military section, Burnaby, British Columbia, Canada. (Photo below courtesy of Forest Lawn Ocean View Memorial Park cemetery)

## 2012 – United with the N/75th Airborne

*Above from left to right back row*: Jeanette and Michael Swisley, Carl Millinder, Herbert Baugh, Jerry Herrera, Richard Baker, Rudy Teodosio *Front row:* Cathy Saint John

The Saxophone Man Fremont St. Las Vegas

## The Brotherhood

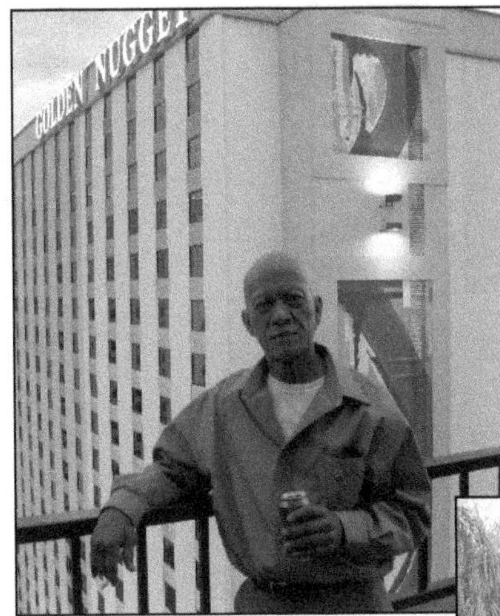


*Left:* Patrick (Tad) Tadina

*Right:* William Jeff Horne

*Left:* John Bryant

*Right:* Don (Chief) Bizadi

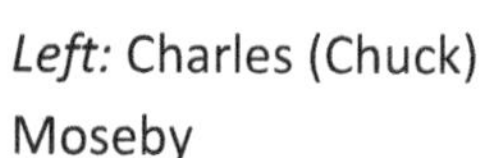

*Left:* Charles (Chuck) Moseby

*Right:* Reed Cundiff

*Above*: Bricks that pave the walkway to the Airborne Ranger Memorial, Fort Benning, Georgia

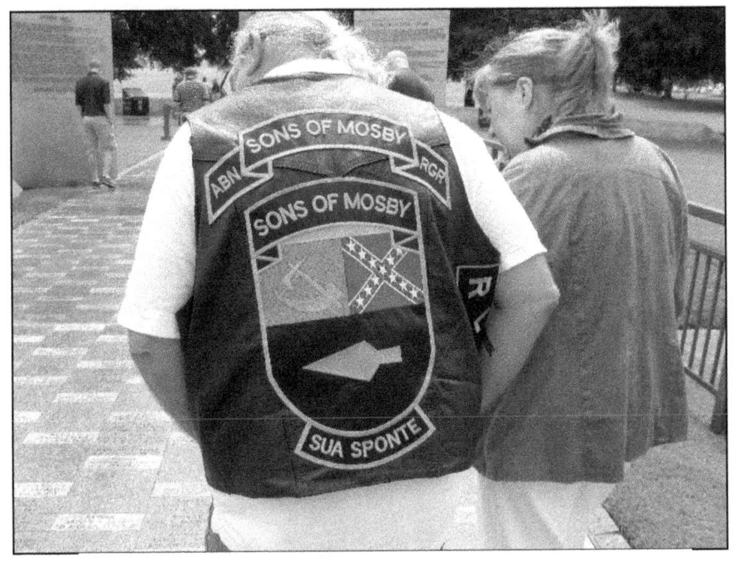


*Above:* Chuck Moseby and Cathy Saint John viewing John's memorial brick

*Above:* The Airborne Ranger Memorial, Fort Benning

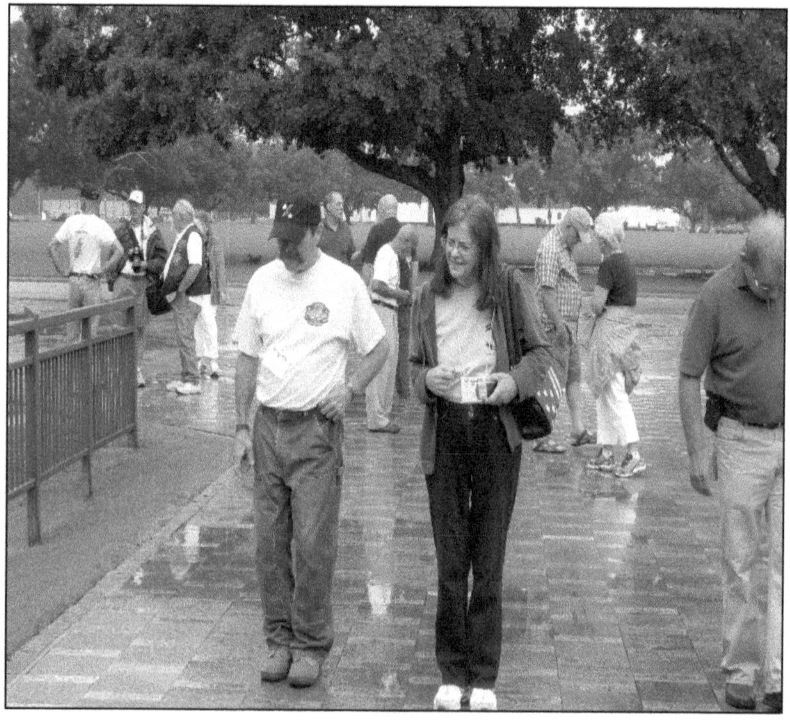

*Above:* Michael and Jeanette Swisley

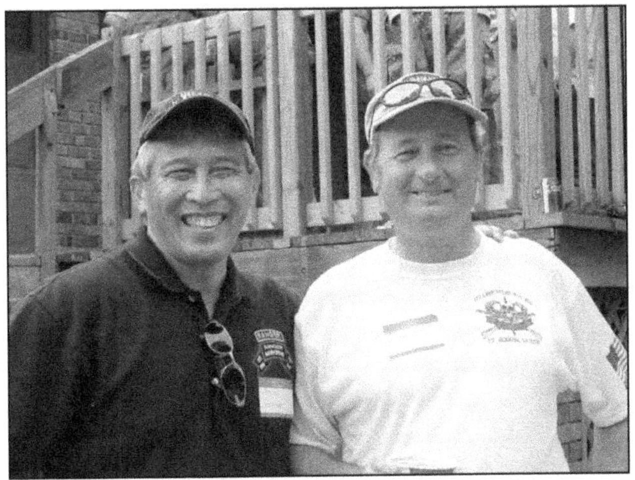

*Above*: Rudy Teodosio and Herbert Baugh at Ranger Browns annual BQ, Columbus, Georgia

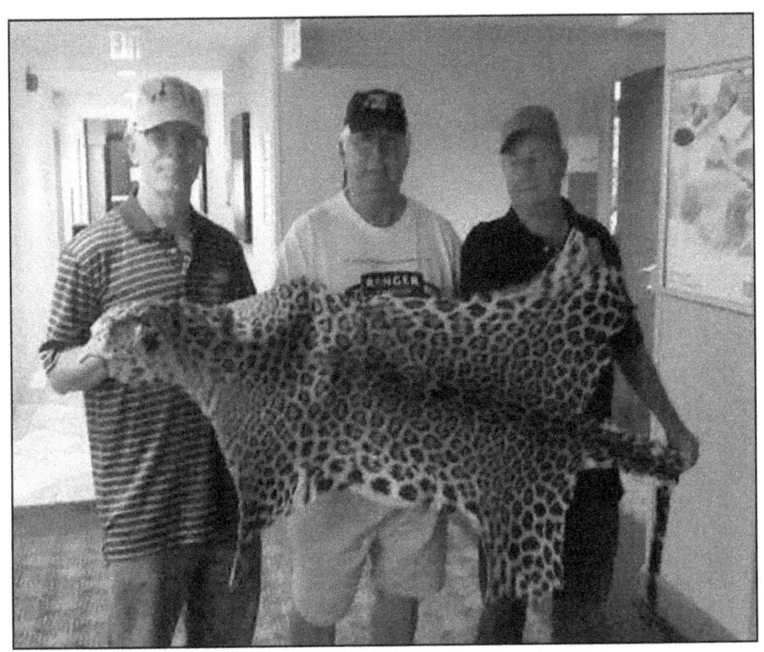


*Above: Left to Right, Jeff Horne, Carl Millinder and Herbert Baugh holding a trophy pelt from Vietnam*

DEDICATED TO
ALL RANGERS WHO
"OF THEIR OWN ACCORD"
HAVE SERVED.
RANGER
U. S.
ARMY
ASSN.
★ RANGERS LEAD THE WAY ★

75 RANGER RGT
CARLETON VENCILL
CHARLES WILLIAMS
RANGER CREED
RANGERS LEAD THE WAY!
RANGERS LEAD
THE WAY!
THE BATTALION IS TO BE AN ELITE, LIGHT
AND THE MOST PROFICIENT INFANTRY
BATTALION IN THE WORLD. A BATTALION
THAT CAN DO THINGS WITH ITS HANDS
AND WEAPONS BETTER THAN ANYONE.
THE BATTALION WILL CONTAIN NO
"HOODLUMS OR BRIGANDS" AND IF THE
BATTALION IS FORMED FROM SUCH PERSONS,
IT WILL BE DISBANDED.
WHEREVER THE BATTALION GOES IT MUST
BE APPARENT THAT IT IS THE BEST...
GEN CREIGHTON ABRAMS
GUIDANCE WHEN FORMING THE
1ST RANGER BATTALION, FALL 1973

*Above:* Roberto Patino, Rachel Blake and Michael Ormiston, Vegas 2016

*Above:* Patrick (Tad) Tadina, Fletcher Ruckman, Michael Swisley, and Chuck Moseby, Fort Benning, Georgia 2013

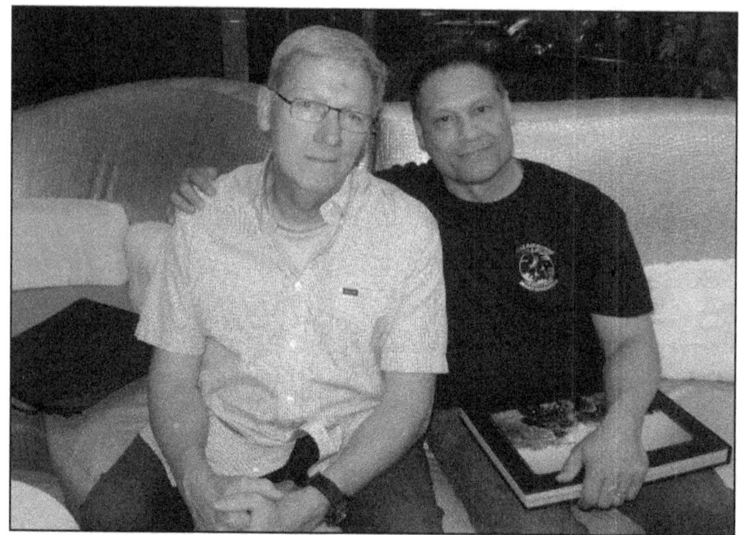

*Above:* Brian Danker and Roberto Patino Vegas 2016

Above: *Left to right: Mikey Potter, Sid Smith, Chuck Moseby, Jeff Horne, Gerald Turner, Freddie Williams, Allen Valkie, Tom Zaruba, Roger Bumgardner, Dave Lang*
*Front row seated: Pat Tadina, Robert Henriksen, Carl Vencill and Larry Cole*

**N/75th Ranger Reunion at Las Vegas, NV 2016**

*Above:* In the group photo from left to right:
1st row: Rachel Blake (John Blake's daughter, Roberto Patino Jr.(son of Patino KIA 10/22/70)
2nd row: Gordon Wax, Frank Bonvillain, John Wilkofsky, Joe Marquez, Robert Henriksen, John Bryant, Jay Borman
3rd row: Dick James, Richard Baker, Allen Phillips, Robert Foti, Tony Novella, Brain Danker, Gordon Baker, Hubie Imhoff, Freddie Williams, Pat Tadina, Ed Zelina, David Carmon, Jim Parkes, Ray Hill, Cliff White, Shane O'Neal, Ed Liptrap
4th row: Mike Swisley, Jim McSorley, John Howard, Robert Clark, John Jersey, Bill Jang

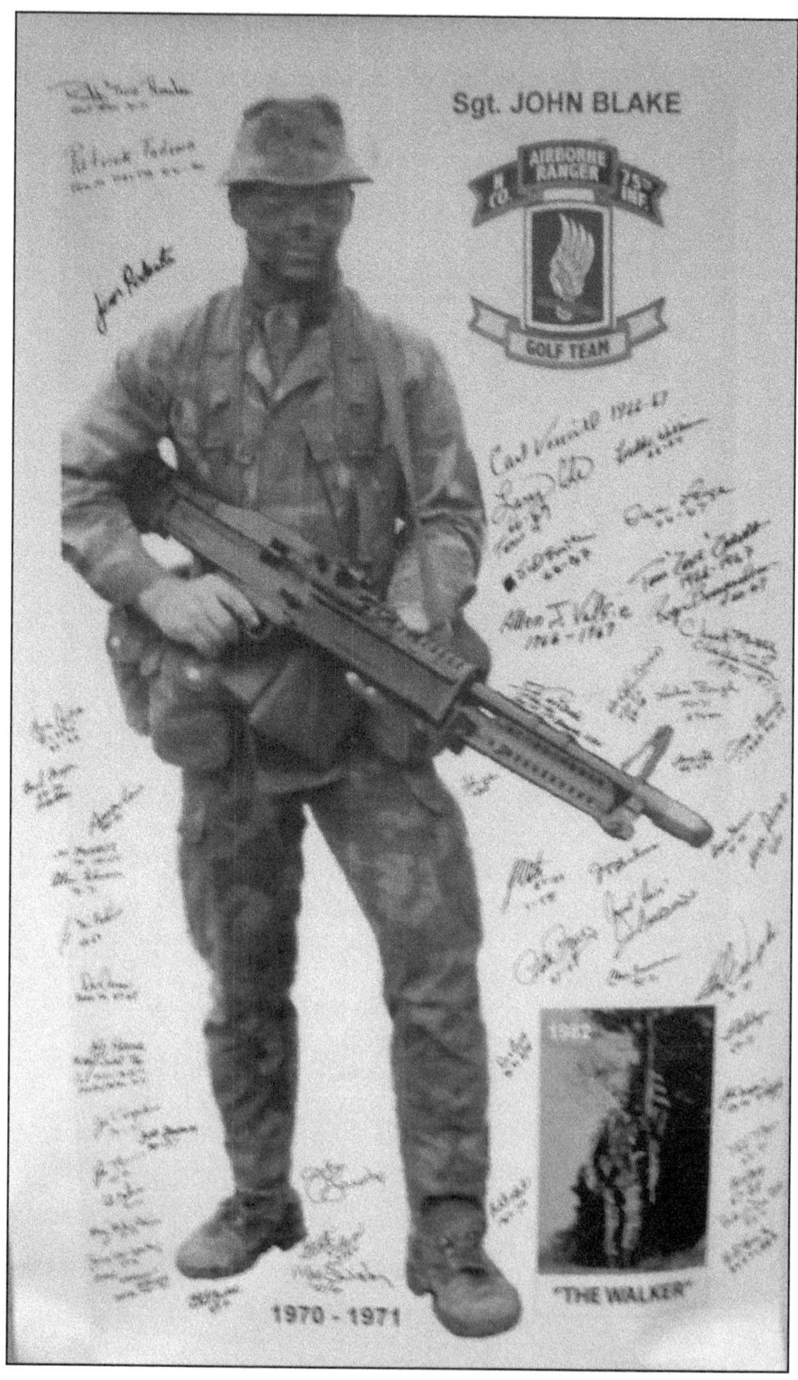
Sgt. JOHN BLAKE
AIRBORNE RANGER
H CO.
75th INF.
GOLF TEAM
1970 - 1971
"THE WALKER"

**Memories are smiling faces...**

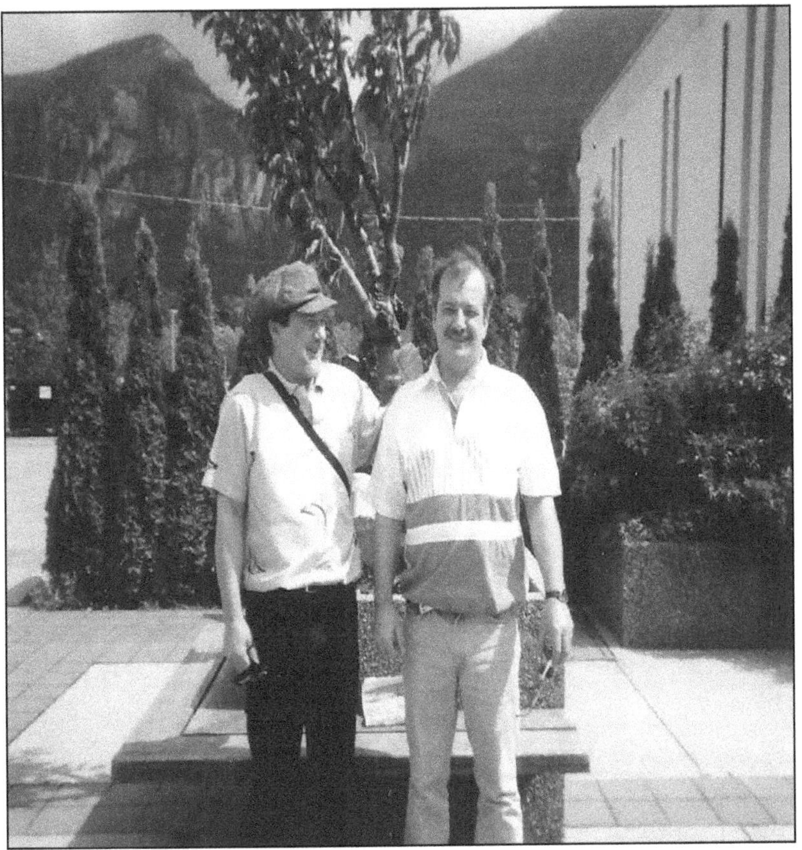

*Above:* The last photo of John (on the left) and David together in Vancouver, British Columbia 1995